Human Becomings

SUNY series in Chinese Philosophy and Culture
―――――――――
Roger T. Ames, editor

Human Becomings

Theorizing Persons for Confucian Role Ethics

Roger T. Ames

Cover: *Xiaodao*, the prime moral imperative in the Confucian tradition that references the intergenerational embodiment of a continuing culture. Calligraphy by Ni Peimin.

Published by State University of New York Press, Albany

© 2021 State University of New York

All rights reserved

No part of this book may be used or reproduced in any manner whatsoever without written permission. No part of this book may be stored in a retrieval system or transmitted in any form or by any means including electronic, electrostatic, magnetic tape, mechanical, photocopying, recording, or otherwise without the prior permission in writing of the publisher.

For information, contact State University of New York Press, Albany, NY
www.sunypress.edu

Library of Congress Cataloging-in-Publication Data

Names: Ames, Roger T., 1947– author.
Title: Human becomings : theorizing persons for Confucian role ethics / Roger T. Ames.
Description: Albany : State University of New York, 2021. | Series: SUNY series in Chinese philosophy and culture | Includes bibliographical references and index.
Identifiers: LCCN 2020023197 (print) | LCCN 2020023198 (ebook) | ISBN 9781438480794 (hardcover : alk. paper) | ISBN 9781438480800 (pbk. : alk. paper) | ISBN 9781438480817 (ebook)
Subjects: LCSH: Confucian ethics. | Human beings. | Confucianism.
Classification: LCC BJ1289.3 .A44 2021 (print) | LCC BJ1289.3 (ebook) | DDC 170.951—dc23
LC record available at https://lccn.loc.gov/2020023197
LC ebook record available at https://lccn.loc.gov/2020023198

10 9 8 7 6 5 4 3 2 1

For the Berggruen Institute
Good People Doing Good Things

Contents

Preface		ix
Introduction		1
Chapter One	The Question of Which Questions to Ask	15
Chapter Two	How Do the Confucian Canons Say "Role Ethics"?	59
Chapter Three	A Narrative Conception of Human Nature	147
Chapter Four	Holography and the Focus-Field Conception of Persons	205
Chapter Five	Relational Autonomy and Thick Choices	275
Chapter Six	Holism, Democracy, and the Optimizing of the Human Experience	317
Chapter Seven	From Human "*Becomings*" to a Process Cosmology	359
Epilogue	Why Theorize Confucian Persons for a Changing World Cultural Order?	401
Bibliography		409
Index		421

Preface

Whence this monograph? Some years ago, much influenced and encouraged by my dear friend and collaborator, the late Henry Rosemont Jr., I embraced the notion that taking Confucian ethics as a sui generis role ethic is the best way to understand the moral discourse found in the early Confucian canons. And over the ensuing years, Henry and I together—and independently, too—have tried our best to elaborate on what we have come to understand as Confucian role ethics. A collection of the papers we wrote in this joint effort recounting the history and development of this idea has been published in a volume entitled *Confucian Role Ethics: A Vision for the Twenty-first Century?*[1] In 2011, I published a monograph that began as the 2008 Ch'ien Mu [Qian Mu] Lectures at the Chinese University of Hong Kong entitled *Confucian Role Ethics*, with the subtitle: *A Vocabulary*. That is, in this book I appeal to the conceptual vocabulary of the tradition itself in my best attempt to allow Confucian role ethics to, quite literally, speak on its own terms.[2] My argument in *Confucian Role Ethics* is that we must begin from an understanding of the vocabulary of Confucian role ethics itself. Only when this has been accomplished and the tradition has been allowed its own voice can we then bring it into a conversation with the contemporary ethical discourse. Said another way, given the long history of Confucian ethics, I was keen to resist the familiar shoehorning of this tradition into

---

1. Henry Rosemont Jr. and Roger T. Ames, *Confucian Role Ethics: A Vision for the Twenty-First Century?* (Taipei: National Taiwan University Press, 2016).

2. Roger T. Ames, *Confucian Role Ethics: A Vocabulary* (Hong Kong: Chinese University of Hong Kong Press, 2011). Chinese translation: 《儒学角色伦理学：一套特色伦理学词汇》 trans. Benjamin Hammer and Tian Chenshan, 孟巍隆译, 田辰山校译 (Jinan: Shandong Peoples' Press, 2017).

our own familiar philosophical categories on the uncritical assumption that the encounter of Confucian ethics with Western moral theory was somehow its defining moment.

Assuming that this publication had made a fair argument for taking Confucian ethics on its own terms, I happily began work on a sequel monograph tentatively entitled "Against Objectivism: Doing Justice to Justice in Confucian Role Ethics." In this second book, my explicit intention was to bring Confucian role ethics into conversation with Western moral theory on the single theme of "justice" and to thus promote an intercultural dialogue on this important topic. In this now stalled book, I began with John Rawls, moved on to Susan Moller Okin, then to Joel Kupperman and Robert Solomon, on to Amartya Sen and John Dewey, and finally to a holistic Confucian conception of social justice. This "justice" monograph has since been deferred. While I was working on this manuscript, responses to *Confucian Role Ethics* came in from some much-respected colleagues within the corridors of Western philosophy, and particularly after the translation into Chinese, from distinguished members of the Chinese academy as well. I was much encouraged by the interest garnered by the idea of role ethics, and in service to clarifying my terms and further refining my arguments, I was grateful to have their critical engagement. While getting much from the comments and criticisms of these scholars, I also came to see that Henry and I, up until now, have been less than successful in stating clearly what we take to be perhaps Confucian philosophy's most important contribution to the contemporary ethical discourse: its relationally constituted conception of persons. That is, I became aware that neither my monograph *Confucian Role Ethics* nor the work I had done in collaboration with Rosemont has provided a sufficiently clear account of how the Confucian relationally constituted conception of persons described in terms of narrative and focus-field holography can serve the contemporary discussion in moral philosophy as a robust alternative to the seemingly default assumption about a foundational individualism.

Simultaneously, Rosemont, with this same concern in mind, undertook a sustained critique of individualism in his monograph *Against Individualism: A Confucian Rethinking of the Foundations of Morality, Politics, Family, and Religion* (2015). In this book, Rosemont mounts a compelling argument that foundational individualism in its various iterations has transitioned from a benign, liberating discourse to become what is now a sometimes malevolent ideology implicated in and aggravating many of the pressing ethical, social, and political problems of our time.³ The overall thrust of Rosemont's thesis in *Against Individualism* can be stated rather simply. The industrial democracies, and by extension most of the rest of the world, are dominated by a corporate capitalism whose interests are served largely by a procedural justice grounded in a foundational individualism that compounds the benefits of a few and marginalizes the possibility of realizing a distributive justice for the many. Hence, the more success academic and political forces have in defending and indeed championing the morality that grounds individualism and procedural justice, the less likely we will be able to make gains in social justice. Or put another way, those of us committed to the primacy of social and distributive justice must confront the fact that individual freedom for an elite and privileged few is being purchased at the expense of substantial justice for an increasing number of the world's peoples.

I join Rosemont's efforts here in arguing that our default individualism constitutes a major underlying and entrenched conceptual problem that is exacerbating the current human predicament—a predicament that I will have occasion to describe below as "the perfect storm." Indeed, this foundational individualism is appealed to first in defining what it means to be a moral person and then extended as a determinate of what it means for this putatively moral person to act justly. The presupposition that defines persons ideally as free, autonomous, rational, and properly self-interested individuals is ubiquitous in much if not most of modern Western moral and political philosophy. And it takes on an analogous form at the extended level of corporate culture and the sovereign state. With its deep roots in the Western philosophical narrative, this foundational individualism dilutes our sense of moral responsibility by allowing us to describe, analyze, and evaluate individual persons—psychologically, politically, and morally—in isolation from others. Yet this ostensibly foundational individual is at every level an ontological fiction. We do not live our lives inside our skins. Moreover, the individual so defined has become an insidious fiction, as it provides the moral and political justification for an increasingly libertarian economic and political system. Indeed, it can be fairly argued that this same libertarian economic system, justified as it is by appeal to individual liberty and autonomy, and far from being the cure for the world's ills, in fact exacerbates the disease itself.

---

3. Henry Rosemont Jr., *Against Individualism: A Confucian Rethinking of the Foundations of Morality, Politics, Family, and Religion* (Idaho Falls, ID: Lexington, 2015).

Like Rosemont, I have come to believe that we need to bring into clearer focus the ways in which the Confucian conception of relationally constituted persons, with all of its far-reaching implications, provides an alternative to this individualism. To this end, I have set aside my "justice book" for the time being to join Rosemont in common cause. I have written this present monograph with the express intention of trying to state as clearly as I can what we have both come to see as the holistic, interdependent, and eventful conception of persons being offered in Confucian philosophy. While Rosemont in *Against Individualism* has focused much of his energies on a sustained critique of foundational individualism, I have taken it as my task to follow up on these efforts and to use the Confucian canons to lay out what we have been calling variously a focus-field, narrative, and relationally constituted conception of persons. That is, I am in these pages trying to theorize the Confucian conception of persons for Confucian role ethics as an alternative to a foundational individualism.

What does it mean to "theorize" persons for the holistic Confucian tradition when, from earliest times, Confucianism has insisted upon the inseparability of theory and practice? It is a commonplace to observe that familiar dualisms that would separate theory from practice, and the formal from the informal, are anathema to the holistic, aesthetic cosmology that serves as interpretive context for the classical Chinese canons. Whatever theorizing might mean here, it does not reference some principle or body of principles we might associate with scientific reasoning proffered to explain phenomena in the abstract. Indeed, these Confucian canons challenge this more familiar understanding of theorizing by beginning from the primacy of practice and by taking theorizing as an intrinsic feature of practical activity itself. Indeed, to get the most out of our practical activities, we must necessarily be self-consciously critical and deliberate. Thus, erstwhile theoretical tools are generally introduced by philosophers in this tradition in media res—that is, from the need to make their practices more productive and intelligent within the context of the practices themselves.

This less familiar understanding of "theorizing" means I must "own" the project in the sense that my own practical narrative provides the concrete and inescapable context out of which my "theorizing" emerges. I am a person of a specific time and place, and my theorizing of the Confucian conception of persons is directed at changing the values and practices of the world to which I belong. And as I will argue, since my world is one in which a perfect storm is gathering on the horizon, it is urgent that we theorize our practices in order to produce the social intelligence needed to address our current human predicament. As I proceed with my own project, it should also become clear that it was this same contextualized sense of theorizing practice that much earlier, and within a very different historical and cultural context, motivated the ancient Chinese philosophers to reflect critically on what it meant to be persons living in a world far away.

An implication of this inseparability of theory and practice in the Confucian philosophical canons is that an understanding of the definitions it provides for key philosophical terms is going to depend in some degree upon the life experience and the existential insights that readers themselves bring to the inquiry. And the cogency of any particular argument in order to be compelling will require reference to specific situations each with their own complex of details providing narrative context.

I am grateful to the Berggruen Institute that provided me with a two-year fellowship 2016–2018 at Peking University. I was provided with an intellectual environment that included a cohort of Beijing-based fellows who have laid the foundation for the Peking University Berggruen Research Center established at the end of 2018: Steve Angle, Bai Tongdong, Daniel Bell, Rajeev Bhargava, Gan Chunsong, Peter Hershock, Jin Li, Viren Murthy, Song Bing, Anna Sun, Zeng Yi, and Zhao Tingyang. The Berggruen Institute itself is a response to the epochal transformations that are reshaping human life, social organization, and the world—transformations that are taking place now, in our own lives, and that will continue in those of our children and grandchildren. The Berggruen Institute's mission is to deepen understanding of these great transformations, the ethical responses they demand, the social decisions they make possible, and how they are seen from different civilizational perspectives, with the objective of having enduring impact on the progress and direction of societies around the world. This book would not have been possible without the generous support of the Berggruen Institute and its commitment to developing and promoting long-term answers to the greatest challenges of the twenty-first century.

I would also like express my thanks to James Peltz and Ryan Morris at the State University of New York Press for their hard work and many professional kindnesses in bringing this project to print.

Introduction

"Rethinking China" (*chongsi Zhongguo* 重思中國): An Asymmetry in Cultural Comparisons

The contemporary Chinese philosopher Zhao Tingyang 趙汀陽, keenly aware of the persistent and pernicious asymmetry in the way we often compare Chinese and Western cultures, has exhorted both Chinese and Western scholars alike to "rethink China" (*chongsi Zhongguo* 重思中國).[1] Emblematic of this asymmetry in cultural comparisons is the question: Who is reading whom? If we go into a Chinese bookstore or explore the collections on the shelves of a good Chinese university library, we find that most avatars of Western culture—old and new, as well as across the disciplines—are readily available in increasingly high-quality translations. Most everything, including the writings of those of us trying to provide our comparative perspectives on the Chinese philosophical tradition, are there in these burgeoning collections. And most significantly, it is the committed readership of young and eager Chinese intellectuals that provides the continuing impetus for this publishing phenomenon.

But upon entering American or European bookstores—or our university libraries—we find that the works of China's best thinkers over the past few centuries, late and soon, are almost totally absent. And what is most disconcerting about this asymmetry is that there is little if any pressure from Western intellectuals to address it. That is, in our world there is a dearth of interest, eager or otherwise, in translations of modern Chinese thinkers reflecting on their own philosophy and culture.

---

1. Zhao Tingyang 趙汀陽, 天下體系: 世界制度哲學導論 [The *Tianxia* system: An introduction to the philosophy of world institution] (Beijing: Peoples' University Press, 2011), 1.

Kwong-loi Shun has made much of how this cultural asymmetry has shaped the way in which comparisons continue to be framed in the scholarship on Chinese and Western philosophical traditions:

> There is a trend in comparative studies to approach Chinese thought from a Western philosophical perspective, by reference to frameworks, concepts, or issues found in Western philosophical discussions.[2]

This troubling asymmetrical assumption of a Western teacher culture overshadowing the Chinese student culture has its history. On the Western side, well-intended Christian missionaries bent on saving China's soul introduced this ancient world into the Western academy by appealing to the vocabulary of their universal faith, ascribing to Confucian culture most of the accouterments of an Abrahamic religion. Early on, traditional Chinese philosophical texts were translated into English and other European languages by missionaries who used a Christian vocabulary to transform these canonical texts wholesale into the liturgy of a second-rate Christianity. James Legge (1815–1897), the great Scottish translator of the Chinese classics on whose broad shoulders twentieth-century Sinology has been built, was a missionary in the field. Legge appealed self-consciously to the theology of Joseph Butler (1692–1752) in the vocabulary he selected as equivalencies for Chinese terms and in his interpretation of the tradition more broadly. In translating *tian* 天 as "Heaven," *dao* 道 as "the Way," *yi* 義 as "righteousness," *li* 禮 as "ritual," *ren* 仁 as "benevolence," and so on, Legge's Confucianism became increasingly familiar to his Christian audience. In his interpretation of Mencius, for example, he wondered aloud about why Mencius did not just use "God" instead of the ambiguous term *tian* and concluded that Mencius's understanding of a benevolent human nature was almost precisely the same as that of anti-Hobbesian theologian Joseph Butler in his *Sermons on Human Nature*.[3]

Thus when we return to those same European and American bookstores and libraries to find translations of the canonical Chinese philoso-

---

2. Kwong-loi Shun, "Studying Confucian and Comparative Ethics: Methodological Reflections," *Journal of Chinese Philosophy* 36, no. 3 (September 2009): 470.

3. *The Chinese Classics*, trans. James Legge (Hong Kong: University of Hong Kong Press, 1960), 2:448, note 1. For an account of Legge's journey, see also Norman J. Giradot, *The Victorian Translation of China: James Legge's Oriental Pilgrimage* (Berkeley: University of California Press, 2002).

phy texts initially translated by Legge, such as the *Analects of Confucius* (*Lunyu*), the *Mencius*, the *Daodejing*, the *Zhuangzi*, and so on, we find that these same titles are catalogued and shelved under the curious rubric of "Eastern Religions" but not found in the more respectable philosophy section. And when we venture into the highest seats of learning in these Western countries, we find that Chinese philosophy is being taught, if at all, in our religion and Asian studies departments rather than within the discipline of philosophy itself. We must also remember that "philosophy," far from being a neutral term, has gravitas and is reserved as an acknowledgment of respect for the quality of human thinking at its best. Historians certainly call themselves "historians" and sociologists "sociologists." But only the most accomplished or self-important of those who "*do* philosophy" or "*teach* philosophy" will have the temerity to make the bold announcement, "I am a philosopher." As a consequence of this cultural reductionism, Confucian philosophy has been literally "converted" into a pseudo-Christianity that at best can only ape the original. From a Western point of view, Confucianism is thus a tradition perceived uncritically as lacking our philosophical bona fides while also being derivative of our own religious sensibilities. Hence, Confucianism can quite comfortably be conceptualized within our Western framework without fear of substantial loss.

The self-understanding that professional philosophy is an Anglo-European narrative with the continuing exclusion of non-Western philosophical traditions is changing slowly in our own time, but it still continues to be challenged within the corridors of professional philosophy. Comparative colleagues Jay Garfield and Bryan Van Norden published a delightfully provocative piece in the *New York Times* (May 11, 2016) suggesting that our departments of philosophy can certainly continue to ignore non-Western philosophical traditions and philosophical diversity generally—and with no troublesome consequences. But in the interests of truth in advertising, these two comparativists recommend that such departments have the courtesy to rename themselves the departments of European and American Philosophy. Excerpting from their op-ed piece entitled "If Philosophy Won't Diversify, Let's Call It What It Really Is," Garfield and Van Norden observe that

> the vast majority of philosophy departments in the United States offer courses only on philosophy derived from Europe and the English-speaking world. . . . Given the importance of non-European traditions in both the history of world

philosophy and in the contemporary world, and given the increasing numbers of students in our colleges and universities from non-European backgrounds, this is astonishing. . . . The present situation is hard to justify morally, politically, epistemically or as good educational and research training practice. . . . We therefore suggest that any department that regularly offers courses only on Western philosophy should rename itself 'Department of European and American Philosophy.' This simple change would make the domain and mission of these departments clear, and would signal their true intellectual commitments to students and colleagues.[4]

John E. Drabinski quickly posted a response to Garfield and Van Norden. He certainly embraces their motivation in this call for a "rectification of names" but wants to further refine their argument. Indeed, he insists that these same philosophy programs are better off acknowledging that they are, in fact, departments of white European and white American philosophy. If Drabinski himself is going to offer courses on "black existentialism" as a corrective, those who teach just "existentialism" ought to acknowledge the pernicious invisibility of "white" in the course title when they are being taught to our increasingly diverse student bodies. Indeed, Drabinski argues that the contemporary philosophical canon is precisely that—*a* particular canon that reproduces *a* particular history and more worrisome, *a* particular way of thinking and living that perpetuates the violence of ignoring:

> What happens in those canonical texts is more than just pursuits of truth and the like. They are also texts that reproduce base ideological forms—or revolutionize them—that are key to reproducing certain kinds of societies. In the case of white Western societies, this means slaving, conquering, and subjugating societies. This is why Locke, Hume, Kant, Hegel, etc. all had theories of race, nation, genesis of human

---

4. Jay Garfield and Bryan W. Van Norden, "If Philosophy Won't Diversify, Let's Call It What It Really Is," New York Times, May 11, 2016, http://www.nytimes.com/2016/05/11/opinion/if-philosophy-wont-diversify-lets-call-it-what-it-really-is.html.

difference, and justifications for all sorts of slavery, conquest, and domination.⁵

And the avalanche of posts responding to Garfield and Van Norden keep coming in, with feminist philosophy also having its say, suggesting that these contemporary philosophy departments acknowledge one more marginalization (if not exclusion) by calling themselves "Departments of Male, White European and White American Philosophy."⁶

If we are going to continue to change professional philosophy and make it a more inclusive discipline, we must acknowledge the exclusions and the distortions as well. One problem, simply put, is the extent to which in both the contemporary Western and Chinese philosophical literature we have in referencing the Chinese philosophical tradition relentlessly theorized it according to Western philosophical assumptions. We have also tended to tailor Chinese concepts to fit inappropriate categories and conceptual structures. We ponder with some philosophical nuance: "Is Mohist utilitarianism an agent-neutral or an agent-relative utilitarianism?" But it would not occur to us to ask whether John Stuart Mill is a latter-day Mohist philosopher. Again, we are now engaged in a continuing debate on whether Confucian virtue ethics is an Aristotelian aretaic ethic or a Hume-inspired sentimentalist ethic. But it would not occur to us to ask if the ethical insights of Aristotle and Hume are, in substance, an ancient and an early modern kind of European Confucianism, respectively.

But this theorizing of China in terms that are not its own is not simply the *déformation professionnelle* of Western philosophers; it has its Chinese history as well. As Shun in describing the cultural asymmetry continues:

> This trend is seen not only in works published in the English language, but also in those published in Chinese. Conversely, in the contemporary literature, we rarely find attempts to approach Western philosophical thought by reference to

---

5. John A. Drabinski, Diversity, 'Neutrality,' Philosophy (website), accessed May 11, 2016, http://jdrabinski.com/2016/05/11/diversity-neutrality-philosophy/.

6. For links to a variety of responses, see http://pages.vassar.edu/epistemologically-wise/2016/05/16/the-debate-over-the-garfield-van-norden-essay-in-the-stone/.

frameworks, concepts, or issues found in Chinese philosophical discussions.⁷

Shun is arguing here that the cultural asymmetry we find in the Western literature on Chinese philosophy is just as marked and egregious when we turn to Chinese-language publications. As Shun has observed, this entrenched asymmetry is as true of contemporary East Asian intellectuals as it is of their Western counterparts. East Asian scholars certainly continue to speak and write in their own vernacular languages, but these languages have been significantly transformed by their encounter with the conceptual structure of a dominating Western modernity. The most astute of our comparative philosophers have been aware of this problem for some time. In articulating the most fundamental problems of translation between these traditions, Cambridge University rhetorician I. A. Richards, for example, observes that trying to understand China on its own terms has "a practical urgency as well as a theoretic interest." Writing in 1932, Richards goes on to worry that

> before long there will be nobody studying Mencius into whose mind philosophical and other ideas and methods of Western origin have not made their way. Western notions are penetrating steadily into Chinese, and the Chinese scholar of the near future will not be intellectually much nearer Mencius than any Western pupil of Aristotle and Kant.⁸

How has this asymmetrical situation come about in East Asia? In the middle and late nineteenth century, the institutional apparatus of Western education was transplanted wholesale to reconfigure East Asian education to its very core. The institutions of European and American education—the public school systems through to the universities with their disciplinary taxonomies and curricula—were imported across the board into the East Asian cultures of Japan, China, Korea, and Vietnam. The Meiji Japanese reformers and then the Chinese, Korean, and Vietnamese intellectuals—at once enamored of and overwhelmed by Western modernity—created their own Sinitic equivalencies drawn largely from traditional Chinese literary resources to appropriate and give voice to the

---

7. Shun, "Studying Confucian and Comparative Ethics," 470.
8. I. A. Richards, *Mencius on the Mind: Experiments in Multiple Definition* (New York: Harcourt, Brace, 1932), 9.

conceptual and theoretical language of the imported Western academic culture. The vocabulary of modernity with its liberating Enlightenment ideas was translated into and transformed fundamentally the vernacular languages of East Asia, prompting these cultures to theorize their own traditions through a largely Western conceptual structure.

Columbia professor Lydia H. Liu 劉禾 has discussed in considerable detail not only the complexity and the politics of this process of synchronizing the East Asian languages with the vocabulary of Western modernity but also the role of Chinese literary tradition as a resource for constructing this vocabulary. In thinking through the impact of this newly emerging conceptual structure as it surfaced and reconfigured the discourse of modern Chinese academic literature, Liu herself probes the "*discursive construct of the Chinese modern.*" "I am fascinated," says Liu,

> by what has happened to the modern Chinese language, especially the written form, since its early exposure to English, modern Japanese, and other foreign languages. . . . The true object of my theoretical interest is the *legitimation of the "modern" and the "West"* in Chinese literary discourse as well as the *ambivalence of Chinese agency* in these mediated processes of legitimation.[9]

Pointedly alluding to Foucault's concern over the definitive role that authority and power relations play, Liu cites Talal Asad who, in offering an appropriate critique of British imperialism, tells the story of a continuing process of self-colonization in our Asian sources. This Asian deference to European knowledge production has immediate relevance to the problem rehearsed here, which is the persisting asymmetry that attends cultural translation more broadly:

> To put it crudely, because the languages of the Third World societies—including of course, the societies that social anthropologists have traditionally studied—are "weaker" in relation to Western languages (and today, especially to English), they are more likely to submit to forcible transformation in the translation process than the other way around. The reason

---

9. Lydia H. Liu, *Translingual Practice: Literature, National Culture, and Translated Modernity—China, 1900–1937* (Stanford, CA: Stanford University Press, 1995), xvi–xviii.

for this is, first, that in their political-economic relations with Third World countries, Western nations have the greater ability to manipulate the latter. And, second, Western languages produce and deploy *desired* knowledge more readily than Third World languages do.[10]

The reductionistic theorizing of China as it has been perpetuated, first through the lens of Christianity and then via the conceptual structures of Western modernity, has been further aggravated by the condescending rhetoric of the powerful and influential philosopher G. W. F. Hegel. For Hegel, the beginning of philosophy in history requires the political freedom for the human will to aspire to the universal. But as we all know so well, opines Hegel, the Oriental character, with its passive spirit immersed in nature and substance, is able to think only in bare particularities. Hegel, in his *Philosophy of History* (and other works), describes China in the most deprecating terms as a primitive culture wholly without *Geist*—that is, without any capacity for internally induced change or confirmation of what is universally right. To Hegel, such a timid spirit does not own the freedom of consciousness necessary for thought to think itself and thus has no role in the historical evolution of philosophy and no place in philosophy's universal and singular system.[11] Hegel's "impact-response" interpretation of a passive, indolent China has dominated the "best" of Western interpretive sources since the nineteenth century. Led by the distinguished Harvard historian John Fairbank in his own time, the language of impact-response became the orthodox and pervasive reading of Chinese history as recently as the 1980s.[12]

This asymmetry in cultural comparisons is the consequence of what has been a double-barreled erasure of Chinese philosophy broadly: first

---

10. Liu, *Translingual Practice*, 3.

11. Wu Xiao-ming, "Philosophy, *Philosophia*, and *Zhe-xue*," *Philosophy East and West* 48, no. 3 (1998): 406–452, esp. 411–419.

12. See the "impact-response" critique of Fairbank by one of his most prominent students, Paul A. Cohen, in *Discovering History in China: American Historical Writing on the Recent Chinese Past* (New York: Columbia University Press, 1984). In fairness to Fairbank, in his later works he gradually distanced himself from this Hegelian interpretation. For a broad account of the evolving interpretation of Chinese history, see David Martinez-Robles, "The Western Representation of Modern China: Orientalism, Culturalism and Historiographical Criticism," *Digithum* 10 (2008), accessed August 22, 2017, http://www.uoc.edu/digithum/10/dt/eng/martinez.pdf.

from without, and then from within. In the Western academy, Chinese philosophy has become a remote and exotic version of an Abrahamic worldview called "Eastern religion" that at least from a Hegelian perspective does not rise to the status of philosophy. And again, with the complicity of the Chinese academy that has itself defined philosophy in Western terms, Chinese "philosophy" can only be legitimate to the extent that it meets the Western criteria of what constitutes philosophy as a professional discipline. This situation has meant that contemporary Western intellectuals—many of whom are inclined to regard their own religious traditions as obsolete, dogmatic, and of little contemporary relevance—have come to see the secular West as the teacher culture and China as having little or nothing to offer a changing world cultural order. And in the wake of their own history of educational self-colonization, contemporary intellectuals in East Asia, evincing little interest in the antiquarianism of their own cultural traditions, are largely inclined to embrace modern liberalism with the good and useful knowledge it continues to produce.

The consequence of this history of cultural reductionism is that the value of the word "Confucianism" in the West, when understood at all, evokes the values of a potted ideology transmitted through unchanging canons, rote learning, patriarchy, hierarchy, footbinding, and other forms of misogyny—a tradition that properly belongs to the past. The Anglo-American process philosopher A. N. Whitehead, who himself had an enormous investment in an ontology that begins from the reinstatement of change as one of its defining characteristics, represents this negative sentiment when he declared that it was Confucius who occasioned "a time when things ceased to change" and who was thus responsible for "the static civilization of China."[13]

---

13. See Lucien Price, ed., *Dialogues of Alfred North Whitehead* (Boston: Little, Brown, 1954), 176–77. Whitehead said, "If you want to understand Confucius, read John Dewey. And if you want to understand John Dewey, read Confucius." Whitehead seems quite oblivious to the process sensibilities of both Confucius and Dewey and in fact dismisses both of them explicitly as "pragmatists" whose commitment to what he considers to be a naïve empiricism precludes any but the most uninteresting of philosophical adventures. Having first criticized Christian theology roundly for banishing novelty through formularizing truth, Whitehead then turns to an assault on both Confucius and Dewey for abjuring questions about the "ultimacies" that underlie the simple facts of experience. Here Whitehead is explicitly criticizing both Confucius and Dewey for being vulgar pragmatists who, in limiting their interest to the bald facts, preclude the fruitful consequences that emerge when we ask "silly" and "superfluous" (i.e., metaphysical) questions and, in so doing, give rise to novelty.

In the Chinese world, too, the term "*ruxue*" 儒學 that we translate as "Confucianism" does not fare much better among contemporary young intellectuals. There has been more than a century of internal Chinese critique of this antiquarian tradition that began in earnest with the May Fourth reformers and their mantra demanding that China "overturn the house of Confucius" (*dadao Kongjiadian* 打倒孔家店). Many of these iconoclasts advocated a process of complete Westernization in which traditional Chinese culture would be abandoned altogether. This internal cleansing continued with the Great Cultural Revolution that sought to purge all remnants of the decadent Confucian tradition. The poignant images of the late 1980s documentary *River Elegy* (*Heshang* 河殤) still linger, with the Yellow River's stagnating silt clogging the pores of a China struggling to make its way to the liberating blue ocean of Western institutions and values. For many among the recent generations of Chinese who have lived through or in the recent wake of these times, any belief in the worth of the indigenous Confucian way of thinking and living has at best worn thin. And recent overt attempts to revive this antique tradition through a collaboration of China's own political and academic forces—with their perceived conservative catechism being foisted upon young China—have been viewed with considerable suspicion. For many if not most of the current generation, *ruxue* as "Confucianism" is little more than someone else's oppressive, xenophobic alternative to the newly emancipating values of a liberal and democratic modernity. Thus it is that a situation has emerged today where, in the minds of many Western and East Asian intellectuals alike, a simple equation can be drawn between the progressive forces of "modernization" on one side and the liberal goals of "Westernization" on the other. Confucian culture has thus come to be viewed as a tired, old-fashioned, and invincibly conservative ideology best left outside the door.

In making this observation about the seeming impotence of Confucian philosophy and culture, there is another asymmetry that needs to be addressed. Today in the Chinese academy we hear the voices of many scholars who espouse liberal values and advocate for the recognition of human rights and the importation of democratic principles and institutions in reconstructing their own cultural tradition. Indeed, most Western scholars, and many if not most among their own Chinese audiences as well, are generally inclined to regard such East Asian liberals as cosmopolitan urbanites who are, with their emancipating values, courageously leading the most educated and progressive of their countrymen into the twenty-first century.

But what about the other way around? Is it aberrant for some contemporary Western thinkers looking for a truly practicable ethics to question complex, abstract, and remote theories that are seemingly irrelevant to our real lives but pretend to serve as explanations for how we ought to achieve and express our moral competencies? Is it naively empirical for these Western scholars to look to our daily practices and reflect on how unrelenting critical attention to the growth in meaning within our everyday roles and relationships might have the power to transform these ordinary affairs of the day into something extraordinary? Is it a mere curiosity that some Western intellectuals with little sympathy for the obsolete supernaturalism and self-abnegating demands of Abrahamic religions would on reflection find their own human- rather than God-centered religious assumptions locating real religious experience within family and community relations aligned in some degree with Confucian values? Again, is it strange for these same Western scholars as modern-day accommodationists who, in aspiring to optimize the rich cultural diversity within their own disparate worlds, find that their own personal commitment to deference and inclusion resonates with the traditional Confucian understanding of a superlative, always hybrid "harmony" that allows alternative cultures who are merely different *from* each other to activate these differences and differ fully *for* each other?

Modernization as Westernization?

Is the equation between modernization and Westernization that marginalizes Confucian culture, both within and without China, humanity's best hope? Or, as we experience the sea change occurring in today's global economic and political order, would we be better off inventorying and taking advantage of all of the cultural resources available, Eastern as well as Western?

In a single generation, the ascendency of Asia, particularly the rise of China, has dramatically reconfigured the global economic and political order. In the same generation since 1989, the Asia Pacific Economic Cooperation (APEC) has grown to include twenty-one Asia-Pacific nations with 40 percent of the world's population. The GDP in this same region has more than tripled, and trade in and with the region has increased exponentially by over 400 percent. The Chinese economy grew over the first few decades at sometimes double-digit rates to overtake Japan as the second-largest economy in the world. And with its continued exponential growth still hovering around 6 percent, China is predicted to become the world's largest economy sometime in the 2020s. Up to now, these economic and political changes have been relatively easy to track. But perhaps such a seismic geopolitical shift will have less visible but also transformative cultural consequences for the human experience.

We might say that we live in the best and worst of times. We can say that these are the best of times because of what we humans as a species have become. That is, a fair claim can be made that world hunger is no longer a problem for us. This magnificent animal known as the human being has now developed the science and the technology that could enable a global initiative to quickly address the world's hunger problem in all of its complexity. We do not have a problem if we already have its solution. Our present predicament, then, is not a technological one; it is ethical. While we clearly have the science to solve world hunger, we lack the moral resolution to act upon it.

On this score then, it is the best of times. But it is also the worst of times. Our recent and dramatic geopolitical reorientation has all the troubling dynamics of a "perfect storm": global warming, pandemics, food and water shortages, environmental degradation, massive species extinction, international terrorism, proxy wars, nuclear proliferation, and the list goes on. Our unprecedented scientific and technological successes are mixed with ever-amplifying environmental, political, and social challenges. Indeed, this perfect storm has several underlying conditions that might encourage us to view our current predicament as requiring a shift from prioritizing technical solutions for world problems to privileging what is ultimately an ethical dilemma—that is, for us to acknowledge our lack of commitment to do what we know is right. After all, the fundamental difference between a problem and a predicament is that where problems are to be "solved," a predicament can only be "resolved" by effecting a radical change in human intentions, values, and practices. If we are to survive, human beings as a species will need to live and think differently.

There are four defining conditions of our current situation. First, human beings and our ways of being in the world are clearly complicit in the predicament we are facing. We are in some important degree responsible for it. Secondly, this predicament is not constrained by national, cultural, or social boundaries. Crises such as pandemics and climate change have global reach and affect everyone regardless of nationality or status. Thirdly, an organic relationship obtains among this set of pressing challenges that renders them in large degree zero-sum—we either address them all, or we can solve none of them. These challenges cannot be met seriatim by individual players engaging them piecemeal but must instead be addressed by the shared commitment of a world community acting in concert. Lastly, the good news is that we human beings probably have sufficient cultural resources to identify and activate the changes in values, intentions, and practices needed to respond immediately and effectively to our current predicament.

Contemporary historian of religion James P. Carse provides us with a distinction between "finite" and "infinite" games that might be useful in beginning to think through how Confucian values might make an important difference in a newly emerging cultural order.[14] In formulating this finite and infinite distinction, Carse uses "games" as an analogy for the many activities that constitute the human experience broadly—for the many things human beings "do" such as business, sports, politics, military security, international relations, and so on. With such finite games the focus is on the agency of single actors engaging in a game played over a finite period in accordance with a finite set of rules that guarantee a winner and a loser. Finite games thus have a defined beginning and end and are played by individual agents with the express purpose of winning. This understanding of game playing seems most immediately relevant to those competitive human activities we think of in terms of means and ends and that are directed at the success of one player over another. Our individualism's pervasiveness and the liberal values that attend this self-understanding of who we are as human beings has made finite games a familiar model of the way we often think about human transactions at every level of scale: as particular persons, as corporations, and as sovereign states.

Infinite games have a different structure and a different desired outcome. There are no beginnings or endings in infinite games. And the focus is on strengthening collaborative relationships within entities to succeed together rather than engaging in a competition among single actors who then play to win. Further, infinite games are played according to rules that can be altered by players as required to serve the purpose of continuing to play the game. Indeed, with no beginnings and no discernable ends, the goal is quite simply a shared flourishing. The relationship among family members might be a good example of the infinite games we play, where a mother is committed to strengthening the relationship

---

14. James Carse, *Finite and Infinite Games* (New York: Ballantine, 1987).

she has with her son, and son with mother, so that together they can effectively manage increasingly complex problems. In the case of infinite games, the interdependence of relationships means that mother and son either coordinate their efforts and continue to succeed together, or they fail together. Infinite games begin from strengthening relations and are thus always a win-win or lose-lose proposition.

When we look for the cultural resources necessary to respond to the global and national predicament I have described as a "perfect storm," we must anticipate the need for a critical shift in our values, intentions, and practices that takes us from the preponderance of finite games played among self-interested, single actors to a new pattern of infinite games played through the strengthening of those relationships at every level of scale—personal, communal, corporate, and those among nation-states as well. We need to move from finite to infinite games to face and hopefully overcome the shared challenges of our day. Priority must be given to those values and practices that will support replacing the familiar competitive pattern of single actors pursing their own self-interest, with the collaboration of players strengthening possibilities for coordinated flourishing across national, ethnic, and religious boundaries.

This monograph argues that the Confucian tradition—particularly the Confucian conception of relationally constituted persons as "human becomings"—has an important contribution to make in this effort as we struggle to resolve our current human predicament. We urgently need a more inclusive world cultural order: one that draws upon all of the resources available to us and can provide the change in our values and practices necessary to guarantee a future for our children, grandchildren, and the generations to come.

Chapter One

The Question of Which Questions to Ask?

Setting the Problem:
Where Should the Discourse on Confucian Ethics Begin?

As I have mentioned in the introduction, the influence of G. W. F. Hegel as a philosopher, for good and for bad, has still not waned almost two centuries after his death. In his introduction to the *Encyclopaedia Logic*, Hegel reflects at great length upon the following questions: Where does philosophy begin? Where does the inquiry start? And in this reverie, he concludes that because philosophy "does not have a beginning in the sense of the other sciences," it must be the case that "the beginning only has a relation to the subject who takes the decision to philosophise."[1] For Hegel, it is the ultimate project of such philosophizing to bring this person—the finite spirit, the single intellect, the philosopher—into identity with God as the object of pure thinking. And for Hegel like Confucianism, the person is not a fact but an achievement that could not become what it does without the structures of the human community. In this inquiry into Confucian ethics, then, I first want to embrace Hegel's concern about the importance of understanding the beginning of our philosophical inquiry, and I also want to heed his injunction to start from those who take the decision to philosophize—that is, human persons. At the same time, I am inspired by the philosophical hermeneutics of John Dewey, who began his long career as a Hegelian but early on abandoned Hegel's teleology and idealism to embrace a process (and in many ways

---

1. G. W. F. Hegel, *The Encyclopedia Logic* (Indianapolis and Cambridge: Hackett, 1991), 41.

Darwinian) pragmatism. Within the philosophical narrative of his own tradition, Dewey challenges substance assumptions that commit us to a superordinate conception of discrete individuals and introduces his own radically disjunctive notion of persons as interpenetrating, irreducibly relational "habitudes."

When we turn to Confucian ethics, we must begin from the expectation that within the ethical discourse of different philosophical traditions there have been significantly different assumptions about how the notion of person has been conceptualized. Heeding Hegel's counsel to question the starting point of the inquiry, identifying and excavating these uncommon Confucian assumptions regarding persons might be a good place to begin. Indeed, taking the concept of persons as our starting point becomes a particularly apposite strategy when we consider what follows from it. That is, the cosmological assumptions that set the alternative interpretive contexts for the classical texts defining the Greek and the Confucian philosophical traditions need to be understood as a correlation between speculations about the life-forms and institutions that structure the daily lives of ordinary people and their respective interpretations of cosmic order. We need only to think of Plato who, in the *Republic* and the *Timaeus*, found a correlation between the harmony that orders the human soul in his formulation of political and cosmic order, respectively. This same assumption is at work in the interpretive studies by some of our most distinguished Sinologists. Nathan Sivin explores these correlations in his "State, Cosmos, and Body in the Last Three Centuries B.C.," and on the analogy of landscape paintings, Michael Nylan makes the argument for soft boundaries and multiple centers and perspectives within the evolving Confucian moral geography (*dili* 地理).[2] In her monograph on *Cosmology and Political Culture in Early China*, Wang Aihe provides a succinct statement regarding this claim about the symbiotic nature of Chinese cosmology:

> Such a correlative cosmology is an orderly system of correspondence among various domains of reality in the universe,

---

2. Nathan Sivin, "State, Cosmos, and Body in the Last Three Centuries B.C.," *Harvard Journal of Asiatic Studies* 55, no. 1 (1995): 5–37; and Michael Nylan, "Boundaries of the Body and Body Politic in Early Confucian Thought," *Boundaries and Justice*, eds. David Miller and Sohail Hashmi (Princeton, NJ: Princeton University Press, 2001), 112–35, reprinted in *Confucian Political Ethics*, ed. Daniel A. Bell (Princeton, NJ: Princeton University Press, 2007).

correlating categories of the human world, such as the human body, behavior, morality, the sociopolitical order, and historical changes, with categories of the cosmos, including time, space, the heavenly bodies, seasonal movement, and natural phenomena.[3]

We can generalize in saying that our world cosmologies, grounded as they are in our alternative conceptions of what it means to become persons, are themselves a reflection of how different cultures have come to understand the human condition. In what follows, I will be relying heavily upon the open-ended process cosmology made explicit in the *Great Commentary* commentary (*Dazhuan* 大傳) to the *Book of Changes* (*Yijing* 易經) as an interpretative context for reading and interpreting the classical Confucian texts. And I will be interpreting this cosmology as having evolved from earliest times in a contrapuntal relationship with an emerging, distinctive, and always changing human ethical, social, and political culture.

With respect to the mainstream discourse on ethics within the Western academy, we are turning a corner and are now at the happy juncture where we can anticipate that Confucian perspectives will be increasingly acknowledged and engaged by mainstream philosophers in the continuing conversation. And like my many colleagues who have been advocates for including Confucian resources in the debate, I also believe that this tradition has a significant role to play and a distinctive contribution to make. In this monograph I argue that the most important contribution Confucian philosophy broadly, and Confucian ethics more specifically, has to make to this conversation is to provide a robust alternative to the notion of the discrete and autonomous individual at a time when a foundational individualism has become a default position in most contemporary ethical discourse.

With respect to our understanding of Confucian ethics itself, there has been some debate among contemporary scholars working in this field over the appropriateness of categorizing this tradition as either a distinctively Chinese version of virtue ethics, or as a sui generis role ethics that belongs to the Confucian tradition itself. The choice between these classificatory alternatives again turns largely on excavating the conception of persons that is presupposed within the interpretive context of classical

---

3. Wang Aihe, *Cosmology and Political Culture in Early China* (Cambridge: Cambridge University Press, 2000), 2.

Chinese philosophy. If our goal is to take the Confucian tradition on its own terms, and in so doing to resist overwriting it with our own cultural importances, we must begin by first self-consciously and critically theorizing the Confucian conception of persons as the starting point of Confucian ethics.

It should be noted that we need the term "role" in the English expression "Confucian role ethics" to make clear the difference this gerundive notion of person has from other ethical traditions. But "role" is actually redundant when we turn to the Chinese language. That is, "role" is already presupposed in the Chinese translation of the term "ethics" itself as *lunlixue* 倫理學, with *lunli* 倫理 meaning specifically "the quality achieved in the patterns of human roles and relations." Again, *lun* is not only used descriptively to mean roles such as "king" or "husband" but also has qualitative implications as "exemplary or ignoble" or "caring or indolent," respectively.[4] An interesting footnote here is that this same term *lun* also means "category" and "class," suggesting that in this cosmology the construction of theoretical discriminations such as "categories" and "classifications" are a function of analogical correlations among things. Such a functional method of organizing experience stands in stark contrast to the classical Greek tradition in which categories are established through positing some assumed essence or selfsame and reduplicative identical characteristic—that is, some *eidos*—shared among members of a particular genus or species.[5] In this Confucian cosmology, categories of things broadly including that of human beings are to be constructed by correlating what they *do* in the various roles they perform in relation to one another rather than by some ontological reference to what they *are*.

---

4. For the Han dynasty sources of this term *lunli*, see Liu, *Translingual Practices*, 316. Although *lunlixue* as a translation of "ethics" is a late nineteenth-century term invented to synchronize the East Asian traditions with the language of Western modernity, the binomial expression *lunli* itself dates back millennia to Han dynasty sources.

5. The later Wittgenstein is making a similar point with respect to language when he insists that words are not defined by core meanings present in all uses of that word. Rather, we should approach words historically and contextually, mapping them through "a complicated network of similarities, overlapping and criss-crossing." See Ludwig Wittgenstein, *Philosophical Investigations (PI)*, ed. G. E. M. Anscombe and R. Rhees, trans. G. E. M. Anscombe (Oxford: Blackwell, 1953), section 66. Wittgenstein surrenders his earlier concern for certainty, exactness, and fixed boundaries when he introduces the expressions "family resemblances" and "language games"—that is, when he appeals to similarities and associations rather than strict identity and formal definitions in language usage.

In the introduction I worried over the problem of an asymmetry in cultural translation that is marked by a constant theorizing of the Chinese tradition by appeal to Western categories. For me, an immediate example of this tendency has been our rush to tailor Confucian ethics to fit the category of virtue ethics. It is at least an interesting coincidence that early on in the Chinese-language literature many of our more influential scholars on Chinese ethics—Mou Zongsan and Lee Ming-huei might be two prominent examples—proffered a principle-based, Kantian interpretation of this tradition. In his survey of Confucian ethics, David Elstein argues that such a deontic interpretation of Chinese ethics has been predominate within Chinese scholarship broadly.[6] But when Elizabeth Anscombe's 1958 publication of "Modern Moral Philosophy" precipitated a revisionist rehabilitation of virtue ethics in the Western ethical discourse, prevailing interpretations of Chinese ethics in our Western sources seemed to follow this new direction in the evolution of Western ethical theory. In her essay, Anscombe accuses rule-based deontology and utilitarianism of being anemically legalistic and lacking any moral psychology. Her seminal critique anticipated Alasdair MacIntyre's *After Virtue* and the avalanche of publications on virtue ethics that followed in its wake.[7] The concerted efforts in Western normative theory to rehabilitate virtue ethics as a significant voice in the discourse occasioned by Anscombe's challenge has also been the story of an interpretive turn in the reading of Confucian ethics within the Western literature. Indeed, the majority of scholars in Confucian philosophy in the Western academy, along with many of their colleagues who do Western ethics, have become more than comfortable in invoking both classical and contemporary developments in virtue ethics as the best way to describe and understand the Confucian tradition.[8] At the same time, many contemporary Chinese scholars themselves who

---

6. David Elstein, "Contemporary Confucianism," *The Routledge Companion to Virtue Ethics*, ed. Lorraine Besser-Jones and Michael Slote (New York: Routledge, 2015), 238.

7. G. E. M. Anscombe, "Modern Moral Philosophy," *Philosophy* 33 (1958).

8. Reflecting on this interpretive turn in Confucian ethics another way, we might recall how in Lewis Carroll's *Through the Looking-Glass*, the White Queen muses that "it's a poor sort of memory that only works backwards." For us to take the recent encounter of Confucian ethics with Western ethical theory as being its defining moment might be a fair example of the White Queen's better kind of memory that remembers forward; that is, now that we have revived virtue ethics as a robust contender in our own ethical discourse, we have "remembered" quite clearly that Confucian ethics is also a form of virtue ethics.

specialize in Confucian moral philosophy remain resistant to any simple equation between Confucian ethics and virtue ethics, beginning from questioning the appropriateness of eliding the distinction between the Confucian notion of *de* 德 conventionally translated as "virtue" and the Greek concept of *arête*.

Aristotle defines *arête* ("virtue") as

> a state concerned with choice, lying in a mean relative to us, this being determined by reason and in the way in which the man of practical wisdom would determine it.[9]

The assumption is that such a virtue—such an excellence or efficacy or ability—is the character trait or settled disposition or state of mind of a particular person. By way of contrast, in the early Chinese cosmology, *de* as a particular "focus" or "insistent particularity" has to be understood in its holographic relationship with *dao* 道 that serves as the specific "field" as it is construed from this particular perspective. And the normative aspect of any particular thing—its excellence, efficacy, or ability—is a function of the quality of the coalescence this particular focus has been able to achieve with all things within its environing field. With respect to persons specifically, *de* does not simply reduce individuals to their character traits or states of mind but rather references the relational virtuosity that such persons evidence within the various activities that in sum come to constitute their life story. Many Chinese commentators would allow that while "virtue" ethics as it has evolved within the Western narrative might have some relevance for understanding Confucian ethics, given the cosmological implications of *de*, such a resonance does not tell the whole story.

I will argue that to the extent the language of virtue ethics broadly, including its many contemporary evolving variations and accretions, still appeals to the familiar vocabulary cluster of agents, acts, generic virtues, character traits, autonomy, motivation, reasons, choice, freedom, principles, consequences, and so on, introduces distinctions that assume some form of foundational individualism as its starting point. In our own time, but having deep roots in the classical Greek philosophical narrative, the individualism assumed in the vocabulary of the deontic, utilitarian, and indeed virtue ethical discourse, while certainly not one thing, has

---

9. Aristotle, *The Complete Works of Aristotle, The Revised Oxford Translation*, ed. Jonathan Barnes (Princeton, NJ: Princeton University Press, 1984), 1106.36–1107.2.

still become a default commonsense assumption, if not an ideology. By "ideology" I mean that when some variant of individualism that appeals to the vocabulary cluster of the discrete person has garnered a monopoly on our consciousness without any serious alternative to challenge it, this variant can best be described as an ideology: in the sense of being the characteristic thinking of an individual, group, or culture.[10]

I will claim that Confucian ethics, by way of contrast with the vocabulary cluster of the discrete individual, begins from the primacy of vital relationality and the wholeness of experience that follows therefrom. Confucian ethics is formulated by invoking its own radically different focus-field cluster of terms and distinctions: "aspiring to become consummate in our roles and relations" (*ren* 仁), "optimizing appropriateness in our roles and relations" (*yi* 義), "seeking relational virtuosity" (*de* 德), "aspiring to propriety in our roles and relations" (*li* 禮), "embodying the tradition through its intergenerational transmission in our roles and relations" (*ti* 體), "bodyheartminding" (*xin* 心), "cultivating our human propensities" (*xing* 性), "resolution and commitment in what we do in our roles and relations" (*cheng* 誠), "pursuing an optimizing harmony or symbiosis within the diversity of our relations" (*he* 和), and so on. Confucian ethics begins from fundamentally different assumptions about how personal identities emerge in our human narratives and how moral competence is expressed as a habituated virtuosity in the roles and relationships that come to constitute us. To fail to distinguish what I will

---

10. We might cite as a counterexample to my claim that individualism has a monopoly on consciousness within the Western philosophical narrative: the fact that social psychologist George Herbert Mead and his fellow traveler John Dewey in their own time developed a revolutionary conception of the relationally constituted person as their own substantial alternative to individualism. But in weighing up this counterexample, we might want to heed A. N. Whitehead's claim that in the philosophical dialectic such counterexamples have to be further assessed on the basis of the actual difference they have made. That is, what influence have such interventions had on changing existing assumptions? Indeed, in having to acknowledge that until very recently this Mead-Dewey conception of a relationally constituted conception of person has made little impact on our contemporary thinking and commonsense assumptions about what it means to be a person, we must allow that, ironically, the counterexample in fact makes the case; that is, an ideology of individualism prevails within the Western discourse. I will argue that it is only as the *intra*subjective conception of person is being thought through by contemporaries such as Charles Taylor, Michael Sandel, and Mark Johnson that such recent scholarship is in some important degree indebted to the classical pragmatists in the revisionist direction they are taking this discussion.

call individual and discrete human "beings" from Confucian relationally constituted "human becomings," then, would mean that we have willy-nilly insinuated a contemporary and decidedly foreign notion of person into our investigation before it has even begun.

The Challenge of Our Times: Theorizing Intrasubjective Persons

Hegel's concern about where a philosophical investigation begins was not a question lost on John Dewey. Almost a century ago, in his *Individualism Old and New*, Dewey worried over the growth in his time of an aberrant form of individualism that had broken with Emerson's promise to conjure forth for us a nonconformist and self-reliant American soul. Dewey rued the fact that real "individuality" as "the most characteristic activity of a self"[11]—that is, the Emersonian project of each of us aspiring to the highest quality of our own personal uniqueness—had degenerated into the then prevailing creed of a self-interested and contentious "individualism." Such a "new" individualism for Dewey is little more than a zero-sum mercantile culture of winners and losers:

> The spiritual factor of our tradition, equal opportunity and free association and intercommunication, is obscured and crowded out. Instead of the development of individualities which it prophetically set forth, there is a perversion of the whole ideal of individualism to conform to the practices of a pecuniary culture. It has become the source and justification of inequalities and oppressions.[12]

Setting up a distinction between his own neologism "individuality" and what had become a then decadent "individualism," he goes on to exhort philosophers in their search for the Great Community to meet the challenge of formulating a new conception of person that embodies the very "idea" of democracy as a personal, social, political, and ultimately religious ideal. Indeed, for Dewey, "constructing a new individuality con-

---

11. John Dewey, *The Later Works of John Dewey*, 1925–1953, ed. Jo Ann Boydston, vol. 7 (Carbondale: Southern Illinois University Press, 1985), 286.

12. Dewey, *Later Works*, 5:49.

sonant with the objective conditions under which we live is the deepest problem of our time."[13]

Dewey felt that we need to aspire to an "individuality" in which full personal realization and the optimal communal flourishing that emerges from these achieved individualities are coterminous and mutually entailing. In his advocacy for this intersubjective "individuality," Dewey can be read as a precursor to prominent contemporary philosophers such as Charles Taylor and Michael Sandel and their reflections on how we become persons.[14] Charles Taylor in his *Sources of the Self* and continuing in his more recent monograph, *The Language Animal*, marries a doctrine of socially embedded persons emerging within "webs of interlocution" who exemplify irreducibly "embodied agency" with a historically and culturally self-conscious form of a communicating communitarianism.[15] In Taylor's view, it is not only that we discover things about who we are through communicating with others, but much more radically, we can only become persons by narrating shared worlds of embodied experience. Taylor's work on person and agency is devoted to a complex and pluralistic understanding of what he terms "hypergoods"—the moral framework within which such identities are formed. If there is a limitation within the parameters of Taylor's compelling exploration of the discursive "sources of the self," he is self-consciously aware that the matrix of objectively real values he references has, through the confluence of communities across time, come to constitute the continuing identity of an evolving and distinctively Western civilization rather than referencing humanity more broadly.

As early as his *Liberalism and the Limits of Justice*, Michael Sandel has also been strongly critical of the deracinated self that serves as starting point for the Kantian-cum-Rawlsian deontological conception of the individual. He describes the Rawlsian person in the following terms:

---

13. Dewey, *Later Works*, 5:56.

14. A. T. Nuyen, "Confucian Role Ethics," *Comparative and Continental Philosophy* 4, no. 1 (2012): 141–150 has most helpfully offered some examples of recent Western ethical theorists who offer a relational and role-based conception of persons: Charles Taylor, *Sources of the Self: The Making of the Modern Identity* (Cambridge, MA: Harvard University Press, 1989); Dorothy Emmet, *Rules, Roles and Relations* (London: Macmillan, 1967); Marion Smiley, *Moral Responsibility and the Boundaries of Community* (Chicago: University of Chicago Press, 1992); and Larry May, *Sharing Responsibility* (Chicago: University of Chicago Press, 1992).

15. Taylor, *Sources of the Self*; and Taylor, *The Language Animal: The Full Shape of the Human Linguistic Capacity* (Cambridge, MA: Harvard University Press, 2016).

> We can locate this individualism and identify the conceptions of the goods it excludes by recalling that the Rawlsian self is not only a subject of possession, but an antecedently individuated subject, standing always at a certain distance from the interests it has. One consequence of this distance is to put the self beyond the reach of experience, to make it invulnerable, to fix its identity once and for all.[16]

And Sandel is clear about the perceived limitations and the consequences of beginning from and building upon such an anemic and isolated conception of individual identity that fails to respect Hegel's previously cited assertion that we only become who we are through our shared social structures. Sandel concludes that

> a self so thoroughly independent as this rules out any conception of the good (or the bad) bound up with possession in the constitutive sense. It rules out the possibility of any attachment (or obsession) able to reach beyond our values and sentiments to engage our identity itself. It rules out the possibility of a public life in which for good or ill, the identity as well as the interests of the participants could be at stake. And it rules out the possibility that common purposes and ends could inspire more or less expansive self-understandings and so define a community in the constitutive sense, a community describing the subject and not just the objects of shared aspirations.[17]

Sandel's search for a more interesting place to start looks to an alternative "intersubjective," or what he terms, perhaps more accurately, as an "intrasubjective" conception of self that the Rawlsian position by implication has clearly ruled out. Sandel is making an important distinction here in invoking "intra-" as a preferred alternative prefix to "inter-," a distinction between a doctrine of internal versus external relations. We commonly use the prefix "inter-" to suggest a joint, external, and open relationship that conjoins two or more separate and in some

---

16. Michael Sandel, *Liberalism and the Limits of Justice* (Cambridge: Cambridge University Press, 1982), 62.

17. Sandel, *Liberalism*, 62.

sense comparable entities. For example, we use our independent and comparable computers to join the "internet" ("inter" + "network") and to get on a "web" with other netizens. "Intra-" by way of contrast, is "on the inside," "within," and references internal and constitutive relations contained within a given entity itself. Sandel insists that intrasubjective conceptions of persons

> allow that for certain purposes, the appropriate description of the moral subject may refer to a plurality of selves within a single individual human being, as when we account for inner deliberation in terms of the pull of competing identities, or moments of introspection in terms of occluded self-knowledge, or when we absolve someone from responsibility for the heretical beliefs 'he' held before his religious conversion.[18]

Were we to follow up on the cosmological implications of "intra" and observe that it has the important organic, ecological implications of an inside without an outside, we might be taking Sandel's distinction further than he intends. In such a world, the focal identity of each of us is holographic; that is, the whole is contained in each unique graph. What really recommends the term "intrasubjective" over "intersubjective" is that rather than referencing the external relations that obtain between or among separately individuated subjects, "intrasubjective" makes persons focal and aspectual within a matrix of organic, internal relations—an extended "field of selves"—that in sum constitute each of our shared, irreducibly social and personal identities. As such, each of us is one specific configuration of relations within the matrix of associations that constitutes the unbounded ecology of social intra-actions.

While Sandel certainly sees his own understanding of this intrasubjective conception of person as potentially more productive than the "unencumbered" deontological self, he still has a persistent worry that this alternative way of conceptualizing persons, especially when taken in the ecological direction I have previously suggested, might become overly diluted and diffused. As such, it would not be anchored in the sufficiently robust sense of individual unity, identity, and moral agency that Sandel requires. The volume Sandel edited along with Paul D'Ambrosio, *Encountering China: Michael Sandel and Chinese Philosophy*, addresses the idea

---

18. Sandel, *Liberalism*, 63.

of Confucian role ethics specifically. While he agrees with Rosemont and Ames that we must reject the idea that "the continuity of our identities over a lifetime is given by an 'essential' self at the core of our being whose contours are fixed once and for all, untouched by the vicissitudes of life," he still wants to distinguish his own position from their claim that persons, rather than being such "selves," are the sum of their roles and relations. Sandel avers that

> what the purely aggregative picture misses, it seems to me, is the role of narrative and reflection (including critical reflection). Not only social roles and relationships, but also interpretations of those roles and relationships, are constitutive of personhood. But narration and interpretation presuppose narrators and interpreters—storytelling selves who seek to make sense of their circumstances, to evaluate and assess the aims and attachments that would claim them. And this interpretive activity, this making of sense, constitutes moral agency.[19]

In responding to Sandel's concern that a sense of autonomous moral agency needs to be maintained, we might begin from a claim developed further in this chapter that the "twoness" in the Confucian notion of consummate person and conduct (*ren* 仁) includes the development of a quality of self-awareness that provides the relationally constituted person with a deliberate and critical perspective on one's own conduct and that of others. At the same time, we might also qualify Sandel's notion of "individual" autonomy and agency with the work of Larry May in *Sharing Responsibility*. May himself largely acquiesces in the moral discourse's strong pull toward a central place for the individual. Even so, he recognizes that in order to appreciate our shared responsibilities as members of a group composed of just such individuals, we must reconceive our familiar ways of thinking about agency in a more pluralistic and communal way:

> Agency should be conceived of in such a way as to include the attitudes and dispositions of those who do not directly perpetrate the act for which responsibility is in question, but whose attitudes and dispositions provide a climate that increases

---

19. Michael J. Sandel and Paul J. D'Ambrosio, eds., *Encountering China: Michael Sandel and Chinese Philosophy* (Cambridge, MA: Harvard University Press, 2018), 274.

the likelihood those acts will be committed. . . . What I am suggesting is that agency should not be conceived of so individualistically. A person's attitudes and dispositions form a context within which that person behaves. The collection of attitudes and dispositions within a community form a climate within which individual behavior occurs.[20]

By way of example, we live in a decidedly racist and sexist world. Even those persons not overtly guilty of being racist or sexist can still inadvertently condone these discriminatory behaviors through normalizing them; they, too, must assume a share of responsibility for the world being what it is. Indeed, May goes so far as to align himself with Heidegger and Jaspers in recognizing that our existential choices are in fact made by persons who are themselves a social construct constituted by "the interplay of history, social conditioning, and the chosen behavior of the individual person."[21] On this basis, May would revive a notion of "existential conscientiousness" that

> urges us to take the kind of enlarged mentality that is barely individualistic, if at all, for it urges us to look at our roles from the perspective of others who are affected by the way we act within those roles.[22]

When Confucius's protégé Zigong asks if there is a single word that can be practiced with profit until the end of one's days, Confucius replies emphatically that it must be the word "deference" (*shu* 恕): literally, "putting oneself in the other's place." For Confucius, this one protean word captures everything he has been trying to convey to his students about the immediate correlation between exercising an educated moral imagination and the possibility of optimizing their relations with others.

Sandel also wants to take the notion of person in a communal direction. Over the years, Sandel has appropriated elements from a range of philosophers, particularly Aristotle and Hegel, and more recently, the Jewish tradition. His project is to formulate an adequately intrasubjective

---

20. May, *Sharing Responsibility*, 52.
21. May, *Sharing Responsibility*, 3.
22. May, *Sharing Responsibility*, 181.

conception of person that allows for a communally constitutive identity that at the same time retains a sufficiently strong sense of personal unity and autonomy. And like Dewey and Taylor, Sandel is committed to a more narrative and relational understanding of persons—that is, persons as "narrators and interpreters" within their particular roles. Such prominent and yet distinctively Western philosophers in their openness to other cultural traditions are an encouragement for engaging the values sedimented into other world philosophies such as the Confucian, Buddhist, Daoist, South Asian, and Islamic cultures that have provided their own human communities with alternative strategies for achieving personal and cultural identity.

In recent decades, in witnessing the dramatic rise and opening of the Asia-Pacific region occurring at the expense of an increasingly isolationist Europe and America, we have quite abruptly found ourselves in a historical moment characterized by a realigning of the geopolitical order of the world. A quantum shift has occurred that has destabilized what was a familiar configuration of the world's economic and political structure and dynamics. The question that arises in our time is this: in the wake of this reconfiguration of the geopolitical order, should we be anticipating a similar sea change in the world's cultural order that will now draw into play previously ignored Asian resources?

Contemporary philosopher Joel Kupperman, whose work is heavily influenced by the Asian traditions broadly, has joined the conversation on ethics and has made his own singularly important contribution to the discourse. His main argument is that ethical philosophy should be structured around the development of character as it begins in family relations and is further developed within the context of community and tradition. In his earlier writings—especially in his seminal monograph *Character*—Kupperman has formulated a doctrine of "character ethics" that he posits as a robust alternative to more familiar versions of virtue ethics. And he sees the Confucian emphasis on personal cultivation as a close analog to his long-term concern with character development. With Kupperman's formulation of this doctrine of character ethics, he is glad to break ranks with those who would advocate for virtue ethics and is further prepared to insist that Confucius himself should be included as a fellow character-ethicist.[23] Kupperman has argued persuasively that his

---

23. Joel J. Kupperman, *Character* (New York and Oxford: Oxford University Press, 1991), 108–9.

"character ethics" is a better model for interpreting Confucian ethics than "virtue ethics" because, in appealing to the unique composite amalgam of virtues and vices that come to constitute any person's character, we are able to respect the multifactorial particularity of persons in a way that is lost when we appeal to a set of monochromatic virtue traits.

While virtues are generally classified and treated separately and simply, Kupperman's appeal to character development requires that we appreciate the interpenetration among personal qualities both good and bad and thus accommodate their multivalence and complexity. In assessing the conduct of persons over their careers, we would do well to take the fusion of both positive and negative qualities into consideration. Furthermore, for Kupperman "selves are constructed during a life rather than being present at birth."[24] With this assertion, he attempts to restore process and duration to the notion of human character, to respect the interpenetration of positive and negative qualities in time, and to abandon any severe distinction between what one does and what is done to one.

Kupperman's robust conception of character development is more specific and personal than a doctrine of virtue traits and has an active, continuous, and particularizing function that both unifies and stabilizes lives through time. In the various dimensions of a developing character, Kupperman wants to understand moral conduct in a vital and more holistic sense by reinstating to a significant degree the processive nature, the always specific context, the particularity, and the growth that are all characteristics of moral conduct. And while appreciative of how Kupperman has taken us in the right direction by restoring many of the continuities in human conduct that have been underrepresented in virtue ethics, Henry Rosemont and I would still contend that he does not go far enough.[25] We are able to identify several remaining disjunctions and dichotomies in his own theory of character ethics that prevent Kupperman, like all the king's horses and all the king's men, from reinstating the wholeness and the capaciousness of our actual moral experience.

First, Kupperman insists on retaining the default concept of a discrete, separate, and reified "self" as the emergent product of character

---

24. Kupperman, *Character*, 37.
25. See our extended discussion of Kupperman's project in "From Kupperman's Character Ethics to Confucian Role Ethics: Putting Humpty Together Again," in *Moral Cultivation and Confucian Character: Engaging Joel J. Kupperman*, ed. Li Chenyang and Ni Peimin (Albany: State University of New York Press, 2014).

development. For Kupperman, "character approximates the nature of self" where his analogies are that "character is to the major matters of life as the nature of self is to all of life."[26] That is, for Kupperman there is a definite, discrete individuality to the self that serves as the ground and the locus of one's character development and that becomes manifest in its more important undertakings.[27] What then is the relationship between this self, its character, and its conduct? To answer this question, Kupperman would retain a clear distinction between the self and the character it has accrued that then "flows" from the character of this self into its actions.

Again, Kupperman's notion of the "self-as-collage" certainly includes "elements derived from outside sources" that have both a causal and a constitutive status along with the sedimenting of "layers that represent the absorption (or sometimes, rejection) of various influences at various stages of life, going back to early childhood."[28] Even though Kupperman often references and seems to appreciate the relational nature of the Confucian person, he is still consistent in maintaining that the character of an individual can be accurately described, analyzed, and evaluated independently of other human beings. With this underlying assumption of an individual and discrete self, Kupperman interprets persons as they are embedded within family narratives in an importantly different way than the role ethics perspective of relationally constituted persons.

In this monograph, I want to join in common cause with Kupperman, Dewey, Taylor, Sandel, and other like-minded contemporaries. In these transitional times, there is some urgency in taking full advantage of all of our global cultural resources, Asian as well as European, to formulate an adequate conception of intrasubjective persons and to advocate for its inclusion in the ethical discourse. More specifically, in this continuing quest to articulate a viable notion of intrasubjective persons for further reflection, I want to invite Confucius with his thick conception of relationally constituted persons to have his seat at the table. With Confucian role ethics, we will discover an alternative notion of persons that contrasts with the many competing versions of the discrete,

---

26. Kupperman, *Character*, 47

27. Kupperman, *Character*, 19.

28. Kupperman, "Tradition and Community in the Formation of Character and Self," *Confucian Ethics: A Comparative Study of Self, Autonomy, and Community*, eds. Kwong-loi Shun and David B. Wong (Cambridge: Cambridge University Press, 2004), 117.

exclusive, and foundational individual currently dominating the discourse in normative ethics.

Angus Graham on Abjuring Substance Ontology in Theorizing Confucian Persons

In turning from these more or less recent excurses in Western moral theory to the conception of person in Confucian ethics, where is the best place to start? What then is a person in classical Confucian philosophy? This would seem to be the obvious, operative question from which we ought to begin our philosophical inquiry. But is it really? Angus Graham quite astutely recognizes that the way we formulate our questions—in this case, for example, our question of *what* is a person in classical Confucian philosophy?—in fact anticipates the answer we will get. The *what* question already prompts and privileges a particular "noun" or "thing" kind of answer while precluding other possibilities. With this in mind, suggests Graham, if we take a step back and examine the language we use to ask our questions, we might be able to discern important conceptual differences in different cultural traditions (and in our case, perhaps even an alternative conception of the human being).

To take just one example of such a difference, in reference to this Confucian conception of "person," Herbert Fingarette would argue that at the very least, we would have to change the question to ask: What are *persons* (plural) in classical Confucianism? Fingarette has famously opined that "for Confucius, unless there are at least two human beings, there can be no human beings."[29] In making this claim, Fingarette is suggesting that "person" in the singular as a discrete individual has little relevance for the relational and irreducibly social notion of persons at play in Confucian philosophy. Persons either come together or not at all. Indeed, endorsing Fingarette's claim that human beings are irreducibly social, I have pluralized "person" in both the subtitle and throughout this monograph: "Theorizing 'Persons' for Confucian Role Ethics."

Graham ascribes unique and evolving categories and conceptual structures to different cultural traditions. In so doing, he is challenging the Saussurian structuralist distinction between *langue* as universal and

---

29. Herbert Fingarette, "The Music of Humanity in the *Conversations of Confucius*," *Journal of Chinese Philosophy* 10 (1983): 217.

systematic linguistic structures and rules governing all languages and *parole* as diverse and open-ended speech acts in any of our natural languages.[30] Like many (but not all) of us, Graham is persuaded that different populations within ever-changing cultural milieus appeal to different concepts and ways of thinking and living.[31] But for Graham, getting at such conceptual differences is not an easy task:

> That people of another culture are somehow thinking in other categories is a familiar idea, almost a commonplace, but one very difficult to pin down as a topic for fruitful discussion.[32]

We might recall Nietzsche's "philosophy of grammar" as having anticipated Graham in this respect. Nietzsche asserts that a particular worldview has over time been sedimented into each member of the family of Indo-European languages to both shape and constrain the semiotic structures of these disparate yet in some ways continuous cultures. As a consequence of this shared history, our culturally specific Indo-European languages

---

30. Saussure uses the analogy of a chess game, where *langue* are the fixed rules that govern the game while *parole* are the actual, varied moves made by different people that come to constitute any particular game.

31. Zhang Longxi, for example, in his commitment to pursuing intercultural understanding, is quite critical of those of us (singling out Jacques Gernet as one primary example) who would describe the tension between Christianity and Chinese as not only one "of different intellectual traditions" but also "of different mental categories and modes of thought." See Gernet, *China and the Christian Impact: A Conflict of Cultures*, trans. J. Lloyd (Cambridge: Cambridge University Press, 1985), 8. Zhang becomes impatient when "the cultural difference between the Chinese and the Western is formulated as fundamentally distinct ways of thinking and speaking, as the ability, or lack of it, to express abstract ideas." Zhang does not recognize that in his giving deracinated abstract and theoretical ideas pride of place as a higher order of thinking, he is advocating for Western philosophical assumptions that are not only absent in the classical Chinese tradition but in fact are under assault as specious within Western philosophy's own ongoing, internal critique. See Zhang's "Translating Cultures: China and the West," in *Chinese Thought in a Global Context: A Dialogue Between Chinese and Western Philosophical Approaches*, ed. Karl-Heinz Pohl (Leiden, The Netherlands: Brill, 1999), 44.

32. A. C. Graham. *Studies in Chinese Philosophy and Philosophical Literature* (Albany: State University of New York Press, 1990), 360.

in their various modes of expression encourage certain philosophical possibilities while discouraging others:

> The strange family resemblance of all Indian, Greek, and German philosophizing is explained easily enough. Where there is an affinity of languages, it cannot fail, owing to the common philosophy of grammar—I mean owing to the unconscious domination and guidance by similar grammatical functions—that everything is prepared at the outset for a similar development and sequence of philosophical systems; just as the way seems barred against certain other possibilities of world-interpretation.[33]

Graham like Nietzsche before him looks to what languages reveal grammatically and by extension, conceptually, to get at the slippery issue of other cultures "thinking in other categories." In thus trying to identify different categories and ways of thinking that would enable us to distinguish Chinese and Indo-European cultures from each other, Graham focuses on how the disparate questions we choose to ask might indeed prompt different answers:

> Since every philosophical answer is shaped by the posing of the question, it may be suspected that the categories within which we think correspond to the basic words available in the language for asking the questions. . . . Can we use the interrogative words to trace differences between Chinese and Western categories?[34]

Graham has consistently warned us that serious equivocations emerge when we elide the distinction between classical Greek ontological commitments and those assumptions grounding a classical Chinese processive, procreative cosmology. Ontology privileges "being *per se*" and a substance language with its "essence" and "attribute" dualism—that is,

---

33. Friedrich Nietzsche, *Beyond Good and Evil*, trans. Walter Kaufmann (New York: Vintage, 1966), 20.
34. Graham, *Studies in Chinese Philosophy*, 3.

substances as property-bearers, and properties that are borne, respectively. Process cosmology, on the other hand, privileges an irreducibly relationally "becoming" and the vital, interdependent, correlative categories needed to "speak" process and its eventful content.

With such teleology and idealism shaping our own common sense, reading *xing* 性 as "nature" suggests to us that human "beings" have as their formal cause "a universal human essence, invariant in all times and places" along with a human *telos* or end as their erstwhile final cause. Indeed, it is precisely this kind of essentialism that has now become the standard reading of Mencius in both the European and Asian language literature, a persistent teleological misreading that Graham over his long career first endorsed, returned to repeatedly for further reflection, and then ultimately rejected.[35]

By contrast with human "beings," the generative and open-ended conception of human "becomings" in the Confucian tradition is itself an answer that requires posing a rather different question. Persons are conceived of as coterminous genealogical narratives-within-narratives, invariably in media res without initial beginnings or final ends. Thus, we should not ask, *What* is a person? We must ask the irreducibly contextual and generative questions, *Whence* and *whither* persons? We need to ask after the story of how evolving personal identities have emerged pari passu within their unfolding narrative contexts, and where the trajectory that such life episodes project will lead them. We must conceive of persons not as abstract "things" or "objects" but rather as generalizable, historical "events." Graham's insight is that in the Confucian context

> *xing* is conceived in terms of spontaneous development in a certain direction rather than of its origin or goal. . . . The *cheng* 成 "completion" of a thing's development which in man is his *cheng* 誠 "integrity," is the interdependent becoming integral rather than the realization of an end.[36]

---

35. For the history of this revisionist reading, see Roger T. Ames, "Reconstructing A. C. Graham's Reading of *Mencius* on *Xing* 性: A Coda to 'The Background of the Mencian Theory of Human Nature' (1967)," in *Having a Word with Angus Graham: At Twenty-Five Years into His Immortality*, ed. Carine Defoort and Roger T. Ames (Albany: State University of New York Press, 2018).

36. Graham, "Replies," 288.

Here Graham is saying that in our spontaneous development our "interdependent" context is continually becoming integral to who we are becoming. Hence, neither persons in their particularity nor humanity as a species can be defined in terms of a discrete beginning or some ultimate end. Graham is keenly aware here of a fundamental contrast between closure and disclosure: between the potential and the actualization of a teleologically driven and substantive human "being," on the one hand, and the continuing emergence of narratively nested human "becomings" informed by the gravitas of an evolving civilization on the other. After all, Confucian persons are events within a continuing transformative, genealogical process wherein their progenitors do not have discrete origins, nor do they suffer ultimate annihilation. On the contrary, these predecessors within a family lineage embody their own antique ancestors—physically, socially, and culturally—at the erstwhile beginnings of their own particular narratives, and then they continue to live on through succeeding generations of their own progeny that carry them beyond any ostensive end.

Aristotle on Asking the Right Questions

Aristotle before Hegel was also concerned about where the philosophical investigation begins. And in looking for this beginning, he took *What is a person?* as his very first question. That is, Aristotle's *Categories* is the first text of the *Organon* in the standard *Corpus Aristotelicum*. And Aristotle's initial project in the *Categories* is to identify the full set of questions that must be asked to give a comprehensive account of what can be predicated of a subject, with his own concrete example of this subject being "the man in the marketplace." In the several different versions of these categories found throughout his corpus the question of *what* is not only his first question but also his primary one. Its primacy lies in the fact that in Aristotle's answer to this question he introduces an ontological disparity by first identifying the necessary essence or substance of the subject (Gk. *ousia*, L. *substantia*)—What "is" a man?—followed then by questions that distinguish this person's various secondary and contingent attributes: What is "in" a man? Aristotle explains this ontological distinction between substance and attribute in the following terms:

> To give a rough idea, examples of substance are man, horse; of quantity: four-foot, five-foot; of qualification: white, grammatical; of a relative: double, half, larger; of where: in the Lyceum, in the market-place; of when: yesterday, last-year; of being-in-a-position: is-lying, is-sitting; of having: has-shoes-on, has-armour-on; of doing: cutting, burning; of being-affected: being-cut, being-burned.[37]

For Aristotle, the *what* question has primacy because it provides us with the essential subject: what identifies the underlying substance of what the man *is*. The various other questions that are prompted by the remaining secondary conditions—quantity, quality, relation, place, time, position, state, action, and affection—seek to provide us with the full complement of attributes that are "in" a subject or can be said "of" a subject that describe it as contingent and conditional predicates, none of which can exist without supervening on this subject. In Aristotle's own language:

> All the other things are either said of the primary substances as subjects or in them as subjects. . . . So if the primary substances did not exist it would be impossible for any of the other things to exist.[38]

It is interesting and important to note that Aristotle's set of questions does not include *how* or *why*. This is because his substance ontology has causal and teleological entailments that already answer the *how* and *why* questions: the subject by definition has the potential that when actualized makes him a man. Aristotle thus assumes a complete propositional description does not require such further explanation, an assumption that we will see is untenable in Chinese process cosmology.

Graham reflects on the extent to which this substance ontology individuates and decontextualizes the man by locating his potentialities as residing essentially within him. In reflecting on Aristotle's strategy for a complete description and what it reveals about his categories, Graham observes the following:

---

37. Aristotle, *The Complete Works of Aristotle, The Revised Oxford Translation*, ed. Jonathan Barnes (Princeton, NJ: Princeton University Press, 1984), 1a25–2b4.
38. Aristotle, *Complete Works*, 2a35–2b5–6.

Aristotle's procedure is to isolate one thing from others, treating even transitive verbs ("cuts," "burns") as objectless, and even the relative ("half," "bigger") as not relating two things but said of one with reference to the other.[39]

We can say of the man in the marketplace that "he-burns" or "he-cuts" as a predicate without the need of stipulating the object of these actions, and we can say "he-is-bigger" as a characteristic of him in reference to a second person rather than describing a relationship between the two. Graham states further:

> Aristotle's thinking is noun-centered; he starts with the substance identified as man, and before introducing any verb but "to be" can already ask "When was he in the market-place?" and "Where was he yesterday?" but not "Whence?" or "Whither?"[40]

Aristotle's ontology allows for a notion of simple location and discrete individuality: the noun form is favored grammatically—the "man" in the marketplace—as the ground for the attributes that can then be ascribed to him. Importantly, the potential of the man's formal essence and his final *telos* as a man makes the explanatory questions of *whence* and *whither* moot.

In his work on social ontology, David Weissman describes Aristotle as asserting the kind of discrete identity that makes us individuals and is the basis of external rather than internal relations:

> Things that have matter and form—primary substance—are freestanding. Each is self-sufficient . . . Aristotle would have us believe that a thing's relations to other things—including spatial, temporal, and causal relations—are incidental to its identity. He reasoned that identity is established by form, so that relations to other things many only support, somewhat disguise, or threaten the thing.[41]

---

39. Graham, *Studies in Chinese Philosophy*, 380.
40. Graham, *Studies in Chinese Philosophy*, 391.
41. David Weissman, *A Social Ontology* (New Haven, CT: Yale University Press, 2000), 95.

One of the corollaries of an Aristotelian substance ontology that privileges such an isolated, individual subject is the experience of the world as populated by discrete things or objects that "object" to us in standing independent of us. And a second corollary of this ontology is the doctrine of external relations it assumes; that is, it construes these various independent objects each with its own essential integrity as first-order, discrete things—what they really are—and then any relations that might conjoin them as only second-order, contingent relations that they subsequently contract.

A Doctrine of Internal, Constitutive Relations

Graham sees this commonsense ontological understanding of the discrete and substantial individual with its doctrine of external relations as standing in rather stark contrast to a classical Chinese process cosmology. In this process cosmology, the world is constituted by the interdependence and interpenetration of "things" (or better, "events") that would require a doctrine of intrinsic, constitutive relations to describe them. Erstwhile "things" do not have a "place" in the sense of simple location, but as "events" in history they are "taking place" with time and space being aspectual descriptors. Referring to this contrast with Aristotle, Graham opines that in Chinese thought

> things appear not as independent but as interdependent . . . and the questions that isolate things from each other have no primacy over those which relate them.[42]

Graham is saying that in Confucian cosmology what something "is" and how it is related to its environing others are two first-order aspects of the same phenomenon. Said another way, the unique individuality of something, far from being exclusive of its relationships, is precisely a function of the quality achieved in those relations; the difference between personal identities and their narratives is simply a matter of foregrounding this focus or that field.

For Graham, the Confucian human being as a dynamic, gerundive "event" refers to a continuously evolving, spontaneous process that realizes

---

42. Graham, *Studies in Chinese Philosophy*, 395.

its own potentialities when properly nourished and unimpeded. But again, we must be careful how we understand "potential" here. In Graham's reading of early Confucian cosmology, something's "own potentialities," far from being substantial and inhering exclusively within the thing itself, are irreducibly relational and inclusive of the dynamic transactions that constitute these relations, with the interdependent context over time "becoming integral" to the thing itself. Vital persons and their ecologies are conterminous.

In clarifying the nature of "relations" that is relevant to this Chinese cosmology, Graham's own language of "concrete patterns" versus second-order abstract "relations between things" introduces a distinction between internal, constitutive relations versus external, contingent relations:

> As for "relationships," relation is no doubt an indispensable concept in exposition of Chinese thought, which generally impresses a Westerner as more concerned with the relations between things than with their qualities; but the concern is with concrete patterns rather than relations abstracted from them.[43]

Graham is thus invoking a distinction between a doctrine of internal relations that is actually constitutive of erstwhile "things" and those second-order external relations that would merely conjoin discrete and independent things. Hence, Graham's understanding of a person's "own potentialities," far from being frontloaded as the latent qualities or abilities inherent in particular individuals available to them for actualization, would make such potential inclusive of and a collaboration with their evolving processual contexts. It is thus that such persons can best be characterized in the language of emergent and genealogical human "becomings."

Peter Hershock sheds further light on the distinction between internal and external relations Graham is alluding to here by giving a clear and uncontroversial account of what is meant by internal, constitutive relations and their implications for how we decode the content of our experience. Hershock diagnoses our problem—a problem that we have seen can be traced back to at least as early as Aristotle's ontology. We have our culturally specific, recalcitrant habit of seeing the world as comprising discrete and isolatable "things" that then enter into external

---

43. Graham, "Replies," 288–289.

relations among themselves. Challenging our penchant for giving primacy to these "things," Hershock observes that

> autonomous subjects and objects are, finally, only artifacts of abstraction. . . . What we refer to as "things"—whether mountains, human beings, or complex phenomena like histories—are simply the experienced results of having established relatively constant horizons of value or relevance ("things"). They are not, as commonsense insists, natural occurring realities or [things]. Indeed, what we take to be *objects* existing independently of ourselves are, in actuality, simply a function of habitual patterns of relationships.[44]

Hershock, using the same "patterns of relationships" language here as Graham does, goes on to offer us what might serve as an intellectual cure for our culturally bound, default assumption that such discrete "things" are primary, allowing us to see "through the conceit that relations are second-order realities contingent upon pre-existing actors." A doctrine of internal relations requires of us a different common sense:

> This amounts to an ontological gestalt shift from taking independent and dependent actors to be first order realities and relations among them as second order, to seeing relationality as first order (or ultimate) reality and all individual actors as (conventionally) abstracted or derived from them.[45]

Both Graham and Hershock are insisting that in this Confucian process cosmology, first-order primacy is given to vital relationality and the unique "events" that are constituted by such relations. And further, "objects" as discrete, independent, and isolatable things are only secondary abstractions from such relations. With respect to persons, they are "events" from which discrete individuals are merely an abstraction.

There is momentum in the contemporary philosophical literature that takes the discussion of persons away from old assumptions about discrete individuals and in the direction of relationally constituted entities

---

44. Peter Hershock, *Buddhism in the Public Sphere: Reorienting Global Interdependence* (New York: Routledge, 2006), 140.

45. Hershock, *Buddhism in the Public Sphere*, 147.

who engage each other through their patterns of relations and "horizons of relevance." Robert Cummings Neville, for example, describes Confucian persons with his theory of "orientations":

> Suppose the self, then, is a continuum beginning from the inner center of responsiveness, that is, the intentionality of orientation, functioning specifically to take on orientations in body and mind to the close things of the intimate body, to things and persons of direct contact such as family, friends, and coworkers, and then to social situations, historical places, nature, and the vast cosmos—the ten thousand things each with its own rhythm, *dao*, and discernible grain.[46]

For Neville, his theory of orientations requires that we reconsider traditional assumptions about the self, locating it within a personal history as a changing yet continuous pattern of purposes and directives:

> In the theory of orientations, the boundaries of the self are functions of differing orientations, and the continuity of the self has to do not with an underlying fixed essence or character but with the history of the person's poise efforts, with the ongoing shifting harmonization of the changing things to which the person must take up or correct orientations.[47]

Such a turn away from a foundational individualism is not limited to the Sinological literature but is becoming increasingly marked within mainstream Western discussions as well. John Henry Clippinger's monograph *A Crowd of One* locates erstwhile individuals within this kind of relational nexus by appealing to biological metaphors. He observes that

> the line between the individual and the group becomes blurred, and the principle of a crowd of one takes effect. Whether it is at the cellular or at the cultural level, highly complex strategies have evolved for signaling, constructing, enforcing, verifying, and coordinating social identities. What

---

46. See Robert Cummings Neville, *Ritual and Deference: Extending Chinese Philosophy in a Comparative Context* (Albany: State University of New York Press, 2008), 159.
47. Neville, *Ritual and Deference*, 160.

becomes striking from the example of the immune system is that identity is not an inalienable, irreducible set of individual qualities or attributes, but rather a composite of attributes derived from interactions and reactions to other bodies. In other words, there is no single, unique, irreducible "identity," but rather many different "identities" that have evolved in different social niches.[48]

In her work in trying to bring sociology and ethics together, distinguished contemporary British philosopher Dorothy Emmet, like most philosophers, acknowledges the important social dimension of the human experience:

> We have noted a common starting point for both sociology and ethics in the fact that people need to live in social relationships with each other, not only for survival but if they are to carry out any of the characteristically human enterprises.[49]

In her efforts to reconcile ethics and sociology, however, Emmet sees the contemporary discipline of sociology following this same logic of "internal relations" rehearsed above by Graham and Hershock, and the various implications for personal identity that comes with it:

> Some Idealist philosophers have held a doctrine of "internal relations," according to which the world is thought of as a system in which everything is so related to everything else, that nothing can be understood except with reference to its total context, every part of which attributes to making it what it is, so that it cannot be transposed to another context without becoming something different. It might be said that sociology is the contemporary refuge of the doctrine of internal relations. This of course gets qualified in practice, . . . and some things may make a lot of difference, some very little.[50]

---

48. John Henry Clippinger, *A Crowd of One: The Future of Individual Identity* (New York: PublicAffairs, 2007), 156.

49. Emmet, *Rules, Roles and Relations*, 33.

50. Emmet, *Rules, Roles and Relations*, 90. Emmet is clearly associating the doctrine of internal relations with Hegel's idealism, but given Hegel's teleology and thus linear

Far from scoffing at such an organic, ecological reading of the cosmos, Emmet worries instead about how such a holographic, focus-field way of looking at the world might compromise our capacities to operate effectively within it. As she continues:

> Indeed, this is probably all quite true; but if we are to talk and act with any effectiveness, we cannot just say there is one big web of reciprocal and ramifying relationships. . . . [I]t is not necessary, even if we admit interconnections, only to think of the world as one great system in which everything is related to everything else.[51]

Such an interpretation of our world is indeed challenging. The interpenetration of roles and relations requires a fundamentally different way of thinking about identity and identity construction. The focus-field conception of persons allows for personal resolution and the critical self-awareness necessary to be deliberate in our enrolled activities but also for us to be fully sensitive to the ecological implications of what we do. Indeed, Clippinger suggests that there are ecological ways of thinking of identity that can bring clarity to such holistic thinking:

> What is needed is a new way of framing human identity in an open but precise manner, one that is free of "holistic obscurism" and yet resonates with our natures. Vernon Smith, the Nobel Laureate economist, advocates the need to get beyond notions of narrow self-interest and to embrace a new kind of rationality, what he calls "Ecological Rationality." . . . An ecological perspective has no "externalities," and it is in the interest of

---

dialectic, there are tensions in Hegel that suggest he is perhaps not the best example. On one interpretation of Hegel at least, his commitment to a strong, objective principle of teleology as an a priori concept provides the explanatory principle needed to discipline our empirical investigations and carry us beyond the limits of our empirical sciences. Hegel's strong teleology, which is decidedly theological in its cast, would bring logic and history together by conceptualizing both nature and history as having an inherent logical necessity, where such necessity vitiates the open-ended, emergent, and aesthetic assumptions that come with a coherent doctrine of internal relations.

51. Emmet, *Rules, Roles and Relations*, 139.

all its members to direct the forces of the invisible hand to fully internalize and reduce actual ecological costs.[52]

Emmet insists that good sociology is able to discern different kinds of horizons within the broader organism and discipline this ecological worldview into meaningful patterns of relationships: these are patterns "of overlapping 'fields,' some of which may be affecting others, but whose special internal properties can be studied."[53] With specific reference to roles, Emmet can be helpful in further illuminating how we might want to understand the complex notion of roles and their social implications. First, for Emmet:

> The notion of role refers to such a special relationship, . . . and in any given society there will be certain ways of enacting a role considered appropriate (as we have already seen, the notion of a role has a reference to a norm of behavior built into it). . . . Within this, there are constellations of roles, e.g. in family relations, and in professional relations, and these are not necessarily coherent; in fact their obligations can and do conflict.[54]

And Emmet is clearly aware that roles are not fixed or final. Old roles are reauthorized, and new roles emerge as society evolves:

> Sometimes changes in circumstances, and sometimes new ways in which some dominant individual plays a role, will establish a new pattern, and make it necessary to form a concept of a new role type, or give a different content to the old one.[55]

Emmet herself puzzles over the question of whether all social behavior does not amount to behavior in a role. Deciding that this is at least partly a terminological question, she herself chooses to reserve the term "role" for relationships sufficiently structured to be classified under a

---

52. Clippinger, *A Crowd of One*, 179.
53. Emmet, *Rules, Roles and Relations*, 140.
54. Emmet, *Rules, Roles and Relations*, 140, 146.
55. Emmet, *Rules, Roles and Relations*, 148.

common name. She introduces a distinction between *persona* and *person*, where the former term captures the generalizable roles, while the latter corresponds to the proper name:

> The notion of *persona* answers to the impersonal aspects of morality; it stands for the detachment from "proper names," the attempt to look objectively at a situation, at rights and obligations and at the requirements of the job to be done.[56]

Such a dualistic distinction between persons and their ostensibly impersonal *persona* or roles can certainly be useful as a tool of social analysis and functionally valuable in allowing for a degree of objectivity in, and even detachment from, our roles. Such distance might be needed for resolving the conflicting demands within our roles and in giving us the space for self-consciously cultivating a personal style or image. Still, given the fact of associated living and the irreducibly social definition of persons, I would argue that Emmet's persona-person distinction can be no more than a question of terminological convenience. To take it any further in reifying "individuals" as being discrete and thus somehow separate from their associations, while perhaps at times functional, is still fallacious thinking and might come at a high cost.

The Discrete "Individual" versus Relationally Constituted "Individuality": A Significant Distinction

Importantly, for clarity's sake and to preclude a fundamental and familiar misunderstanding of our claim that "individuals" are second-order abstractions from their relations, we will need to appeal to a distinction between a foundational individualism with its numerically discrete "individual," on the one hand, and John Dewey's unique "individuality" as previously introduced. In ordinary parlance, the contrast is between "individuals" as discrete and separate "things" or "objects" and "individualities" as relationally constituted and distinctive "narratives" or "events." We have argued that Confucian persons are constituted by their relations—or using Angus Graham's language, patterns of relations—and that in the absence of such patterns they do not exist. The commonsense intuition

---

56. Emmet, *Rules, Roles and Relations*, 171.

of many of our interlocutors in response to such a claim begins from the assumption that persons by definition must have an autonomous, unified, and independent identity. For them, this Confucian-diffused, relational conception of person without a superordinate and substantial self to anchor it threatens the important commitment persons ought to have to their own personal integrity and uniqueness. We would argue, on the contrary, that it is the conception of the relationally constituted person that carries with it a much stronger sense of integrity and uniqueness than our uncritical, commonsense notion of the discrete individual.

With substance ontology informing our best intuitions, the self-same reduplicative essence or form (*eidos*) defining each person and the species as a whole, means that all members of a class are fundamentally and essentially the same—and they are only incidentally different. We might also remember that in Aristotle's time, such categorical thinking essentialized and naturalized differences in race and gender, which produced a discriminatory consciousness that has persisted until modern times. While our common sense might have this specific referent, this same ontological notion of strict identity carries over in a contemporary, more liberated dress: for example, into the legal status of all persons in the courtroom, where the convention is that everyone, regardless of the contingencies of gender, generation, race, religion, class, and so on, are ostensibly equal before the law. To argue thusly that our many differences are at best contingent attributes grounded in a shared and essential sameness offers us a much-truncated version of unique identity and personal integrity.

On the other hand, the relationally constituted model of persons asserts that each of us is an inimitable matrix of vital, concrete relations all the way down, without any assumed shared essence. On that basis, this model would further claim that the commonalities of our class membership are dependent upon overlapping relations and complex analogies rather than any notion of strict identity, thus advancing a conception of persons that carries a much stronger sense of unique identity.

Hence, when we claim that the "individual" is a second-order abstraction, we want to preclude a possible equivocation between what we might call the abstracted and derivative discrete "individual," one that is assumed in most variations of a foundational "individualism," and a concrete and first-order relationally constituted "individuality" that we associate with Confucian persons. There is an important distinction being made here. There is the second-order, formal abstraction of discrete "individuals." For example, there is the formal legal status of a deracinated

Henry Rosemont unencumbered by race, gender, or generation, as one more example of an independent and autonomous individual who on this basis has entered into legal contracts with many other autonomous individuals. And then there is the first-order "individuality" of relationally constituted, unique persons. Indeed, there is the one and only Henry Rosemont whom we have all loved dearly as this unique, distinctive, and distinguished person whose complex, Emersonian identity has been shaped over the course of a lifetime through living this singular and exemplary narrative.

Invoking a doctrine of internal relations in our roles and relations with others is not to ignore the unique individuality of particular persons but is rather to argue that such individuality, far from excluding these relations, is a function of the quality achieved in them as they come to constitute this person's focal identity. Henry is who he is because of the many roles he lived and because of the quality he has achieved in the mutuality of the relationships he has shared with each of us. And we have in these relations become as integral to his identity as he is to ours. I use the example of Henry Rosemont here because, although sadly he has passed, as person who had a most eventful career and made a transformative impact on so many people, he is very much with us in how we continue to live our lives. Said another way, persons such as Henry are unique focal events that are defined relationally within their own continuing histories rather being delimited as separate, individual entities. In order to register these two different senses of "individual," we will need to respect a distinction between the relationally constituted "individuality" of Confucian persons as being the first-order, concrete actuality, and discrete "individuals" as being merely derivative, second-order abstractions from that actuality.

Parity Among the Questions: Reinstating *Whence* and *Whither*

With this distinction between first-order individuality and the second-order discrete individual in hand, we can return to Graham's initial insight that in order to explore the idea that different cultures have different categories and modes of thinking, we might begin with Graham's observation that the questions cultures ask shape the answers they get. But we might further clarify this intuition by adding that the cosmology or worldview of any particular culture would also shape our expectations of the answers we get in asking our questions. That is, when we ask the *what* question of a world understood in terms of substance ontology, we will expect to learn analytically what is essential about any given thing. That is, we are promised *episteme*: apodictic knowledge about things in the world. But the seemingly same *what* question when asked of a world understood as a processual cosmology promises much less. With the *what* question we will only be able to separate and give diremption to specific events within a continuing, organic process without any expectation that the answer will provide a fixed or final object of knowledge. Indeed, we might worry that the answer to the *what* question, in interrupting the very flow of experience, distorts our understanding of it by isolating elements within it while ignoring their mutual interpenetration, conjunction, and transitivity.

Even though the *what* question gives us a much-diminished answer given the holistic, focus-field, and ecological nature of Chinese cosmology, we must acknowledge that we will need to ask all of the questions to do justice to the complexity of the human experience. We must rely upon each of the questions to foreground one more aspect of experience, with the expectation that all of them in sum will provide us with the most information, while none among them alone will promise some final truth. And although each question might foreground and bring into focus some different aspect of experience, we must allow that ultimately each question is organically related to the others, and thus each question entails all of them. The *what* question asked of an "event" rather than of a "thing," for example, instead of terminating the inquiry by giving us knowledge of what something really is, will only serve functionally to abstract the event from the context of a continuing process. In order to get to the best explanation, the *what* question requires that we continue our interrogation with *how, whence, whither,* and so on, thus making the most "comprehensive" answer that illuminates the event in all of its complexity our best answer.[57]

The epistemic critique that we find in many of the classical Confucian texts, rather than relying heavily upon the language of true and false

---

57. It is interesting that the term *quan* 全 that we translate as "comprehensive" is defined in the early lexicons qualitatively and aesthetically as well as quantitatively. The *Shuowen*, for example, defines *quan* as *wan* 完 meaning "complete," where "complete" has both the meaning of "full" or "total" (*bei* 備) as well as "completely beautiful" (*wanmei* 完美). It also defines *quan* as pure and flawless jade 純玉曰全.

that would follow from a reality-appearance and essence-attribute kind of ontological dualism, often takes the form of insisting that someone knows only one aspect of a situation while being insufficiently aware of the others. For example, the *Xunzi* has a chapter entitled "Dispelling Obsessions" (*jiebi* 解蔽) that opens with the following charge: "The affliction most people have is that they are obsessed with one corner and cannot see the big picture."[58] Xunzi then goes on to criticize his contemporaries Mozi, Shen Dao, Shen Buhai, and Hui Shi, accusing each of them in their doctrines of grasping only one corner of the whole. Indeed, Xunzi takes Zhuangzi as an example, saying of him that "being so obsessed with 'nature' (*tian* 天), he does not know human beings."[59] Of course, as we will have occasion to remark, this is the same Xunzi who constructed an extended and amplified Confucianism (a more "comprehensive" Confucianism) by freely imbibing and digesting the doctrines of competing lineages of thought from within what is now in retrospect called the Hundred Schools of the pre-Qin period (*zhuzibaijia* 諸子百家), reshaping these same ideas to make them his own. Xunzi's greatest contribution to the Confucianism that would emerge as state doctrine a century later in the Western Han dynasty was his transmission of an eclectic and fortified Confucianism—one that aspired to the fullest degree of comprehensiveness (*quan*). And a fair argument can be made that the strength of Confucianism across the centuries has been its continuing porousness and subsequent hybridity. It continues to have the capacity to absorb doctrines that would compete with it, with Buddhism being one of its earliest "Western" encounters and then subsequently, down to the present day, the many more recent iterations of "Western" learning.

There is a popular proverb in modern Chinese that translates as, "I cannot see the true face of Mount Lu because I am standing within this mountainscape."[60] While everyone uses this phrase, I think most people misunderstand it. This expression is usually read as asserting that an external, more objective perspective is better than one from the inside. As the *Zhuangzi* says, "A father will not act as matchmaker for his son because whatever the father might say in praise of his son is not

---

58. 《荀子. 解蔽》曰: "凡人之患, 蔽於一曲而闇於大理."
59. 《荀子. 解蔽》莊子蔽於天而不知人.
60. 不識廬山真面目, 只緣身在此山中.

as persuasive as it would be coming from someone else."⁶¹ Perhaps we might offer a salutary corrective on the internal-external understanding of this proverb that begins by looking at the whole Su Shi poem rather than just the last two lines. Su Shi's famous verse, "Written on the Wall of the Western Forest Temple" 提西林壁 reads:

> Horizontally I see the ridges, vertically, the peaks;
> Far or near, high or low, each affords a different view.
> I cannot see the true face of Mt. Lu
> Because I am standing within this mountainscape.⁶²

Indeed, the poem begins first by asserting that there are a countless number of competing vistas within the changing landscape of Mount Lu. Further, and most profoundly, asserts that there is never an "outside" of this mountainscape but only an inside, seeing it from one perspective or another. And again, following the same logic, the most comprehensive view that includes as many perspectives as possible is the best way of looking at Mount Lu or anything else in the human experience. This then is an argument for an epistemology of "comprehensiveness" (*quan* 全) where, in the end, the best we are entitled to is not truth or certainty but only an intelligent and edifying conversation that provides us with the most panoramic view of things.

One way of formulating the holistic Confucian alternative to the priority Aristotle gives to the ontological *what* question is to look at the scope of the Chinese question particle, *an* 安, as it functions in the classical canons. Parsed according to specific contexts, the particle *an* seems to mean *how* in the *Book of Songs*; *where* and *what* in the *Zuo Commentary*; and quite famously *whence* and *whither* as we try to make sense of the "happy fish" story in the *Zhuangzi*. But in fact this same question particle, while seemingly delimited by different contexts, always carries the full range of questions simultaneously. Each of these questions references one aspect of the same phenomenon, and in the proliferation into many different questions, they in sum provide us with a panoramic overview of the multivalence and the complexities of our experience. Indeed, the fullest answer to any one of these questions requires an answer to all of them.

---

61. 《莊子》寓言篇: 親父不為其子媒。親父譽之，不若非其父者也.
62. 橫看成嶺側成峰，遠近高低各不同。不識廬山真面目，只緣身在此山中.

Thinking further about priorities among the questions asked within the Confucian process cosmology, the *what* question predicates events rather than things. The *what* question in this fluid context in some ways provides the least satisfying answer. Far from promising us truth by revealing what is ontologically essential and thus knowable, the *what* question has the effect of arresting and delimiting a temporally and spatially focal event having implicated within it all of its previous history, as well as everything that would follow. Indeed, in this process cosmology, the questions of *whence* and *whither* that would allow us to assay *an event over time* become the primary questions to be asked. And this *whence* question form carries over into the modern Chinese language where the conventional way of asking "Do you know?" (*ni zhidao ma*? 你知道嗎?) means, quite literally, "Do you know whence and whither?" The *where* and *when* questions that only provide putative *points in place and time*, like the question of *what*, are merely conventional abstractions from and indeed distortions of what comes to us as both continuous and eventful in the flow of our experience.

This observation regarding the priority of the questions to be asked within this process cosmology is borne out by the fact that its epistemic vocabulary seeks a "mapping" of the context that allows for a productive "forging ahead" within it, thus promising only practical rather than apodictic knowledge: "realizing our way" (*zhidao* 知道), "unraveling the patterns within the context" (*lijie* 理解), "seeing with full clarity" (*liaojie* 瞭解), "getting through with facility" (*tongda* 通達), "being well acquainted with everything" (*baishitong* 百事通), and so on.

Turning more specifically to the questions we might ask to know particular persons, the project of coming to really know someone requires an appeal to a narrative, processual, and generative understanding of their identity with all of the transitivity and conjunctions integral to the course of who they have become and who they are becoming. Persons thus understood are to be likened more to historical events than to marbles in a jar. And when we ask after historical events—the Civil War, for example—we are more inclined to ask, "How did it come about?" (*whence*) and "What were its consequences?" (*whither*) rather than "*What was the Civil War?*" That is, as we have seen, Aristotelian "things" are invested with an assumed generic *eidos* and *telos* that implicitly provide us with the *whence* and *whither* in their evolving process of actualization. But in order to provide an adequate description of any resolutely particular event in the Chinese cosmology, the explanatory *whence* and *whither* questions that Aristotle would abjure in describing his subjects and their predications are immediately relevant as providing information not otherwise available. This eventful nature of persons is the first inkling of the holographic, focus-field conception of persons that inhabits Confucian role ethics and that we will return to in some detail.

The centrality of the *whence* and *whither* questions in this narrative epistemology of "realizing our way" (*zhidao* 知道) is not lost on contemporary New Confucian philosopher (*xinruxuejia* 新儒學家) Tang Junyi 唐君毅 in his extensive work on the key philosophical concept of "cultivating our natural human propensities" (*xing* 性). In pondering the classical Confucian conception of what it means to become something—and in particular, what it means to become a person—Tang registers a great sensitivity to the existential force that propels us. In trying to understand and explain *xing*, he prioritizes the vital "propensities" that animate the trajectory of the narrative over the given native conditions that something might have. For Tang, the *whither* answer would seem to give us more important information than the *what*:

> Take the fact that a concrete existent is vital. In speaking of its natural propensities (*xing*), what is important is not remarking on *what* the *xing* of this entity is, but in assaying *the direction of its existence*.[63]

Tang is certainly insightful here. Asking the *whence* and *whither* questions provides the most information about both the content and the nature of experience, especially with respect to the experience of becoming human. But importantly, in a holistic cosmology, we must not undervalue the *what*, *when*, and *where* questions. These abstracting and isolating questions, when asked about the Civil War, for example, come to have increased significance when we are called upon to draw comparisons between the Civil War as one particular example of a military campaign and others in different times and places. The importance of these analytic questions emerges from the need to register some degree of integrity, determinacy, and intelligibility in experience. These delimiting

---

63. Tang Junyi 唐君毅, *Complete Works* 唐君毅全集, vol. 13 (Taipei: Xuesheng shuju, 1991), 28: 然就一具體存在之有生, 而即言其有性, 則重要者不在說此存在之性質性相之爲何, 而是其生命存在之所向之爲何.

questions are functional in providing us the convenience of parsing the continuous flow of experience into eventful units with tentative beginnings and consummating endings. These "abstracting" questions provide us with the felicitous distinction between the flow of process and the meaningful integrity of particular events within that continuing process, where both flow and particularity are vital to our understanding. Asking such abstracting questions serves us in the production of meaning that emerges as we parse the flow of experience and impose an intelligible order upon it. To the extent that the process of experience is eventful, the identities of these events as particular foci are a function of both unique disclosure and punctuating closure, with the most meaningful events among them exhibiting the distinctiveness of a uniquely executed work of art or a virtuosic performance of a piece of music. Such closure comes along with the ostensive beginnings and endings of experiences and allows these events to achieve their own provisional consummation even while they open out onto further stages in the ever-evolving process of experience.

The meaning and complexity of our experience emerges from the cadence and quality of these distinctive events. The distinctive episodes are at once mutually imbricated and yet determinate, and while sometimes ephemeral like momentary eddies in a stream, they are also sometimes persistent like the banks of the stream that produce these same eddies and give definition to the stream's ceaseless flow. An analogy between how such eventful experience unfolds and how we use language comes immediately to mind. When we think of the carefully turned works of William Shakespeare, all of his crafted and economical expressions and sentences, his paragraphs, and his entire plays and poems have their beginnings and endings and their degrees of determinacy. And yet Shakespeare's world of language has an always interpenetrating determinacy in which the full meaning of each linguistic unit has implicated within it the entire corpus of his work and much, much more.

We have seen that Aristotle, with the primacy of his *what* question within his "thing" substance ontology, gives grammatical privilege to the noun. Graham finds a distinct contrast with Aristotle in Chinese process cosmology in arguing for the privileging of the verb:

> If . . . one starts from the action, then duration and direction are already inherent in the verb; action is as much *from* and *to*

as *in*, and as much *to*, *from* and *in* [my italics added] things and persons as places. . . . We may link this asymmetry with the verb-centeredness of Chinese language and thought.⁶⁴

Graham is asserting that in this "eventful" Chinese cosmology, human becomings as "events," for example, are better understood as fluid and inclusive verbs rather than as static and exclusive nouns. We might take inspiration from Graham's insight here and suggest that on further reflection it is perhaps the gerund form as the more inclusive verbal noun that might be a better choice than the verb—that is, a notion of "person-ing" that does not separate "persons" from "what they do." In any case, Graham offers us a holographic understanding of this Confucian world in which radically situated persons cannot be extricated from the temporality and fluid locale of their continuing narratives as these stories are "taking place." As we will see, Graham will come to advocate for what we might call a "narrative" understanding of the expression "cultivating our natural human propensities" (*xing* 性)—conventionally translated as "human nature"—in which, as we make our way in the world, person and world evolve together temporally and spatially in a dynamic, contrapuntal relationship. Graham is alluding to just such a narrative understanding here:

> One notices the special interest of Chinese thinkers in the circumstances one "happens on" (*yu* 遇) and the action which is "timely" (*shih* [*shi* 時] used verbally). The categorical distinction which emerges from the question forms would seem to be between, not places and times, but the way (*tao* [*dao*] 道) one is on, coming from and proceeding along, and the times (*shih*) [*shi*] that one meets on the way.⁶⁵

Graham here notes rather explicitly the keen interest Chinese thinkers seem to invest in the *whence* and *whither* questions in being attentive not as much to "time" and "place" as to the journey they are on and to the timely and thus important events they happen upon along that way. Graham is remarking here on a clear awareness in these texts of the fact that the accidents and imponderables within a life often introduce

---

64. Graham, *Studies in Chinese Philosophy*, 391.
65. Graham, *Studies in Chinese Philosophy*, 391.

significant twists and turns we have little control over. Certainly, a major theme in the Confucian literature is *ming* 命, "the force of circumstances" or "the propensity of things" that we all inevitably encounter as our lives unfold. We should also note that perhaps the shared axis of these same texts is the emphasis they place upon assiduous personal cultivation (*xiushen* 修身) required in the face of even the direst of circumstances. The Confucian project itself is defined in terms of the deliberate resolve that must attend our capacity for "broadening and extending our way through life" (*hongdao* 弘道) and that must motivate us to the achieved musicality necessary to make this same human way both harmonious and most fully our own (*zhonghe* 中和).[66] "Waymaking" for Confucian persons is living deliberately in the face of contingency and engaging with what we happen upon with a quality of responsiveness that makes us exemplary in spite of whatever challenges might arise. And it is of course Confucius himself who is most typically advanced as the best example of someone who overcame the most unfortunate of times to become a model for the ages.

"Aspectual" and "Analytic" Language: Complementarities in the Discourse

Parity among the questions to be asked within the Confucian cosmology is made necessary because the different questions asked provide information about different aspects of experience. Inspired by Marcel Granet, who makes much of the idea of "aspect" in the correlative or associative thinking so prominent in Confucian cosmology, I have had occasion to make a distinction between "aspectual" and "analytic" language in thinking through the question forms we find in the Confucian literature. The alternating deployments of aspectual and analytic language serve the processual cosmology, requiring as it does a strategy for denoting both the continuity of process and the punctuation of this process with particular events. In this process cosmology, the notions of "time" and "place" can only serve functionally as separate dimensions that can be parsed respec-

---

66. See, for example, *Analects* 15.29, 1.12, and *Zhongyong* 25 and 1. The translations for both of these texts are adapted from the Ames and Rosemont translation of the *Analects* and the Ames and Hall translation of *Focusing the Familiar* (*Zhongyong*), respectively.

tively as discrete moments and as the simple locations of individuated things. Indeed, in this cosmology, time and place (or perhaps better, "timing" and "taking place") are more importantly to be understood as inseparable "aspects" of the *whence* and *whither* of the diverse currents of events within the ceaseless flow of the human experience. At the same time, as with the relationship between continuous process and determinate event, there is also an important role for our analytic and discriminating sensibilities that allows for the punctuating of the lived experience, and in so doing, to thus appreciate both its cadence and its multivalence.

In invoking "aspectual" language to "speak" this cosmology, we are identifying different yet mutually entailing ways to talk about what is in fact the same phenomenon. For example, we can use the aspectual language of "forming and functioning" (*tiyong* 體用) to describe different perspectives on a living person, where the persistently formal and determinate aspects (body, language, ritual, life patterns, institutions, roles) can be distinguished from the vital, informal, and indeterminate ones (growth, creativity, passion, shame, skill, taste, insight, spirit). Such differences can be readily observed and experienced, but as different perceptions of the same phenomenon—this particular person—they cannot be isolated and separated analytically. Human persons are at once determinate and vital. At the same time, however, although these aspects cannot be separated out, the very different perspectives are integral to the meaning of the phenomenon itself, providing complexity and intensity to the same unique and continuous quantum of human experience. This multiplicity of aspect in its function of providing additional information is analogous to the additional predicates of Aristotle's man in the marketplace that tell of place, time, state, position, and of having, doing, being affected by, and so on, which in fact provides us with many coterminous perspectives on the same unfolding event.

We might appeal to the phenomenon of Ludwig Beethoven as a way of thinking about aspectual language. Beethoven is a composer of a time and place, but his corpus has expanded radially over the centuries. Initially it was music that Germany's elites enjoyed; yet Beethoven's works would eventually be celebrated by disparate cultures everywhere. In the global reach of this appreciation, Beethoven becomes a much bigger, more complex, and increasingly meaningful phenomenon by taking on many different aspects. The music of Beethoven's Choral Symphony with its "Ode to Joy," for example, was adopted as the Anthem of Europe first by the Council of Europe and then by the European Union. And beginning as early as World War I, this same Ninth Symphony has gradually become the theme song of Japanese New Year celebrations with some fifty performances across the country every year. Being "appreciated" from different cultural sites means value added. Beethoven has become a larger and more complex phenomenon as his corpus is now entertained from so many different perspectives.

This aspectual nature of language is revealed in the structure of many Chinese linguistic expressions themselves. As an example, the binomial that denotes our human "world" (*shijie* 世界) is constructed by combining a diachronic aspect, *shi* 世 "worlding-as-intergenerational-temporal-succession," with a synchronic aspect, *jie* 界 "worlding-as-the-traversing-of-spatial-boundaries." Similarly, the binomial for "cosmos" (*yuzhou* 宇宙) combines a synchronic aspect, *yu* 宇 "cosmos-as-eaves-extending," and a diachronic aspect, *zhou* 宙 "cosmos-as-temporally-enduring." Importantly, each of these aspects is altered by both its dyadic relationship with the other and the vitality of a process cosmology. The inseparability of time and place, of form and flow, becomes the measured cadence and musicality of the human experience. Flow that cannot be separated from place becomes events as "taking place," and form that cannot be separated from time becomes the rhythm of life.

Again, in this Confucian cosmology, there is no "outside" of the "time-space" world—only the perspective of "worlding" that is internal to it. As Tang Junyi insists:

> When Chinese philosophers speak of the world, they are thinking of the world that we are living in. There is no world beyond or outside of the one we are experiencing. . . . They are not referencing "*a* world" or "*the* world," but are simply saying "world," where the fact that "world as such" does not have an article in front of it is extremely significance.[67]

And dynamics of the flux and flow of such "worlding" are integral to itself without the need to appeal to something foundational and causal:

> In the minds of Chinese people, the cosmos has always been nothing more than a continuous stream, a kind of flow; all

---

67. Tang Junyi, *Complete Works*, 11:101–3: 中國哲人言世界, 只想著我們所處的世界。我們所處的世界以外有無其他的世界. . . . 中國的哲人說世界不說我們的世界是一世界 A World, 亦不說是這世界 This World, 而只是說世界, 天地, World as Such 前而不加冠詞, 實是有非常重大的意義的.

of the things and events of the cosmos are just a continuing process. And beyond this process there is not some other fixed substratum that supports it.[68]

By way of closure for this chapter, I might appeal to the aspectual language of "changing and persisting" or "persistence in change" (*biantong* 變通) as it is developed in the *Book of Changes* (*Yijing*) to think about how an always changing and yet persistent worldview is over time sedimented into and conveyed in both the structure and the content of the world's many different languages. I have followed Angus Graham in using Aristotle and the classical Confucian canons in trying to argue that excavating these resilient substrata from our natural languages provides us with some insight into how different traditions have parsed the human experience to establish their own persistent identities and common sense—and more specifically how by extension they have come to conceptualize the notion of persons in importantly different ways. Further, to identify and excavate this cosmology in the form of a set of underlying, always protean cultural assumptions—Aristotelian ontological commitments versus a Chinese process cosmology have been my two examples herein—far from opening up an incommensurable gap between traditions, in fact serves us well as a hedge against the essentialism and reductionism that are the hallmarks of a pernicious cultural relativism. We come to know ourselves and the other better as we come to know them both.

With this contrast between substance and process in hand—respectively, *What* is a human being? and *Whence* and *whither* are these human becomings?—we can now turn to the main question to be addressed in this monograph. What language can we find to articulate the irreducibly social, relationally constituted, generative conception of "persons" that can be excavated and theorized from the Confucian canons and serve as an alternative to the ideology of individualism?

---

68. Tang Junyi, 中国人心目中之宇宙恒只为一种流行，一种动态；一切宇宙中之事物均只为一种过程，此过程以外别无固定之体以为其支持者 (substratum).

Chapter Two

How Do the Confucian Canons Say "Role Ethics"?

Persons as an Achieved Relational Virtuosity

While certainly having important theoretical implications, the Confucian project (and the process cosmology that grounds it) is compelling because it proceeds from a relatively straightforward account of the actual human experience. We have found that rather than appealing to ontological assumptions about fixed, essential natures or supernatural speculations about immortal souls and salvific ends—all of which would take us outside of the world of our empirical experience—the Confucian project focuses instead on the possibilities for enhancing personal worth available to us here and now through enchanting the ordinary affairs of the day. In this Confucian ethic, there is a tacit awareness of what Bernard Williams concluded over his own long career as an ethicist. In his search for "thick," "world-guided," and "action-guiding" ethical concepts, Williams is famous for having reservations about the capacity of any moral theory to tell us what is right and wrong and what we ought to do. In the preface to *Moral Luck*, Williams announces:

> There cannot be any very interesting, tidy or self-contained theory of what morality is, nor, despite the vigorous activities of some present practitioners, can there be an ethical theory, in the sense of a philosophical structure which, together with

some degree of empirical fact, will yield a decision procedure for moral reasoning.[1]

Williams is saying here that no ethical theory, no ready-made set of rules, no moral system, can in any particular situation instruct us on the right course of action to take. The best responses to our moral quandaries must emerge out of intelligent reflection on the specific conditions of experience, where much of human flourishing is dependent upon dexterity in the exercise and application of our moral imagination. Williams is quite rightly setting limits on our expectations for moral theory. But in our search for doing what is most appropriate, the abstract and theoretical, as they emerge out of practice, are certainly important in providing an opportunity to reflect on and think critically about our conduct, thereby making it more productive and intelligent.

Confucius developed his insights around the most basic and enduring aspects of the ordinary human experience: personal cultivation in family and communal roles, family reverence, deference to others, propriety achieved in our roles and relations, friendship, a cultivated sense of shame, moral education, a communicating community, a family-centered religiousness, the intergeneration transmission of culture, and so on. In so doing, Confucius has guaranteed the continuing relevance of this accumulating wisdom. In addition to being focused on such perennial issues, one further characteristic of Confucian philosophy present in the words of Confucius himself that makes his teachings so resilient in this living tradition is the porousness and adaptability of his philosophy. His enduring contribution was simply to strive to take full ownership of the cultural legacy available in his time and place, to adapt this compounding wisdom from the past for the betterment of his own present historical moment, and then to recommend to future generations that they continue to do the same.[2]

The *Analects* and the other canonical texts do not purport to lay out some generic formula by which everyone should live their lives. Rather, the personal model of Confucius that is remembered in these documents recalls the narrative of one special person: how he in his

---

1. Bernard Williams, *Moral Luck: Philosophical Papers 1973–1980* (New York: Cambridge University Press, 1981), ix–x.
2. *Analects* 7.1: 子曰:「述而不作,信而好古,竊比於我老彭。」The Master said, "Following the proper way, I do not forge new paths; with confidence I cherish the ancients—in these respects I am comparable to Old Peng."

relations with others cultivated his humanity and how he lived a fulfilling life, much to the admiration of those around him. Indeed, in reading the *Analects*, we encounter the relationally constituted Confucius making his way through life by living his various and sometimes conflicted roles as best he can: his roles as a strict and at times judgmental teacher and mentor; as a scrupulous and incorruptible scholar-official; as a caring family member; as a concerned neighbor and member of the community; as an always critical and sometimes reluctant political consultant; as the grateful progeny of his progenitors; as an enthusiastic heir to a specific, living cultural legacy; and indeed, as a member of a chorus of joyful boys and men singing their way home after a happy day on the River Yi.[3] The teachings of Confucius, which have been passed on from generation to generation and recall the events of his life, portray him as someone more inclined to appeal to the narratives of historical models than to invoke abstract principles; to reference specific, concrete analogies rather than apply putatively systematic theories; and to express deeply felt exhortations more than issuing imperatives. While Confucius seems keenly aware of the critical value of theorizing our practice in search of further intelligence, he is also cognizant of the primacy of practice itself as both the source of the theorizing and the warrant for endorsing its results. As I will endeavor to show in this monograph, the power and lasting value of Confucius's insights lie in the fact that many of these ideas are intuitively persuasive and readily adaptable to the conditions of ensuing generations, including our own.

Indeed, what makes this Confucian tradition more empirical than empiricism—that is, what makes Confucianism a *radical* empiricism—is

---

3. *Analects* 11.26. 子路、曾皙、冉有、公西華侍坐。子曰:「以吾一日長乎爾,毋吾以也。居則曰:『不吾知也!』如或知爾,則何以哉?」...「點!爾何如?」鼓瑟希,鏗爾,舍瑟而作。對曰:...「莫春者,春服既成。冠者五六人,童子六七人,浴乎沂,風乎舞雩,詠而歸。」夫子喟然歎曰:「吾與點也!」Zilu, Zengxi, Ranyou, and Zihua were all sitting in attendance on Confucius. The Master said, "Just because I am a bit older than you do not hesitate on my account. You keep saying, 'No one understands me!' but if someone did understand you, how would you be of use to them?" . . . "And what about you, Zengxi?" asked the Master. Zengxi plucked a final note on his zither to bring the piece to an end, and setting the instrument aside, he rose to his feet. "I would choose to do something somewhat different from the rest. . . . At the end of spring, with the spring clothes having already been finished, I would like, in the company of five or six young men and six or seven children, to cleanse ourselves in the Yi river, to revel in the cool breezes at the Altar for Rain, and then return home singing." The Master heaved a deep sigh, and said, "I'm with Zengxi!"

the fact that while grounded in the soil of an antique culture, it is also prospective and evolutionary in respecting the uniqueness of the omnipresent particular. Indeed, it alludes to the particular narrative of this one special person, Confucius, who lived such an exemplary life. Rather than advancing doctrines as universal principles or organizing experience around a taxonomy of natural kinds grounded in some notion of strict identity, Confucian philosophy proceeds from analogy with, and always provisional generalizations derived from, those *particular* historical instances of successful living. Confucius's signature neologism, "aspiring to consummate conduct in my roles and relations" (*ren* 仁), for example, is not an appeal to some higher-order, antecedent principle, or generic virtue but is rather a vision of the exemplary human life as it is aspired to through assiduous personal cultivation in one's relations that in its achievements can provide succeeding generations with a guiding source of value. Of course, any exemplary narrative is nested within and informed by a continuing confluence of the particular narratives of exemplary persons over time, including the life story of Confucius himself. And as a consummate exemplar who grows in meaning through the patterns of deference that define the social fabric of ensuing generations, Confucius serves as a role model within this living tradition to shape the way in which people come to live their own particular lives.

Confucian Role Ethics and a Narrative Understanding of Persons

What we refer to as "Confucian role ethics" begins from the primacy of vital relationality within our lived roles and relations. Stated simply, it assumes (rather than argues for) the bare fact of associated living. The initial claim here is that no one does anything by themselves. All of our physical, conscious, and social activity is collaborative and transactional. We walk because we have the ground, breathe because we have the air, and see because we have the sun. And we exchange opinions, share insights, and dismiss rumors because we live in families and communities. But whereas transactional associations are merely descriptive, once such associations are identified and stipulated as occurring within the specific roles we live with others, they become normative. Our different roles then—the activities of daughters and grandpas, teachers and neighbors, shopkeepers and lovers—are simply specific modes of association that in their specificity take on value and a clear normative cast that prompts critical reflection: Am I a good daughter? Am I a good teacher? Am I a good grandmother? And while this grandmother's love for her grandson is one of the most familiar and ordinary things we will ever encounter, in Confucian role ethics it is a profound source of moral education for her grandson and is highly valued as one of the most extraordinary products life has to offer. After all, her grandson can only learn to love others by being loved himself, and there can be no higher value in the human experience than our love for one another.

Confucian role ethics appeals to a "gerundive" understanding of persons in this tradition—that is, persons are something we do rather than what we are, as well as something we do together or not at all. Such a holistic, relationally constituted conception of persons as focal identities within continuing personal narratives resists our seemingly default assumption that discrete individuals are concrete, exclusive existents rather than second-order abstractions from their narratives. It eschews the belief that persons can be accurately described, analyzed, and evaluated independently of their contextualizing environments, including first and foremost those environments in which they deal with other human beings. Role ethics begins from the notion that in any interesting moral or political or religious sense, persons cannot be understood apart from the other family and community members with whom they interact over their lifetimes and beyond. Indeed, persons are best understood and measured critically by themselves and others in terms of the specific roles that guide their conduct in their transactions with these specific others.

Simply put, moral conduct itself is nothing more than behavior that conduces to growth in the roles and relations we live together with others, and immoral conduct is the opposite. Being considerate, listening attentively, acting upon an empathetic imagination, looking for ways of being helpful, being committed in one's relations, lending encouragement, living up to one's word—these very ordinary gestures are the substance of morality. All of these behaviors are deliberate and require critical reflection. Being self-absorbed, ignoring the interests of others, being dismissive, failing in our commitments, being thoughtless or obstructive, being inflexible, lacking resolution—these are negative, immoral dispositions that lead to diminution in our relations. From this perspective, it is easy to see how the grandmother's love for her grandson can be morally didactic, not only in deepening her grandmotherly relationship with him but also in modeling for him how to best exhibit moral competence in growing his relations with others.

This moral "growth" that is effected through personal cultivation in our roles and relations is expressed explicitly and vividly in an expansive, radial vocabulary that is pervasive in the Confucian canons. While "small, petty persons" (*xiaoren* 小人) are morally retarded people who resist such growth, "grand persons" (*daren* 大人) and "developed persons" (*chengren* 成人) are those who have grown in their relations to become morally achieved persons. Virtuosity (*de* 德) is "getting and gaining" (*de* 得) through deference to others. Spirituality (*shen* 神) is "stretching and extending" (*shen* 伸) in reach and influence. Mere persons (*ren* 人) grow to become consummate as persons (*ren* 仁) through achieved coalescence (*du* 度) in the activities that define their lived roles and relations together and so on. Most of the cluster of terms that define human morality in Confucian philosophy allude to the effective and deliberate communicating within family and community that is the source of this personal growth and that makes us like-minded and wholehearted in our associations. For example, the character for exemplary persons (*junzi* 君子) is written with the mouth signific, the relationship of trust and credibility (*xin* 信) with the speech signific, the dynamics of empathetic deference (*shu* 恕) with the mouth and the heartmind (or "thinking and feeling") signific, the attainment of true sincerity and resolution (*cheng* 誠) with the speech signific, the expression of moral virtuosity (*de* 德) with the heartmind signific, and so on.

As I have observed, the vocabulary of virtue ethics in appealing to the cluster of agents, acts, generic virtues, character traits, autonomy, motivation, reasons, choices, freedom, principles, consequences, and so on, assumes the discrete individual human being as its starting point. By contrast, Confucian role ethics is grounded in a more holistic and eventful "narrative" understanding of persons. As David B. Wong reports:

> The *Analects* thus shows a group with Confucius at the center, engaged in moral cultivation, each with a different configuration of strengths and weaknesses, not theorizing about it or giving philosophical justifications for it, but rather through their interactions providing a basis and inspiration for sub-

sequent theorizing and justification by Confucius' successors in the Chinese philosophical tradition.[4]

Taking the irreducibly social nature of persons as our starting point, we have tried to articulate and to bring clarity to Confucian role ethics not as an alternative "ethical theory" but as a capaciousness, sui generis vision of the moral life that begins from, and ultimately seeks its warrant in, a relatively straightforward account of the human experience as we find it described in the *Analects* and other early Confucian texts. Integral to living well is an educated imagination and the critical reflection that must attend our conduct within the roles we live with others. Indeed, the normativity of role ethics arises from whole persons aspiring to live whole lives.

Ren 仁 as a Way of Saying "Role Ethics" in the Classical Chinese Canons

A starting point for Henry Rosemont and me in trying to find an adequate vocabulary to bring clarity to Confucian role ethics was to reflect upon the stubborn ambiguity that attends the term "aspiring to consummate conduct in roles and relations" (*ren* 仁) as it first occurs in and then is developed as a defining philosophical idea in the *Analects of Confucius*. Of course, the character *ren* 仁 does appear as early as the Zhou bronzes *[i]* in which the graph is composed with "corpse body" (*shi* 尸) as an alternative way of writing "person" (*ren* 人), coupled with the number two (*er* 二).[5] From its context we can discern that *ren* in its earliest form clearly means "love" or "kindness." While there are several such early although infrequent occurrences of the character *ren*, this term only accrues substantial philosophical import with its development as a key term of art in the *Analects*. The character *ren* is also found on the Guodian bamboo strips (*ca.* 300 BCE), where the graph is similar to

[i]

---

4. David B. Wong, "Cultivating the Self in Concert with Others," *Dao Companion to the Analects*, ed. Amy Olberding (Dordrecht, The Netherlands: Springer, 2014), 175.

5. Image taken from Tze-wan Kwan, "Multi-Function Character Database": 中山王鼎 284, http://humanum.arts.cuhk.edu.hk/Lexis/lexi-mf/.

66 | Human Becomings

[ii]

[iii]

its modern form *[ii]*.⁶ But it also frequently appears with an alternative graphic composition *[iii]* that combines "lived-body" (*shen* 身) with the "heartmind" (*xin* 心) beneath it.⁷

Confucius's creative investment of new meaning in *ren* is borne out by a survey of its infrequent and relatively unimportant usage in the earlier corpus. *Ren* only occurs infrequently in the ancient classics and in its appearance is absent a significant philosophical relevance. This unexceptional usage compares with 105 occurrences in the *Analects* in more than 10 percent of its passages: that is, 58 of the 499 sections. Given that *ren* denotes the qualitative transformation of a *particular* person, it is made more ambiguous because it must be understood relative to the specific concrete conditions of that person. There is no generic formula, no ideal. Like a work of art, *ren* is a process of disclosure rather than closure, resisting fixed definition and replication. Insight into the nature of consummate conduct is provided first in modal terms such as "resolutely" (*cheng* 誠), "conscientiously" (*zhong* 忠), "credibly" (*xin* 信), "wisely (*zhi* 知), "appropriately" (*yi* 義), and so on: the way, manner, or mode in which something is done rather than stipulating in abstract language the specific actions themselves. Indeed, such modalities are resistant to general prescription in defining the substance of exemplary conduct and are often brought into focus by an appeal to and critical reflection on specific historical episodes and concrete exemplars.

It is a commonplace that the present character *ren* 仁 in being composed of "person" and the number "two" is semantically revealing in locating the process of becoming consummately human within the pattern of relations we have with others. Consistent with this emphasis on relationality is an alternative graphic form of *ren* found on the bamboo strips where the graph for "lived-body" (*shen* 身) in its prestylized form is depicted as the body of a pregnant woman *[iv]*.⁸ Composed of a woman's pregnant body and the heartmind or "thinking and feeling" signific, this alternative way of writing *ren* points to perhaps the most intimate form of human relationality: the symbiotic feelings felt by a mother with child and those felt by a child within its mother's womb. In this warm world of amniotic fluid, synergetic exchange is effected between woman and child, and through osmotic and hydrostatic forces,

[iv]

---

6. Kwan, "Database," 馬王堆, 五十二病方, 230.

7. Kwan, "Database," 上博竹書五, 君子為豊, 1.

8. Kwan, "Database," 逆鐘 (西周晚期) CHANT 63.

the woman is transformed into her child's mother and the child into her mother's daughter. In understanding *ren* by reference to the inextricable and even sacred bonds formed between mother and child in this most intimate relationship, we are given some insight into its profound religious import. The *Analects* would aver that such visceral family feelings certainly begin at home. But when extended radially into all of our roles and personal relationships, from our professional associates to the commonest of persons, attentiveness to *ren* has the power to elevate mere associated living into a veritable sacrament:

> Zhonggong inquired about consummate conduct (*ren*). The Master replied, "In your public life, behave as though you are receiving honored guests; employ the common people as though you are overseeing a great sacrifice."[9]

When we ask after the meaning of *ren* as it appears in the Confucian canons, it seems that this evolving and complex notion will not give itself up immediately to the *what* question so often asked of it: what does *ren* mean? Indeed, in trying to find some clarity, we must ask if *ren* is one cardinal virtue among many as suggested by the conventional translations as "benevolence," "love," "altruism," "humaneness," and "humanity"? Or is it a "general virtue"—Confucianism's supreme moral principle or *summum bonum*? Or, as suggested by Wing-tsit Chan long ago, is it both and much more?[10] Or do we need a more holistic, narrative understanding of *ren* primarily as the moral property of communities and only derivatively an individual property as proposed by Alex McLeod?[11] Or is it, as Karyn Lai would argue, all that in sum makes up an exemplary human life?[12]

In the more than one hundred instances in which *ren* appears in the *Analects*, there seems to be a persistent eliding if not an erasure of a set of familiar, rather useful distinctions guaranteed at least in part by the grammar and inflections of our own English language: the distinguishing

---

9. *Analects* 12.2: 仲弓問仁。子曰:「出門如見大賓, 使民如承大祭。。。。」
10. Wing-tsit Chan, "The Evolution of the Concept *Jen*," *Philosophy East and West* 4, no. 1 (January 1955): 295–319.
11. Alex McLeod, "*Ren* as a Communal Property in the *Analects*," *Philosophy East and West* 62, no. 4 (October 2012): 505–528.
12. Karyn Lai, "*Ren* 仁: An Exemplary Life," *Dao Companion to the Analects*, ed. Amy Olberding (Dordrecht, The Netherlands: Springer, 2014).

of an inner self from an outer world, agents from their actions, selves from others, individual dispositions from communal properties, the means from the ends, mind from body, a person's character from the whole person, virtuous character traits from those actions that follow from them, psychological dispositions from the behaviors that are informed by them, specific virtuosic actions from an exemplary life, the abstract concept itself from the concrete narrative from which it is derived, specific instances of conduct from higher-order generalizations made about them, and so on. What seems clear from a close reading of our texts is that on different occasions and in different contexts, *ren* can be parsed as referencing any and all of these aspects of moral conduct, thus defying the distinctions made among them. Then we must ask ourselves: What is the status of these functional, often convenient distinctions we bring to the term *ren* in parsing the broad spectrum of meaning we associate with it?

Most if not all of these overlapping linguistic distinctions that break up the continuity of personal experience are meaningful for us because of our commonsense realist and intellectualist penchant for first internalizing our minds as individual persons and then separating ourselves subjectively from a putatively mind-independent world. In so doing, we separate ourselves from one another as discrete individuals and then again separate ourselves as agents with specific character traits from what we do. The function of these familiar and psychologically severe distinctions, serving as they do our need for clarity and precision, is to abstract and isolate one or more aspects of persons from the unity and continuity of their concrete experience. As we have seen with Aristotle's *Categories*, this is a habit of thinking that has deep roots in the ontology of our philosophical narrative. Indeed, it has been my continuing worry that such a fragmenting of persons and their conduct is a persistent and uncritical assumption being made by those who would argue that Confucianism offers a virtue ethics with Chinese characteristics; that is, those who would claim that the classical Greek notion of *arete* can be equated with the Confucian term *de* 德 and thus that the core ethical terminology in early Confucian ethical writings can by extension be comfortably rendered into an aretaic vocabulary.

As we witness with this term *ren*, the *Analects* in fact seems to eschew any severe separation between persons and their world, persons as discrete individuals, and persons and their conduct. No one can become consummate in their conduct (*ren*) by isolating themselves from their world, withdrawing from their interactions with other people, or performing some generic and reduplicative *ren* action. Given that none of these distinctions has any finality, perhaps the aspectual language captured in the expression "forming and functioning" (*tiyong* 體用) would be helpful in organizing the many dyadic associations that can be drawn out of the narrative contexts within which *ren* is used. *Ren* parsed as an abstract character trait, for example, might seem to fall on the more determinative "form" (*ti*) side, while *ren* as a specific virtuosic activity would seem to be more vital and thus be more "functional" (*yong*). The value of such distinctions is that they allow for the necessary distance from our specific practices to be reflective and to exercise our critical judgment without vitiating the primacy of practice and the focus-field holography wherein the entire narrative is implicated in each aspect. That is, relational virtuosity is fully implicated in the glowing complexion of our physicalities, the possibilities of our outer worlds are fully implicated in our achieved subjective identities, each determinate act of kindness is fully implicated in the exemplary narrative of a consummate person, and so on. What recommends this focus-field language as a way of understanding *ren* is that the meaning of any particular action within any particular situation can only be properly evaluated by reference to the entire narrative.

When we reflect on *ren* as it is used in the *Analects* as a way of "saying" role ethics, we must acknowledge that the meaning of *ren* is different for different people in different contexts. For example, in the *Analects* it is recorded that Yan Hui, puzzled by the Confucius's frequent use of his *ren* neologism, asks after its meaning: "Yan Hui inquired about *ren*." In comparing the Master's answer to Yan Hui with the response he gives to precisely the same question when it is asked in other passages by equally nonplussed Zhonggong, Sima Niu, Fan Chi, and Zigong, we might begin by reflecting on the question form—the interrogative term.[13] That is, rather than uncritically assuming that the protégées are asking "What is *ren*?," we might infer that they are instead asking, "How given my narrative do I become *ren*?" And hence the Master has very different answers for each of them. Even when the "same" Fan Chi on a second occasion repeats the same question, he gets a much different answer.[14]

---

13. Yan Hui, *Analects* 12.1: 顏淵問仁. Zhonggong 12.2, Sima Niu 12.3, Fan Chi 12.22 and 13.19, and Zigong 15.10.

14. Fan Chi comes across as an avid inquirer, asking about *ren* and wisdom in 12.22 and 13.19. He is not a quick study, repeatedly asking his fellows what Confucius has meant in his responses. Indeed, on one occasion when Fan Chi asks Confucius how to grow a garden (13.4), Confucius gets sorely impatient with him, calling him "a petty person" who clearly does not understand the difference in priority between growing yourself as a person and growing your vegetables.

Clearly Confucius is not responding to a *what is ren* question that might prompt him to give a generic answer to cover all instances of this term. Rather he is drawing his different answers from his understanding of the evolving narratives of his many students—that is, where are they "coming from" and where are they going as specific persons? He is responding to the *whence* and *whither* of their lives and how a particular understanding of *ren* might serve them as their narratives continue to unfold. Seeing that Yan Hui and the other protégés are so diverse in their capacities and temperaments, the always specific answers Confucius chooses to give each one of them must mirror the perceived differences he sees in the always unique situations and vicissitudes that together make up their different lives. And his different answers as they are received by each of his students serve as a point of deliberation and critical reflection on their relations with others.

In another case remembered in the *Analects*, Confucius is asked a question by each of his two students, Ranyou and Zilu: "On learning something, should I act upon it?" In response, Confucius gives each of them not only a different answer but indeed precisely the opposite: "yes" to Ranyou and "no" to Zilu. When Confucius is then asked by a perplexed witness why he would give clearly contradictory counsel to his two students, his response is that he must consider what is most appropriate to the habituated dispositions of the questioners: "Ranyou is diffident, and so I urged him on. But Zilu has the energy of two, and so I sought to rein him in."[15]

From these and other examples we could cite, we must allow that *ren* seems to be both situation specific and person specific. At the same time, however, each situation is interpreted in terms of perceived personal

---

15. *Analects* 11.22: 子路問:「聞斯行諸?」子曰:「有父兄在, 如之何其聞斯行之?」冉有問:「聞斯行諸?」子曰:「聞斯行之。」公西華曰:「由也問聞斯行諸, 子曰『有父兄在』; 求也問聞斯行諸, 子曰『聞斯行之』。赤也惑, 敢問。」子曰:「求也退, 故進之; 由也兼人, 故退之。」Zilu inquired, "On learning something, should one act upon it?" The Master said, "While your father and elder brothers are still alive, how could you, on learning something, act upon it?" When Ranyou asked the same question, the Master replied, "On learning something, act upon it." Gongxi Hua said, "When Zilu asked the question, you observed that his father and elder brothers are still alive, but when Ranyou asked you the same question, you told him to act on what he learns. I am confused—could you tell me what you mean by this?" The Master replied, "Ranyou is diffident, and so I urged him on. But Zilu has the energy of two, and so I sought to rein him in."

differences and within the framework of perceived habits of conduct and thus also has a holistic, narrative quality. That is, *ren* is only achieved in any particular situation when the virtuosity of whole persons (*ren* 人) as it is expressed through the full range of their different roles is considered. Again, just as the evolving definition of what it means to be human as a species emerges out of the confluence of human experience in the broadest sense, such generalizations about what it means to act consummately can also be made. The text *Focusing the Familiar* says as much: "Aspiring to consummate conduct in your roles and relations (*ren* 仁) is becoming a person (*ren* 人); and loving your family members is what is of greatest consequence."[16] And the *Mencius* also says the same thing: "Aspiring to consummate conduct in your roles and relations (*ren* 仁) is becoming a person (*ren* 人); and when these two words—consummate conduct and your person—can be spoken together, you are walking the proper way."[17] Of course, while "walking the proper way" (*dao* 道) might have a more generic reference, at the same time it refers to excelling in one's own particular narrative. Indeed, I would argue that this holistic, normative, role-based, and narrative meaning of *ren* allows us to claim that *ren* itself is one clear way that role ethics is being referenced in classical Confucianism.

To be clear on this, *ren* denotes the aspiration to an achieved virtuosity in the unique roles and relations that constitute our specific continuing narratives. And further, these particular roles, like erstwhile "principles," function as abstract guidelines that find their evolving definition as they are shaped by and emerge out of the collective confluence of our concrete behaviors. As such, roles as they are lived produce generalizations for succeeding generations about how past exemplars in their actions might serve literally as "role models" to guide our present conduct and to assist us in the evaluation of it.

I find welcome corroboration for this claim about the narrative reference of *ren* in the fact that in her essay "*Ren* 仁: An Exemplary Life," Karyn Lai is in her own way making a similar point. She argues that *ren* is best understood as an expansive, always context-specific quality of conduct discernible in those morally exemplary lives that share a commitment to the well-being of others and hence that are lived in a way that fosters growth in relations. Such persons develop and come to express

---

16. *Zhongyong* 20: 仁者人也, 親親為大。
17. *Mencius* 7B16: 仁也者人也, 合而言之, 道也。

this quality of conduct biographically in the roles and behaviors that are first associated with a family environment and are then extended into the community more broadly. Lai insists on an underlying holism that brings unity to the various capacities of such persons as this habituated disposition to foster personal growth is evidenced in their virtuosic conduct. She contrasts her own organic, situational, and dynamic reading of *ren* in this essay with Tu Wei-ming's more analytic, theoretical, and abstract understanding, where for Tu *ren* becomes "a higher order concept" and "an inner morality." Lai argues that such reductionistic descriptions of *ren* that invoke these fragmenting distinctions tend to overly theorize and psychologize what she takes to be irreducibly concrete and thus always specific qualities of lives lived well.[18]

Lai's understanding of *ren* would require that such exemplary lives be ultimately evaluated by an appeal to more holistic and inclusive aesthetic criteria. Abstract standards of conduct such as an appeal to specific reduplicative principles, to the calculation of goods, or to the cultivation of generic virtues that themselves have their ultimate origins in our concrete human narratives: these can only be instrumental and provisional tools serving us at best as rules of thumb. The appropriate role of theorizing is its intimate and inseparable relationship to intelligent practice.

When we reflect on our exemplary teachers, for example, we are more inclined to remember particular situations or specific events as emblematic of their virtuosity rather than to invoke thin, abstract character traits such as honesty, prudence, or courage. "We loved old Angus dearly—he was such a temperate man" is an unlikely thought (certainly made more so because it was Angus). On the other hand, an all too familiar kind of recollection might be: "Do you remember when old Angus, with a length of rope holding up his trousers, announced to his class that this semester during his posted office hours he is to be found at the appointed time under a palm tree at the Sans Souci ('No Worries') Beach in Waikiki—and please bring the beer and pupus?"

As I have noted, the now standardized character for *ren* 仁 in being composed of "person" (*ren* 人) and the number "two" (*er* 二) is semantically revealing in locating the discursive process of becoming consummately human in our relations with and in our relating to both ourselves and others. Such an etymological analysis underscores the Confucian assumption that one cannot become a person by oneself. From our inchoate beginnings,

---

18. Lai, "*Ren* 仁: An Exemplary Life," 83–94.

we are irreducibly social: narratives nested within narratives. We have seen that this "duplicity" or "twoness" in the prestylized graph is represented in several different ways. "Duplicity" from the Latin *duplicare* means first "twofold, having two parts," and then only by extension, something being other than what it purports to be. It is in this latter sense that "duplicity" has come to connote deceit. Such an inference is particularly compelling in a tradition informed by a substance ontology that defines particular things as having an essential individual integrity. What then are the implications of this "duplicity" that attends the project of becoming consummate in one's conduct as a person (*ren* 仁)?

In understanding this "twoness," we must acknowledge the primacy of vital relationality: in taking the dynamic context as integral to the identity of things, vital relationality makes all things including human persons uniquely one and focally many at the same time. No one does anything by themselves. Said another way, in this holographic cosmology, anything is what it is at the pleasure of everything else. The agency and actions of a son are not the conduct of some discrete person. Rather, implicated in such eventful "son" activity is not only the parenting of his parents but the living on of the distinctive physical qualities and the cultural and ethical values of the remotest of his progenitorial ancestors. Much of who and what this son is gets determined by the others with whom he interacts, just as his efforts determine in part who his parents are, and indeed, who his ancestors were as well. At least one significant dimension of our personhood, of our identity, is that it is in important measure conferred upon us by others, just as we make our contribution in conferring identities upon them.

As a corollary to this primacy of vital relationality, the "twoness" recalls the assertion in *Focusing the Familiar* that every happening in the cosmos is indelibly and uniquely one of a kind:

> The ways of heaven and earth can be fully captured in one phrase: Since things and events of the world are never duplicated, their proliferation is beyond comprehension.[19]

This is not a claim merely for the uniqueness of each thing but a statement that precludes any discreteness and independence among them. In speaking of the way of the heavens and the earth, in addition

---

19. *Zhongyong* 26: 天地之道可一言而盡也: 其為物不貳則其生物不測。

to affirming unreduplicated particularity, this passage is also acknowledging the continuity that all things have with each other. This means that erstwhile "things" are both one and two at the same time. They are what they mean for themselves and for the cosmos as a whole. There is always duplicity in identity formation, with the "integrity" of human becomings best being understood as the continuing "integration" of a two-becoming-one: someone who is one and two at the same time.

One criticism directed at the term "role" in role ethics is that "playing a role" introduces a certain distance between "actors" themselves and the roles or "characters" they play. But we might use this same insight (again taking duplicity in its original sense) to appreciate the necessary distance there must be between protégés and their mentors, where it is incumbent upon the students to seize upon whatever inspiration they can find in their intimate relationships with their teachers and elders and adapt this stimulation in whatever direction will best nourish their own personal growth. There is deference to our teachers in the sense of being inspired by them, but there is also deference to the particularities that are defining of each and every situation.

Such "twoness" is a factor in the need for those who would be consummate in their conduct to imaginatively adapt the inspiration of their mentors to shape their own project of becoming uniquely who they would become. The "duplicity" in the term "role" reflects the qualitative distance between role models and those who are inspired by them who must seek in their own projects a comparable standard that is always unique to themselves. In this Confucian tradition, deference to exemplary persons available within historical narratives does much of the work of abstract "principles" in serving as a guide for proper conduct but differs from the principle-based model in that the project of habituating consummate conduct must always be a uniquely personal undertaking. That is, consummate conduct (*ren*), far from being reduplicated actions or generic virtues, is always a unique achievement by particular persons under particular circumstances. We can and should be properly inspired by our role models, but consummate conduct does not brook replication. It should also be noted that, conversely, becoming a mentor is itself a collaboration; persons can only become mentors by virtue of the deference accorded to them by those who are inspired by them.

Again, this duplicity or "twoness" has direct reference to the way of thinking whereby persons actually become consummate. As stated explicitly in the *Analects*, "Correlating one's conduct with those near at hand can be said to be the method of becoming consummate in one's conduct" 能近取譬，可謂仁之方也已.[20] Such an understanding of the continuing and open-ended shaping of personal identity stands in stark contrast to the "oneness" of essentialist, substance models in which a person actualizes an already present, innate potential. Such a correlative method, whereby persons forming their emergent identities pursue optimally appropriate correlations with others, is closely related to the "dramatic rehearsal" required in "putting oneself in the place of others" (*shu* 恕) in determining the best course of action.

And again, we can appeal to this "twoness" as an explanation of the evolution of human self-consciousness with the positive meaning and the important role of a keen, critical self-awareness. There is an important sense in which Chinese processual cosmological order is both cyclical and recursive. Tang Junyi's proposition, which would seem to resonate with the underdeterminacy of emergent order, is the notion that "there is no advancing without reversion 無往不復觀."[21] Whatever persons are and whatever putative "individuals" might or might not be, they cannot be the separate and isolated things without reference to past and current relations that our retrospective thoughts might assume they are. Persons are not present at birth but are emergent in the relations that constitute them from this initial stage, shaping and being shaped in their roles and relations. As they become increasingly social, they also become increasingly reflective and self-conscious through communicating in the families and communities in which they live and where the production of the erstwhile "self-" within a distinctively human self-consciousness is arguably in imitation of their more primary social interactions. That is, persons have discursive relations with others, and under such influence and with reference to such a discursive model, they then gradually come to be reflective and engage in introspective conversation with themselves:

> The Master said, "When you meet persons who are truly worthy think to stand shoulder to shoulder with them; on meeting persons who are otherwise, look inward and examine yourself."[22]

---

20. *Analects*, 6.30.
21. Tang Junyi, *Complete Works*, 11:11.
22. *Analects* 4.17: 子曰：「見賢思齊焉，見不賢而內自省也。」

In *The Concept of Mind*, Gilbert Ryle seems to be making a similar point regarding the social origins of our self-awareness:

> The trick of talking to oneself in silence is acquired neither quickly nor without effort; and it is a necessary condition of our acquiring it that we should have previously learned to talk intelligently aloud and have heard and understood other people doing so.[23]

We might further observe that there is a direct correlation between the quality of one's critical self-awareness together with the sense of shame that attends it, on the one hand, and conduct that might be deemed consummatory on the other. Conversely, the shameless conduct of aberrant individuals reflects a lack of awareness that connects one's own conduct to the narratives of others. "Petty persons" (*xiaoren* 小人) who are a major persona in the *Analects* are retarded not only in their relations with others but also in their degree of critical self-awareness. We might recall Hannah Arendt's seemingly mild indictment of the genocidal monster Adolf Eichmann as being "thoughtless"; it was her considered view that Eichmann lacked the critical self-awareness to see the world from another's point of view. In Confucianism, the mantra is not "I think therefore I am" but rather should be "through communicating we are becoming together" as well as "through communicating I am becoming a critically self-conscious 'we.'" This always collaborative, discursive process of becoming persons is why the language of roles is so powerful in expressing what is indeed a more robust, narrative notion of agency.

If there is one term that captures the spirit of the Confucian tradition, it is perhaps "deference." The fabric of the Confucian family and community is constituted by the always mutual patterns of persons deferring to each other that define the roles of daughter and neighbor (*li* 禮), of uncle and shopkeeper. The need to be inclusive of the interests of all concerned (*yi* 義) means of course that grandmothers must defer to their grandsons and vice versa. The intergenerational transmission of the

---

23. See *The Concept of Mind* (New York: Routledge, 2009), 16. I am indebted to Kevin J. Turner for having pointed this out to me.

living culture captured in the character for "family reverence"—*xiao* 孝 as the combination of *lao* 老 + *zi* 子, "elders" + "juniors"—requires that each generation be one and two at the same time. It requires deference by each generation to those who have come before.

Another implication of this duplicity or "twoness" is that terms such as *ren* are aspectual and have immediately implicated in them the full cluster of terms that are integral to becoming consummate in conduct. The fact, for example, that throughout the *Analects*, *ren* and *zhi* 知 ("wise," "living wisely," "knowing," "realizing") repeatedly appear in tandem suggests that wisdom and morality are interpenetrating and coterminus—that morality transforms mere knowledge into living wisely and that living wisely is an expression of moral "competence." Similarly, the collateral relationship between *ren* and *yi* 義 ("being optimally appropriate," "being meaningful") reflects the reflexivity, inclusiveness, and growth in relation to others entailed by consummate conduct. Again, the persistent association between *ren* and *li* 禮 (aspiring to a ritual propriety in roles and relations) locates the project of becoming consummate within the cultivation of first family and then communal relations.

If we defer to early Chinese cosmology broadly as providing the interpretive context for reading the *Analects* and the other classical Confucian texts—that is, as providing a processual cosmology that first and foremost gives primacy to vital, relationality-constituted persons—we must question the relevance of our own commonsense distinctions that would separate persons from their worlds, persons from each other, and agents from their conduct. After all, when we begin from this primacy of relationality, the introduction of retrospective and post hoc dissections, while often functional and pragmatic, also violate the fundamental wholeness and continuity of experience. Said another way, the narrative ground of all ethical discourse in Confucian philosophy renders such fragmenting distinctions post hoc abstractions made from concrete and continuous episodes of associated conduct. While we might be inclined as a matter of convenience to distinguish erstwhile "individuals" from their "virtuous actions," and "concepts" from their "narrative sources," we must also allow that within our actual lives such abstractions are manifested and "had" initially as continuous aspects of the same experience. And most importantly, such aspects are interpenetrating and coterminous. That is to say, who we are and the lives we live are really one and the same thing.

Xiao 孝 as Another Term for "Role Ethics" in the Confucian Canons

Another key term pervasive in the Confucian corpus that expresses this notion of role ethics is nothing less than "family reverence" (*xiao* 孝), perhaps the prime moral imperative in this continuing tradition. *Xiao* 孝 has conventionally been rendered "filial piety" in English, but Henry Rosemont and I have translated it as "family reverence." What recommends "family reverence" as a translation is that in degree it disassociates *xiao* from the duty to God implied by "piety" and from the unilateral obedience that is assumed in paterfamilias. "Family reverence" is collateral, with the elder generation receiving appropriate deference from their younger members within their family lineages and the younger generation deriving pleasure from deferring to those who have given both meaning and substance to their lives. The term "family reverence" at the same time retains the sacred connotations that are certainly at play in the ritualized culture of ancestral sacrifices.

The collaterality of "familial reverence" (*xiao* 孝) is captured in the character itself, constituted as it is by the combination of the graph for "elders" (*lao* 老) and that for the diminutive "son, daughter, child, youth" (*zi* 子). As with the term *ren* 仁 that resists any formulaic understanding, *xiao* requires us to access and to build upon our own existential sense of what it means to optimize our specific roles within family and community. *Xiao* has immediate reference to our lived experience within the narrative of succeeding generations as we remember our own parents and grandparents and as we attend to our own children and grandchildren. *Xiao* quite literally describes and makes normative the lived roles and relationships that constitute the communities of elders and youth across successive generations, and the thick relations that obtain between the present generation and those generations that have gone before. It references the continuing process of physical and cultural embodiment from one generation to the next and thus the inseparability of grandparents and grandchildren, fathers and daughters, progenitors and progeny, and how such familial roles can only be learned and lived together. In fact, when we examine the earliest form of the character for "elders" (*lao* 老) as it is found on the oracle bones, we find that it depicts an old person with long, disheveled hair, leaning on a walking stick *[v]*, bringing immediately to mind the famous photograph of Albert Einstein with his dandelion hair.[24] In the

[v]

---

24. Kwan, "Database," 甲骨文合集 CHANT 0039A.

small seal script this same graph becomes stylized as *[vi]*, anticipating its present form as 耂. In comparing this character for "elders" (*lao* 老) with the earliest instance of the character for "family reverence" (*xiao* 孝) found later on the bronzes *[vii]*, we discover that the image of a young person has quite literally taken the place of the walking stick as the support elders can lean upon, thereby constituting this character as "elders" together with their "young."²⁵ While *xiao* certainly references the aid and comfort that succeeding older generations can enjoy as it is provided by the progeny that succeeds them, the complement flows in the other direction as well. That is, *xiao* is also the vital process whereby the members of the younger generation are transformed into and become a novel yet persistent embodied variant of those elders to whom they have deferred. The older generation is a reservoir of culture from whom the succeeding generation can draw sustenance and meaning, and in so doing, this younger generation provides their progenitors with a conduit to live on both in the bodies and in the lived, cultural experience of a continuing lineage.

[vi]

[vii]

The centrality of *xiao* in the Confucian project of aspiring to consummatory conduct in one's roles and relations (*ren* 仁) becomes immediately apparent on examining one familiar passage from the *Analects*:

> Exemplary persons (*junzi*) concentrate their efforts on the root, for the root having been properly set, the proper path in life (*dao*) emerges therefrom. As for family reverence (*xiao*) and fraternal deference (*ti*), these are, I suspect, the root of becoming consummate in one's roles and relations (*ren*).²⁶

What then does it mean to take the practical activities of revering family members (*xiao* 孝) and of deferring appropriately to elders (*ti* 弟) to be the *root* (*ben* 本) of becoming consummate in one's roles and relations (*ren* 仁)? Much commentarial ink has been spilled trying to argue against the claim found in this passage that "family reverence" (*xiao*) is the root of "consummate conduct" (*ren*). The Southern Song philosopher Zhu Xi 朱熹 who fused the key concepts of the Northern Song thinkers in his own commentary on the *Analects* worries over this problem. He endorses the interpretation of his philosophical predecessors, the Cheng

---

25. Kwan, "Database," 西周晚期 CHANT 3937.
26. *Analects* 1.2: 君子務本，本立而道生。孝弟也者，其為仁之本與.

brothers 二程, who go to great lengths to challenge this reading. In their commentary, the Cheng brothers argue for a distinction between "practicing *ren*" (*xingren* 行仁) and "becoming *ren*" (*weiren* 為仁), insisting that *ren* in being integral to "human nature" must be prior to *xiao* and that *xiao* only provides us with a forum to "practice" *ren* rather than serving as a resource to "become" *ren*.[27] *Xiao* for the Cheng brothers must be the fruit of *ren* rather than its root.

But previously we saw that the association between *ren* and "family" is clear in the alternative graphic form of the character found on the bamboo strips, with *ren* being the combination of a woman's pregnant body coupled with "heartmind" *[viii]*.[28]  Clearly, any conception of family must begin from woman with child. Allowing that human narratives are always in media res as narratives nested within narratives, I would argue that *ren* as "consummate person/conduct" cannot be taken to describe the content of some essential, ab initio notion of "human nature" (*xing* 性). Indeed, and following from this claim, I would resist any means-end reduction that would introduce a severe separation between "practicing" what it means to be consummate and "becoming" consummate as a person. Getting an education and being educated have the same content. Thus, as I have suggested, *ren* has no meaning or possibility independent of our family and community relations. Such *xiao* and *ti* activities—the various things done in being this proper son to this loving mother, in being this solicitous youth to this congenial elder—are the content of a consummate narrative (*ren*). In a parallel way, as I will argue in some detail, the Confucian notion of "cultivating one's natural propensities" (*xing*) conventionally translated as "human nature" is better understood as in large measure referencing the narrative *content* of the life experience rather than some isolatable "nature" as the erstwhile reduplicative *source* of human conduct. Both *ren* and *xing*, too, are in important measure something that we "do" as an aesthetic achievement rather than denoting something that we already "are." Or perhaps said more clearly, our narratives and our persons, rather than entailing some means-and-end distinction, are one and the same thing.

John Dewey makes this same point in resisting what he calls "*the* philosophical fallacy." This is the fallacy of decontextualizing and essentializing one element within the continuities of experience such as "human nature" and then making this element foundational and causal:

---

27. See the discussion in Ames, *Confucian Role Ethics*, 88–90.
28. Kwan, "Database," 上博竹書五, 君子為豊, 1.

The reality is the growth-process itself; childhood and adulthood are phases of a continuity, in which just because it is a history, the later cannot exist until the earlier exists ("mechanistic materialism" in germ); and in which the later makes use of the registered and cumulative outcome of the earlier—or, more strictly, is its utilization ("spiritualistic teleology" in germ). The real existence is the history in its entirety, the history just as what it is. The operations of splitting it up into two parts and then having to unite them again by appeal to causative power are equally arbitrary and gratuitous.[29]

"Family reverence" (*xiao*) certainly entails deference to elders. Confucius repeatedly insists on the importance of duty and compliance when the young are serving in an official capacity and again on the continuing weight of deferential conduct throughout one's life:

> Those today who are filial are considered so because they are able to provide for their parents. But even dogs and horses are given that much care. If you do not respect your parents, what is the difference?[30]

While Confucius is surely claiming that these patterns of interpersonal behavior are necessary for family flourishing and societal harmony, he is equally guiding his protégés toward such deference as a path of spiritual cultivation in which appropriate conduct expressed through a reverential attitude to family elders is an opportunity for personal refinement.

Two points of clarification are needed here. First, as I have previously remarked, we must resist any simplistic equation between family reverence (*xiao*) and blind obedience. *Xiao* must be distinguished clearly from paterfamilias that we associate with Roman law as the juridical *patria potestas* or power and privilege of the father. Indeed, there are times when being truly filial within the family, like being a loyal minister within the court, requires courageous remonstrance (*jian* 諫) rather than automatic compliance. And indeed, such remonstrance is not perceived merely as a possibility or an option one might choose but as a stern if not sacred obligation. We have seen that one aspect of the "two-ness" of consummate

---

29. Dewey, *Later Works*, 1:210.
30. *Analects* 2.7: 子曰:「今之孝者,是謂能養。至於犬馬,皆能有養;不敬,何以別乎?」

person/conduct (*ren* 仁) that parallels this role of remonstrating with one's elders is the cultivation of a critical self-awareness and a sense of shame that can serve as a perspective from which to critique one's own roles along with those of others.

In *The Chinese Classic of Family Reverence*, Master Zeng, who is to become the paragon of family reverence in the Confucian tradition, after having benefited from a full fourteen chapters of instruction on *xiao*, asks Confucius explicitly if strict obedience is the substance of family reverence:

> Master Zeng said, "Parental love (*ai*), reverence and respect (*jing*), seeing to the well-being of one's parents, and raising one's name (*ming*) high for posterity—on these topics I have received your instructions. I would presume to ask whether children can be deemed filial (*xiao*) by obeying every command of their father."[31]

Confucius responds to Master Zeng's query with a disappointed impatience, making the argument that such an uncritical attitude of automatic compliance to one's elders, far from being the substance of family reverence, can conversely be a source of gross immorality in conduct:

> "How could you? What on earth are you saying?" said the Master, "If confronted by reprehensible behavior on his father's part, a son has no choice but to remonstrate with his father, and if confronted by reprehensible behavior on his ruler's part, a minister has no choice but to remonstrate with his ruler. Hence, remonstrance is the only response to immorality.

---

31. Henry Rosemont Jr. and Roger T. Ames, *The Chinese Classic of Family Reverence: A Philosophical Translation of the* Xiaojing 孝經 (Honolulu: University of Hawai'i Press, 2009), chapter 15: 曾子曰：「若夫慈愛、恭敬、安親、揚名，則聞命矣。敢問子從父之令，可謂孝乎？」Master Zeng is best remembered as a proponent of "family reverence" (*xiao*)—the devotion and service that the younger generation directs to their elders and ancestors, and the pleasure that they derive in doing so. A natural extension of this affection for one's family is friendship, and Master Zeng is portrayed in the *Analects* as being able to distinguish between the sincerity of fellow student Yan Hui and the rashness of another student, Zizhang.

How could simply obeying the commands of one's father be deemed filial?"[32]

Indeed, the *Xunzi* takes on this issue and devotes an entire chapter to multiple stories providing examples of how blind obedience to the older generation, far from reflecting family reverence, offends against this very same value by producing consistently dire consequences.[33]

And the second point to be made here in clarifying the meaning of family reverence is that the immediate family is only the beginning of such deference. *Xiao* must become a pattern of conduct that with unrelenting attention is extended out from family to include all members of the community, the polity, and ultimately even nature itself. Indeed, in the "Three Powers" chapter of *The Chinese Classic of Family Reverence*, *xiao* has cosmic reference, correlating the relationships that obtain among the heavens, the earth, and the human world within this *xiao* moral imperative. It is because these three powers are mutually implicated in each other that such cosmic relations, providing as they do a context for the human experience, have themselves a moral aspect that can serve as a model for the proper accord to be achieved within our human institutions:

> "Incredible—the profundity of family reverence!" declared Master Zeng. "Indeed," said the Master. "Family reverence is the constancy of the heavenly cycles, the appropriate responsiveness (*yi*) of the earth, and the proper conduct of the people. It is the constant workings of the heavens and the earth that the people model themselves upon. Taking the illumination (*ming*) of the heavens as their model and making the most of the earth's resources, they bring the empire into accord (*shun*). This is the reason that education can be effective without being severe, and political administration can maintain proper order without being harsh."[34]

---

32. *Classic of Family Reverence*, chapter 15: 子曰：「是何言與! 是何言與! . . . 當不義, 則子不可以不爭於父, 臣不可以不爭於君。故當不義則爭之。從父之令, 又焉得為孝乎! 」

33. See *Xunzi*, ch. 29.

34. *Classic of Family Reverence*, chapter 7: 曾子曰：「甚哉! 孝之大也。」子曰：「夫孝、天之經也, 地之義也, 民之行也。天地之經而民是則之, 則天之明, 因地之利, 以順天下。是以其教不肅而成, 其政不嚴而治。

Relationally constituted persons are born into the broadest swath of family, community, and cosmic relations. They cannot exist exclusive of these relations, nor can they grow without them. By locating the notion of persons within the relational ecology that serves as interpretive context for these texts, we can argue that terms such as "root," "potential," "cause," and "source," which are at times taken as disjunctive and exclusive terms to be associated with some underlying cosmic teleology, have to be reconceived as referencing always multilateral, symbiotic, and reflexive processes. Such an alternative understanding of the project of civilizing experience is immediately relevant in thinking through the intergenerational, genealogical, and holographic implications of family reverence (*xiao*) that would construe persons as radial centers within an unbounded cosmic ecology.

The "root" metaphor, for example, means that in these ongoing transactional processes of associated living, the cultivation of one's unique person within one's specific and often changing relations is the "root" from which a full canopy of interdependent personal bonds grows. These bonds define the various radial spheres of family lineage, neighborhood, community, village, polity—and, ultimately, cosmos—with each of these mutually implicated dimensions making its own contribution to the prevailing social ethic. As the *Expansive Learning* (大學 *Daxue*) enjoins us in the singularly important project of becoming consummate persons, personal cultivation in the relations that constitute us is fundamental, and we must thus make it our highest priority:

> From the emperor down to the common folk, everything is rooted in personal cultivation. There can be no healthy canopy when the roots are not properly set, and it would never do for priorities to be reversed between what should be invested with importance and what should be treated more lightly.[35]

It is necessary to understand the underlying focus-field holism here. Continuing this familiar root-and-branches metaphor, root and canopy must

---

35. Ian Johnston and Wang Ping, eds., *Daxue and Zhongyong: Bilingual Edition* (Hong Kong: Chinese University Press, 2012), 46. 自天子以至於庶人，壹是皆以修身為本。其本亂而末治者否矣，其所厚者薄，而其所薄者厚，未之有也! I have borrowed this translation of the title of the *Daxue* as *Expansive Learning* rather than the familiar *Great Learning* from Jung-Yeup Kim because it captures the expansive radiality of the Confucian project as it is rehearsed in this foundational text.

grow together, with the tree spreading its roots outward beneath the earth and simultaneously stretching its branches upward toward the sky. While the root is certainly growing the tree, the tree is also in turn growing its roots. The root and its flourishing canopy are perceived as aspects of an interactive and organic whole that grow together symbiotically or not at all. In the same way, the aspiration to become consummate in our conduct as persons (*ren*) is the expansive process of persons becoming increasingly rooted in virtuosic habits of conduct and extending themselves outward synergistically in their relations within family, community, and cosmos. Indeed, the *Record of Rites* (*Liji* 禮記) version of the *Expansive Learning* fascicle concludes the excerpt earlier cited by declaring that personal cultivation sets the root deeply and securely while fostering the social intelligence needed for a flourishing world. In the words of the text itself:

> This resolve in one's personal cultivation is called both the root and the magnitude of wisdom.[36]

Here again, the project of personal cultivation eschews exclusive means-ends distinctions. The "root" and its erstwhile product, "wisdom," are perceived as an organic whole that in growing together are two ways of viewing the same phenomenon. This is just to say that the practice of personal cultivation and the wisdom that thereby comes to characterize one's conduct are aspectual abstractions from the concrete narrative of living consummately within the relations of family, community, and cosmos.

This perception of the root and the tree as a symbiotic process stands in stark contrast to thinking of, abstracting, and thus isolating the root as some independent, single source and has important ecological implications. Such symbiotic thinking reflects the holistic cosmological assumptions that would anticipate an always situated answer to our most fundamental and perennial philosophical questions: what is the "source" of meaning, and how is it conveyed? By way of contrast, in the Abrahamic traditions the answer is simple: meaning comes from a divine "source" beyond and independent of the human community. Yahweh or God or Allah provides us with a continuing vision of life's purpose, and each of us must return to this source when we lose our way. For the Confucian project, on the other hand, with no appeal to some independent, external

---

36. D. C. Lau and Chen Fong Ching, eds., *Liji* 禮記 [Record of rites], *A Concordance to the* Liji (Hong Kong: Commercial Press, 1992), 43.1/164/30: 此謂知本, 此謂知之至也。

principle, meaning arises pari passu from a vital network of meaningful relationships in the process of the intergenerational transmission and embodiment of a living civilization. Human narratives are "rooted" in their genealogical and cultural lineages and grow therefrom. A personal commitment to achieving relational virtuosity within one's own family relationships is both the starting point and the ultimate source of personal, social, and indeed, cosmic meaning. In cultivating our own persons through aspiring to and extending robust relations as they evolve in our families and beyond, we enlarge the cosmos by adding meaning to it, and in turn, this increasingly meaningful cosmos provides an ever more fertile context for the project of our own personal cultivation.

Given this primacy of relationality exemplified by the centrality of family reverence (*xiao*) as the prime moral imperative, if *religare* as the Latin root of "religious" does mean "binding tightly" (as reflected in the cognates "ligament," "obligation," "league," and "ally")—then we can see that "family reverence" (*xiao*) so described has a profoundly religious import as well, referencing as it does those familial, communal, and ancestral bonds that together constitute a resilient and enduring social fabric.[37] And it is this profoundly religious sense of "binding tightly"—that is, the strengthening of family and communal bonds—that we would appeal to in interpreting the Master's autobiographical response to Zilu's question about what Confucius would most like to do:

> I would like to bring peace and contentment to the aged, share relationships of trust and confidence with friends, and to love and protect the young.[38]

In *The Chinese Classic of Family Reverence*, Confucius begins by elevating *xiao* to be Confucianism's highest moral imperative, declaring that this "way of family reverence" is the very substance of morality and education: "It is family reverence (*xiao*) that is the root of moral virtuosity, and whence education (*jiao*) itself is born."[39] The opening chapter of this same text goes on to provide us with the familiar radial progression from

---

37. Sarah F. Hoyt, "The Etymology of Religion," *Journal of the American Oriental Society* 32, no. 2 (1912): 126–129. Hoyt provides some interesting textual evidence for this very old and sometimes disputed etymology.

38. *Analects* 5.26: 子路曰：「願聞子之志。」子曰：「老者安之，朋友信之，少者懷之。」

39. *Classic of Family Reverence*, chapter 1: 子曰：夫孝，德之本也，教之所由生也。

a determinate center to an unbounded extreme that we find consistently in the Confucian literature, beginning from respect for one's own person as what is closest at hand, extending such concern to the care for one's family and kin, and then culminating in dedicating one's service to one's ruler and to posterity. In this passage, King Wen—that is, King "Culture" (*wen*)—is once again singled out as the source from which the current generation draws its inspiration and to whom, with the cultural dividends it has accrued, makes appropriate return.

> Your physical person with its hair and skin are received from your parents. Vigilance in not allowing anything to do injury to your person is where family reverence begins. Distinguishing yourself and walking the proper way (*dao*) in the world; raising your name high for posterity and thereby bringing esteem to your father and mother—it is in these things that family reverence finds its consummation. Such family reverence then begins in service to your parents, continues in service to your lord, and culminates in distinguishing yourself in the world. In the "Greater Odes" section of the *Book of Songs* it says: "How can you fail to remember your ancestor, King Wen? You must cultivate yourself and extend his virtuosity."[40]

The charge in this passage to keep the body intact certainly refers to a person's own carnal physicality, but it also lends itself to an important broader, cultural reading; that is, each succeeding generation has the responsibility of keeping whole and alive the corpus of culture that it comes to embody. Indeed, we might offer the following as an alternative reading of the concluding citation from the *Book of Songs*: How can you fail to embody the culture of your ancestors? You must cultivate yourself and extend its reach and influence.

Confucian role ethics in substance is perpetuated through family lineages that have complex political, economic, and religious functions. In the following section, I will have occasion to appeal to two cognate characters that are integral to the dynamics of "family reverence" (*xiao*) in the intergenerational transmission of the continuities of the family lineage:

---

40. *Classic of Family Reverence*, chapter 1: 身體髮膚, 受之父母, 不敢毀傷, 孝之始也。立身行道, 揚名於後世, 以顯父母, 孝之終也。夫孝, 始於事親, 中於事君, 終於立身。《大雅》云:『無念爾祖, 聿脩厥德。』; *Book of Songs*, 235.

ti 體 ("embodying," "body," "forming and shaping," "category," "class") and *li* 禮 ("ritual," "achieving propriety in one's roles and relations"). Without the formal and determinate dimension provided by embodied living (*ti* 體), and by the social grammar afforded by meaningful roles and relations (*li* 禮), there is a very real question as to whether the significant refinement that is aspired to through such embodied life-forms would even be possible. Put simply, determinate forms in their many different variations—body, ritual, language, the institutions of family and ancestral reverence, and so on—are a necessary condition for cultural refinement. The "living body" (*ti* 體) and its "embodied living" (*li* 禮) is the narrative site of the conveyance and the continuing refinement of the culture through which a living civilization is perpetuated: its language, its mores and values, its religious rituals, its aesthetics of cooking, song, and dance, and so on.

An important dramatis persona in the *Analects* who in his own conduct underscores this primacy of relationality is Confucius's protégé, Master Zeng 曾子, whom we have already met as the paradigmatic figure most closely associated with the fullest expression of "family reverence" (*xiao* 孝):[41]

> Master Zeng was gravely ill, and when Meng Jingzi asked after him, Master Zeng said to him, "Baleful is the cry of a dying bird; felicitous are the words of a dying person."[42]

In this passage, Master Zeng, plainly aware of his own impending demise, begins by exhorting his listener to pay serious attention to what he is about to say, for Master Zeng on his deathbed believes that his last words as he will utter them are of real consequence:

> There are three habits that exemplary persons consider of utmost importance in their vision of the moral life. By maintaining a dignified demeanor, such persons keep violent

---

41. In reading the *Analects* and exploring the meaning and function of the term *xiao* to shed light on this key philosophical term, one can complement such an analysis by an appeal to the many references to Master Zeng himself where he appears as the personal embodiment of *xiao*.

42. *Analects* 8.4: 曾子有疾，孟敬子問之。曾子言曰：「鳥之將死，其鳴也哀；人之死，其言也善。」

and rancorous conduct at a distance; by maintaining a proper countenance, they keep trust and confidence near at hand; by taking care in their choice of language and their mode of expression, they keep vulgarity and impropriety at a distance. As for the details in the arrangement of ritual vessels, there are minor functionaries to take care of such things."[43]

Master Zeng's message then is that all three of the habits of deportment considered by exemplary persons to be vital to the moral life—that is, a dignified demeanor, a proper countenance, and a commitment to effective communication—are essential to the productive growth of interpersonal relations. And it is such growth in relations that is the substance of Confucian morality. On the other hand, a failure to cultivate such dispositions precipitates vulgarity, impropriety, and violent, rancorous actions. This kind of untoward behavior is an immediate source of diminution and disintegration in one's relations, and as such, is for the Confucian the substance of immoral conduct. By way of contrast with the vital concern Master Zeng would invest in the cultivation of the quality of personal relations, he regards the formal and material trappings of a refined life to be of relatively marginal significance. The example given here is the arrangement of ritual vessels that can be taken care of by minor attendants. It is thus that the familial and social roles are seen to have normative force, serving us as concrete guidelines for how we ought to proceed, and quite felicitously, for determining what we ought to do next. Indeed, it is this continuing process of elevating, refining, and deepening our lived roles and relations to make the most of our associated lives that prompts us to describe Confucian morality as an ethics of roles and to claim that Confucian role ethics is, in our view, a sui generis vision of the moral life.

In Confucian role ethics, the assumption is that social and political order broadly construed is rooted in and emerges from personal cultivation as it is first and foremost actuated within the institution of the family and then extended to one's family lineage and beyond. The renowned sociologist Fei Xiaotong reflects upon the contemporary configuration of the Chinese kinship-based sociopolitical model of governance that can be attested to as early as the bronze inscriptions and canons of the

---

43. *Analects* 8.4:「君子所貴乎道者三：動容貌，斯遠暴慢矣；正顏色，斯近信矣；出辭氣，斯遠鄙倍矣。籩豆之事，則有司存。」

early Zhou dynasty.[44] Fei introduces distinctions that would contrast Western and Chinese models of social organization. Fei identifies "the organizational mode of association" (*tuantigeju* 團體格局) as groups of discrete individuals with their rule-governed social organizations functioning within clearly defined boundaries with Western individualism. The image Fei uses for this organizational mode is of individual straws collected and bound together to form a haystack—a bundle of discrete entities. He contrasts this mode of organization with the Chinese kinship model that he calls "the differential mode of association" (*chaxugeju* 差序格局).[45] Fei's analogy for the differential mode is "the concentric circles formed when a stone is thrown into a lake," a relational image that is reinforced by the fact that the character for "ripples" or "rippling" (*lun* 淪) is cognate and homophonous with the graph for "relational order" (*lun* 倫). One important feature in Fei's distinction between these two modes of association is the existence of a common organizing principle binding persons together in the organizational mode of association that makes them equal (some variation on the concept of "law" or as "God" in the broadest sense). This notion of being equal before the law or all children of God stands in contrast with the interrelated, hierarchical, and graduated differences in personal roles and relations—the *li* 禮—that emerge and are at play in the differential mode. This equality/hierarchy distinction is very much in evidence in the alternative ways of thinking about the construction of personal identity: a contrast between asserting one's perceived rights and entitlements, on the one hand, and managing one's personal connections—one's *guanxi* 關係—on the other.

Fei Xiaotong insists that Confucian ethics must be conceived of as always unique "centers fanning out into a web-like network" that are "composed of webs woven out of countless personal relationships."[46] He would further claim that this predominant pattern of kinship relations with its hierarchically defined roles and relations produces its own distinctive kind of morality in which "no ethical concepts . . . transcend

---

44. Yiqun Zhou, *Festival, Feasts, and Gender Relations in Ancient China and Greece* (New York: Cambridge University Press, 2010), 147. Yiqun Zhou argues that "the home, where one engaged in daily practices of kinship-centered moral precepts and religious ceremonies, was the site for the most fundamental education in Zhou society."

45. Xiaotong Fei, *From the Soil: The Foundations of Chinese Society* [in Chinese] (Berkeley: University of California Press, 1992), 63.

46. Fei, *From the Soil*, 68, 78.

specific types of human relationships."⁴⁷ That is, kinship as the root of human relations is defined by the values of "family reverence" (*xiao* 孝) and "fraternal deference" (*ti* 悌). And friendship as the way of extending this pattern of kinship relations to include nonrelatives is pursued through an ethic of "commitment and resolve" (*cheng* 誠), "doing one's utmost" (*zhong* 忠), and "making good on one's word" (*xin* 信).⁴⁸ All such ethical values are aspired to as the way of reconciling the tensions among and promoting the accommodations made within the specific personal relationships of family members and community.

Dorothy Emmet echoes several of Fei Xiaotong's insights in her reflections upon the relationship between sociology and ethics. Emmet, like Fei, acknowledges the centrality of social roles:

> Whether every social relation should be described as a role relation may be a matter of logic, as defining how a term is being used, . . . but whether or not role relationships are seen as omnipresent in social life, at least they form its recognizable patterns.

This being the case, Emmet declares that "what people think they ought to do depends largely on how they see their roles, and (most importantly) the conflicts between their roles."⁴⁹

This intimate relationship between ethical values and social roles brings to mind a passage from the *Mencius* in which the vocabulary of role ethics is historicized, taking these terms back to the earliest stages in the evolution of human civilization. During the reign of Yao and then Shun, the land was cleared, and Yu drained the waters to make the cultivation of crops possible.

---

47. Fei, *From the Soil*, 74.
48. See, for example, *Analects* 1.4 and 1.8. There is an ambiguity in the expression "associates and friends" (*pengyou* 朋友) as it is used in the documents of the Western Zhou and Spring and Autumn period where these texts do not distinguish nonrelated friends from agnatic male relatives—that is, paternal relatives such as brothers, uncles, nephews, cousins, and so on. Some scholars have argued that *pengyou* becomes a term commonly used to denote non-kin friends specifically only in the Warring States period. See Zhou, *Festival, Feasts, and Gender Relations*, 110–111 and 137–139.
49. See Emmet, *Rules, Roles and Relations*, 13, 15.

> [The minister of Shun and legendary cultural hero] Houji 后稷 taught the people how to sow and reap their crops, and how to plant and grow the various grains. When these grains ripened, the people flourished. But human beings have their proper way, and even when they have full stomachs, warm clothing, and comfortable housing, without education they are little more than animals. These sage rulers were much concerned about this situation, and sent Xie as Minister of Education to teach the people by appealing to propriety in human roles and relations: that is, there is affection to be found in the roles of father and son, optimal appropriateness to be found in the roles of lord and minister, proper distinctions to be found in the roles of husband and wife, a productive hierarchy to be found in the role of elders and juniors, and fidelity to be found in the role of friend and friend.[50]

It is because the entry point for developing moral competence in the Confucian vision of the moral life is family relations in the broadest sense that *xiao* 孝 as "family reverence" has its singularly important place in the *Analects*. It is for this reason that to better understand the notion of *xiao* itself, we need to clarify the nature and the significance of the institution of family within this Confucian context. Again, Fei Xiaotong draws a contrast between the nuclear "family" that for anthropologists takes on its major significance as the site of reproduction and the dominant pattern of premodern Chinese families and clans. Such Chinese families have historically been lineages of persons with the same surname (*shizu* 氏族 or *jiazu* 家族) and by extension have been communities (*zu* 族 or *minzu* 民族) made up of several lineages who have different surnames. While such extended lineages certainly have the function of reproduction, Fei insists that within the Chinese experience they have the singularly important institutional role as "a medium through which all activities are organized."[51] That is, in addition to the perpetuation of the family, such lineages have complex political, economic, and religious functions that are expressed along the vertical and hierarchical axis of the father-

---

50. *Mencius* 3A4: 后稷教民稼穡。樹藝五穀，五穀熟而民人育。人之有道也，飽食、煖衣、逸居而無教，則近於禽獸。聖人有憂之，使契為司徒，教以人倫：父子有親，君臣有義，夫婦有別，長幼有序，朋友有信。

51. Fei, *From the Soil*, 84.

son and mother–daughter-in-law relationships. Lineage relations are again reinforced socially and religiously through the institutions of ancestor reverence, which is a continuing practice that archaeology tells us dates back at least to the Neolithic Age.[52]

In the early Shang, the ancestors—at least those of the king and the noble families—were believed to be directly responsible for the good or ill fortune in the lives of their descendants, necessitating a propitiating of these progenitors through sacrifice. That this belief was persistent helps to explain Confucius's comment that "sacrificing to ancestral spirits other than one's own is being unctuous."[53] One of Confucius's important insights was to appreciate the fact that even though the supernatural raison d'être for performance of these ritual sacrifices might no longer be broadly credible among the intelligentsia, such rituals as a celebration of past generations living on in the present could still continue to provide a good deal of meaning for human lives and serve as a binding force in the family and community overall.

Of course, given the fact that particularly over the past century the structure of Chinese family lineages has changed dramatically, such generalizations must be qualified by time and place, as well as by regional and temporal variations. Having acknowledged this, Yiqun Zhou marshals scholarly consensus behind her claim that premodern Chinese society was "for several thousand years largely a polity organized by kinship principles."[54] In weighing the extent to which social and political order was derived from and dependent upon family relations, Zhou insists that in contrast with the Greeks, "The Chinese state was never conceived as a

---

52. See David N. Keightley, "Shamanism, Death, and the Ancestors: Religious Mediation in Neolithic and Shang China, ca. 5000–1000 B.C," *Asiatische Studien* 52 (1998): 763–828. Yiqun Zhou's analysis of the dominance of kinship and the inalienable bond between ancestors and their progeny in early Zhou society points out that "nearly one-sixth of the *Odes* pertain to ancestral sacrifices, including the ceremony proper and the subsequent feast. These pieces demonstrate the central importance of the ancestral banquet for our understanding of the Zhou discourse of sociability." And Zhou states further that "ancestor worship entails not only memorial rituals that are regular, systematic, and continuous, but also, more important, incorporation of the dead into a descent group as permanent members endowed with an essential role in forging group solidarity." See Zhou, *Festival, Feasts, and Gender Relations*, 104 and 112.

53. *Analects* 2.24: 非其鬼而祭之，諂也。

54. Zhou, *Festival, Feasts, and Gender Relations*, 19.

political community that equaled the sum of its citizens" and that "the relationship between the rulers and the ruled was considered analogous to the relationship between parents and children," or an isomorphism between family and state (*jiaguotonggou* 家國同構).⁵⁵ This contrast immediately recalls Fei Xiaotong's distinction between "the organizational mode of association" (*tuantigeju* 團體格局) and "the differential mode of association" (*chaxugeju* 差序格局).

Confucius himself is making an astute observation when he asserts that within this cultural tradition, the proper functioning of the institution of family is integral to the production of the sociopolitical order of the state:

> Someone asked Confucius, "Why are you not employed in government?" The Master replied, "The *Book of Documents* says: 'It all lies in family reverence. Being filial to your parents and finding fraternity with your brothers is in fact carrying out the work of governing.' In doing these things I am participating in government. Why must I be employed in government?"⁵⁶

Zhou Yiqun again cites the late Qing scholar Yan Fu, who claims that sociopolitical order in the two millennia of imperial China was from its beginnings "seventy percent a lineage organization and thirty percent an empire."⁵⁷ Indeed, it is this persistent family-based sociopolitical organization of Chinese society that has within this antique culture elevated the specific family values and obligations circumscribed by the term *xiao* to serve as its governing moral imperative.

Ru 儒 as Role Rather than Doctrine

"Family reverence" (*xiao*) serves as the primary cultural imperative that makes the roles lived by each and every human being significant in serving as the living conduits through which the culture is transmitted—that is,

---

55. Zhou, *Festival, Feasts, and Gender Relations*, 17–18, note 51.

56. *Analects* 2.21: 或謂孔子曰:「子奚不為政?」子曰:「《書》云:『孝乎惟孝、友于兄弟、施於有政。』是亦為政, 奚其為為政?」

57. Zhou, *Festival, Feasts, and Gender Relations*, 19, note 55.

the always evolving yet persistent Confucian way of becoming human (*rendao* 人道). And as we have seen in the first chapter of *The Chinese Classic of Family Reverence*, the culmination of *xiao* is performed by those who are able to raise their names high for posterity, and in so doing, bring esteem to their family lineages. It is these exemplars as role models who, in every age and over the eons, have enabled their progeny, in transcending their animality, to intensify the human experience with the elegance and refinement of culture in its most noble sense. There is thus a parallel between the function of *xiao* that references the intergenerational embodiment and transmission of family lineages broadly and of *rujia* 儒家 as the literati or lettered class (*wenren* 文人) that functions as literally an additional important stratum of family within the family lineages. The *ru* family describes one elite layer in the population responsible for embodying and transmitting the high literary tradition from one generation to the next. And it is to the role of this elite class of literati exemplars in perpetuating the persistent yet always transforming social, political, and ethical orthodoxy of this cultural core—what is called the *daotong* 道統—that we now turn.

The early philosopher and teacher Kongfuzi 孔夫子, Latinized as "Confucius," lends his name to the English (but not to the Chinese) expression of this tradition called "Confucianism."[58] Confucius was certainly a flesh-and-blood historical person who lived, taught, and died some twenty-five centuries ago, consolidating in his own time a formidable legacy of wisdom that has been passed down and applied through the ages to shape the character of an entire culture and beyond. In and of itself, the profoundly personal model of Confucius remembered by his protégés through those intimate snapshots of his life collected in the

---

58. Tim Barrett in "Chinese Religion in English Guise: The History of an Illusion," *Modern Asian Studies* 39, no. 3, (2005): 518 has identified Sir John Francis Davis (1795–1890), the second governor of Hong Kong, as the first person on record to have used the word "Confucianism." See Sir John Francis Davis, *The Chinese: A General Description of the Empire of China and its Inhabitants* (London: Charles Knight & Co., 1836), 45. It is perhaps interesting that just as with the term "Confucianism" as a decidedly Western intervention into Chinese culture, the mountain peak in Hong Kong that remembers Davis as "Mount Davis" in English still continues to be known in Chinese by its own name: "Star-scrapper Peak" (*Moxingling* 摩星嶺). See also Nicolas Standaert, "The Jesuits did NOT Manufacture 'Confucianism,'" *East Asian Science, Technology and Medicine* 16 (1999), 115–132 for a detailed discussion of the *ru* tradition and its questionable interpretation as "Confucianism" that absolves the Jesuits of this problematic equation.

middle chapters of the *Analects* and other canonical texts, has its own value and meaning. But then, as cited earlier, Confucius reportedly said of himself that most of what he had to offer his students had ancient roots and that he was inclined to follow the established path rather than strike out in new directions.[59] Indeed it is perhaps for this reason that in the Chinese language itself, the tradition is not identified specifically with the person Confucius as "Confucianism" but rather with the social, political, and religious role of the ongoing *ru* 儒 literati class who over the centuries has provided the cultural tradition with its evolving "literati learning" (*ruxue* 儒學). The point I want to make here is that what we call "Confucianism" and conventionally interpret as a particular doctrine or stipulated set of values is first and foremost a continuing sociopolitical class of literati whose role within the family lineage has always been the embodiment and perpetuation of the living cultural tradition—a tradition that reflects markedly different content in different epochs as it continues to travel across the generations.

The earliest occurrence of this term *ru* in our extant corpus is found in a single passage of the *Analects*:

> The Master remarked to Zixia, "You want to become the kind of *ru* literatus who is exemplary in conduct, not the kind that is a petty person."[60]

The etymology of the character *ru* 儒 itself is cognate with the graphs *ru* 腝 as "pliant, soft," *ru* 孺 as "child, weak, mild," and "weak, timid" (*nuo* 懦), fairly describing a class of "gentle" literate people who emerged and flourished as early as the Shang dynasty (1600–1046 BCE) at least thirty generations before Confucius. And it is this same lettered class including the scholars and intellectuals still at work today that continue to thrive some eighty generations after Confucius's death. This gentry class of intellectuals—across the ages, and in different ways at different times—has contributed its own best thoughts to this "literati learning" as a continuous, living tradition. Consistent with Confucius's own premises, this scholarly legacy called *ruxue*—the always porous core of an elite,

---

59. *Analects* 7.1.

60. *Analects* 6.13: 子謂子夏曰:「女為君子儒, 無為小人儒。」

accumulating Chinese culture—is both vital and corporate. What we now have come to call "Confucianism" is in fact a shared and evolving culture corpus that has been appropriated, reinterpreted, commented upon in great detail, further elaborated upon and extended by always "new" Confucians, and then reauthorized in each succeeding generation. And the *ru*, far from being doctrinaire advocates of some specific dogma, have at different times across the centuries reflected different values and embraced an ever-evolving range of ideas and cultural practices. While there has certainly been a continuing, self-conscious identity over the centuries, there are also importantly different degrees of innovation and creative advance that have occurred with the passing of each generation.

One way of interpreting the role of this *ru* literary class is to rehearse its narrative as it emerges as an elite social stratum in the Shang dynasty. These early *ru* of the Shang began in earnest to aestheticize urban life in their social and political institutions, a story that can be told through the casting of mass quantities of exquisite bronze vessels that are today displayed in museums around the world as emblematic of ancient Chinese culture. Much can be learned about this literati class by going back and relocating these bronze artifacts within their own historical context—thus retrieving their original iconic status and function.

To begin with, we can speculate on how the development of this bronze production was catalytic in the emergence of Chinese civilization itself. The Shang dynasty achieved a high degree of metalworking mastery within a few centuries of its founding, and the vessels cast within this cultural site served as markers of social, political, and indeed religious power that distinguished city-dwelling nobles from a rural peasantry. In his history of Chinese aesthetics, Li Zehou reports that "though bronzes were actually cast by manual laborers and even slaves, and though the origin of some bronze designs can be traced back to primitive totems and pottery, such designs were primarily expressions of the will and power of the rulers of early hierarchical society."[61] Indeed, these bronzes help to tell the story of the bronzes' owners who had both the privileges and the responsibilities signified by these sacred castings. The Shang people had a well-developed written language that provides us with the earliest recorded history of life in ancient China. This script was recovered in

---

61. Li Zehou, *The Path of Beauty: A Study of Chinese Aesthetics* (Oxford: Oxford University Press, 1994), 28.

the early twentieth century as an oracle bone script (*jiaguwen* 甲骨文) written on the physical medium of bovid scapula and turtle plastrons used for divinatory practices. During the subsequent Western Zhou dynasty (1056?–770 BCE), significant events of the court were sometimes inscribed for posterity on the inner walls of commemorative bronze vessels using a later generation of these same graphs—the second medium for writing called the bronze inscriptions (*jinwen* 金文).

The oracle bones inscriptions contain a rich vocabulary of over five thousand characters that are unintelligible to most contemporary people. Indeed, even trained paleographers have now after a century of painstaking analysis only been able to decipher less than a quarter of these ancient inscriptions. The complexity and scope of this early language is startling when we consider that educated Chinese persons today might have a reading vocabulary of about four thousand characters with a writing competency of something less. The commemorative inscriptions on bronze vessels or *jinwen* 金文 dating from the Western Zhou dynasty are written in a seal script only decipherable by the learned few.

By reflecting on the truly vast collections we have of these Shang dynasty bronze vessels, we can come to understand life in early China from many different cultural perspectives. From a sociological vantage point, for example, these bronzes tell the story of hierarchical kinship structures and institutions dominated by a hugely literate aristocratic bureaucracy that lent its labors and counsel to a hereditary Shang house. This royal house was supported in this world largely by the labors of farmers and fishermen and watched over from the next world by a pantheon of former Shang kings. With respect to the role of the *ru* literati in this advanced culture, the historian Paul Wheatley observes that "the overwhelming impression left by a survey of Shang technology is that its progress was a response to, not a determinant of, the emergence of a social class whose primary concerns were with ritual and ceremony."[62]

By reading these bronzes from a religious perspective, we learn of how this aristocratic population expended its wealth and time on complex programs of ancestor reverence and used its resources to develop

---

62. Paul Wheatley, *The Pivot of the Four Quarters: A Preliminary Enquiry into the Origins and Character of the Ancient Chinese City* (Chicago: Chicago University Press, 1971), 74.

an extraordinary culture in which, unlike many other civilizations of the same period, most bronze metal was used for ritual vessels rather than weaponry. Such ceremonial instruments were the accouterments that attended regular sacrifices and libations in the various ancestral temples and that ornamented mantic practices linking this world to the next. These ceremonies provided a conduit for communication between this living population and the ancestors who assisted them from beyond. Still, as civilized as the Shang people were, one dimension of their increasingly ritualized life was a huge appetite for death; that is, the Shang court practiced large-scale blood sacrifices as an integral component of their religious experience. As proof, we have the recovery of dozens of human skulls together with equally numerous bronze vessels from the cornerstone foundations at building sites.

By reading these bronzes from the perspective of the economy, we are able to correlate the metal-winning efforts of this population living in the Yellow River basin with the magnitude of its surpluses and how they were expended. The placement of the quarters and workshops of bronze-working artisans in desirable urban locations also tells us of the growing prestige of their craft. We are able to trace a transition from low volume metalworking to large-scale metal production at fabrication centers that reflects an exponential growth in technological competence. As Shang dynasty historian Ursula Franklin recounts, "In the context of early China, the sheer scale of bronze production is as impressive as the quality of the craft. Such a level of bronze production demands, as a prerequisite, a well-organized large-scale mining and smelting industry."[63] And we know that such industrial scale could only be achieved and maintained by employing a ready-to-hand population of forced laborers captured by incursions into the neighboring tribal regions and who then became indentured workers and candidates for sacrificial rituals.[64]

---

63. Ursula Franklin, "On Bronze and Other Metals in Early China," *The Origins of Chinese Civilization*, ed. David N. Keightley (Berkeley: University of California Press, 1983), 287.

64. See *Cambridge History of Ancient China: From the Origin of Civilization to 221 B.C.*, ed. Michael Loewe and Edward L. Shaughnessy (Cambridge: Cambridge University Press, 1999). In this edited volume, the essays by Robert Bagley ("Shang Archaeology") and David N. Keightley ("The Shang: China's First Historical Dynasty") tell the fascinating story of these Shang bronzes.

From these bronzes, we learn much about the lives of the Shang people who established a profoundly "aestheticized" way of being in a world that had begun with the production and institutionalization of ritual vessels by an elite group of literati at the Shang court. This same social class can be associated with the development of a program of religio-political practices (*li* 禮)—an elaborate social grammar that reinforced the status of the highest stratum of the population. The Zhou dynasty (1056?–256 BCE) that followed the Shang initially comprised a federation of tribal peoples who over time conquered the Shang but also perpetuated its high culture. The Shang religio-political ceremonies provided the ground and the impetus for the extension of this evolving pattern of ritual life-forms and institutions (*li* 禮) to the population more broadly during the extended Zhou dynasty. The role of the *ru* literati class over these ensuing centuries was to serve as the embodiment of this constantly evolving, complex notion of *li* that in the fullness of time was to become the heart and blood of Confucian philosophy.

The point is well made that *ruxue* as "literati learning" is a living, corporate tradition with deep roots in the tradition that cannot be reduced to any one historical person. It is not "Confucianism." At the same time, the man Confucius has become a cultural paragon who has more than lived up to his own exhortation that everyone ought to aspire to become an "exemplary literatus" (*junziru* 君子儒). There is a well-known passage in the *Analects* referenced earlier that we return to here in which Confucius describes his personal role in the transmission of the literati learning in the following terms:

> The Master said: "Following the proper way, I do not forge new paths; with confidence, I cherish the ancients—in these respects I am comparable to our venerable Old Peng."[65]

When Confucius allows that in "following the proper way, I do not forge new paths," he is clearly disassociating himself from the term *zuo* 作. *Zuo* is conventionally translated as "initiating," but respecting the significance of the pervasive "path" metaphor in the text, I have translated it as "forging." Allowing that this term *zuo* throughout the canonical texts is often coupled with the "sages" (*shengren* 聖人) and what they have uniquely been able to accomplish, one interpretation of Confucius's

---

65. *Analects* 7.1: 子曰: 述而不作, 信而好古, 竊比於我老彭。

demurring from this association might be his sincere deference to the cultural innovations of the sages, and at the same time, yet another expression of his familiar modesty.

But there are commentators across the centuries who have read this passage literally as a portrait of Confucius as a cultural fundamentalist. As early as the *Mozi*, for example, Confucius is taken at his word as being wholly a transmitter and is criticized roundly for offering the world a lifeless conservatism:

> Again, the Confucians say: "Exemplary persons follow and do not innovate." But we would respond by saying: "In ancient times, Yi introduced the bow, Yu introduced armor, Xizhong introduced the carriage, and the tradesman Qiu introduced the boat. Such being the case, are today's tanners, smiths, carriage-makers, and carpenters as followers all exemplary persons, and are Yi, Yu, Xizhong, and the tradesman Qiu as innovators simply petty persons? Further, since whatever it is the Confucians are following had to be introduced by someone, doesn't this mean that what they are in fact following are the ways of petty persons?"[66]

The logic of this Mohist criticism is impeccable if we take Confucius's self-description to be expository rather than as an expression of his profound deference to the cultural tradition and again as a token of his personal modesty. And just such a Mohist criticism of Confucian traditionalism is alive and well in the commentarial tradition as it has continued to the present day. The contemporary political philosopher, Hsiao Kung-chuan [Xiao Gongquan] 蕭公權, for example, describes this ostensive Confucian conservatism at length as the project of "emulating the past" (*fagu* 法古).[67] More recently, Edward Slingerland, in interpreting this same passage from the *Analects*, aligns himself with a retrospective understanding of a Confucianism that harkens back to the Golden Age of the Zhou dynasty. Slingerland observes:

---

66. *Mozi* 墨子 Harvard Yenching Sinological Series, Supplement 21 (Beijing: Harvard-Yenching Institute, 1948), 63/39/19: 又曰:「君子循而不作。」應之曰:「古者羿作弓, 杼作甲, 奚仲作車, 巧垂作舟, 然則今之鮑函車匠皆君子也, 而羿、杼、奚仲、巧垂皆小人邪？且其所循人必或作之, 然則其所循皆小人道也?」See also 81/46/50.
67. Hsiao Kung-chuan, *A History of Chinese Political Thought*, trans. F. W. Mote, vol. 1 (Princeton, NJ: Princeton University Press, 1979), 79–142.

It is more likely that transmission is all that Confucius countenanced for people in his age, since the sagely Zhou kings established the ideal set of institutions that perfectly accord with human needs.⁶⁸

In opposition to this fundamentalist and purist reading of Confucius—a position that I must disagree with profoundly—I want to suggest that this passage speaks rather to Confucius's understanding of the nature and the dynamics of both intergenerational and genealogical transmission. And in this process of transmission, the patterns of deference captured in the notion of "family reverence" (*xiao*) serve as a key factor.

Borrowing the language of the *Book of Changes* (*Yijing*), I would argue that Confucius as he is remembered historically is in fact a particularly good example of the cosmological assumptions that ground this canonical text. Consistent with the language of the *Book of Changes*, Confucius assumes that the unfolding of the natural and cultural narratives can best be expressed in terms of "continuity and change" or "continuity in change" (*biantong* 變通) and of "ceaseless procreation" (*shengsheng buyi* 生生不已). Describing Confucius in these terms, with his constant appeal to the core canons of the tradition, is not to deny that he is anything but a most effective transmitter of a persistent worldview and of an abiding common sense. Indeed, his personal gravitas lies with the authority he embodies through the traditional assumption that it was he who compiled (or at least edited) the canonical *Five Classics*. At the same time, however, with Confucius's own unique contribution to the development of a specific and sometimes novel philosophical vocabulary, he is also an exemplar of creative new insights within a living tradition. Indeed, while appreciating his modesty here in demurring at the suggestion that he has been an innovator and is thus a sage, we still have substantial evidence to comfortably assert that although Confucius was without question an effective transmitter, he was also an innovator of the first order who took the tradition in significantly new directions.

Turning to the text, the self-understanding of Confucius in broad strokes is that he self-consciously sees himself as continuing an antique tradition reaching back into the second millennium BCE:

---

68. Edward Slingerland, trans., *Analects: With Selections from Traditional Commentaries* (Indianapolis: Hackett, 2003), 64.

The Master said: "The Zhou dynasty looked back to the Xia and Shang dynasties. Such a wealth of culture! I follow the Zhou."[69]

The source of Confucius's education as this Zhou tradition lives on in the lives of the people of his own day has been the compounding culture of the many generations that have come before. Traveling through the district of Kuang on his way from the state of Wei to Chen, he is confronted by a perilous situation and says the following:

> With King Wen (literally, King "Culture") long dead, does not our cultural heritage reside here in us? If *tian* were going to destroy this cultural legacy, we latecomers would not have had access to it. If *tian* is not going to destroy this culture, what can the people of Kuang do to us![70]

While Confucius was a dedicated intermediary within a living tradition, he has also been singularly responsible for introducing, redefining, and elaborating upon a set of key terms as the authorized philosophical vocabulary for an evolving Confucianism: *ren* 仁 (aspiring to consummate conduct in one's roles and relations), *junzi* 君子 (exemplary persons), *yi* 義 (an optimizing appropriateness), and *li* 禮 (achieving propriety in one's roles

---

69. *Analects* 3.14: "'周監於二代，郁郁乎文哉! 吾從周。'" See also *Analects* 8.20: "舜有臣五人而天下治。武王曰：'予有亂臣十人。'孔子曰：'才難，不其然乎? 唐虞之際，於斯為盛。有婦人焉，九人而已。三分天下有其二，以服事殷。周之德，其可謂至德也已矣。'" Shun had only five ministers, and the world was properly governed. King Wu also said, "I have ten ministers who bring proper order to the world." Confucius said, "As the saying has it: 'Human talent is hard to come by.'" Isn't it indeed the case? And it was at the transition from Yao dynasty to Shun that talented ministers were in greatest abundance. In King Wu's case with a woman, perhaps his wife, among them, there were really only nine ministers. The Zhou, with two thirds of the world in its possession, continued to submit to and serve the House of Yin. The excellence of Zhou can be said to be the highest excellence of all.

70. *Analects* 9.5: 文王既沒，文不在茲乎? 天之將喪斯文也，後死者不得與於斯文也; 天之未喪斯文也，匡人其如予何? According to the biography of Confucius, Confucius had left Wey and was on route to Chen when he passed through Kuang. The people of Kuang had recently been ravaged by Yang Huo, also from the state of Lu, and mistook Confucius for Yang Huo. See Sima Qian 司馬遷, Shiji 史記 [Records of the historian] (Beijing: Zhonghua shuju, 1959), 1919. See also *Analects* 11.23.

and relations). Again, it is Confucius who promotes personal cultivation as defining of the Confucian project and who grounds Confucian role ethics and the vision of the consummate life in "family reverence" (*xiao* 孝). This being the case, it is not surprising that when Zhu Xi selects the *Four Books* as the core texts of the tradition, he describes *Expansive Learning* (*Daxue* 大學) as the most basic text that sets the Confucian project as a regimen of personal cultivation within the context of family and community relations. He then canonizes the *Analects* and the *Mencius* as the second and third of the *Four Books* respectively. The explicit reason given is that these texts provide the fundamental vocabulary for this Confucian project and also offer the tradition a narrative example of such personal cultivation in the persons of Confucius and Mencius. Again, Zhu Xi celebrates the fourth of the *Four Books*, with *Focusing the Familiar* (*Zhongyong* 中庸), as the highest and most exuberant statement of the Confucian project. This text again remembers Confucius by centering its message on his own term "focusing the familiar" (*zhongyong* 中庸) and remembers Mencius as well with his idiosyncratic cosmic use of the term "resolve" (*cheng* 誠). We find it is the person of Confucius himself who is described as the very embodiment of the "massive transformations" that occur in the evolving cosmic order:

> Confucius revered Yao and Shun as his ancestors and carried on their ways; he emulated and made illustrious the way of Kings Wen and Wu. He modeled himself above on the rhythm of the turning seasons, and below he was attuned to the patterns of water and earth. He is comparable to the heavens and the earth, sheltering and supporting everything that is. He is comparable to the progress of the four seasons, and the alternating brightness of the sun and the moon. All things are nurtured together and do not cause injury to one another; the various ways are traveled together and are not conflicted. Their lesser virtuosity is to be seen as flowing streams; their greater virtuosity is to be seen as massive transformations. This is why the heavens and the earth are so grand.[71]

---

71. Roger T. Ames and David L. Hall, *Focusing the Familiar: A Translation and Philosophical Commentary on the* Zhongyong (Honolulu: University of Hawai'i Press, 2001), 30: 仲尼祖述堯、舜, 憲章文、武; 上律天時, 下襲水土. 辟如天地之無不持載, 無不覆幬, 辟如四時之錯行, 如日月之代明. 萬物並育而不相害, 道並行而不相悖, 小德川流, 大德敦化, 此天地之所以為大也.

Several corollary entailments that give further focus to the innovative Confucian project adumbrated in the *Four Books* can be drawn from the primacy of lived family and community relations that serve as the ground for Confucian role ethics: corollaries that can be readily summarized and illustrated by passages selected from the *Analects*. For example, the *Analects* insists that there is a fundamental uniqueness of persons as they are defined by their specific patterns of relations and an interdependence among such persons as they live these relations.[72] There is a correlative, engaging, and reflexive nature to all human activities, and there is an underlying processive and emergent conception of both the natural and the social orders.[73] As we have seen, there are also mutually entailing historical and cosmological implications that follow from this primacy of relations. For example, there is the holistic, unbounded, and nested nature of relationships and a holographic conception of persons as they are defined in focus-field rather than part-whole terms. Further, Confucianism, as a philosophical aestheticism, registers all of the relationships that collaborate in constituting each person as being relevant in degree to the totality of the effect as it is comes into focus as someone's personal identity.

---

72. *Analects* 15.36: 子曰:「當仁不讓於師。」The Master said, "In striving to be consummate in your person, do not yield even to your teacher"; *Analects* 6.30: 夫仁者, 己欲立而立人, 己欲達而達人。能近取譬, 可謂仁之方也已。」As for consummate persons, they establish others in seeking to establish themselves; they promote others in seeking to get there themselves. Correlating one's conduct with those near at hand can be said to be the method of becoming consummate in one's conduct.

73. *Analects* 7.8: 子曰:「不憤不啟, 不悱不發, 舉一隅不以三隅反, 則不復也。」The Master said, "I do not open the way for students who are not driven with eagerness; I do not supply a vocabulary for students who are not trying desperately to find the language for their ideas. If on showing students one corner they do not come back to me with the other three, I will not repeat myself." And 7.22: 子曰:「三人行, 必有我師焉。擇其善者而從之, 其不善者而改之。」The Master said, "In strolling in the company of just two other persons, I am bound to find a teacher. Identifying their strengths, I follow them, and identifying their weaknesses, I reform myself accordingly"; *Analects* 9.17: 子在川上, 曰:「逝者如斯夫! 不舍晝夜。」The Master was standing on the riverbank, and observed, "Isn't life's passing just like this, never ceasing day or night!"; 2.11: 子曰:「溫故而知新, 可以為師矣。」The Master said: "Reviewing the old as a means of realizing the new—such a person can be considered a teacher." and 15.29: 子曰:「人能弘道, 非道弘人。」The Master said: "It is persons who are able to broaden the way, not the way that broadens persons."

It is clear that many of the most significant personal relationships obtain among and between family members, and for this reason, much of anyone's personal identity will be derived therefrom. But in this Confucian project, the relationships also extend outward synchronically from family lineage to the larger social order. Again, diachronically, the relationships are also resolutely intergenerational and genealogical in the broadest sense and must be understood in terms of the alternating roles persons have as benefactors and beneficiaries too. Further, these relations with the preceding pantheon of ancestors and cultural heroes reach beyond the immediate social and political order to inspire the tradition's family-centered religiousness. The *Analects* seems to be saying consistently that a full and flourishing human life requires that some of our relations be with those younger than ourselves and some with our peers. Further, the *Analects* also requires us to have relations with those generations that have preceded us, those who live on in our own persons, and those continuing in our progeny.

Li 禮, *Ti* 體, and *He* 和 as an Aspectual Cluster for "Role Ethics"

I have translated Confucius's neologism *ren* 仁 that is first developed as a key philosophical term in the *Analects* as "aspiring to consummatory conduct in one's roles and relations." The argument rehearsed previously is that this term *ren*, which is composed of the character "person(s)" (*ren* 人) and the number "two" (*er* 二), is an explicit expression of Confucian role ethics. Again, *xiao* 孝 as the prime moral imperative governing the intergenerational embodiment and transmission of the genealogical tradition in the roles persons live within the family lineage again references this notion of role ethics. And further, at an elite social and political level, the role of the *ru* 儒 literati class across the millennia has been to embody, transmit, and perpetuate the highly aestheticized Confucian culture.

I want to add one more important vocabulary cluster that gives expression to Confucian role ethics in the canonical texts: the aspiration to "an optimizing harmony" (*he* 和) through an "achieved propriety" (*li* 禮) in the "embodied living" (*ti* 體) within one's roles and relations. This "aspectual" cluster again has an immediate relationship with the vocabulary of *ren*, *xiao*, and *ru* discussed previously. Perhaps the best way of understanding the dynamics of "family reverence" (*xiao* 孝) as the prime moral imperative in the process of intergenerational transmission, for example, is to appeal to these two cognate characters that speak to the physical, cultural, and narrative continuities within the enduring family lineage: *li* 禮 as "embodied living" and *ti* 體 as "lived body." These two terms *li* and *ti* are further informed by the qualitative dynamic "harmony" (*he* 和) we find pervasive in Confucian cosmology. While this term is conventionally translated simply as "harmony," it is perhaps better understood as the aspiration to optimize the creative possibilities of any particular situation—in the case of Confucian ethics, for example, the concerted effort to make the most of the roles as they are lived in family and community.

Although we will find that "optimizing harmony" (*he*) is a generic idea with wide application in all human activities from the kitchen to the cosmos, what needs to be emphasized here is the Confucian assumption that when such aspirations have reference to human flourishing specifically, the harmony must necessarily be mediated through familial roles and relations for it to be robust, genuine, and enduring. The family is the ultimate source and the indispensable ground of an achieved propriety (*li* 禮) in all of our roles and relations. The *Analects* makes this point explicitly:

> An optimizing harmony (*he*) is the most valuable function of achieving propriety in our roles and relations (*li*). In the ways of the Former Kings, the sustaining of this quality of harmony through achieving propriety in their roles and relations made them elegant, and was a guiding standard in all things large and small. But when things are not going well, to realize harmony just for its own sake without regulating the situation through an achieved propriety in roles and relations, will not work.[74]

Morality so understood describes the cultivation of a quality of conduct that is directed at making familial bonds stronger, thicker, and more enduring. But without such accord among persons being properly negotiated through our lived roles and relations, our actions can be meaningless or worse. That is, a putative "harmony" that is achieved by

---

74. *Analects* 1.12: 禮之用，和為貴。先王之道斯為美，小大由之。有所不行，知和而和，不以禮節之，亦不可行也。See also 12.1 and 12.15.

imposing external mechanisms and constraints as a means of enforcing order—the application of laws, policies, or rules—is dehumanizing to the extent that such "harmony" precludes personal confirmation and participation. To take a textual example, Confucius would insist that important social values such as deference, circumspection, bravery, and candor can only rise above the thin and indeed perverse dispositions of lethargy, timidity, rowdiness, and rudeness when they are properly transformed and legitimated through aspiring to propriety in our personal relations:

> The Master said, "Deference unmediated by achieving propriety in our roles and relations (*li*) is lethargy; circumspection unmediated by such propriety is timidity; bravery unmediated by such propriety is rowdiness; candor unmediated by such propriety is rudeness. Where exemplary persons are earnestly committed to their parents, the common people will aspire to consummate conduct; where they do not neglect their old friends, the people will not be indifferent to each other."[75]

The goal of healthy living is a lived equilibrium in which we avoid both excess and insufficiency in our giving and getting, in our doing and undergoing, and in our shaping and being shaped. This pursuit of the superlative in our conduct is explained by medical anthropologist Zhang Yanhua in the following terms:

> Harmony defined here is related to the Chinese sense of *du* 度 (degree, extent, position) . . . In other words, in a dynamic interactive environment, harmony is brought about when each particular unfolds itself in its unique way and to an appropriate *du* such that "each shines more brilliantly in the other's company" (*xiangdeyizhang* 相得益彰).[76]

---

75. *Analects* 8.2: 子曰:「恭而無禮則勞，慎而無禮則葸，勇而無禮則亂，直而無禮則絞。君子篤於親，則民興於仁；故舊不遺，則民不偷。」

76. Zhang Yanhua, *Transforming Emotions with Chinese Medicine: An Ethnographic Account from Contemporary China* (Albany: State University of New York Press, 2007), 51.

How Do the Confucian Canons Say "Role Ethics"? | 109

We are only able to get the most out of the ecology of the human experience by achieving full measure (*du* 度) in both the particularities and the scope of our transactional activities.

Going back to the high culture of the Shang dynasty, formally prescribed rites and rituals were performed at stipulated times to reinforce the political and religious status of the royal participants within the extended family lineages and to punctuate the seasons of the life at court. For that group of officials responsible for the casting of the bronzes and for the choreography of the court functions that used them, "ritual propriety" (*li*) meant quite literally knowing one's place in the formalities and thus knowing where to stand. The graph for *li* 禮 is found on the oracle bones as *[ix]* and on the bronzes as *[x]*, a pictograph with two pieces of jade in a ritual vessel depicting a sacrificial offering made by the court to seek the blessings and good fortune from its ancestral lineage.[77] Originally, ritual performances were formal and narrowly defined religious procedures enacted by the ruling classes and their entourage to fortify their relationship with both nature and the other world. These rituals were often constituted in imitation of perceptible cosmic rhythms as a means of strengthening the coordination of the human, natural, and spiritual environments—and they were also used to reinforce a sense of human participation in the regular operations of the cosmos.

[ix]

[x]

If bronze production adumbrates the story of the Shang dynasty, it is the evolution and broad dissemination of this notion of "observing ritual propriety in roles and relations" (*li*) as a pervasive cultural value that provides a window on the millennium-long narrative of the Zhou dynasty. First, the increasingly widespread propagation and performance of a kind of institutionalized propriety within the society broadly took place during the Zhou dynasty. Gradually over the ensuing centuries these ritual activities were extended outward from the ruler himself to the community more broadly. And with this expanding reach came an increasingly important significance for social and political order. In these amplified ritual observances, participants would have their proper status and their place, their *wei* 位. If persons did not understand the details and spirit of the ritual procedures, they would quite literally not know where to stand (*li* 立) or what to do. Thus, the term "stance" or "standing" (*li*) found on the oracle bones *[xi]* and on the bamboo strip

[xi]

---

77. Kwan, "Database," 甲骨文合集 CHANT 2809 and 西周早期 CHANT 6015, respectively.

manuscripts *[xii]* is closely associated with one's "rank, position, status" (*wei*) *[xiii]*.[78] In Confucius's account of his own personal growth, he states that "by fifteen I had set my purposes on learning, and by thirty I had taken my stance (*li* 立)," referring thereby to his commitment to the assiduous effort need to fund his continuing project of personal cultivation.[79] Importantly, throughout the *Analects*, such physical and spatial terminologies are closely linked to the governing metaphor of "advancing resolutely on one's way" (*dao* 道). It is repeatedly stated that it is "ritual propriety" (*li*)—also frequently translated as "rites," "ceremony," "etiquette," "decorum," "manners"—that enables persons to determine, consolidate, and display virtuosity in the relational transactions of their daily lives. Indeed, education in its broadest sense was learning where to stand and what to say:

> Chen Gang asked Boyu, the son of Confucius: "Have you been given any kind of special instruction?"
> "No," he replied. "but once my father was standing alone, and as I was hastening across the courtyard, he asked me, 'Have you been studying the *Book of Songs*?' I replied, 'Not yet,' to which he remarked, 'If you do not study the *Songs*, you will be at a loss as to what to say.' I deferentially took my leave and am now studying the *Songs*.
> On another occasion, my father was again standing alone, and as I was hastening across the courtyard, he asked me, 'Have you been studying the *Record of Rites*?' I replied, 'Not yet,' to which he remarked, 'If you do not study the *Rites*, you will be at a loss as to where to stand.'" I deferentially took my leave and am now studying the *Rites*."[80]

But not everyone, not even Confucius's rather unremarkable son, can "live" *li* in an equally felicitous way. It is ultimately the quality of

---

78. For a fuller description of this extension of *li* to the population broadly, see Robert M. Gimello, "The Civil Status of *li* in Classical Confucianism," *Philosophy East and West* 22 (1972), 203–211.

79. *Analects* 2.4: 吾十有五而志于學，三十而立。

80. *Analects* 16.13: 陳亢問於伯魚曰：「子亦有異聞乎?」對曰：「未也。嘗獨立，鯉趨而過庭。曰：『學詩乎?』對曰：『未也。』『不學詩，無以言。』鯉退而學詩。他日又獨立，鯉趨而過庭。曰：『學禮乎?』對曰：『未也。』『不學禮，無以立。』鯉退而學禮。

particular persons as it is registered in the virtuosity of their roles and relations that is expressed in the meaning and the musicality of the ritually aestheticized life:

> The Master said: "What have persons who are not consummate in their conduct (*ren*) to do with achieving ritual propriety in their roles and relations? What have persons who are not consummate in their conduct to do with the playing of music?"[81]

Such passages in the *Analects* can be used as a heuristic from which to glean several insights into what "ritual propriety" had come to mean by the time of Confucius at some five hundred years removed from the fall of the Shang dynasty. Although an achieved propriety in one's roles and relations clearly has a formal and redundant structure, still the preponderant significance of these activities in defining family and communal life lies in those informal, personal, and particular aspects that are necessary for real meaningful experience. Pursuing such refinement through the performance of *li* must be understood in light of the uniqueness of each participant engaged in the profoundly aesthetic project of becoming this exceptional and always inimitable person.

In our exploration of *li*, we must begin from the holistic and thus reflexive assumptions of the process cosmology that serves as the interpretive context. What recommends the translation of *li* as "propriety" is that along with other words such as "appropriate," "proper," and "property," it is derived etymologically from the Latin *proprius* with its core meaning of "making something one's own." The substance and depth of *li*, unlike formal regulations, is dependent upon a process of personalization. This process involves the aspiration to take the unique role of this particular daughter in her relationship with this particular father and to make it into something moving and magical. What makes ritual performance profoundly different from law or rule is this sustained effort to make the tradition and its institutions one's own. As noted earlier, the Latin *proprius*, "making something one's own," gives us a series of reflexive cognate expressions that are useful in translating key Confucian philosophical terms to capture this sense of participation, reflexivity, and personalization: *yi* 義 is not "righteousness" as compliance with some external divine directive but rather is an optimal "appropriateness" as "the sense of what is most fitting

---

81. *Analects* 3.3: 子曰:「人而不仁, 如禮何? 人而不仁, 如樂何?」

for all concerned" in this particular communal context. *Zheng* 正 is not merely "rectification" or "correct conduct" as an appeal to some external standard but "proper conduct" as it can best be determined by persons as they are embedded within any particular situation. *Zheng* 政 is not simply "government" but "governing properly given these particular conditions," and *li* 禮 is not just "what is ritually appropriate in one's roles and relations" but *personally doing* what is ritually appropriate in such relations. It is the necessity for personalization that prompts Confucius to observe:

> The expression "sacrifice as though present" is taken to mean "sacrifice to the spirits as though the spirits are present." But the Master said: "If I myself do not participate in the sacrifice, it is as though I have not sacrificed at all."[82]

As a footnote to this understanding of *li* as "making something one's own," we have to allow that one important factor that is integral to the quality of our understanding of these Confucian canons is our own lived experience. Theoretical explanation and cognitive insight are certainly important, but they cannot do all of the work of making the function of *li* clear to an apprentice. That is, the expository limits of these canonical texts lie in their tacit assumption that readers will evoke their own life experience to inform and amplify the themes under discussion. At the same time, the expectation of these documents is that they will certainly provide their readers with cognitive clarity when it comes to reflection on moral issues. But more importantly, readers will, by refining their own lives through reference to these texts and a continuing regimen of elevating their practices, do nothing less than transform their persons into morally competent human beings (*jiaohua* 教化).[83]

Again, the concern for achieving ritual propriety in one's own roles and relations works in complex ways to promote order and elegance in the communal living of irreducibly relational persons. Michael Ing's *The Dysfunction of Ritual in Early Confucianism* introduces the important

---

82. *Analects* 3.12: 祭如在，祭神如神在。子曰: 吾不与祭，如不祭。

83. I. A. Richards allows that the seeming ambiguity that we register in reflecting upon the Mencian conception of "native human tendencies" (*xing* 性) arises from the expectation of the text that the reader's own experience as a human being will be called upon to fill in the existential details needed to bring clearer definition to this idea. See Richards, *Mencius on the Mind*, 6 and 49.

caveat that when compared with the integrity provided by "rule" or "law," it can be fairly argued that this Confucian ethic of ritual brings with it a degree of flexibility, adjustment, and innovation. At the same time, however, such ritualized roles are also a source of moral ambiguity and a personal vulnerability having both positive and negative consequences for the Confucian project of personal cultivation.[84]

A careful reading of the classical Confucian literature uncovers a way of life carefully choreographed down to appropriate facial expressions and physical gestures, a world in which a life is a performance requiring enormous nuance and attention to detail. Importantly, this *li*-constituted performance begins from the insight that personal refinement is only possible through the discipline provided by formalized roles and behaviors. Form without personalization is the external imposition of coercive and thus dehumanizing regulation, while creative personal expression without form is randomness at best, and license at worst. It is only with the appropriate combination of form and functional personalization (*tiyong* 體用) that behavior within family and community can be self-regulating and increasingly refined.

With respect to Confucius himself, *li* is a resolutely personal performance revealing his worth to both himself and to his community. It is a public discourse through which he is able to constitute and reveal himself qualitatively as a unique individual and a whole person, doing what he does for the benefit of everyone, including himself. Importantly, there is no respite. *Li* requires the utmost attention to every detail of what Confucius does at every moment he is doing it: from the drama of the high court to the posture he assumes in going to sleep, from the reception of different guests to the proper way to comport himself when alone, and from how he behaves in formal dining situations to appropriate extemporaneous gestures when encountering friends.

In our reading of the *Analects*, there is a tendency to give short shrift to the middle books 9–11 that we have had occasion to visit as a series of intimate portraits depicting the historical person of Confucius. If such personal information is considered at all, we are inclined to pass over it quickly as insufficiently philosophical to be relevant to the Confucian project of personal cultivation. But in fact, in overlooking these personal details, we are in danger of missing the real substance of

---

84. Michael David Kaulana Ing, *The Dysfunction of Ritual in Early Confucianism* (Oxford: Oxford University Press, 2012).

114 | Human Becomings

Confucius's moral vision. It is precisely these passages recalling the specific moments in the exemplary life of Confucius himself that most reveal the extent to which the appropriate conduct of a scholar-official participating in the daily activities of the court were choreographed: the cut of his robes, the cadence of his stride, his keen sense of context and requisite proprieties, his posture and facial demeanor, his profound expression of reverent attention, his tone of voice, his gestures of deference, and even the rhythm of his breathing. In the *Analects* Confucius is described in precisely such terms:

> On passing through the entrance way to the Duke's court, Confucius would bow forward from the waist, as though the gateway were not high enough. While in attendance, he would not stand in the middle of the entranceway; on going through the passageway he would not step on the raised threshold. On passing by the empty throne, his countenance would change visibly, his legs would bend, and in his speech, he would seem to be out of breath. He would lift the hem of his skirts in ascending the hall, bow forward from the waist, and hold in his breath as though ceasing to breathe. On leaving and descending the first steps, he would relax his expression and regain his composure. He would then glide briskly from the bottom of the steps, and returning to his place, would resume a reverent posture.[85]

We must not lose sight of the fact that Confucian role ethics ultimately and invariably has to do with specific persons in their specific situations. While laws and formal institutions can certainly serve as important guidelines for conduct, it is ultimately analogy and correlation with family members, role models, and cultural heroes that serve as the greatest motive forces in promoting the flourishing community. This being the case, the deferential yet authoritative life habits of Confucius himself and the emulation of this role model over succeeding generations can be an object lesson in understanding the real workings of role ethics. One compelling image we have of Confucius, for example, is the

---

85. *Analects* 10.4: 入公門，鞠躬如也，如不容。立不中門，行不履閾。過位，色勃如也，足躩如也，其言似不足者。攝齊升堂，鞠躬如也，屏氣似不息者。出，降一等，逞顏色，怡怡如也。沒階趨，翼如也。復其位，踧踖如也。

self-conscious display he makes of his dedication to official duties even from his sick bed:

> When ill, and his lord came to see him, Confucius reclined with his head facing east, and had his court robes draped over him with his sash drawn.[86]

Indeed, these many seemingly random snapshots of Confucius reveal an image of a person aspiring in the conduct of the largely routine events of his daily life to express a quality of relational virtuosity that is sufficiently robust to transform and indeed to enchant the ordinary affairs of his life. This passage and many other similar ones should make it clear that propriety in our roles and relations cannot be reduced to generic, formally prescribed "rites" and "rituals" performed at stipulated times to announce status and to punctuate the seasons of our lives. The *li*—the realization and expression of propriety through our roles and relations—are much more than such performances.

One way to distinguish the inclusive and holistic Confucian role ethics from more formalized and thus reductionistic principle-based ethical theories is to give an account of how the particular, informal, and contextualizing aspects of experience in this Confucian moral vision, far from being discounted or marginalized, in fact take on a central importance as resources that can be drawn upon to maximize the productive outcome of always particular human activities. Certainly, the formal aspect in all of its guises has an indispensable role in theorizing our practices and the refinement of conduct. But this aesthetic dimension—the need for elegance and moral artistry in ethics—is also integral to this holistic understanding of human conduct in which all aspects of the life experience have more or less relevance and thus have some value for determining a worthwhile outcome. It is because the moral vision of Confucian role ethics is concerned with coordinating the contribution of each aspect of experience in achieving the totality of the effect that the normative language to which it appeals and the sense of order to which it aspires

---

86. *Analects* 10.19: 疾, 君視之, 東首, 加朝服, 拖紳。 The bed for the master of the house was usually on the western side of the southern window. When one's lord would visit, the lord would approach by ascending the stairs from the east. The eastern stairs would be the place of the "host," but since the lord himself is the proper host of the entire country, he would ascend and descend from these same eastern steps.

are in the Whiteheadian sense fundamentally aesthetic.[87] The effect itself is most often characterized in these texts in the language of authenticity or duplicity rather than by appeal to the rationalizing language of right and wrong, or good and evil. There is a perceived inseparability in the relationship between elegance and morality, and conversely, between baseness and immorality. On being asked about family reverence (*xiao* 孝), for example, Confucius would insist that this moral imperative cannot be satisfied by some set of formally prescribed, reduplicative activities that would resolve to a binary right or wrong but rather is dependent upon the specific attitude expressed as the actions are being carried out:

> The Master said: "Family reverence (*xiao*) lies primarily in showing the proper countenance. As for the young contributing their energies when there is work to be done, and deferring to their elders when there is wine and food to be had—how can merely doing such things be considered being properly filial?"[88]

This ethics of proper responsiveness is elaborated upon in great detail in these middle books of the *Analects* wherein the life habits of Confucius are displayed as a model for the ages:

> In sleeping, he did not assume the posture of a corpse, and if at home alone, he did not kneel in a formal posture as though he were entertaining guests. On encountering someone in mourning dress, even those with whom he was on intimate terms, he would always assume a solemn visage. On coming across someone wearing a ceremonial cap or someone who is blind, even though they were persons of frequent acquaintance, he would invariably pay his respects. On meeting up with a person in mourner's attire, he would bow forward on the crossbeam of his carriage. He would do the same on encountering an official with state census records on his back. On being presented with a sumptuous table, he would always take on a solemn demeanor and rise to his feet.

---

87. A. N. Whitehead, *Modes of Thought* (New York: Macmillan, 1938), 53–60.
88. *Analects* 2.8: 子曰：「色難。有事弟子服其勞，有酒食先生饌，曾是以為孝乎？」

On experiencing a sudden clap of thunder or fierce winds, he would change his countenance. In mounting his carriage, he would always stand upright and grasp the cord. While riding in the carriage, he would not turn his head to look inward, speak hastily, or point at things.[89]

This detailed portrait of Confucius rehearses a succession of images that reveals his unrelenting attention to proper countenance and a quality of responsiveness to particular circumstances. It discloses a pattern of proper conduct on the part of this particular human being in the particular circumstances of his life. And at the end of this series, the text then naturalizes these ritualized behaviors by ascribing just such a responsive pattern of conduct to the life of the animal world as well:

Sensing their approach, the bird took to flight, and soared about them before alighting. The Master said, "Look at that hen-pheasant on the mountain bridge—what timing! what timing!" Zilu clasped his hands together and saluted the bird, which flapping its wings three times, took to the air once again.[90]

Since morality itself is nothing more than those modalities of acting that conduce to the enhancement of relations, any kind of conduct that has a disintegrative effect on the fabric of family or community is perceived as fundamentally immoral. Lifestyle takes on crucial import when we consider the corrosive consequences on the community of those who live lives without style. Carelessness becomes a major concern when we have to worry about those who could care less. And ignorance in the sense of ignoring others and their needs, far from being detached or neutral, is in fact to inflict a violence upon the persons of our friends and neighbors.[91]

---

89. *Analects* 10.24–26: 寢不尸, 居不容。見齊衰者, 雖狎, 必變。見冕者與瞽者, 雖褻, 必以貌。凶服者式之。式負版者。有盛饌, 必變色而作。迅雷風烈, 必變。升車, 必正立執綏。車中, 不內顧, 不疾言, 不親指。色斯舉矣, 翔而後集。曰:「山梁雌雉, 時哉! 時哉!」子路共之, 三嗅而作。

90. *Analects* 10.27: 色斯舉矣, 翔而後集。曰:「山梁雌雉, 時哉! 時哉!」子路共之, 三嗅而作。

91. Vrinda Dalmiya, "Linguistic Erasures." *Peace Review* 10, no. 4 (1998).

Graciousness, on the other hand, has gravity when we reflect on the relevance that charm and deportment have for an overall sense of fittingness and propriety. Morality is much more than formal correctness, emerging as it does importantly from poise and demeanor in our discursive transactions with others. The *Analects*, for example, reflects the always transactional nature of this Confucian philosophy as a "face" or "shame" culture. "Face" itself as a discursive social phenomenon is performed in our roles in "giving face," "saving face," and "losing face," where the effects of such conduct are both felt and seen. As I have previously remarked, this sense of shame reflects a cultivated and critical self-awareness integral to consummate conduct (*ren*) in our roles and relations. This wholeness and integrative nature of the moral experience means that a socially responsive "sense of shame" (*chi* 恥) is highly valued in the Confucian culture; after all, it is a robust sense of shame that is the clearest evidence of one's commitment to the family and community nexus. Shame is such a powerful expression of moral awareness that when properly nurtured it can become a galvanizing value that promotes social and political solidarity to the extent that it can also enable the community to become self-regulating.[92]

Confucius himself as he is portrayed in the canonical literature has a well-developed sense of shame and the feelings of belonging that accompany it. Shamelessness by contrast is poison in the well, unleashing aberrant individuals to roam freely and to act arbitrarily without reference to the roles and relations that would properly secure them within their families and community. Such selfish, morally retarded individuals erode the communal solidarity on which the moral life depends.

Turning from *li* 禮 as "embodied living" to the somatic aspect of a visceral "knowing" in this Confucian role ethic, we can correlate "lived body" (*ti* 體) and "aspiring to propriety in one's roles and relations" (*li* 禮) as cognate characters by arguing that they express two ways of shaping, embodying, and thus "realizing" our personal identities: these two characters reference "a living body" and "embodied living," respectively. This relationship between "knowing" and "body" is carried over into the modern language in which "knowing bodily or viscerally" (*tihui* 體會 and *tiyan* 體驗) means to know something through practicing and experiencing it and, in this way, fully "realizing" it.

---

92. *Analects* 2.3.

The notion of *li* 禮 denotes a continuing, complex, and always novel pattern of invested institutions and significant behaviors that is embodied, authored, and reauthorized by succeeding generations as the persistent cultural authority serving to unify the family lineages (*shizu* 氏族 or *jiazu* 家族) and communities (*zu* 族) as a specific yet extended body of people (*minzu* 民族). For this holistic Confucian philosophy, our unique persons in their entirety penetrate so deeply into the human experience that it would be a nonstarter to try to separate out some reality that stands independent of them. Put another way, in Confucianism our reality is our lived, embodied experience and nothing else.

In the pre-Qin documents, the graph for "embodying" (*ti* 體) appears with three alternative semantic classifiers—*shen* 身 that alludes to the lived, vital, and irreducibly social body; *rou* 肉 as the flesh and hair, carnal body; and *gu* 骨 that references the "bones" and formal, skeletal structure. We can appeal to these different ways of writing the graph as a heuristic for attempting to give fuller value to the notion of how each succeeding generation has the responsibility of coming to know and to thus embody the cultural corpus that has come before.[93]

Ti with the "lived body" classifier (*shen* 身) *[xiv]* is the earliest form of this character that is found on the early Warring States bronzes (*ca.* 400 BCE), and references the vital and existentially aware dimension of the embodied experience in its dynamic social relations with others.[94] The body depicted in the prestylized *shen* graph is that of a pregnant woman, an image of perhaps the most intimate and visceral of all human relations. The "duplicity" or "two-ness" of the pregnant body carries over with *shen* referencing the subjective as well as a more objective dimension of experience: an inner voice as well as an external profile. We come to know and express what it means to become fully human intuitively as well as more objectively, where feelings in our various social lived-body relations are first "had" before we then struggle to organize and make sense of them.

[xiv]

---

93. For a fuller discussion of this sense of embodiment, see Roger T. Ames, *Confucian Role Ethics*, 102–113. For more on the *ti* body, see Deborah Sommer, "Boundaries of the *Ti Body*" in *Star Gazing, Fire Phasing, and Healing in China: Essays in Honor of Nathan Sivin*, ed. Michael Nylan, Henry Rosemont Jr., and Li Waiyee, Asia Major, 3rd series, 21.1 (Taipei: Academy Sinica, Institute of History and Philology, 2008).

94. Kwan, "Database," 戰國早期 CHANT 9735.3b.

Ti with the "flesh" classifier (*rou* 肉) *[xv]* is found on the Guodian bamboo strips (ca. 300 BCE), and references the carnal body—the body as flesh, hair, and bone.[95] The modalities of our experience are rooted in and are always mediated through a unique localizing physicality and are temporally and spatially constrained by this fact. All of our thoughts and feelings are grounded in a complex physical sensorium of seeing, hearing, touching, smelling, and tasting. This sensorium makes specific demands on our conduct and registers our pleasure and pain. Philosopher Richard Shusterman has made much of what he has called a "somaesthetic," which is the opportunity that the lived body provides us for aestheticizing the human experience by educating our bodies: through developing a keen eye for art, an acute ear for music, a fine sense of touch on the piano keys, an awakened nose for good wine, and a discriminating palate for haute cuisine.[96]

The familiar, traditional form of the character *ti* with the "bones" classifier (*gu* 骨) that is still used today in places where simplified characters have been resisted *[xvi]* does not occur in our current records until the Mawangdui silk manuscript (168 BCE). Our persons are described as "discursive bodies" that engage in "structuring," "configuring," and "embodying" our experience not only cognitively and affectively but also viscerally.[97] We might reflect on the difference implied by "seeing" versus "knowing" the world as a distinction between experience as immediately *had* and reflective and deliberate experience that has been mediated through human epistemic structures. Each of us inherits a worldview and a cultural common sense and collaborates with the world to discriminate, conceptualize, and critically theorize the human experience, embodying and giving Apollonian form to the contents of our culture, language, and habitat. And in this continuing process, our various environments speak to us in much the same way as we relate to them.

A traditional cursive form, and now the Chinese simplified graph and the standard Japanese character for body, is *ti* 体 with 躰 and 軆 variants that all include the graph for "root" or "trunk" (*ben* 本). A hugely significant factor, then, to consider in the process of focusing a persisting, personal identity and its coherent horizons of relevance is the extent to

---

95. Kwan, "Database," 郭店簡, 窮達以時, 10.

96. See, for a representative example, Richard Shusterman, *Body Consciousness: A Philosophy of Mindfulness and Somaesthetics* (Cambridge: Cambridge University Press, 2008).

97. Kwan, "Database," 馬王堆. 五十二病方, 376.

which the structure of our understanding and our habitude is "rooted" in and shaped by the fact of our embodied experience in its visceral connection to the world. In addition to being a determinate aspect of personal identity, the body itself is the site of the ongoing "embodying" (*ti* 體) processes of our always "discursive" bodies. Given the correlative relationship between "body" and "mind" (*shenxin* 身心) in this process cosmology, it should not be surprising that Deborah Sommer, in summarizing her analysis of the uses of the *ti* body in the classical literature, uses language immediately reminiscent of the holography made explicit in the *Mencius*. When Mencius says, "The myriad things of the world are all implicated here in me," he is averring that the cosmic totality is implicated in each vital impulse of embodied lives as they are lived by always unique persons.[98] In similar language, Sommer concludes that the *ti* body is

> a polysemous corpus of indeterminate extent that can be partitioned into subtler units, each of which is often analogous to the whole and shares a fundamental consubstantiality and common identity with the whole.... When a *ti* body is fragmented into parts (literally or conceptually), each part retains in certain aspects, a kind of wholeness or becomes a simulacra of the larger entity of which it is a constituent.[99]

At the most primordial level, the body via these three mutually entailing modalities—vital, carnal, and discursive bodies—serves as the conveyance that coordinates our subjectivity with our environments and that mediates our processes of thinking and feeling with our demonstrable patterns of conduct.

At a genealogical level, our bodies and the process of human procreativity provide the birthing of distinctive and unique persons from those who have come before. And the "embodied knowing" and "living

---

98. *Mencius* 7A4: 孟子曰: 萬物皆備於我矣。

99. Sommer, "Boundaries of the *Ti* Body," 294. Whereas the metaphor we associate with "body" in European languages is a "container" or "structure" image, the meaning in the earliest classical Chinese sources is the organic (rather than geometric) form of animal and plant bodies, where in certain contexts it has a horticultural reference as plant vegetation (roots, stalks, foliage) in general, and more specifically, as a rhizome or tuber.

on" that is taking place is not meant merely rhetorically. Even more obvious and significant than the transmission of physical likenesses are the continuities of the cultural tradition itself: its language, institutions, and values.[100] Within this ongoing, overlapping process of intergenerational embodiment, the earlier progenitors literally persist in this continuing process as they are physically and culturally transformed into their progeny. That is, while persons emerge to become specifically who they are as unique individuals, the parents, grandparents, and ancestors of such persons continue to live on in them, most obviously in their physicality but also in terms of how they think, feel, and live their lives. And the eventful process continues as their progeny also live on in their own descendants. The focus-field language we have proposed as a way of thinking about the relationship between particulars and the totality seems immediately relevant to this holography, in which the entire field of the physical and cultural experience is implicated in the moment-by-moment narrative of each person.

In the Confucian tradition, the body is understood as an inheritance from our families and as a vital current in a genealogical stream that reaches back to our remotest ancestors. The body brings with it a sense of continuity, contribution, belonging, and importantly a sense of felt worth: the feelings that most immediately inspire our religious sensibilities. The *Record of Rites* recounts:

> The Master said: "Among those things born of the heavens and nurtured by the earth, nothing is grander than the human being. For the parents to give birth to one's whole person, and for one to return this person to them intact is what can be called family reverence (*xiao*). To avoid desecrating your body or bringing disgrace to your person is what can be called keeping your person whole."[101]

---

100. The sense of immortality implied by the expression "living on" is difficult to see if the body is taken as "belonging" only to an individual. The opening chapter of *The Chinese Classic of Family Reverence* makes clear that for Confucius, the body is an inheritance and on loan from one's family lineage and that the first obligation we have to this lineage is to maintain its integrity by avoiding any kind of desecration or disgrace.

101. *A Concordance to the* Liji 25.36/128/6: 夫子曰: 天之所生, 地之所養, 無人為大。父母全而生之, 子全而歸之, 可謂孝矣。不虧其體, 不辱其身, 可謂全矣。

To show respect for our own bodies—both the physical body and its function as the residence of the cultural corpus that our lineage has bequeathed to us—is to show reverence for our ancestors embodied therein and for the relationship we have with them. Again, to disrespect our bodies by treating them lightly is to be doubly shameless: we first fail to acknowledge our debt to our family lineage, and further, we bring shame instead of honor upon those who have come before. What is significant in this reflection on our embodied persons is that physically, socially, and religiously, our bodies are a specific matrix of nested relations and functions that are a collaboration between our own persons and the extended web of our many familial, social, cultural, and natural relations. Nobody and no "body"—neither the vital, the carnal, nor the discursive body—does anything by itself.

It should be clear that what we are referencing here is not simply the transmission of a physical lineage—although it is that as well. The living body and our embodied living is the conveyance of the cultural corpus of knowledge through which a living civilization itself is preserved and extended: linguistic facility and proficiency, religious doctrines and mythologies, the aesthetics of refined living, the modeling of mores and values, instruction and apprenticeship in cognitive technologies, and so on. Our bodies are certainly our physicality, but they are also conduits through which the entire body of culture is inherited, interpreted, elaborated upon, and reauthorized across the ages.

There is an important passage in the *Analects* in which Master Zeng, the paragon of family reverence in the classical corpus, surrounded by his students on his deathbed, expresses a deep sense of relief in having come to the end of his life with his body still intact:

> Master Zeng was ill, and summoned his students to him, saying, "Look at my feet! Look at my hands!
> The *Book of Songs* says:
> > Fearful! Trembling!
> > As if peering over a deep abyss,
> > As if walking across thin ice.[102]
>
> It is only from this moment hence that I can at last know relief, my young friends."[103]

---

102. *Book of Songs*, 195.
103. *Analects* 8.3: 曾子有疾, 召門弟子曰:「啟予足! 啟予手!《詩》云『戰戰兢兢, 如臨深淵, 如履薄冰。』而今而後, 吾知免夫! 小子!」

This passage is usually interpreted as Master Zeng expressing profound relief that he has been able to live to a point where he can now anticipate returning his carnal body to his ancestors without issue. The first chapter of *The Chinese Classic of Family Reverence* (*Xiaojing* 孝經) provides us with important commentary on this exchange between the dying Master Zeng and his students that might prompt us to read something more into this concern for the body. *The Chinese Classic of Family Reverence* certainly does declare that "your physical person—literally, 'your vital and discursive body' (*shenti* 身體)—with its hair and skin are received from your parents." But when the text goes on to assert that "vigilance in not allowing anything to do injury to your person is where family reverence begins," it perhaps lends itself to an understanding of "body" in a broader cultural sense.[104] I would argue that Confucius's elaboration upon the importance of "family reverence" (*xiao*) is not simply referencing respect for the carnal body but is also alluding to the function that the body has as the site of intergenerational cultural transmission—that is, the "vital body" and the "discursive body." Confucius defines the substance of education as the serious responsibility of each generation to transmit the culture they have inherited to the generations that follow in all its fullness and without diminution. In so doing, he reinforces his claim in this same chapter that *xiao* is indeed "the root of human virtuosity, and whence education (*jiao*) itself is born."[105] Thus, keeping the cultural "body" intact is the process of embodying the tradition fully, drawing upon it creatively as a resource for distinguishing oneself in the world, and contributing dividends to its resources by establishing a name for oneself and one's family that will be remembered by posterity. In this way, the evolving corpus of the cultural tradition—the civilization itself—is continued in each person, embodied in each succeeding generation, and is thus perpetuated for those that follow.

In his essay "American Civilization," Ralph Waldo Emerson provides us with a rather simple physical image of a carpenter hewing wood, which makes a profound statement about the intergenerational march of a continuing civilization:

> Civilization depends on morality. Everything good in man leans on what is higher. This rule holds in small as in great.

---

104. *Classic of Family Reverence*, chapter 1: 身體髮膚, 受之父母, 不敢毀傷, 孝之始也。
105. *Classic of Family Reverence*, chapter 1: 夫孝德之本也, 教之所由生也。

Thus, all our strength and success in the work of our hands depend on our borrowing the aid of the elements.[106]

Emerson remarks on the ineffectiveness of individuals striking out and "going it alone" in this world:

> You have seen a carpenter on a ladder with a broad-axe chopping upward chips and slivers from a beam. How awkward! at what disadvantage he works![107]

For Emerson, such aberrant individuality stands in a marked contrast with the indomitable felicity of squaring civilization behind our shoulders and living lives that are propelled by the moral and cultural gravitas provided by the impulse of a shared and continuing cultural tradition:

> But see him on the ground, dressing his timber under him. Now, not his feeble muscles, but the force of gravity brings down the axe; that is to say, the planet itself splits his stick.[108]

Emerson's image of lives empowered by the weight and momentum of a common civilization recalls the key Confucian exhortation that "it is persons who are able to broaden the way" (*ren neng hong dao* 人能弘道)[109]—a shared way of life that each generation is obligated to broaden and extend as it builds its own connector. As we have seen, in this Confucian tradition the intergenerational transmission of civilization is the responsibility of two different but related conceptions of "family" (*jia* 家). There is the continuing civilization of the *daotong* 道統 or "orthodox way" embodied in the elite social stratum of "the literati family lineage" or *rujia* 儒家. And then more broadly, but informed by the orthodox way of the literati lineage, there is the *xiaodao* 孝道 or "way of family reverence" that guides the lives of everyone within their extended family lineages or *jiazu* 家族.

---

106. Ralph Waldo Emerson, "American Civilization," *Atlantic Monthly*, April 1862, 502–11.
107. Emerson, "American Civilization."
108. Emerson, "American Civilization."
109. *Analects* 15.29.

There is a textual example that underscores the singular importance of continuing the embodied culture from one generation to the next:

> Mencius said: "There are three ways of failing to observe family reverence, and to be without progeny is the most serious among them. It is because Shun's taking a wife without first asking his parent's permission was done to guarantee his issue that exemplary persons interpret his case as if he had in fact gotten their approval."[110]

For a family to be without progeny is not only a failure to continue the blood lineage but also a failure to produce the human conduits necessary for the transmission of the living cultural tradition itself. It is an offense not only against a person's parents for whom the continuity of sacrificial offerings will be broken but also against the collective ancestors who were the distant founders and transmitters of the civilization itself. Given that Confucian morality is nothing other than continuing growth in relationships, to lack the progeny needed to attend to one's ancestors in this broadest sense is considered an acute moral lapse.

Again, there is a historical example that might provide us with further insight into this extended cultural meaning of "body" and "embodying." We can immediately relate the exhortation to be vigilant "in not allowing anything to do injury to your person" to the poignant story of Grand Historian Sima Qian 司馬遷 (145 ca.–86 BCE) of the Han dynasty. When Sima Qian was in his mid-thirties, he was called back from a military expedition to the deathbed of his father, Sima Tan 司馬談, who had in his time undertaken the ambitious project of compiling a comprehensive history of the preceding two thousand years. In that solemn moment, Sima Qian rose to the occasion and promised his father he would carry on and complete this important work on behalf of their family name. Sima Qian began at once and in earnest his efforts to fulfill his promise to complete the compilation of a grand history that would raise the name of "Sima" for all posterity.

Some ten years later an incident occurred at court that nearly brought both Sima Qian and his history project to an untimely end. General Li Ling, under the orders of Emperor Wu, had been dispatched to quell the

---

110. *Mencius* 4A26: 孟子曰:「不孝有三,無後為大。舜不告而娶,為無後也,君子以為猶告也。」

Xiongnu tribes who were fierce and brutal adversaries forever making incursions into the western regions of Han China. The emperor was incensed to learn that the Han army had been routed and General Li captured by the enemy, putting the blame squarely on Li's military incompetence. In his role as a court counselor, Sima Qian was the only one who dared to speak up in defense of General Li. And a livid Emperor Wu, incensed by this perhaps courageous but impolitic intervention, sentenced Sima Qian at first to death and then commuted his punishment to castration. Accepting this physical and social humiliation only because of his promise to his father, Sima Qian returned from prison several years later to live on as a disgraced and friendless outcast at the court. Working tirelessly over the next decade, he was able to bring to completion the *Records of the Grand Historian* (*Shiji* 史記), a monumental work in 130 chapters of over half a million characters. This opus, a singular model of scholarship and literary elegance, has been passed on from generation to generation and has had an enormous influence not only on China's historiography but also on the historiographies of Korea and Japan as well.

Given this narrative as described here, a question might be raised as to Sima Qian's filiality in accepting the defilement of his body rather than a noble and liberating death. He clearly violated the first precept of "family reverence" (*xiao*), which is "vigilance in not allowing anything to do injury to your person." But the argument on Sima Qian's behalf must begin from the assertion that true "family reverence" (*xiao*) must be attended by the stern obligation a child or a minister has to remonstrate (*jian* 諫) with the parent or ruler, respectively, when persuaded they are straying from the proper course. Secondly, under excruciating circumstances, Sima Qian stepped up like a truly filial son, fulfilling his promise to his father to complete the comprehensive history on behalf of the Sima family. Perhaps the most compelling argument beyond the filial obligation to remonstrate and keep a promise to his father, however, would be that while Sima Qian suffered his own physical desecration at the hands of an angry emperor, by completing the *Records of the Grand Historian* he selflessly and courageously gave of himself in preserving the body of the traditional culture intact. Sima Qian himself made the following observations:

> We have netted up and gathered the old knowledge of the world that had been dispersed and lost. We have, in a total of one hundred and thirty chapters that are composed of

everything from charts and letters to biographies, reflected upon the full compass of past deeds and events to fathom their patterns of success and failure, and their vicissitudes. Our desire was to get to the bottom of all that has happened between heaven and man, to understand thoroughly the changes that have occurred from the past to present, and to compile all of this as the contribution of a single family. But before even completing an initial draft, I encountered the worst calamity that could befall a person. And it was only because I felt a deep sense of regret that I had not yet been able to finish this work that I was willing to suffer this extreme punishment without acrimony. When I have at last brought this manuscript to its conclusion, I will store it up in a sacred mountain. If this work can be transmitted down to others and spread from the towns to the great cities, then were this disgrace that I have suffered be a thousand times such a mutilation, how could I possibly feel any regret?[111]

We must allow that Sima Qian clearly failed in the first dictate of family reverence that requires him to keep his physical body intact. But then he accomplished the more difficult charge of giving service to his parents and his lord, and he further succeeded in the ultimate goal of "family reverence": he raised his name for posterity and brought fame to his family lineage by distinguishing himself in the world.

As a peerless figure who faced down adversity and won fame and glory for his family, Sima Qian was exceptional in defining what filiality (*xiao*) really means. At an abstract level, we can also appeal to his complex and conflicted life as providing us a segue to a second philosophical term that is frequently evoked to express a more general sense of human flourishing: the achievement of an "optimal harmony" (*he* 和). This

---

111. Sima Qian, "A Letter in Reply to Ren An" 《報任少卿書》網羅天下放失舊聞，考之行事，綜其終始，稽其成敗興壞之理，上計軒轅，下至于茲，為十表，本紀十二，書八章，世家三十，列傳七十，凡百三十篇，亦欲以究天人之際，通古今之變，成一家之言。草創未就，適會此禍，惜其不成，是以就極刑而無慍色。僕誠已著此書，藏諸名山，傳之其人通邑大都，則僕償前辱之責，雖萬被戮，豈有悔哉！ A monograph entitled *The Letter to Ren An and Sima Qian's Legacy (or, Why Write History?)* by Stephen Durrant, Wai-yee Li, Michael Nylan, and Hans van Ess, dedicated to exploring the authenticity of this letter and its implications for an interpretation of the *Shiji* is presently at press.

kind of achieved "harmony" is not simply the mutual accommodation of difference that would attenuate dissonance, but more importantly, it references the creative and productive consequences of coordinating such differences to optimum effect—that is, the achievement of a human and cosmic "musicality." The composition of the earlier and more complex graph for "optimal harmony" (*he* 和) found on the oracle bones is *[xvii]* and on the bronzes is *[xviii]*. This character is composed of a *yue* 龠 wind instrument constructed out of reed pipes, with "growing grain" (*he* 禾) as the phonetic element, alluding to the playing of music as one metaphorical way of understanding this highly aesthetic sense of harmony.[112] And in fact, early twentieth-century reformer Lu Xun 魯迅, in describing Sima Qian's *Records of the Grand Historian*, appealed to just such hyperbolic terms, calling this great work "the historians' most perfect song" (*shijia de juechang* 史家的絕唱).

[xvii]

[xviii]

With respect to how we might understand the consummatory nature of experience, we can draw commonalities and contrasts between this Confucian notion of superlative "harmony" (*he* 和) that seeks to optimize the possibilities of "lived body" (*ti*) and "embodied living" (*li*) within the Confucian process cosmology, on the one hand, and the strong sense of teleology that has motive force in substance ontology (that has its roots in ancient Greece) on the other. Both harmony and teleology have an important albeit different function in explaining the organization, evolution, and completion of events within the human experience. Teleology gives impetus and direction to a cosmos informed by an overarching and predetermined design. Such teleology, with its formal and final causes directing the actualization of order to a given end, is linear and front-loaded in the sense of being to an important degree predetermined. By contrast, the Confucian idea of an achieved "optimal harmony" within its own process cosmology is without a given design, a presumed beginning, or a predetermined and final end. Moreover, it is ever emergent in the sense of focusing on the capacity and responsibility of the most exemplary of human beings to make the most of the cosmic possibilities in their continuing present. This being said, the pursuit of such harmony does much of the work of teleology as a determining factor in the flourishing and consummation of the human experience. This optimizing harmony, resourcing the historical past as its reservoir for analogy and projection,

---

112. Kwan, "Database," 甲骨文合集 CHANT 1490 and 戰國早期 CHANT 17, respectively.

draws upon human resolve and imagination to forge ahead in new ways. Our capacity for design, purpose, and direction assumed in this Confucian sense of harmony gives human beings a vital and prominent role in the evolution of an emergent and always provisional cosmic order.

One reason "harmony" is less than a good translation of *he* 和 is the alternative understanding of "harmony" as it functions within the teleological understanding of cosmic order. In favoring *ratio* over *oratio*, this notion of harmony tends to be reductionistic in the Whiteheadian sense of a "rational" or "rationalized" order, referring to a process of closure in "tuning" Y to X as opposed to a process of disclosure in the mutually "attuning" and accommodating of the differences between X and Y.[113] That is, the predetermined goal X disciplines the evolution of the many according to the privileged and thus rationalizing order, making the details that collaborate to constitute the cosmic order relevant only to the extent that they contribute to the completion of the predetermined order. To give an example of such a rational order, the construction of a triangle needs three points to complete it, where such points can alternatively be coins, cabbages, or Caledonians, and where such obvious and interesting differences among these three "points" (collectors, cultivars, and kilts) have no relevance or value for the desired order. That is, the concrete many are reduced to an abstract, reduplicated one as they are disciplined and rationalized to constitute a single-ordered world. Moving from the triangle to some grand, divine design, the *kosmoi* as many are rationalized to become a single *kosmos*, and the *pluri*-verse as many are rationalized to become a single "*uni*-verse."

The Confucian optimizing harmony, by contrast, is an example of the Whiteheadian holistic and inclusive "aesthetic order" in the sense that everything without remainder is relevant to the achieved totality of the effect. Because each unique thing conduces to the flourishing of every other unique thing, order has to be conceived of in terms of *equity* or *parity* among things in the heightening realization of their dynamically shared well-being. And the *diversity* to be aspired to in this sense of order is the full appreciation of the creative possibilities of any situation through the conserving, activating, and accommodating of those differences that make each ingredient unique and thus uniquely relevant.[114]

---

113. Whitehead, *Modes of Thought*, 53–60.

114. I am using "equity" here in the Aristotelian sense of serving as a corrective on the notion of universality that is necessary because of the insistent particularity of things in practical affairs. In the *Nicomachean Ethics*, Book 5, Aristotle observes that "the equitable

Perhaps the most prominent example in the Chinese cultural tradition that illustrates the centrality of this aesthetic, superlative sense of "harmony" (*he*) is role that the institution of family occupies as its pervasive and governing cultural metaphor. Family is a model of order that when optimally functional is one and many at the same time. A healthy family is that powerful social nexus to which its members are most inclined to give themselves utterly and without remainder. That is, when required, persons are disposed to give their families their time, their fortunes, their body parts, and even their lives. The Confucian promotion of this institution of family with its primary moral imperative of "family reverence" (*xiao* 孝) as the governing cosmological trope is surely a deliberate strategy to maximize the creative possibilities available within all of the human activities that are rooted in family and extend outward socially, politically, and religiously from this resilient core.

As mentioned earlier, *Focusing the Familiar* (*Zhongyong*), the fourth among Zhu Xi's *Four Books*, has been celebrated across the centuries in this tradition as the highest statement of the Confucian vision of the moral life. This seminal text appeals directly to this superlative sense of "harmony" in its own iteration of the holistic and aspirational Confucian project of optimizing familial, political, and cosmic relations. Eastern Han dynasty philosopher Wang Chong 王充 summarizes the fundamental value that this Confucian tradition has traditionally invested in the institution of family as its strategy for the pursuit of optimal harmony in the following terms:

> Sages take the whole world as their family without distinction of near or far, of domestic or foreign. . . . In their undertakings, the sages seek what is optimally appropriate . . . The most sagacious among us would "family" the whole world.[115]

---

is just, but not the legally just but a correction of legal justice. The reason is that all law is universal but about some things it is not possible to make a universal statement which will be correct. . . . And it is none the less correct; for the error is not in the law nor in the legislator but in the nature of the thing, since the matter of practical affairs is of this kind from the start." See Aristotle, *Complete Works*, 1137b1120. Peter Hershock makes much of this superlative, aesthetic sense of order as the Buddhist *kusala* conduct in his monograph, *Valuing Diversity: Buddhist Reflection on Realizing a More Equitable Global Future* (Albany: State University of New York Press, 2012).

115. 王充, 論衡16.7–8: 聖人以天下為家, 不別遠近, 不殊內外。。。。聖人舉事求其宜適也。。。。賢聖家天下。

Confucian role ethics is a radial way of thinking about the moral life, with human feelings grounded as they are at a focal familial center to then be extended outward by cosmic waymakers in their best effort to "family" the world in which we live. Our warrant for translating the title of the text, "*zhongyong*" 中庸, as *Focusing the Familiar* is the fact that "familiar" and "family" share the same etymological root: L. *familiaris* "domestic, private, belonging to a family, of a household." A close reading of *Focusing the Familiar* here will help us bring this important aspiration for optimizing the human experience into clearer focus.

The Confucian ethic of roles as an alternative to rule-based ethics begins from its recognition of the native human capacity to collaborate creatively with our environments in pursuit of a consummatory, aesthetic end. As the *locus classicus* among the Confucian canons in celebrating human beings as having both the office and the responsibility to be full cocreators with the heavens and the earth, *Focusing the Familiar* opens with the oft-cited passage:

> What *tian* commands is called our native human propensities; acting upon these propensities is called way-making; advancing this way is called education.[116]

---

116. Ames and Hall, *Focusing the Familiar*, 89: 天命之謂性, 率性之謂道, 修道之謂教。An alternative translation of this same passage by Scottish "commonsense" missionary James Legge reads: "What Heaven has conferred is called The Nature; an accordance with this nature is called The Path of duty; the regulation of this path is called Instruction." While Legge thought that his own theistically inspired reading of this opening passage gave it a good beginning, he wrote a scathing indictment of the hubris he found in rest of the document and condemned the entire work with utter derision:

> It begins sufficiently well, but the author has hardly enunciated his preliminary apothegms, when he conducts into an obscurity where we can hardly grope our way, and when we emerge from that, it is to be bewildered by his gorgeous but unsubstantial pictures of sagely perfection. He has eminently contributed to nourish the pride of his countrymen. He has exalted their sages above all that is called God or is worshipped, and taught the masses of the people that with them they have need of nothing from without. In the meantime it is antagonistic to Christianity. By-and-by, when Christianity has prevailed in China, men will refer to it as a striking proof how their fathers by their wisdom knew neither God nor themselves. (Legge, *The Chinese Classics*, 1:55)

One possible reading of this opening line when the text is located within its own historical context would be to interpret it dialectically as a Confucian argument against the Mohist camp, a philosophical lineage that constituted a pervasive and powerful polemical force during this pre-Qin period.[117] A Mohist interpretation of this line would have construed the relationship between *tian* and the human being in a decidedly conservative, "theistic" direction by suggesting that "Heaven" (*tian*) largely imposes its natural and moral order on the human world from without (*wai* 外).[118] Chris Fraser provides a summary description of this Mohist understanding of the intentions or "purposes of 'Heaven'" (*tianzhi* 天志) as constituting and making available to human beings an externally grounded, objective standard:

> The Mohists justify their consequentialist ethics by appeal to the intention of Heaven (*Tian*), which they believe provides an objective criterion of morality. . . . The crux of the Mohists' appeal to Heaven is that as the highest, wisest moral agent, Heaven conducts itself in a way (a *dao*) that unfailingly sets an example of correct ethical norms. Its intentions are consistently or reliably humane and right. To obtain an objective criterion of moral right and wrong, then, we can observe Heaven's conduct and notice the norms it is committed to and enforces.[119]

To be clear, I would argue (and I think Fraser would agree) that the "external" standard of the Mohist is a publicly determined and implemented objective norm, and while certainly conservative and impositional, this idea still remains as one possible extreme within the assumed framework of a correlative relationship between *tian* and the human world. That is, the "purposes of *tian*" are negotiated and function within the parameters

---

117. A good example of how the interpretive context makes a difference in our interpretations of these early texts is the recent work by scholars such as David Wong, Chris Fraser, James Behuniak, Dan Robbins, Hui-chieh Loy, Ben Wong, and so on, who have done much to reinstate the *Mozi* as integral to the intellectual debates that flourished during the pre-Qin period.

118. This Mohist claim that moral order is ultimately derived from an external source is the basis of a frequently encountered debate in the Confucian texts, with the *Mencius* being perhaps the clearest case in point. See, for example, the *Mencius* 6A chapter.

119. Chris Fraser, "Mohism," *The Stanford Encyclopedia of Philosophy*, ed. Edward N. Zalta (Stanford, CA: Stanford University Press), http://plato.stanford.edu/archives/fall2012/entries/mohism/.

of "the continuity and inseparability of the human and the cosmic orders" (*tianrenheyi* 天人合一). Thus as a putatively objective standard it is of a fundamentally different quality of "objectivity" than that derived from the dualistic, two-world order we would associate with the conventional Abrahamic notion of the perfection and thus the aseity or self-sufficiency, of an independent, transcendent God.

In arguing against the Mohist assertion that cosmic order is divinely imposed upon the human world, the Confucians are not simply advancing the claim that human beings are active in the production of cosmic order. Indeed, the Confucians go on to insist that human beings, in this aspiration to live inspired lives, contribute in an intense and inimitable way to the refulgent spirituality of the cosmos. Moreover, this spirituality, far from being unilateral or singular in purpose as is implied by the Mohist notion of "the purposes of 'Heaven'" (*tianzhi* 天志), is multivalent, pluralistic, and inclusive. The myriad things obey no single unifying principle but achieve their harmony and diversity through resourcing the interpenetrating differences that obtain among them to make a difference for each one of them. Stated more simply, according to this text, the Confucian vision of the moral life is enhanced, and all things in the world flourish when powerful human feelings coalesce in their relations with their environing others and are orchestrated together with them into a productive, optimal harmony.

In translating this opening line as "What *tian* commands is our native human propensities," I am following the interpretation of the term "native human propensities" (*xing* 性) that Tang Junyi endorses in his extensive commentary on this theme generally and on this passage specifically. Tang insists that

> what is meant in this opening passage by such a claim is not that *tian* according to some fixed fate determines the conduct and progress of human beings. On the contrary, *tian* endows humans with our native human propensities (*xing*) that, being more or less free of the mechanical control of established habits and of external intervening forces, undergo a creative advance within their contextualizing situation that is expressive of this spontaneity.[120]

---

120. Tang Junyi, *Complete Works*, 4:100: 所謂天命之為性，非天以一指定命運規定人物之行動運化，而正是賦人物以多多少少不受自己過去之習慣所機械支配，亦不受外界之來感之力之機械支配，而隨境有一創造的生起而表現自由之性。

The two paragraphs that follow from this opening statement each offer a complementary interpretation of this first line that can be read as a succinct and explicit summary of the main thesis of *Focusing the Familiar*. *Focusing the Familiar* is, from beginning to end, a celebration of the continuing contributions of those human beings who embrace and take responsibility for their cocreative role in the cosmos, which is captured in the mantra, "the continuity and inseparability of the human and the cosmic orders" (*tianren heyi* 天人合一). Expanding upon this central message, these two introductory paragraphs provide us with several cosmological corollaries that follow from the primacy invested in vital relationality. The first paragraph reads:

> As for this way-making, we cannot quit it even for an instant. Could we quit it, it would not be proper way-making (*dao*). It is for this reason that exemplary persons are so concerned about what is not seen, and so anxious about what is not heard. There is nothing more present than what is imminent, and nothing more manifest than what is inchoate. Thus, exemplary persons are ever concerned to consolidate their virtuosic habits as an inner disposition for action.[121]

---

121. Ames and Hall, *Focusing the Familiar*, 89: 道也者,不可須臾離也,可離非道也。是故君子戒慎乎其所不睹,恐懼乎其所不聞。莫見乎隱,莫顯乎微。故君子慎其獨也。Liang Tao, on the basis of recently recovered archaeological texts, has argued convincingly that the meaning of the last phrase in this passage—故君子慎其獨也—is to internalize and consolidate the five modes of virtuosic conduct as a habitual disposition for acting with moral virtuosity. The commentary included in the Mawangdui version of *Wuxingpian* is explicit in defining this familiar phrase:

> 慎其独也者,言舍夫五而慎其心之谓也。独然后一,一也者,夫五为囗(一)心也,然后得之.
> The expression *shenqidu* means accommodating these five modes of virtuosic conduct within and focusing them carefully in one's heartminding. Having consolidated these five modes of conduct, they become one, where this "one" then refers to the five modes of virtuosic conduct having been consolidated as the [one] heartminding that then becomes one's own identity.

See Liang Tao 梁涛, "Zhu Xi dui 'shendu' de wudu ji qizijingxue quanshizhong de yiyi 朱熹對"慎獨"的誤讀及其在經學詮釋中的意義, *Zhexueyanjiu* 哲学研究 (2004), 第期, 48–54.

We human beings are taken to be integral to the creative cosmic process, and as we cultivate and enculturate ourselves, we have a recursive relationship within the context of this generative advancing of cosmic order, shaping and being shaped at the same time. And we cannot extricate ourselves from this responsibility. Importantly, it is the inchoate and thus underdetermined penumbra of the emerging cosmic order that provides cultivated persons with the opening and the opportunity to function as cocreators and to collaborate fully with the heavens and the earth to achieve a flourishing world. Moreover, through the reflexive internalization and consolidation of this virtuosic conduct in their own persons, in this focus-field dynamic they come to have this entire flourishing cosmos implicated in their personal project of becoming fully who they are.

Indeed, the capacity of exemplary persons through personal cultivation and an achieved inner resolve to produce increased significance in all of the relations that constitute them and their world illustrates the Confucian assumption that creativity is always a situated, collaborative undertaking as *creatio in situ*. Given that Confucian morality is nothing more or less than deliberate growth in relations, these exemplars are thus able to achieve cosmic stature as a continuing source of moral meaning in their increasingly intimate relationship with their world. That is, any reticence with respect to the remoteness, vastness, and externality of the cosmos gives way to an awareness of an increasingly mutual and indeed "social" coalescence with this world that is funded by feelings of deference, belonging, and trust.[122]

This opening chapter of *Focusing the Familiar* then continues in a second paragraph by restating this same theme, albeit in different terms, of "the continuity and inseparability of the human and the cosmic orders" (*tianren heyi*):

> The moment at which joy and anger, grief and pleasure, have yet to arise is called a nascent equilibrium; once these feelings have arisen, that they find coalescence is called an optimiz-

---

122. It is this same sense of the inseparability of the human and the natural worlds that is inspiring the contemporary movement in the social sciences and humanities to herald an Anthropocene epoch by challenging the nature/social dualism and, remembering the etymology of "social" as "company" and "alliance," embracing nature as a social category. See Gisli Palsson et al., "Reconceptualizing the 'Anthropos' in the Anthropocene: Integrating the Social Sciences and Humanities in Global Environmental Change Research," *Environmental Science & Policy* 28 (April 2013): 3–13.

ing harmony. This notion of coalescence is the great root of the world; an optimizing harmony then is the advancing of way-making in the world. When coalescence is sustained and an optimizing harmony is fully realized, the heavens and the earth maintain their proper places and all things flourish in the world.[123]

This second passage, then, begins from a description of our initial conditions—those latent, native, but as yet unexpressed feelings—that provide us with the relational resources for engaging the world and for enchanting the cosmos. And it is because we are able to cultivate ourselves as responsive, feeling creatures that we can develop the capacity to become a truly transformative force suffusing the ceaseless process of procreation. The notion of "feelings" here has to be read as a human responsiveness that has the potential to function in a deepened, capacious, and inclusive way. As David Wong and others have argued, we do not find the Greek separation of emotions and reason in these classical Confucian texts or any assumed tension between these capacities that might follow from such a disjunction.[124] Our feelings in this broad, cosmic sense seek their

---

123. Ames and Hall, *Focusing the Familiar*, 89–90: 喜怒哀樂之未發謂之中; 發而皆中節謂之和; 中也者, 天下之大本也; 和也者, 天下之達道也。致中和, 天地位焉, 萬物育焉。Zisizi 子思子 aka Kong Ji, 孔伋, the grandson of Confucius, is traditionally identified as the author of *Focusing the Familiar*. In the opening line of this chapter, we have encountered three of the five philosophical terms that have, through recent archaeological finds, come to be associated with the philosophy of Zisizi: *tian* 天 (conventionally translated as "Heaven"), *ming* 命 ("commands"), and *xing* 性 ("native human propensities"). An argument can be made that even though the additional two Zisizi terms—"feelings" (*qing* 情) and "heartmind" (*xin* 心)—do not appear in this second paragraph explicitly, they are implicit in what is being said about the intimate role of human feelings in cosmic flourishing. That is, the semantic content if not the two remaining Zisizi terms themselves—the "feelings" (*qing* 情) that constitute and empower the human "heartmind" (*xin* 心)—are also referenced obliquely, making up the full complement of five key terms with these surrogates. And then later in the text, the increasing centrality of *cheng* 誠—"sincerity, honesty, integrity, resolve"—that is elevated to cosmic proportions as a kind of "cocreativity" reinforces the claim that human "feelings" have a prominent role in shaping the cosmos.

124. David B. Wong, "Is There a Distinction Between Reason and Emotion in Mencius?" *Philosophy East and West* 41, no. 1 (1991): 31. Myeong-seok Kim disputes Wong's claim in her subsequent essay, "Is There No Distinction between Reason and Emotion in *Mengzi*?," *Philosophy East and West* 64, no. 1 (2014).

own satisfaction by pursuing a productive continuity within the contours of the concrete world as we actually come to embody it.

But such feelings become a powerful resource only when they are properly cultivated to achieve both coalescence (*zhongjie* 中節) and a superlative harmony (*he*) in these expansive relations, and in so doing, to give rise to the personal resolution needed to produce a flourishing world. It is only through deepening and achieving proper measure (*du* 度) in the correlative "human and cosmos" relationship (*tianren* 天人) and thus transforming this relationship into one of sociality—and indeed of an evolving religiousness—that these exemplary persons can make their profound contribution to cosmic meaning. Such achieved harmony and clear resolution in our relationships is the very root from which the flourishing world order emerges and as such contributes to the life force that guides the entire cosmos, with all of its bounty, on its proper course. And on the human side, it is our unique sense of felt worth and belonging within this dynamic cosmic life force that is the substance of real religious experience and that gives *Focusing the Familiar* as a text its profound religious significance.

Far from being some remote speculation on the turning of the heavens, cosmology in general are typically a projection onto the world of an order initially derived from ordinary activities of the everyday human experience: love and strife, law and chaos, friend and foe, and so on. In the cosmology implicit in early Confucian philosophizing, the pursuit of cosmic harmony begins with cultivating family and community relations at home and then ripples out to suffuse the polity and the furthest horizons of the cosmos that are both construed as a direct extension of familial relations. As the text itself insists, the thriving family is a precondition for a flourishing world:

> The proper way of exemplary persons is to realize that in traveling a long way, one must set off from what is near at hand, and in climbing to a high place, one must begin from low ground. As it says in the *Book of Songs*:
>
> The loving relationship with wife and children
> Is like the strumming of the zither and the lute;
> The harmonious relationship between older and younger
>   brothers

Is the source of an abundance of enjoyment and pleasure.
Do what is fitting in your domestic affairs
And find joy in your wife and progeny.
"And how happy the parents will be as well!" said the Master.[125]

These middle chapters of *Focusing the Familiar* provide a detailed historical account of the cultural heroes who have constructed the institutions and embodied the values as they are then passed on from generation to generation. And as role models, these heroes are themselves available for emulation. But perhaps in response to the challenge of Daoist cosmology, *Focusing the Familiar* goes further than the earlier Confucian texts. While the *Analects*, for example, focuses primarily on the human world, *Focusing the Familiar* extends the compass of Confucian concern beyond such limits to ascribe the transformative force of human feeling to the cosmos more broadly:

> Thus, exemplary persons cannot but cultivate their own persons, and in cultivating their persons, cannot but serve their kin. In serving their kin they cannot but come to realize the human world, and in realizing the human world, cannot but come to realize the cosmic *tian*.[126]

In many ways, the structure of *Focusing the Familiar* serves as an object lesson in a Confucian cosmology that requires of human cocreators the production of added significance, and in so doing, the expansion of the cosmic order. It exhorts its readers to exercise their capacity of *ars contextualis*—"the art of contextualizing"—to strive with imagination to take full advantage of both the indeterminate energy that honeycombs the determinate world and the profound differences always unique human beings can activate in their relations with those things present-to-hand. The first fifteen chapters following the opening statement co-opt the authority of Confucius himself to support its interpretation of the cosmic

---

125. Ames and Hall, *Focusing the Familiar*, 95–96: 君子之道，辟如行遠必自邇，辟如登高必自卑。《詩》曰：「妻子好合，如鼓瑟琴；兄弟既翕，和樂且耽。宜爾室家，樂爾妻帑。」子曰：「父母其順矣乎!」

126. Ames and Hall, *Focusing the Familiar*, 100–1: 故君子不可以不修身；思修身，不可以不事親；思事親，不可以不知人；思知人，不可以不知天。

force of human feelings. These chapters expound on the term *zhongyong* 中庸, a vague binomial that had appeared only once prior to *Focusing the Familiar* from the mouth of the Master himself as he is remembered in the *Analects*:

> The Master said, "It takes the highest degree of virtuosity to bring focus to what is familiar in the ordinary affairs of the day. That such virtuosity is rare among the people, is an old story."[127]

Some of these early *Focusing the Familiar* chapters are an attempt to define *zhongyong* explicitly.[128] A few other passages attempt to illuminate what is meant by the character *zhong* 中 by itself as "focus" or "coalescence."[129] What is clear is that the chapters in this first portion of the text attempt to link the notion of *zhongyong* with full human participation in the "waymaking" (*dao* 道) of the cosmos.

The text begins from the ordinary lives of people in their families and communities as these lives have been informed and inspired by the model provided by the exemplary persons who have come before.[130] In the chapters that follow, the felt lives of the ordinary people being thus transformed serve as a motive force as they are implicated in the epochal lives of the sages. That is, the sages become sages only through their capacity to transform ordinary lives into extraordinary ones. These towering paragons then raise their voices on behalf of humanity as a whole to sing the joyful music of the cosmos. Chapter 12 of *Focusing the Familiar* provides an initial and clear statement of this radial and interpenetrating transformative process:

> The way-making of exemplary persons . . . has as its start the simple lives of ordinary men and women, and at its zenith can be discerned by the entire world.[131]

---

127. *Analects* 6.29: 子曰:「中庸之為德也, 其至矣乎! 民鮮久矣。」
128. Chapters 2, 3, 7, 8, 9, and 11.
129. Chapters 6 and 10.
130. Chapters 10, 11, 12, 13, and 15.
131. Ames and Hall, *Focusing the Familiar*, 92–93: 君子之道 . . . 造端乎夫婦, 及其至也, 察乎天地。」

The middle chapters of the text recount how the sages and cultural heroes have taken the everyday human experience within family and ancestral lineages and, by promoting the pursuit of a ritualized propriety in family and community relations (*li* 禮), have aestheticized this experience in attempting to transform the ordinary into the extraordinary. In so doing, they have to an important degree elevated and enchanted the lives of the people. A particular important point is made repeatedly: *Tian*'s bounty has been and continues to be shared with the human world in direct proportion to the achieved virtuosity of those in positions of social and political authority. Appealing to the paronomastic relationship between the homophonic terms "virtuosity" (*de* 德) and "getting" (*de* 得), we can say that there is a contrapuntal relationship between human virtuosity and the largesse of *tian*. A pervasive dynamic in these Confucian canons, simply put, is that in the lives of exemplary persons, there is an immediate correlation between their achieved resolution rooted within and their expansive reach and influence without:[132]

> Thus, those of the greatest virtuosity (*dade* 大德) are certain to gain status, emoluments, reputation, and longevity. For the generosity of nature (*tian* 天) in giving birth to and nurturing things is certain to be in response to the quality of the things themselves. . . . Those of the greatest virtuosity are thus certain to receive *tian*'s charge.[133]

Thus, in recounting the history of the collaborative origins of human culture, the text marshals the hoary sages and cultural heroes to join Confucius himself in endorsing its Confucian interpretation of the transformative cosmic force of human feelings.

Chapter 25 of *Focusing the Familiar* provides a straightforward and substantial statement of several cosmological assumptions that further expand upon the theme expressed in the opening chapter: that it is the indeterminate aspect of our experience together with human resolution that provides the opening for humans to participate as responsible players in the creative cosmic advance. The chapter itself is an elaboration

---

132. In the language of the *Analects* 14.35: 下學而上達。"Study what is near at hand and aspire to what is lofty."
133. Ames and Hall, *Focusing the Familiar*, 96–97: 故大德必得其位，必得其祿，必得其名，必得其壽。故天之生物，必因其材而篤焉 . . . 故大德者必受命。

on a passage found in the *Mencius* that has elevated the term *cheng* 誠, translated here as "resolve," to cosmic status as a source of transformation:

> Resolve is the way-making of *tian*, reflecting with resolution on things is the way-making of the human being.[134]

The *Mencius* here is ascribing the potential to become a powerful force in shaping cosmic order to the resolve achieved in our intense human feelings. This correlation between human resolve and creative cosmic advance is again elaborated upon in this seminal passage of *Focusing the Familiar*:

> Resolve (*cheng* 誠) is self-consummating and its way-making is self-directing. Resolve is the beginning and the end of things, and without this resolve, there would be nothing. It is thus that, for exemplary persons, it is resolve that is prized. But resolve is not simply the self-consummating of one's own person; it is what consummates everything. Completing oneself is achieving virtuosity in one's roles and relations (*ren* 仁); completing all things is advancing wisdom in the world (*zhi* 知). Such is the virtuosity achieved in one's natural propensities and the way-making that integrates what is more internal and

---

134. *Mencius* 4A12: 是故誠者天之道也，思誠者人之道也。In this seminal passage, we witness the repeated image of an inner intensity and resolve and its vast outer cosmic reach and compass. This cosmic association of *cheng* 誠 with creativity and resolve has been anticipated in Ames and Hall, *Focusing the Familiar*, 16: 夫微之顯，誠之不可掩如此夫。

> Such is the way that the inchoate is made manifest and that resolve cannot be repressed.

It occurs again in Ames and Hall, *Focusing the Familiar*, 20:

誠者，天之道也；誠之者，人之道也。誠者不勉而中，不思而得，從容中道，聖人也。誠之者，擇善而固執之者也。

> Resolve is the waymaking of *tian*; applying resolve is the waymaking of becoming human. Resolve is achieving equilibrium and coalescence without coercion; it is succeeding without reflection. Freely and easily traveling at the center of waymaking—this is the sage. Resolve is selecting what is efficacious and holding on to it firmly.

what is more external. Thus when and wherever one applies this virtuosity, it is fitting.[135]

We should note here that *cheng* is first and foremost a human sentiment usually translated as "sincerity," "honesty," or "integrity." In the *Mencius* and these middle passages of *Focusing the Familiar* it is elevated and projected onto the cosmos to describe the process of procreation itself, making the resolve of intense human feelings not only integral to its operations but also a source of the world's boundless capacity for growth. It is because of the cosmic power of this sentiment that resolve (*cheng*) is revered by all exemplary people who understand most profoundly that the process of personal consummation (*ren* 仁) is at once collaborative and reflexive, a source not only of family and community solidarity but also of critical self-awareness. Such personal growth is coterminous with the growth of a joyful wisdom that inspires a flourishing world (*zhi* 知). Here also we have the explicit statement, contra the Mohists, that subjectivity and objectivity (*neiwai* 內外) in the achieved virtuosic relationships constituting our insistent particularity as unique persons (*de* 德) are a matter of aspect rather than exclusivity, a matter of degree rather than kind. What is subjective and objective are inseparable aspects of the waymaking (*dao* 道), enabling us in the process of coalescing with the content of our environments to achieve what is optimally fitting in these relations (*yi* 宜) on the objective side, while more subjectively, to find and dispose ourselves in the most appropriate way in these same relations (*yi* 義).[136] Moral appropriateness is the source of meaningful relations, bringing them internally into focus and resolve and making them externally available as a source of cosmic flourishing. In this development of the uniquely Mencian reading of human resolution as a cosmic force, the text has added Mencius to Confucius and the early sages as one more sponsor for its Confucian interpretation of the cosmic reach and influence of human feelings.

---

135. Ames and Hall, *Focusing the Familiar*, 106: 誠者自成也，而道自道也。誠者物之終始，不誠無物。是故君子誠之為貴。誠者非自成己而已也，所以成物也。成己，仁也；成物，知也。性之德也，合外內之道也，故時措之宜也。

136. Earlier in the text in Ames and Hall, *Focusing the Familiar*, chapter 20, "what is optimally appropriate" (*yi* 義)—that is, what is the source of moral growth—has been defined paronomastically as "what is most fitting" (*yi* 宜) in any particular situation, providing a warrant for reading this character here as what is optimally appropriate as a source of moral as well as phenomenal significance.

Focusing the Familiar, with Confucius, the cultural heroes, and Mencius all endorsing its interpretation of the Confucian project, has only to bring in the compelling voice of the *Book of Songs* to complete its score. It is the *Book of Songs* as the anonymous and commonly shared songs of the people, in having absolute veracity and powerful affective force, that typically serves as the ultimate *quod erat demonstrandum* (QED) endorsement within many if not most of the Confucian canonical texts.

As we move through the final succeeding chapters of *Focusing the Familiar*, the bottomlessness and the boundlessness of the heavens and the earth that provide the natural context for the human experience are described in hyperbolic language (chapter 26). An important cosmological point made explicitly here that we have had reason to mention before is that each particular event emerging as integral to cosmic order is unique and without replication, making the process of procreation unlimited in its bounty:

> The way of heaven and earth can be captured in one phrase: since events are never duplicated, their proliferation is unfathomable.[137]

With quickening pace and animation, the text goes on to describe the human complement to these natural processes of procreativity through the contributions made by sages and exemplary persons who spread the proper way throughout the world (chapter 27). It is through the exemplary rulership of the True King (chapter 28) that the role of the human actor is extended both culturally and politically to the furthest reaches of the cosmos. These more generic descriptions then give way to the specific and concrete example of Confucius himself (chapter 30) who is portrayed in grand, celestial language that makes his life a counterpart to the cosmic process of procreation itself in which the human and the natural operations converge as one:

> He modeled himself above on the rhythm of the turning seasons, and below he was attuned to the patterns of water and earth. He is comparable to the heavens and the earth,

---

137. Ames and Hall, *Focusing the Familiar*, 106–7: 天地之道，可壹言而盡也。其為物不貳，則其生物不測。

sheltering and supporting everything that is. He is comparable to the progress of the four seasons, and the alternating brightness of the sun and the moon.[138]

Making the point that this cosmic process continues unabated, the penultimate chapters 31 and 32 describe in majestic and exuberant language the singular transformative impact of "those of utmost sagacity in the world" (天下至聖) and "those of utmost creative resolve in the world" (天下至誠), respectively. Finally, the last chapter (chapter 33) registers perhaps most dramatically the now galloping momentum of the generative procreative process. The text breaks out into the celebratory, full-throated verses of the *Book of Songs* and moves rapidly toward its crescendo in a veritable "Ode to Joy." It is these verses that draw upon the powerful emotion of the people and the genuineness of their songs to serve as the last and most compelling endorsement for the Confucian reading of this text: the celebration of the power of intense human feelings in the collaborative processes of cosmic procreativity.

With this close reading of *Focusing the Familiar*, I have tried to show how the "aspectual" notions of "achieved propriety in one's roles and relations" (*li* 禮), "embodied living within one's roles and relations" (*ti* 體), and the aspiration to "an optimizing harmony" (*he* 和) provide the framework for the highest statement of the Confucian project. Without appeal to any strong sense of cosmic teleology, this Confucian project requires a different, open-ended, and provisional language. It challenges us to think in a processual way, collaboratively and creatively, in exercising ourselves as relational human "becomings" who have some real responsibility for cosmic waymaking rather than conceiving of ourselves as ready-made human "beings" disposed to actualizing some given human potential within a linear and teleologically driven historiography.

---

138. Ames and Hall, *Focusing the Familiar*, chapter 30, 111–112: 仲尼。。。上律天時，下襲水土。辟如天地之無不持載，無不覆幬，辟如四時之錯行，如日月之代明。

Chapter Three

A Narrative Conception of Human Nature

A Human "Being" or Human "Becomings"?

The contemporary philosopher Li Zehou 李澤厚 makes a distinction between "morality" (*daode* 道德) and "ethics" (*lunlixue* 倫理學) by appealing to Kant and Hegel, respectively. For Li, Kant's philosophical psychology makes "morality" a function of comporting oneself according to the dictates of our innate reason and its moral imperatives, while Hegel takes a philosophy of history perspective and locates "ethics" within the parameters of the relationships that obtain within family, community, and country. The important question for Li is whether human "beings" are born with some universal moral faculty that makes them good. Or do "human becomings" become morally good as the product of their personal cultivation? While many contemporary interpreters of the debate between Mencius and Xunzi might ascribe the former innatist, psychological position to Mencius and the latter appeal to personal cultivation and refinement to Xunzi, I am glad to have the corroboration of Li Zehou. He also sees both Mencius and Xunzi as advocating for the latter position. Zehou insists that

> Mencius and Xunzi are consistent with Confucius in both advocating for "education." The first chapter of *Xunzi* is "Encouraging Education." And Mencius observes that "what distinguishes people from the brutes is ever so slight, and while the common run of people might lose this difference, exemplary persons preserve and develop it." Hence this

distinguishing human characteristic has to be sought after or it will be lost. Both Mencius and Xunzi emphasize *aposteriori* cultivation and learning. The distinguishing characteristic of Confucianism is that what is fundamental to the human experience is not some fixed nature, but a process of ceaseless change and growth. Learning to become human is a key precept in Confucianism.[1]

What is a human "being"? This was a perennial Greek question asked in Plato's *Phaedo* and in his *Republic*, and as we have seen, in Aristotle's *Categories* as well. And there were many different answers, two of which are pointed at metonymically in Raphael's famous *School of Athens* fresco by the "up" and "down" pointing gestures of Plato and his student Aristotle. One persistent answer to this question was an ontological one. It predated Plato's psyche with the Egyptian transfiguration of the *ka* and *ba* life forces animating the spiritual entity *akh* in the afterlife and with the Pythagorean doctrine of the reincarnation of an immortal soul that anticipates and informs Plato's *Phaedo*. From these deep historical roots, the "being" of a human being has come to be understood popularly in Christian doctrine as some variation on a permanent, ready-made, self-sufficient soul. Early on in the narrative, "know thyself," as the signature exhortation of Socrates' doctrine of "recollection" (*amnanesis*), is an exhortation to remember, recover, and thus fully know this soul. Each of us *is* a person; and from conception we have the integrity of *being* an individual person.

How or *in what way* (*dao* 道) do persons in their roles and relations—and in their cultivated, critical self-awareness—*become* consummately human (*ren* 仁)? This was the perennial Confucian question asked explicitly in the *Four Books*: in *Expansive Learning* (*Daxue*), in the *Analects of Confucius*, in the *Mencius*, and again in *Focusing the Familiar* (*Zhongyong*). And the answer even before the time of Confucius was a moral, aesthetic, and ultimately religious one. Persons (always and necessarily plural) *become* humans by cultivating those thick relations that

---

1. Li Zehou in his "An Explanation of the Summary Chart on Ethics" (关于"伦理学总览表"的说明) 所以我说孟、荀统一于孔, 即"学"。荀子有《劝学》作为首篇, 孟子也讲"人之所以异于禽兽者几希, 庶民去之, 君子存之", 所以要"求放心", "求则得之, 捨则失之"。孟荀双方都重视后天的培养和学习。孔学的特点就是认为人的本性并不是固定的nature, 而是一个总在不断成长、变化的过程。从而"学做人"始终是孔学要义之一。

constitute our native conditions and that shape the trajectory of our life narratives; that is, these relations guide the whence and whither of our life's journey within family, community, and cosmos.² In this Confucian tradition, because we depend upon our associated lives lived in the roles of family and community to become persons, our assertive "I" is always a "we," and our socialized "me" is always an "us." And "cultivate your persons" (*xiushen* 修身) as the signature exhortation of the Confucian canons is described as the root of the Confucian project—that is, of becoming consummate as those unique and critically self-aware persons we aspire to be (*ren*). We are to cultivate our conduct assiduously as it is expressed through the specific family, community, and cosmic roles and relations we live together.

Of course, to insist on a narrative understanding of persons does not preclude the necessary generalizations about persons and our evolving cultural values that we need to describe, analyze, evaluate, and ultimately to use in guiding human experience. As Borges's "Funes the Memorius" and Plato before him would insist, such generalizations are necessary for the thinking process itself; after all, we cannot think particularity.

In the Confucian texts we find frequent reference to the values of courage (*yong* 勇); living up to one's word (*xin* 信); family reverence (*xiao* 孝); conscientiousness (*zhong* 忠); empathetic deference and dramatic rehearsal (*shu* 恕); cherishing learning (*haoxue* 好學); an optimizing, superlative harmony (*he* 和); achieving propriety in one's roles and relations (*li* 禮); wisdom (*zhi* 知); and many more such normative abstractions. What we must understand, however, is that such generalities about the human experience ultimately emerge from human lives lived and thus the general emerges from the specific rather than the other way around. Far from beginning from some teleological notion of a fixed human nature with antecedent, determinative principles to guide our conduct, such functional generalizations about persons and their values are post hoc abstractions from the continuing confluence of particular narratives and the patterns of conduct expressed therein. As such, these generalizations are always provisional, revisionist, and constantly being theorized out of our practices to make these same practices more productive and intelligent. The "journey or way-making we have undertaken together"—our *dao* 道—is the classical Chinese expression of personal narratives, where the *genus* of

---

2. See *Analects* 12.1: "Through self-discipline and achieving propriety in one's roles and relations one becomes consummate in one's conduct." 克己復禮為仁.

this term that purports to describe humans in a general way (*rendao* 人道) emerges continuously out of the history of a confluence of the specific and always unique lives lived. And emulation of the exemplary models that arise in this same history provides human "becomings" with the more concrete inspiration for living a consummate human life (*rendao* 仁道).

The important adjustment in thinking that a narrative understanding of persons requires is that we must avoid what John Dewey has called *the* philosophical fallacy: abstracting one element out of the continuing process of experience, reifying it, and then making this second-order "principle" first order by claiming that it is antecedent, causal, and determinative. Dewey references this fallacy specifically with reference to the notion of "good":

> There is no morality in my ethics i.e., there is no apart morality. Good conduct (once conduct is defined as activity which is an end to itself) seems to me a pleonasm. Conduct, full activity, is the good. . . . Now the usual idea of the Good seems to be an abstraction which has been frozen. It denotes full activity, but then it [is] abstracted and put over by itself and then frozen in its isolated apart from the content of specific activities which first gave it meaning.[3]

We are guilty of this fallacy of "pleonasm" or redundancy when the notion of "potential" as cause, root, source, or nature is reduced to some antecedent teleological principle that is then reduplicated in the process of growth. We are also guilty of this fallacy when reasoning becomes rationalism, desiring becomes volitionalism, and "bodying" becomes materialism. We dissect the human experience and then try to splice it back together by making causal and idealist claims about some isolated source.

And in turning specifically to the Confucian notion of "good" (*shan* 善), rather than referencing some antecedent, generic "virtue," it actually means primarily "moral growth" achieved through effective communication and a critical self-awareness in one's roles and relations. It is not some qualitatively superior action or a character trait derived from

---

3. John Dewey to Thomas Davidson, in *The Correspondence of John Dewey, 1871–2007* (Charlottesville, VA: IntelLex), Past Masters Database, vol. 1, 1871–1918, 1891.03.14 (00453), http://www.humanities.com/collections/132#:~:text=List%20of%20Contents,Carbondale%2C%20is%20the%20electronic%20editor.

some prior and higher virtue of "goodness" that inheres "in" a person, or some general principle of "goodness" that informs and supervenes on an action as it is "done" by a person. Indeed, as the shared and efficacious life path one is walking together with others (*zhishan zhi dao* 至善之道), *shan* is most concretely imputed to the narrative rather than to the person as it contrasts with the paths of those whose narratives are less so. "Good" is in the first instance "good with," "good to," "good in," "good for," "good at," and then only abstractly and in summary "good." "Good" in this sense of moral growth begins from discursive activities within the continuing narrative and only then can serve as a description of a person or action. *Shan* is the gregarious activity of growing our relations and making them "meaningful" by "relating" to each other and communicating effectively. This discursive source of *shan* is made evident in the graph as it is found on the bronzes and in the small seal script *[ixx]* where it is written with at least two and occasionally three "speech" radicals (*yan* 言), prompting philosopher-philologist Kwan Tze-wan 關子尹 to suggest the following:

> This kind of repetition of the speech radical might reflect the fact that when the ancients talked about *shan* they were not referring to "good" in itself, but "good" as it obtains in the relations among people. Thus, putting the auspicious sheep and multiple speech components together gives us the meaning of two persons speaking face-to-face with warmth and affection.[4]

Of course, the identities of persons are certainly grounded in their thick native beginnings within the environing relationships of family and community. As a received and thus retrospective inheritance integral to who they are, a person's native endowment needs to be both nurtured and protected from loss or injury. And the conduct of such persons is certainly guided by the normative generalizations that a cultural tradition has best remembered in its customs and institutions. But such identities and the realization of their highest aspirations only emerge prospectively in the process of these initial relationships achieving thick resolution as they are cultivated, grown, and consummated over their particular lifetimes and as the normative generalizations are continually being retheorized to

---

4. Kwan, "Database," 善夫吉父鬲 (西周晚期) CHANT 704. 凡此種種, 可能反映古代談《善》都不指獨善, 而指人際關係中的善, 故羊、詰合起來意會二人好言相向(關子尹)。

refine its practices. The potential of persons, far from being an antecedent given, in fact emerges most significantly in the always transactional events that in sum constitute lives lived in the world.

Again, the "potential" for becoming human is not a causal "beginning" or teleological "end": it is not an inborn, essential potential exclusive of context and family relations, nor is it a potential that is actualized as the ineluctable process of growth toward some predetermined ideal. To begin with, in this Chinese natural cosmology, there are no such deracinated, individual persons who could be described as living outside the context of family relations. Persons do not live their lives inside their skins; they exist only in their associations. And since persons in their nested narratives within narratives are constituted by these evolving, eventful relations, the "potential" of persons and their achieved identities in fact emerge pari passu from the specific contingent transactions of their lives. Thus, the best sense we can make of "potential" here is that it certainly has a retrospective reference to native conditions within an evolving narrative. But rather than being understood as wholly antecedent as a set of given defining factors, such potential is most significantly prospective and contingent, evolving and compounding within the ever-changing ebb and flow of circumstances. Rather than being generic or universal, such potential is unique to the career of this specific self-aware and relational person. And rather than existing simply as an inherent and defining endowment, the full measure of such potential can only be known post hoc after the unfolding of the particular narrative—a shared narrative that usually continues long beyond the putative demise of specific persons.[5]

In our own contemporary world, where variations on a foundational "individualism" have become an ideology without any seemingly robust alternatives, it behooves us to ask whether the vocabulary cluster that gives expression to our own default, commonsense assumptions about the human experience and the discrete human "beings" that populate

---

5. For Dewey, too, "Potentialities cannot be known till after the interactions have occurred. There are at a given time unactualized potentialities in an individual because and in as far as there are in existence other things with which it has not as yet interacted." See *Later Works*, 14:109. Lincoln is not Lincoln independent of the circumstances of history, nor are the circumstances of history the making of Lincoln. Indeed, Lincoln is a collaboration between person and circumstances expressed as thick habits of conduct. "The idea that potentialities are inherent and fixed by relation to a predetermined end was a product of a highly restricted state of technology." See *Later Works*, 14:110.

it makes sense within the Confucian project of human "becomings." Indeed, the Confucian conception of persons as "human becomings" was developed within the natural process cosmology that has served this alternative tradition as the context for such personal growth. And within this holographic process cosmology, our familiar dualistic understandings of concepts closely related to this notion of "potential" such as "root," "cause," "source," and "human nature" have to be reconsidered. As Joseph Needham has observed, this Chinese process cosmology "has its own causality and its own logic."[6] In this chapter, therefore, we will turn specifically to the concept of "human nature" as one of these allusions to an antecedent "being" conventionally ascribed to the Confucian tradition. We will look at how this concept must be revised in narrative terms to be consistent with the assumptions that ground this alternative cosmological context.

A Prelude: A Confucian Conception of Human Culture

Metaphors matter. George Lakoff and Mark Johnson have famously argued that cultural metaphors not only make our thoughts more vivid and interesting, but they actually structure the perceptions and understandings of events as they emerge in our experience.[7] And of course, it is a commonplace that different cultures in different times and places appeal to different cultural metaphors.

But taking one step back, we must first ask the following questions: What do different cultural traditions actually mean by "culture" in its relation to "nature" as this familiar distinction itself is grounded in their alternative "cultural" metaphors? That is, what is the perceived relationship between culture and nature, between the artificial and the natural, and between what is cultivated through human intervention and what purportedly grows of its own accord? And more specifically in reference to persons, how has the relationship between human nature and human culture been understood in different traditions? Resisting the tendency to overwrite this Confucian tradition with assumptions not its own, we

---

6. Joseph Needham, *History of Scientific Thought*, vol. 2, *Science and Civilisation in China* (Cambridge: Cambridge University Press, 1956), 280.

7. George Lakoff and Mark Johnson, *Metaphors We Live By* (Chicago: University of Chicago Press, 1980).

must allow that Confucian conjectures about "human nature" grounded in its own cultural metaphors are going to be immediately relevant to how the conception of persons has been theorized and understood.

Thus, as a prelude to exploring the dominant Confucian conceptions of "human nature," I want to begin by exploring how we now use the term "culture" within the Western academy and how the use of this term differs significantly from the Confucian tradition. Such a reflection on "culture" will serve us in anticipating the influence our own assumptions might have on our commonsense understanding of the terms "nature" and "human nature" and on the perceived relationship that obtains between them. That is to say, it might behoove us to reflect carefully on the metaphorical associations surrounding the occupations of agriculture, horticulture, and husbanding as they are implicated in our term "culture" and the teleological assumptions that attend this idea as its use has evolved within our own narrative. More specifically, such teleological assumptions are wont to persuade us uncritically that the "cultivation" of human "culture" by analogy with horticulture and the rearing of stock has to do with conserving, nurturing, and actualizing a specific set of inborn potentialities that are driven by a given goal (*telos*) or inherent design (*eidos*). As our common sense would have it, seed corn is cultivated to become cornfields, and nursing calves are raised to become cows. Clearly, seed corn cannot sprout pigs nor can piglets be raised to become fields of wheat.[8] And because we tend to default to these same generic assumptions when we think about human beings and the actualization of their human nature, we stand in danger of inadvertently projecting just such a teleological understanding of both culture and human nature onto the Confucian tradition. In fact, as I will argue, the Confucian tradition appeals to a much more open-ended and particularistic metaphor for culture and for human nature, too, and to a much different synergistic relationship between these two terms. And for the Confucian tradition, it is an aesthetic rather than a horticultural metaphor behind both the art of becoming human and the production of culture that is integral to this process.

---

8. Of course, this might not be quite so clearly the case if we resist our own teleological assumptions to consider the fact that maize, cracked corn, corn cobs, and husks can also be an integral part of good pig feed and that early in the spring growing season, a deep-pit swine finishing manure can serve as an ideal top-dress fertilizer for the wheat fields.

In his *Keywords: A Vocabulary of Culture and Society*, Raymond Williams has famously described "culture" as one of the two or three most complicated terms in the English language.[9] He attributes this complexity in part to the relative recency with which the meaning of "culture" has been metaphorically extended from its original sense of the physical processes of nurturing and cultivation—that is, the perhaps mundane yet vital practices of agriculture that include both horticulture and husbandry—to point toward a characteristic mode of human material, intellectual, spiritual, and aesthetic development. Just as our common sense would dictate, we tend to see these horticultural and husbanding practices as teleologically motivated in bringing to fruition those characteristic forms inherent in the objects of our cultivation, where human intervention serves as a source of discipline and control and as an external facilitation. The assumption is that the plant or animal will flourish if it is protected, unimpeded, and properly nourished.

According to Williams, it was only in the eighteenth century that "culture" was first used consistently to denote the entire "way of life" of a people. And it was only in the late nineteenth and early twentieth centuries that culture was identified with specific civilization-distinguishing patterns of practices and values. In this latter case, it was used in the context of theories of progressive "social evolution" as a metric that sets apart and divides societies, making one person or class more cultured than another and one "culture" more advanced than another. Contemporary vestiges of this sense of contest can be found not only in the tension (and sometimes hostility) between high art (culture) and popular entertainment but also in the contemporary media's frequent characterization of multicultural tensions in the curricula of our educational institutions as "culture wars."

As in Europe, there was no single term in the languages of the premodern Sinitic cultures—Chinese, Japanese, Korean, or Vietnamese—that had a conceptual reach comparable to that of our modern, now extended uses of the word "culture." But the term that emerged in the nineteenth century throughout this geographical region as an equivalency to translate and appropriate this modern Western concept differs markedly in its metaphorical implications from those assumed with the English word "culture." The languages of these traditionally agrarian Asian

---

9. Raymond Williams, *Keywords: A Vocabulary of Culture and Society* (New York: Oxford University Press, 1976).

societies abound with terms that like "culture" are rooted in instrumental physical processes of cultivation and nourishing: for example, *yang* 養 (providing for, keeping, growing), *xu/chu* 畜 (raising domestic animals), *pei* 培 (cultivating, training), *xiu* 修 (cultivating, trimming, pruning), *yu* 育 (rearing, raising, bringing up), *zai* 栽 (planting and growing), and so many more. But in constructing an erstwhile equivalency, such agricultural terms are bypassed as points of metaphorical departure in favor of 文化 (*wenhua*), a compound expression that combines the two characters for (1) the "transforming" (*hua* 化) of the human experience effected by (2) "the inscribing and embellishing processes undertaken by literary, civil, and artistic traditions" (*wen* 文). This modern expression *wenhua* 文化, created to synchronize Chinese with Western modernity's word "culture," is an allusion to the *Book of Changes*, which states: "Through observing carefully the heavenly patterns we can gain insight into the changing seasons; through observing carefully the embellishments made by human beings (*wen*), we can transform (*hua*) the world."[10] In a word, *wenhua* is the civilization and aestheticization of the human experience in all of its parts. Human pedagogy is understood as emerging from close attention to the changing patterns and designs of the world around us and then correlating these images critically with the establishment of those human technologies and institutions needed to optimally regulate the human experience.

Having metaphorically rooted "culture" in the agricultural practices of plant and animal domestication invites us to see cultural norms as having a transcendent disciplinary force with respect to what is being "cultured," thereby enabling us to regulate its spontaneous growth. *Wen* by contrast was understood (with significant political implications) as the disclosing processes of civilization: *collaborating* with nature's beauty; *elaborating* upon it; *elevating* it; and through a critical self-awareness, *achieving* a decidedly aesthetic if not spiritual product. In this contrast between culture driven by teleology and culture as *wenhua*, we have an important distinction between a tendency to understand culture in terms of rationalized closure rather than aesthetic disclosure, a tendency that might assume a retrospective necessity (what is predetermined and then actualized), as opposed to a prospective possibility (what is imagined and then realized).

As demonstrated by the provenance of the expression *wenhua* in texts dating to the Han dynasty (202 BCE–220 CE), this term is an

---

10. 《周易. 賁. 彖》:「觀乎天文, 以察時變; 觀乎人文, 以化成天下」

ancient one. Pronounced *bunka*, the modern Japanese *kanji* term meaning "culture" is derived from classical Chinese use of *wenhua* that first appears explicitly as early as the court bibliographer Liu Xiang's 劉向 (77–6 BCE) *Garden of Stories* (*Shuoyuan* 說苑). In this text we read that "it is only when our civilizing efforts (*wenhua*) fail to bring the people up to the appropriate standards that punishments are to be imposed."[11] And by at least the fifth century CE, Chinese literary theorists such as Liu Xie 劉勰 (465?–522?) associated human *wen* practices explicitly with the self-arising (*ziran* 自然) and ceaselessly creative dynamics (*shengsheng buxi* 生生不息) at the intersection of the human and natural worlds (*dao* 道). This association affirmed that nature and nurture, far from being in opposition, together constitute a coevolving, contrapuntal process at the heart of realizing a symbiotic and mutually entailing natural and societal harmony.

This disparity between European and Asian languages in the cultural metaphors in which the term "culture" itself is embedded is certainly related to an indelibly skewed understanding of "creativity" in the Abrahamic traditions: teleologically informed design in the former case and a fundamentally open-ended, aesthetic process in the latter. In the evolution of our common sense, ex nihilo creativity ("creativity from nothing") properly belongs to a self-sufficient Creator God.[12] And when such ex nihilo creativity is usurped and then exercised by the idiosyncratic and audacious human genius—by eccentrics such as Goethe's Faust, Shelley's Frankenstein, Milton's Satan, and Nietzsche's Übermensch, for example—it becomes dark, dangerous, and deliciously depraved: a promethean offense against God's natural and moral order. We might be inclined (although with our children at a safe distance) to admire the rakish charms of someone deemed "morally creative." Scientists deemed creative in their experiments might find it hard to win grants from the National Science Foundation. We might be attracted (although with enormous caution) by the offer of "creative financial instruments." And we might find ourselves curious about (although embarrassed by) the bizarre ritual performances of "new" religions. Even in our contemporary times of radical innovation and entrepreneurship, our commonsense understanding of the core human occupations of morality, science, economics, and religion still have

---

11. 文化不改，然後加誅。

12. As *Psalms* 24.1 insists: "The earth is the Lord's and the fulness thereof, It is He that has made us and not we ourselves."

a strong teleological cast that seems resistant to the idea of "creativity." Instead, this term "creativity" usually prompts an association with more marginalized aesthetic interests such as the creative arts and the writing of entertaining "fiction."

By contrast, we find that in the Confucian worldview as evidenced in Confucian role ethics, singular value is invested in the quality of the moral imagination, and the critical self-awareness that would exercise it, needed to inspire real artistry in our moral lives. Indeed, as we have seen in our previous close readings, the Confucian project as defined in the cosmology of the core canonical texts such as the *Book of Changes* (*Yijing*) and *Focusing the Familiar* (*Zhongyong*) requires of human beings in their "the heartminding of the cosmos" (*tiandizhixin* 天地之心) nothing less than both the imagination and the deliberate refinement needed to stand together with the heavens and the earth as cocreators of the cosmos.

Reflecting further on the genealogy of *wen*, dating back more than a millennium earlier than the passage previously cited from the Han dynasty *Garden of Stories*, *wen* has consistently been contrasted explicitly with the coercive, destructive, and dehumanizing use of martial force (*wu* 武) as it arises in the human experience. *Wen* so understood, in a sharp departure from our contemporary use of "culture wars" as a metaphor for cultural tensions, is indeed the antithesis of war in all of its parts. *Wen* denotes the expansively civil and civilizing dimension of the lettered class of each succeeding generation as they respond to the pressing issues of their day. *Wen* is the refinement of the human experience that emerges when the life of a community is guided by an aesthetically and critically enriching counterpoint between persistent canonical texts and the interlinear commentaries that are continuously being written on them. Martial force is regarded even in the militarist *Sunzi: The Art of War* literature as a sometimes necessary but always losing proposition that should only be considered as a last resort (*budeyi* 不得已). This deprecatory attitude contrasts sharply with how the use of force is often celebrated as a source of glory and honor in classical Greek and Roman cultures, respectively.

In sum, the conceptual genealogy of the Chinese term *wenhua* implies that culture emerges through an *intrinsic* relationship between continuity and change (*biantong* 變通), a symbiotic relationship described at great length in the *Book of Changes* between a determinate and enduring tradition and the ambient forces of transformation as we continue to theorize and thereby elevate our practices. Cultural conservation and prospective change, far from opposing each other, are complementary and mutually enhancing. As I will argue, it is this complementary, symbiotic, and synergetic dynamic between persons and world that has immediate relevance for the Confucian notion of *xing* 性, a term in this case perhaps better rendered as the realizing of our "human propensities" rather than "human nature." In his evolving interpretation of the *Mencius*, Angus Graham explicitly challenges and sets aside the idea that *xing* references some "transcendent origin" or some "transcendent end" as familiar and yet unfortunate teleological misreadings of this seminal text.[13] Indeed, following Graham, I will argue that *xing* is much more than simply a retrospective, antecedent conception of "human nature" as is commonly assumed: it is importantly prospective as the realizing of human propensities and requires of us deliberate elaboration and refinement in the continuing aestheticizing of the human experience.

The "Ontological" and "Developmental" Understandings of the Human "Being"

Historically, Mencius's concerted attempt to formulate the conditions required to achieve the consummate human experience has not been well served by his commentators and interpreters. Mencius's nemesis, Xunzi, living a generation or two after Mencius and following his own agenda, is perhaps the earliest philosopher remembered by history to give Mencius's notion of *xing*, conventionally translated as "human nature," a skewed, naturalistic reading. Indeed, such a naturalistic conception of *xing* as "what you are born with makes you good" is not only incongruent with Mencius's own definition but is one that he himself flatly rejects. As previously mentioned, one aspect of Xunzi's historical importance that has become a signature of the Confucian tradition itself is Xunzi's willing appropriation and reinterpretation of those thinkers who would compete with him. In his time, such adversaries were the Mohists, the School of Names, the Militarists, as well as rival Confucians such as Mencius. Xunzi draws upon these eclectic resources to produce a hybrid and fortified Confucianism that through this process of expansion and renewal emerges during the Han dynasty several centuries after his death to become the state doctrine. This doctrine then persists as a political orthodoxy for some two millennia thereafter.

---

13. Rosemont, *Chinese Texts and Philosophical Contexts*, 287.

Xunzi, following Confucius in arguing for the assiduous effort it requires to achieve moral competency, caricatures Mencius's position on *xing* as an understanding of human morality that is otherwise:

> Mencius says that "since human beings can be educated, their *xing* is good." I would argue that this is not so. Mencius in his lack of understanding of the human *xing*, is unable to discern the distinction between *xing* itself and deliberate activity (*wei* 偽). Speaking generally, *xing* is what is given by nature; it can neither be learned nor acquired. Moral dispositions such as aspiring to propriety in our roles and relations (*li* 禮) and seeking what is optimally appropriate in any situation (*yi* 義) are the products of the sages, and hence are something that can be learned and applied, acquired and mastered. What cannot be learned and cannot be acquired but is simply inherent in persons is what is called *xing*.[14]

In criticizing Mencius, Xunzi begins by assuming that his own understanding of *xing* as being an unlearned "given" is incontrovertibly what *xing* actually means. Such being the case, according to Xunzi's logic, when Mencius says *xing* enables us to be good, Mencius is at the same time asserting that being good is unlearned and does not require deliberate effort. Being good is as easy as just being and acting human. Of course, this naturalistic interpretation of *xing* that Xunzi is imputing to Mencius—what you are born with makes you good—is explicitly rejected by Mencius as a reductio ad absurdum when it is proposed in another context by Mencius's contemporary, Master Gao:

> Master Gao asserted: "It is what you are born with (*sheng* 生) that is meant by *xing* 性."

---

14. *Xunzi*, 23: 孟子曰:「人之學者, 其性善。」曰: 是不然。是不及知人之性, 而不察乎人之性偽之分者也。凡性者, 天之就也, 不可學, 不可事。禮義者, 聖人之所生也, 人之所學而能, 所事而成者也。不可學, 不可事, 而在人者, 謂之性 。Although Xunzi is making a distinction between what we are born with and what is deliberately acquired, we must resist translating Xunzi's naturalism into a metaphysical claim that would align Xunzi with the dualistic realism of a Plato or an Aristotle in which some self-same and immutable "form" or *eidos* that is "inherent in persons" separates human beings from their world.

"Is saying that 'what you are born with is what is meant by *xing*' the same thing as saying that 'white' is what is meant by 'white'?" responded Mencius.¹⁵

"Indeed, so it is." replied Master Gao.

"Then is the whiteness of white feathers the same as the whiteness of snow, and the whiteness of snow the same as the whiteness of jade?"

"Yes it is." replied Master Gao.

"Would it follow then that the *xing* of a dog is the same as the *xing* of an ox, and the *xing* of an ox is the same as the *xing* of a human being?"¹⁶

In this passage and elsewhere we find Mencius's emphatic rejection of this tautological naturalism that suggests humans are good because they are good. And yet just such an impoverished teleological interpretation of Mencius that *xing* is an unlearned given that makes us good has not only persisted in the literature after Xunzi but in fact largely prevails among commentators even today. The mantra *xingshan* 性善, understood as "human nature is good," is an interpretation that persists in the contemporary commentary on Mencius, both Western and Chinese alike.

Michael Sandel, in his search for a robust *intra*subjective alternative to a deracinated individualism, pointedly observes that for most Western commentators

> to speak of human nature is often to suggest a classical teleological conception, associated with the notion of a universal human essence, invariant in all times and places.¹⁷

---

15. As D. C. Lau points out, because *sheng* 生 and *xing* 性 are used interchangeably in these early texts and were close in pronunciation, Mencius is able to impute a tautology to Master Gao: "A is A." This tautology allows Mencius to draw the reductio analogy that just as "white is white," the *xing* of one thing is the same as another. See D. C. Lau, *Mencius* (Hong Kong: Chinese University Press, 1984), 225.

16. 6A3: 告子曰:「生之謂性。」孟子曰:「生之謂性也, 猶白之謂白與?」曰:「然。」「白羽之白也, 猶白雪之白; 白雪之白, 猶白玉之白與?」曰:「然。」「然則犬之性, 猶牛之性; 牛之性, 猶人之性與?」

17. Sandel, *Liberalism*, 50.

Indeed, the uncritical assumption for many if not most commentators is that for Mencius, *xing* references a universal, inborn, fixed, self-sufficient endowment in all human beings that programs us naturally to be moral in what we do.

Lee Yearley's comparison of Mencius with Thomas Aquinas questions this assumption and looks to refine this notion of a given human nature by making an important distinction between an ontological or discovery model of *xing*—one that he would reject as a familiar yet mistaken interpretation of both Mencius and Aquinas—and a developmental or biological model that he would endorse as the better reading of them both. Of the former ontological or discovery model, Yearley says the following:

> In a discovery model . . . human nature exists as a permanent set of dispositions that are obscured but that can be contacted or discovered. People do not cultivate inchoate capacities. Rather they discover a hidden ontological reality that defines them. The discovery model reflects, then, ontological rather than biological notions. An ontological reality, the true self, always is present no matter what specific humans, particular instances of it, are or do.[18]

Yearley argues that this conception of human nature as an ontological given is a misreading of both Mencius and Aquinas. Instead, he advocates for the developmental or biological understanding described as follows:

> What can be called a biological framework informs Mencius's ideas on human nature and its characteristic successes and failures. . . . To speak of the nature of something within such a framework is to refer to some innate constitution that manifests itself in patterns of growth and culminates in specifiable forms.[19]

While the developmental model of the Mencian *xing* is certainly more compelling than the discovery model, it is still strongly Aristote-

---

18. Lee Yearley, *Mencius and Aquinas: Theories of Virtue and Conceptions of Courage* (Albany: State University of New York Press, 1990), 60.
19. Yearley, *Mencius and Aquinas*, 58–59.

lian in its teleological understanding of human potential as the innate and self-defining "capacities humans possess" that are then redundantly manifested and actualized in determining who we will become.[20] One association that recommends this developmental model to Yearley and others is Mencius's frequent appeal to a horticultural analogy in which, for example, seeds of barley if uninjured and nurtured will achieve the characteristic form of barley.[21]

Indeed, in the *Mencius* and other canonical Confucian texts, the appeal to agricultural metaphors is often construed as reinforcing the teleological idea that plants and animals, in growing to become what they essentially are, are simply actualizing the potential inherent in their "seed" or "root." But is such classical Greek teleology and idealism also integral to early Chinese cosmology? If not, or at least if not in the same degree, what alternatively might make these horticulture and husbanding analogies appropriate for capturing the growth of relationally constituted "human becomings" is the acute dependence in farming and the raising of livestock on a contrived environment and the concentrated human imagination and effort needed to succeed in such an enterprise. In the *Book of Changes* and elsewhere, the initiation of these technologies is associated with the legendary sage Shen Nong 神農 and other cultural avatars as part of the continuing civilization of the human experience. Most seeds, far from becoming what they "are," become anything and everything else without sustained, radical, and deliberate human intervention. While we must allow that an acorn does not usually become a chicken, we must also allow that only one in a million acorns actually becomes an oak tree. And the million-minus-one acorns left over in fact become something else. Indeed, the "seed" of anything and what it will become is fundamentally a transactional process. The "seed" might have the initial genetic conditions from which something "begins," but what it becomes is the internalization of the possibilities made available through whatever intensive cultivation there might be, along with the many contingencies in the other circumstances that attend its growth. The point here is that on reflection, even in agriculture, context really matters.

---

20. Yearley, *Mencius and Aquinas*, 60.
21. Yearley, *Mencius and Aquinas*, 59.

Graham's Initial Developmental Understanding of the Mencian *Xing*

As we have seen, Graham has lamented that later interpreters of Mencius continue to ascribe to him a doctrine of "human nature" (*xing* 性) that has a "transcendent origin" and a "transcendent end." In this present discussion, "we" (because I must include my collaborators David Hall and Henry Rosemont as having embraced this same effort) want to join cause with our teacher, colleague, and old friend Angus Graham to save Mencius from the now all-too-familiar essentialist misreadings of *xing*—that is, from both the "discovery" and the perhaps more interesting but still stunted "developmental" model of *xing* as well. We will argue that Graham's interpretation of the *Mencius* evolved over time to arrive at a third position that we will call a "narrative" interpretation of *xing*. In this narrative understanding of *xing*, as is the case in the traditional Confucian understanding of "culture," we will find that person and world evolve together in a symbiotic, dynamic, and contrapuntal relationship. The identities of persons are certainly grounded in the native conditions of family and community, and these environing relationships need to be both nurtured and protected from loss or injury. But such increasingly complex identities as profoundly unique aesthetic and spiritual accomplishments only emerge in the process of these relationships achieving thick resolution as they are cultivated, grown, and articulated over their lifetimes. Their distinctive and unique potential as persons, far from being a given, in fact emerges pari passu in the always transactional events that in sum constitute lives lived in the world.

In our own times in which individualism has become an ideology with a seeming monopoly on intellectual consciousness, we must question whether our own default commonsense assumptions about the *individual* human "being" are consistent with the Mencian project as it was situated and developed within the natural *qi* cosmology that serves this tradition as the context for such personal growth. Is a narrative understanding of person not in fact a better reading of this ancient Confucian philosopher? As we will see, Graham asked and over time answered this question for himself, first setting aside his own commonsense assumptions and then formulating an understanding of person that is consistent with the Confucian interpretive context.

But Graham did not come to his narrative understanding of the Mencian *xing* quickly or easily. Early on he had endorsed the developmental model of *xing* for Mencius by associating it quite explicitly with an Aristotelian understanding of a given human potential and the subsequent process of actualization this potential undergoes. Graham's earliest sustained foray into exploring the Mencian notion of *xing* was in his 1967 essay "The Background of the Mencian Theory of Human Nature," in which he allows that we can best understand Mencius by acknowledging the fact that

> Aristotle was pursuing a similar line of thought with the much greater logical rigour of the Greeks. Indeed it is difficult to write of *hsing* [*xing*] in English without resorting to the Aristotelian terminology of "potentiality" and "actualization," and the former word has several times slipped into the present study.²²

Graham, appealing to *Focusing the Familiar* (*Zhongyong*) for his textual proof to support this essentialist, Aristotelian reading of Mencius, argues in this early essay that *xing* denotes the self-sufficient and self-completing nature of things:

> Each thing has its nature, and "becomes complete" (成 *ch'eng* [*cheng*]/*DIENG) by fulfilling the capacities of its nature. In man this state of maturity, by which we act wholeheartedly according to our nature and become in the full sense men, is 誠 *ch'eng* [*cheng*]/*DIENG "wholeness, integrity," defined in *Chung Yung* [*Zhongyong*] by "Integrity is self-completion" (誠者自成也).²³

The passage Graham is citing here, using his translation of *cheng* 誠 as "integrity," states:

---

22. A. C. Graham, *Studies in Chinese Philosophy and Philosophical Literature* (Albany: State University of New York Press, 1990), 55. This collection of essays was first published in 1986 by the Institute of East Asian Philosophies, National University of Singapore. Importantly, the specific essay included in this anthology, "The Background of the Mencian Theory of Human Nature," was published much earlier in *Tsing Hua Journal of Chinese Studies* 6.1–2 (1967).

23. Graham, *Studies in Chinese Philosophy*, 55.

> Integrity (*cheng* 誠) is self-completing just as *dao* is self-directing. Such integrity is the beginning and end of things, and without such integrity there would be nothing.[24]

Of course were Graham to have cited this same *Focusing the Familiar* passage in its entirety, he would have had to admit that this text, far from corroborating his claim that things with their integrity are "self-completing," is in fact making precisely the opposite point: *cheng* 誠 cannot and *does not* mean merely "self-completion" in the exclusive sense being suggested here by Graham. As the text goes on to state rather clearly:

> But *cheng* 誠 is *NOT* simply the self-consummating of one's own person; it is what consummates everything. Completing oneself is achieving virtuosity in one's roles and relations (*ren* 仁); completing all things is advancing wisdom in the world (*zhi* 知). Such is the virtuosity achieved in one's natural propensities and the way-making that integrates what is more internal and what is more external. Thus, when and wherever one applies this virtuosity, it is fitting.[25]

If we want to translate *cheng* 誠 as "integrity" as Graham chooses to do here, we might observe that in Aristotle's substance ontology, the integrity of persons—the immutable, reduplicated *eidos* that is immanent in matter as form and that directs the teleological structure of individual existents—guarantees self-actualization through the realization of a given set of real capacities and their potential to produce a human "being." But if we respect the holography of the Chinese process cosmology that

---

24. *Zhongyong* 25: 誠者自成也，而道自道也，誠者物之終始，不誠無物。 This *Focusing the Familiar* passage can be read in two different ways. It could be that the phrase Graham is appealing to here in making his case for an essentialist reading of *xing* is merely rhetorical and thus flatly contradicted by what follows. Or it could be that the "self" in the expression "self-completing" (*zicheng* 自成) in this opening line is being used in the inclusive, symbiotic sense in which "self" and "other" are together "self-completing." Given the parallel between *cheng* and the holistic notion of *dao* described as "self-directing" in this opening line, a notion that clearly precludes any exclusive "other," I would think that the inclusive reading of "self-" (*zi*) in the first line makes better sense of the passage.

25. *Zhongyong* 25: 誠者非自成己而已也，所以成物也。成己，仁也；成物，知也。性之德也，合外內之道也，故時措之宜也。

Focusing the Familiar has as its interpretive context, such "integrity," far from being a self-sufficient given, would also have to include the entire process of such persons pursuing full integration within their intractable and indeed boundless social, cultural, and natural environments. That is, the potential of persons would emerge within the transactions and possibilities as they unfold within their continuing narratives. Such persons and their environing others would thus be "aspectual" in the cocreative process of becoming-one-together.

The point of *Focusing the Familiar* in the passage cited here is to dispute any suggestion that persons can be "self-completing" in some isolated and exclusive sense. It quite specifically defines the virtuosity of *xing* itself as what coordinates the external and the internal in allowing all things to find their fit and to thus coalesce productively with each other as we advance wisdom in the world. Far from defining *cheng* 誠 as "self-completion" in some exclusive sense of "self," the text argues that such personal cultivation is invariably a collaborative attempt to optimize the possibilities available at the vital intersection between purposeful persons and their environing conditions. *Cheng* gives human beings the capacity to both shape their world and to respond efficaciously to the pressures of this same world as it shapes them. As we have previously seen in exploring the dynamic of an optimizing harmony (*he* 和), *Focusing the Familiar* provides a clear account of how it would interpret this responsive collaboration between persons and world to be the ground of all cosmic flourishing.

Graham's Evolving Narrative Understanding of *Xing*

But Graham in his later writings becomes dissatisfied with and indeed repudiates his earlier essentialist "developmental" reading of *xing*. Reflecting on the turn that has brought him to a more situated and evolutionary understanding of *xing*, Graham offers us a novel, revisionist interpretation that begins from citing and disputing the interpretation of *xing* posited by Arthur Waley, his predecessor among London's most famous Sinologists:

Waley says that "*hsing* [*xing*] (nature) meant in ordinary parlance the qualities a thing has to start with,"[26] and I have

---

26. Arthur Waley, *Three Ways of Thought in Ancient China* (Stanford, CA: Stanford University Press, 1939), 205.

myself in previous publications translated the definition 生之謂性 by "Inborn is what is meant by 'nature.'" Yet early Chinese thinkers who discuss *hsing* [*xing*] seldom seem to be thinking of fixed qualities going back to a thing's origin . . . ; rather they are concerned with developments which are spontaneous but realize their own potentialities only if uninjured and adequately nourished. Mencius in particular seems never to be looking back towards birth, always forward to the maturation of a continuing growth.[27]

We have seen that Graham here clearly wants to distinguish himself from any discovery model of *xing* in introducing language that might on first reading seem to favor the developmental alternative. But to understand his interpretation more clearly, such a prospective, processual, and developmental interpretation of the maturation of an "uninjured and adequately nourished" *xing* needs to be located within Graham's understanding of early Chinese process cosmology more broadly.

For Graham, proper attention to the interdependence and irreducibly contextual nature of all things will enable us to disambiguate some of the key philosophical vocabulary of classical Chinese philosophy such as *tian* 天 and *dao* 道. We do this by identifying equivocations that emerge when we elide the distinction between cosmological presuppositions indigenous to the classical Chinese worldview with our more familiar classical Greek ontological assumptions. On Graham's reading:

> In the Chinese cosmos all things are interdependent, without transcendent principles by which to explain them or a transcendent origin from which they derive. . . . A novelty in this position which greatly impresses me is that it exposes a preconception of Western interpreters that such concepts as *Tian* "Heaven" and *Dao* "Way" must have the transcendence of our own ultimate principles; it is hard for us to grasp that even the Way is interdependent with man.[28]

Graham cautions us about such frequent equivocations, using as his specific example the tendency commentators who, in appealing to the

---

27. Rosemont, *Chinese Texts and Philosophical Contexts*, 287.
28. Rosemont, *Chinese Texts and Philosophical Contexts*, 287.

language of "human nature," had to treat the Mencian *xing* as referencing some "transcendent origin," which for Mencius "would also be a transcendent end."[29] Rejecting the relevance for Mencius of an essentializing Greek idealism and the radical teleology that follows from it, Graham would locate his notion of *xing* within the generic features of an early Chinese process or "event" ontology in which putative "things" and their contexts are interdependent and thus inseparable. What it means to become human, far from referencing an antecedent given that takes us back to our origins (*eidos*) or forward to some given, predetermined end (*telos*), is in fact a provisional and emergent process within the context of an evolving cosmic order. It is just such a worldview that I and my collaborators following Marcel Granet, Tang Junyi, Joseph Needham, and Graham himself have argued for at length as the most appropriate interpretive context for understanding classical Confucianism.[30]

What is at stake here is the deliberate Mencian answer to perhaps our most fundamental philosophical question: what does it mean to become fully human? Further, how do we explain the birth, life, and growth of the human "being"? Do we appeal to reduplicative causal accounts (the infant is a ready-made adult), by teleological accounts (the infant is simply preliminary to the existing ideal)? Or do we posit the notion of human "becomings" that appeals to a contextual, narrative account available to us through a phenomenology of reflective and purposeful personal action? How do we define what it means to be a human "being"? Do we offer speculative assumptions about innate, isolatable causes that locate persons outside of the roles and relations in which they live their lives? Or alternatively, do we explain their having "become" human by taking full account of the native conditions and context within in which persons are inextricably embedded and then assaying the full accretion of consequent and deliberate action as their life stories unfold?

We have seen that for Graham, *xing* as a dynamic gerundive concept references an erstwhile "developmental" process that is spontaneous

---

29. Rosemont, *Chinese Texts and Philosophical Contexts*, 287.

30. See, for example, David L. Hall and Roger T. Ames, *Thinking from the Han: Self, Truth, and Transcendence in Chinese and Western Culture* (Albany: State University of New York Press, 1998), 23–78; and Roger T. Ames and Henry Rosemont Jr., *The Analects of Confucius: A Philosophical Translation* (New York: Ballantine, 1998), 20–45. See also Roger T. Ames, *Confucian Role Ethics: A Vocabulary* (Honolulu: University of Hawai'i Press, 2011), esp. chapter 2, "An Interpretive Context for Understanding Confucianism."

and realizes its own potentialities when it is nourished and unimpeded. But here we see that Graham wants to damp down any of our familiar assumptions about the antecedent beginnings and endings we associate with such a developmental model. And as we have seen, Graham's understanding of early Confucian cosmology assumes a doctrine of internal relations constitutive of events rather than external relations that merely conjoin discrete and independent things. Hence, his interpretation of "their own potentialities" would make such potentialities contextual, historicist, particularistic, and genealogical. Indeed, Graham's clarification of what kind of "relation" is relevant to this Chinese cosmology introduces precisely this distinction between the concrete patterns of relations that constitute things and those secondary relations abstracted from otherwise independent things:

> As for "relationships," relation is no doubt an indispensable concept in exposition of Chinese thought, which generally impresses a Western as more concerned with the relations between things than with their qualities; but the concern is with concrete patterns rather than relations abstracted from them.[31]

Again, Graham has already counseled us to acknowledge some fundamental equivocations commentators must avoid in their understandings of the terms available for theorizing classical Chinese cosmology. Early Chinese concepts, says Graham, often "tend to be more dynamic than their closest Western equivalents, and that English translation freezes them into immobility."[32] It is only over the past century, with the insights of contemporaries such as Ludwig Wittgenstein and more recently George Lakoff and Mark Johnson, that we have called into question the assumption that concepts can serve us as a univocal currency to guarantee the cogency of our arguments. Indeed, we have now largely abandoned the expectation that concepts can be a source of univocity, and along with it, certainty. Instead, given the perceived inseparability of language and action in our "language games," we have come to understand language as being irreducibly interdependent with an always evolving practical context that at best offers us "family resemblances" among the categories we

---

31. Graham, "Replies," 288–289.
32. Graham, *Studies in Chinese Philosophy*, 8.

might appeal to in our attempts to best theorize our experience. Graham makes the following remarks on this recent transition:

> We are losing the faith, except in logic and mathematics, that a concept can be established by precise definitions which free the word from the analogies which guide its ordinary usage.[33]

In our search for cultural equivalencies in comparative philosophy, we might speculate that our earlier essentialist assumptions about the univocal nature of concepts themselves might have arisen from a substance ontology that naturalizes form and stasis and thus favors the more stable, decontextualizing noun as making available to us the unchanging object of knowledge. Such assumptions contrast rather clearly with any attempt to theorize a dynamic process cosmology that is committed to the inseparability of a rhythmic, contrapuntal forming and functioning (*tiyong* 體用) and thus favors the contextualizing gerund (or verbal noun): not as the object of knowledge per se but as the source from which we can draw the best reconnoitering information required to advance most expeditiously on our prospective journey.

Indeed, as we have seen, Graham's narrative conception of *xing* locates this key term as always contextualized within a process cosmology in which persons and context are mutually shaping, or in Graham's own words, we find "the interdependent becoming integral rather than the realization of an end."[34] Graham abjures the assumed teleological assumptions that would define *xing* in terms of antecedent design or predetermined end and instead invokes the more important role of deliberate, prospective action. In so doing, Graham offers us an understanding of *xing* as a vital and responsive conatus that in its narrative growth is self-directing and aware; yet it is also collaborative in shaping and being shaped by its environments. In Graham's own words:

> Still riding my own hobby-horse, might one distinguish *xin* "heart" and *xing* "nature" as the centres of awareness and spontaneity respectively? . . . With the exercise of the heart for thinking, spontaneous inclination shifts away from the

---

33. A. C. Graham, *Disputers of the Tao: Philosophical Argument in Ancient China* (La Salle, IL: Open Court, 1989), 120.
34. Graham, "Replies," 288.

direction in which it is pulled by the mere action of the perceived thing on the senses. . . . In unawareness you know only present inclination; it is by full exertion of the heart to understand the things which act on you that you come to know what Heaven has ordained as the spontaneous preference of your nature in full awareness of them.[35]

Graham's sense of a radically situated and contextualizing center of awareness and the spontaneous growth it directs would be lost if we were to understand *xing* 性 as simply referencing a "natural endowment at birth." In such a retrospective, innatist reading of *xing*, we would be reducing the *sheng* 生 that is constitutive of *xing* 性 to simply "being born" as opposed to its broader meaning of "being born, living, and growing." This extended meaning requires that we include along with a putative "birth" the prospective life and growth of these native conditions within their constitutive relationships.

But to make to make too severe a distinction between "heartminding" (*xin*) as the guiding center of "awareness" and *xing* as the "spontaneity" that is thus guided, we might overlook the fact that *xin* itself is also an integral aspect of the character *xing*; that is, the graph *xing* 性 comprises a combination of *xin* 心 and *sheng* 生, making both the awareness and the spontaneity integral to *xing* itself. Using Graham's own language, if *xin* is a center of "awareness," then *xing* would have to be that center of "awareness" together with the animating "spontaneity," thus making *xing* an animated and evolving center of awareness. *Xing* would seem in sum to reference the vital, intentional, and deliberate unfolding of the life and growth of our native conditions: the human narrative in its wholeness.

For Mencius, at least, *xin* by itself at times refers to the initial native conditions that are captured in the "four inclinations" (*siduan* 四端) formula of the inchoate *xin*. That is, *xin* is our native inclination toward consummate conduct (*ren* 仁), appropriate behavior (*yi* 義), an achieved propriety (*li* 禮), and wisdom (*zhi* 智) as these tendencies are expressed in our roles and relations. The "four inclinations" are the multivalent aspects of *xin* referencing our preliminary and at first inchoate pattern of roles and relations in the ambient family, community, and culture that constitute our focal identity at birth and that are then thickened as our narratives unfold. We will see that it is an appreciation of this

---

35. Graham, "Replies," 290–91.

irreducibly relational and intentional understanding of *xin* together with the vital, generative import of *xing*—what Graham has described as the complementary center of "awareness" and "spontaneity"—that might save us from the common misinterpretations of Mencius.

Familiar Misreadings of the *Mencius* on *Xing*

One familiar misreading of Mencius on *xing* occurs when, on the analogy of default metaphysical conceptions of an essential "human nature," we decontextualize and detemporalize *xin* or "heartminding" and treat such generalized features captured in the expression "four inclinations" (*siduan* 四端) as innate, internal, fixed, independent, and isolatable conditions. As we have seen, far from being some inborn and exclusive "nature" that discrete individuals are defined by, *xin* is the concrete pattern of vital, constitutive relations that serves as a general description of the native inclinations of always unique yet radically situated human becomings. These "inclinations" as currents within an event describe irreducibly familial and social bonds that are integral to relationally constituted persons who at birth are already embedded within their families and communities as still inchoate narratives nested within mature narratives. But *xin* is more than just such "inclinations." As integral to *xing* 性 itself, these inchoate sprouts are then available for the project of further nurturance and growth (*sheng* 生) in the transactions that constitute a life: what the *Mencius* refers to specifically as the process of "making the most of the *xin*" (*jinxin* 盡心).

Attributing to Mencius a notion of an essential "human nature" as a principle of individuation is a misreading of *xin* on at least two counts. First, it is certainly a counterintuitive assertion within the context of a holistic *qi* 氣 cosmology that begins from the primacy of process and vital relationality. In this cosmology, the assumption is that change is pervasive, and as such, everything is disposed to transformation. By referencing the initial conditions and propensities of human "becomings," *xin* 心 acknowledges that in loving families and communicating communities, infants are born into roles informed by "consummatory conduct" (*ren*), "appropriateness and meaning" (*yi*), "a sense of propriety" (*li*), and "intelligence and wisdom" (*zhi*). Radically situated within these fecund and discursive associations, such infants through participating in the various discourses of life are inclined to efficacious growth (*shan* 善).

This nonanalytic *renyilizhi* language of "the four inclinations" is "aspectual" in that each term provides a particular perspective on the same relationally constituted, vital phenomenon. Each term also anticipates how this incipient, socially embedded infant, located within a grammar of familial and cultural conditions, will be inclined to grow and mature discursively as a source of communal and ultimately cosmic meaning.[36]

We might take the roles of the infant as they are informed by intelligence and wisdom (*zhi* 智) as an example. Such an attribution is not a claim that infants have some internal and innate repository of a priori knowledge that they then apply to the situations of their lives. Rather, wisdom is a quality of conduct that arises gradually within the social activities of which infants are a part, informed as these activities are by the persistent yet changing values of their families, their communities, and the mature culture into which they are born. Reading "conduct" etymologically as *con-* ("together, "with") and *duct* ("leading"), such wisdom (or maybe "wise-ing") is a profoundly participatory activity manifested in the ongoing transactions infants have with their environing others and the interactions their environing others have with them. Indeed, without ready access to a mature wisdom, the lives of infants would likely be perilous and short.

Again, *xin* as "four inclinations" is no more an essential and inborn "given" than the tendency that infants have toward "consummate conduct in their roles and relations" (*ren* 仁). Such consummate conduct is initially no more than an incipient relational disposition, an inclination, a tendency. But with assiduous effort within this matrix of relations, these inclinations gradually evolve into a cultivated self-awareness and an acquired virtuosity in their roles as they unfold within the personal narratives of family and community. Over time and with the continuing growth of what are initially only tentative dispositions, these "four inclinations" can be aptly described as native conditions that gradually become qualitatively achieved habits of conduct in the roles and relations that constitute our persons.

---

36. In *Just Babies* (New York: Random House, 2014), Paul Bloom argues that humans, rather than being blank slates, are hardwired with a sense of morality. The problem with this understanding of morality is that it locates such feelings exclusively in the babies themselves rather than in the relationally informed narrative of the baby—babies that are inchoate narratives emerging within larger continuing narratives.

A second, related misreading of Mencius is to ascribe to Mencius a kind of individualism by appealing to either *xin* or *xing* as a doctrine of innate and universal human nature that would serve as a principle of individuation. While a conception of persons as discrete and isolatable individuals is an all-too-familiar uncritical assumption in much of our contemporary philosophical discourse, it is at the same time being repudiated as a fallacious understanding of person within the internal critique being waged by some of our most progressive thinkers, several of whom we have just encountered. Given the principle of charity, we might want to worry about imputing such an individualism to Mencius when it seems that we ourselves are trying to get past it.

For the philosopher Whitehead, for example, as a prominent spokesperson for process thinking, the notion of the discrete individual assumed in much of the liberal theorizing of person is a specific and persistent example of the philosopher's *deformation professionelle* and is described by him as a prominent case of not one but two fallacies. First, it is a prime and powerful example of what he terms the "fallacy of simple location": the familiar and yet fallacious claim that isolating, decontextualizing, and analyzing things as simple particulars is the best way to understand the content of our experience. For Whitehead, such theorizing is fatally reductionistic and suffers from what he further describes as "the fallacy of misplaced concreteness" where we equate the abstracted and independent "thing" with what is real but ignore the genuine connectivity and transitivity of such "things" that animate them in the transactional events of ordinary experience. This fallacy of misplaced concreteness is to regard abstracted entities presumed to have a simple location as being what is concrete while ignoring the vital and processual transitivity that attends all things in our experience of them.[37] Allowing that persons experience each other within the narratives of events that in sum constitute our shared lives together, Whitehead is insisting that we treat persons as interpenetrating "events" rather than as standing outside each of other as discrete "things."

Indeed, Charles Hartshorne elaborates upon Whitehead's fallacy of simple location by problematizing our commonsense understanding

---

37. A. N. Whitehead observes: "This presupposition of individual independence is what I have elsewhere called, the 'fallacy of simple location.'" See A. N. Whitehead, *Process and Reality: An Essay in Cosmology* (New York: Free Press, 1979), 137.

of our ostensive "inner" and "outer" domains that would place persons "outside" and independent of each other. As an alternative, he offers us his version of an interpenetrating, focus-field conception of persons:

> As Whitehead has most clearly seen—individuals generally are not simply outside each other (the fallacy of "simple location") but in each other, and God's inclusion of all things is merely the extreme or super-case of the social relativity or mutual immanence of individuals.[38]

Hartshorne is insisting here on the holographic and mutual implication and interpenetration of persons in their relations with others. Of course, in the Confucian case, using Hartshorne's language, it would be an unsummed *dao* that would do the work of God as the "super-case" of the inclusive yet unbounded field as it is comes to be construed from the perspective of each "individual."

A third, related misinterpretation of Mencius on *xing* arises with the frequent eliding of the distinction between "heartminding" (*xin* 心) and *xing* 性 and the treatment of them as equivalents in referencing some given "human nature" that stands antecedent to the process of growth. If the *Mencius* parses *xin* as a general description of our contextualizing native conditions (and it certainly does), and if *xing* is understood as denoting an innate "human nature" without further qualification (which it does for most commentators), then this equivocation seems unavoidable.

Zhang Dainian, for example, suggests that "since the sage is also a man, the *xing* that the sage has is the *xing* that all people have."[39] Since *xin* in Mencius can serve as a general description of those native human conditions available to all people for cultivation, Zhang is certainly justified in asserting that the sage's *xin* in this sense can be described as a generic human condition. In fact, the *Mencius* describes the *xin* as a "function" (*guan* 官) on the same plane as the offices of sight and hearing, all being standard issue in our biological sensorium.[40] But Zhang's assumption here in his eliding of the distinction between *xin* and *xing* seems to be that

---

38. Charles Hartshorne, *A History of Philosophical Systems* (New York: Philosophical Library, 1950), 443.

39. Zhang Dainian 張岱年, 中國哲學大綱 [An outline of Chinese philosophy] (Beijing: Chinese Academy of Social Sciences Press, 1982), 250–253.

40. *Mencius* 6A15.

xing, as with his understanding of *xin*, is a given, latent potential shared by all persons in their definition as persons and that the sage is simply the one who most successfully actualizes it.

Tang Junyi is more rigorous and more traditional in his reading of *xing*, arguing that in our understanding of becoming human we must give appropriate value to the growth and life force (*shengli* 生理) integral to the process. As previously noted, the character *xing* 性 is quite literally a combination of *xin* 心—initially "heartminding" as the native conditions available for growth—and *sheng* 生, the spontaneous and vital birth, growth, and life that makes the most of the possibilities of this same *xin* within a specific narrative. Tang's understanding of *xing* resonates with the position of Graham cited previously; that is, for Graham "*xin* 'heart' and *xing* 'nature' " in a reading he arrived at quite independently of Tang are best understood as "the centres of awareness and spontaneity respectively."[41]

Importantly, we need to introduce two clarifications here. First, if we register fully the "birth, growth, and life" that comes with the term *sheng*, the possibilities *xing* entails do not lie solely within things themselves; rather the *xing* of human beings in particular, while certainly deliberate, self-aware, and resolute when properly directed by *xin*, references the continuing process of a diffused and creative collaboration of persons with and within their various familial, social, and natural environments. And secondly, while *xin* certainly references our native human conditions, it is also the locus of the growth and the consummation of persons that enables them to act deliberately within this process of consummation. Tang Junyi underscores the vital, collaborative, and emergent nature of this process of human "becoming":

> Within Chinese natural cosmology what is held in general is not some first principle. The root pattern or coherence (*genbenzhili* 根本之理) of anything is its "life force" (*shengli* 生理), and this life force is its *xing* 性. The *xing* is expressed in the quality of its interactions with other things and events. The *xing* or "life force" then entailing spontaneity and transformation has nothing to do with necessity. . . . The emergence of any particular phenomenon is a function of the interaction between its prior conditions and other things

---

41. Graham, "Replies," 290–91.

and events as external influences. So how something interacts with other things and events and the form of this interaction is not determined by the thing itself. . . . Thus, the *xing* of anything itself is inclusive of this process of transformability in response to whatever it encounters.[42]

I. A. Richards makes the same point perhaps more explicitly in his *Mencius on the Mind* when he insists that

the phrase "human nature"—with its suggestion of something ultimate, given, and unalterable—is notoriously misleading here.[43]

Rather, observes Richards, we must allow that since "man is after all the most versatile, plastic, adaptable of the animals," we must understand that "human nature"

must be, for Mencius, an artificial product of man's life in society. And we will be the less likely to dissent the more clearly we perceive how little that we recognize as distinctive of the human mind would remain if the shaping influences of society were removed.[44]

As we can see, *xin* and *xing* as native conditions and ultimate product, respectively, have a clearly different reference at the beginning of the process of situated personal growth, and at this stage, the distinction between them must not be elided. But as the process unfolds, they gradually converge as terms denoting the same result; that is, the consummate *xin* is the emerging product of the spontaneous process of growth, and *xing* is the spontaneous process of growth that has produced the consummate *xin*. This point is made explicitly in the *Mencius* when the

---

42. Tang Junyi 唐君毅. *Complete Works*, 4:98–100: 中國自然宇宙論中, 共相非第一義之理。物之存在的根本之理為生理, 此生理即物之性。物之性表現於與他物感通之德量。性或生理, 乃自由原則, 生化原則, 而非必然原則。. . . 蓋任一事象之生起, 必由以前之物與其他之交感, 以爲其外緣。而一物與他物之如何交感或交感之形式, 則非由任一物之本身所決定。. . . 因而一物之性之本身, 即包含一隨所感而變化之性。

43. Richards, *Mencius on the Mind*, 78.

44. Richards, *Mencius on the Mind*, 78.

text insists that "those of us who make the most of their 'heartminding' (*xin*) realize their *xing*."⁴⁵ *Xin* can be parsed at first as the initial, native conditions (what Mencius calls the "four inclinations" [*siduan*]) available for growth. Then in "making the most" of this resolute and deliberate *xin* through assiduous effort and a cultivated self-awareness, the *xin* as the product of this cultivation becomes the same referent as *xing*. So, then at the stage of full consummation when the process of growth has run its course, there is no equivocation in ascribing a shared identity to *xin* and *xing* with the distinction between them analogous to persons and their narratives.

A fourth misreading of Mencius on *xing* is prompted by the frequent analogy appealed to in the *Mencius* between our desire to nurture the "body" and our similar impulse to nourish the process of our "heartminding" (*xin*). Influenced by our own persisting common sense, we are inclined to assume uncritically that the outcome of personal cultivation is a kind of intellectual and spiritual ascent, elevating us above our mundane physical experience. But such dichotomous mind-body, intelligible-sensual, spirit-flesh thinking is dualistic and anathema to Mencius.

Sinologists have become generally aware that the Mencian *qi* cosmology is nondualistic. Realizing that our familiar separation of the cognitive and the affective has little relevance for Mencius, they have also attempted to overcome this familiar dualism by standardizing the translation of *xin* as some variant of the neologism "heartmind." However, while this is certainly an appropriate gesture, it is at best just a beginning. In addition to resisting this cognitive-affective dichotomy (which we certainly should do), we must allow that Mencius's notion of *xin* also precludes the relevance of our other familiar dualisms as well: mind-body, agent-action, inner-outer, subject-object, self-other, nature-nurture, part-whole, and so on. Such distinctions are certainly functional, allowing us to foreground one aspect of *xin* while backgrounding others. But we must also appreciate the fact that *xin* has both an intellectual and a physical aspect: it feels and is the feelings themselves, it encompasses at once our inner selves and our outer world, and so on. With such an acknowledgment, we might be doing greater justice to the complexity of *xin* if we read this term not merely as "heartmind" but gerundively (if not ungrammatically and playfully perhaps) as "vital, resolute, and self-conscious bodyheartminding within our particular field of experience." In any case, we will need to

---

45. *Mencius* 7A1: 盡其心者知其性也。

reconceive *xin* in this more vital and holistic direction if we are going to rescue it from our otherwise suppressed dualistic assumptions.

Using the *Mencius* to Restate Graham's Insights into the Narrativity of *Xing*

Where are we today in our received reading of the *Mencius*? In spite of Graham's important insights into this alternative, narrative understanding of *xing*, his intervention seems to have made little difference in how the *Mencius* continues to be read and understood. Although Graham abandoned his earlier essentialist reading and has provided a relatively full account of this more capacious narrative interpretation of *xing* in his magnum opus, *Disputers of the Tao*, these same insights continue to be either ignored or misunderstood. At the very least, we need only to note that in the interpretive literature, Graham's revisionist, narrative reading of Mencius's *xing* has failed to replace the persisting understanding of it as a default, inborn, and morally good "human nature."

One significant factor in this persistent misreading of Mencius is the seemingly invincible commitment to a default individualism in our contemporary culture to the extent that we have some real difficulty in allowing that the *Mencius* might have an alternative conception of persons on offer. And again, as we have witnessed, Graham's own evolving narrative interpretation of *xing* is itself hardly a model of clarity. Indeed, it is only by building upon excerpted fragments drawn from his later publications more broadly that we have been able to reconstruct the appropriate interpretive context for the *Mencius* and to attempt to bring Graham's dynamic and irreducibly contextual "narrative" interpretation of *xing* into clearer focus.

At the same time, like Graham and other philosophers of culture such as Tang Junyi, Granet, and Needham who came before him, we have also sought to register the importance of this same interpretive context as a necessary condition for understanding Confucian ethics. As argued previously, role ethics begins from the fact of associated living; and on that basis it contests foundational individualism by advancing a radically different relational understanding of what it means to become persons. And what we will suggest is that a reading of the *Mencius* that respects its interpretive context will show an alignment between Graham's narrative understanding of the Mencian *xing* and our own concept of role ethics. The most important questions to address here are first whether or not the *Mencius* being read within its own interpretive framework will give us this narrative reading of our human propensities (*xing*), and then secondly, whether or not this narrative reading of how we become human is consistent with Confucian role ethics. These are the two questions to which we now turn.

In moving from our reconstruction of Graham on Mencius to the text of *Mencius* itself, we will argue that a close reading of this philosophical canon confirms Graham's argument that the project of becoming consummately human for Mencius, far from merely acting out who we are, is hard work. Contra Xunzi who would impute to Mencius a kind of moral naturalism—that is, the position that simply to be human is to be good—Mencius begins and ends with advocating assiduous and deliberate personal cultivation in our roles and relations as the source of our moral growth. That is, the Mencian project for vital human "becomings" seems to demand not only motivation and real purposeful effort on our part but also imagination and creative responsiveness to the constraints set by our ever-changing circumstances.

We might begin this close reading of some passages of the *Mencius* from what the text calls our incipient "four inclinations" (*siduan* 四端): the native, constitutive conditions that Mencius generalizes about the human experience and that he identifies with the inchoate heartmind (*xin* 心). The *Mencius* provides a clear description of these four inclinations as they stir us to moral conduct:

> Our heartmind in feeling pity at perceived suffering disposes it toward consummate conduct in our roles and relations; our heartmind in feeling shame at perceived crudeness disposes it toward appropriate conduct in our roles and relations; our heartmind in its feelings of modesty and deference disposes it toward propriety in our roles and relations; our heartmind in feeling a sense of approval and disapproval disposes it toward wisdom in our roles and relations. Persons have these four inclinations (*siduan*) just as they have their four limbs.[46]

---

46. *Mencius* 2A6: 惻隱之心，仁之端也；羞惡之心，義之端也；辭讓之心，禮之端也；是非之心，智之端也。人之有是四端也，猶其有四體也。

Commenting on this passage, Graham observes that the analogy between cultivating our four inclinations and nourishing our bodies is an apposite one:

> It is essential to Mencius' case that although moral education is indispensable it is, like the feeding of the body, the nourishing of a spontaneous process.... A man becomes bad, not because the incipient impulses are missing from his constitution, but because he neglects and starves them.[47]

Graham underscores the analogy here between physical and moral growth. In both cases such growth occurs because of the natural conditions of the organism and the effort at nourishment that must be invested in its development. And the terms "constitution" and "incipient impulses" used here to describe these natural conditions are important because Mencius is referencing the native inclinations we have within our relations as human beings:

> Mencius said: "Great persons are those who do not lose the heartmind of the newborn babe."[48]

We must resist an expository reading of this passage that might essentialize and reify heartmind; it is perhaps better to understand Mencius here as simply making a point. And the point being made is that activating the native inclinations of the relationally constituted infant who is defined relationally rather than essentially is a necessary condition upon which the project of ultimately becoming exemplary in our persons depends. Mencius's description of incipient "inclinations" not only introduces the radically embedded newborn babe as the locus of the growth of these "inclinations" but further defines the "constitution" of this infant in terms of these same organic relations. That is, the newborn babe emerges in media res as an inchoate narrative nested within the larger pattern of the more mature narratives of family and community.

The growth of an infant born into the concrete matrix of the family and communal relations of a mature culture can be captured both descriptively and prescriptively by an appeal to the intense socializing

---

47. Graham, *Disputers of the Tao*, 126, 129.
48. *Mencius* 4B12: 孟子曰：「大人者，不失其赤子之心者也。」

impulses of these constitutive bonds. The *Mencius* uses the metaphors of a runaway fire and surging water to emphasize the precipitous nature of this moral growth:

> Now acknowledging that these four inclinations are defining of us, the process of realizing the development and fruition of them is like a fire beginning to blaze or a spring of water beginning to gush forth. Persons who are able to bring them fully to fruition can vouchsafe everyone within the four seas, while persons unable to do so cannot even be of service to their own parents.[49]

Graham comments here that this inexorable progression of moral growth is motivated by the agreeable feelings we derive from it:

> The process once launched accelerates, like fire catching, because we discover the pleasure of it.[50]

For this infant, the four inclinations that anticipate moral growth are the thick, irreducibly biological, familial, social, and cultural action-guiding conditions that define it. These discursive bonds are thus by nature resolutely relational and inclusive and in their activation and growth are a source of rapid moral articulation (*shan* 善). As I have suggested, *shan* as "good" in the sense of this moral growth being stimulated by (to use Charles Taylor's felicitous expression) the "webs of interlocution" within the continuing narrative. It is only from this continuing discursive process that "good" can be abstracted as a summary description of either persons or their actions. In other words, newborns as concrete facts are constituted by the relations that define them. And as newborns follow the discursive promptings of the matrix of these relations, they grow their various roles into their emerging personal identities. Infants in these relations are animated and projective, and they develop their inflected and reflexively aware sense of themselves within the expansive intrasubjective roles and relations that come to constitute them.

Importantly, it is the radial, constitutive, and transactional nature of relations themselves and their propensity to produce meaning that

---

49. *Mencius* 2A6: 凡有四端於我者，知皆擴而充之矣，若火之始然，泉之始達。苟能充之，足以保四海；苟不充之，不足以事父母。
50. Graham, *Disputers of the Tao*, 126.

first locates newborns within an inchoate habitude and thus disposes them to positive moral growth. Given its irreducibly relational nature, an infant conceived of as a discrete and independent "individual" is nothing more than a retrospective abstraction from this same manifold of relations. And further, the erstwhile "goodness" (*shan* 善) of infants, far from being some innate and isolatable endowment, is the compounding dividend produced as they activate the vital disposition they have toward social growth. *Shan* refers to the outcome of the semiotic processes and symbolic competencies that come to shape them as human "becomings."

Mencius on the Role of Assiduous Personal Cultivation

For Mencius, the gregarious impulse that prompts growth in relations and guides us in the direction of efficacious moral conduct is at first only incipient and is certainly at risk of being lost, as we have seen. But contra Xunzi's caricature of Mencius as offering a naturalistic interpretation of *xing*, for him becoming "great persons" requires so much more than simply avoiding the loss of our initial impulse to relate meaningfully. In the *Mencius*, there is in fact an inordinate emphasis on the role of unremitting personal cultivation in growing and consolidating the virtuosic habits that are expressed in and characteristic of an exemplary life. This process at one end begins from our initial animality with the minimalist human advantage of the incipient "four inclinations" and extends at the other end to the possibility of attaining the habitude of full-blown, epoch-changing human sagacity as our loftiest prospect.

Mencius makes a frequently found distinction between just doing something that is prompted by the approbation of others, and by contrast, acting consistently out of a cultivated, evolving moral habitude:

> Mencius said: "What distinguishes people from the brutes is ever so slight, and while the common run of people might lose this difference, exemplary persons preserve and develop it. Shun was wise to the way of all things and had real insight into human roles and relationships. He acted upon his moral habit of being consummatory and optimally appropriate in

his conduct rather than merely doing what was deemed consummatory and appropriate by others."[51]

We need to register the vital distinction being made here between persons who are merely able to follow conventional values by acting in a way deemed virtuosic by the community and a sage like Shun who through assiduous personal regimen actually becomes consummatory in his roles and relations and acts from this cultivated habitude of virtuosity. We also need to be careful how we parse the human journey from animality to sagehood. Commenting on the assumed inseparability of physical and moral growth, Graham observes:

> Moral inclinations belong to nature in the same way as the physical growth of the body. They germinate spontaneously without having to be learned or worked for, they can be nourished, injured, starved, they develop if properly tended but their growth cannot be forced.[52]

The familiar and oft-repeated analogy in the *Mencius* between the "four inclinations" and the "body with its four limbs" is important in at least two respects. First, the growth in our personal relations and of our bodies is profoundly but not exclusively physical (rather than metaphysical) and is prompted by the agreeable feelings we have as we participate in the ongoing conversation of the always social heartmind. Like the body, our moral habits find nourishment and growth when they are exercised regularly.

And secondly, the qualitative virtuosity that emerges in the radial growth of our relations, inspired as it is by the promptings of the inchoate heartmind, produces a qualitatively transformed moral physicality (what Richard Shusterman has called a "somaesthetic") that elevates the embodied human experience into something refined and elegant.[53] Stated simply, the distinction between human animality and sagacity is not one grounded in the differences between our physical and intellectual qualities. Indeed, the sensual and the intellectual as complementary aspects of our persons

---

51. *Mencius* 4B19: 孟子曰：人之所以異於禽獸者希。庶民去之，君子存之。舜明於庶物，察於人倫，由仁義行，非行仁義也。See also 6A8.
52. Graham, *Disputers of the Tao*, 125.
53. For a representative example, see Shusterman, *Body Consciousness*.

are, in fact, no more than two different ways of viewing and evaluating the same phenomenon. Virtuosic conduct is necessarily embodied, and as it is habituated, it is expressed through a quality of action that is at once physically and intellectually compelling:

> Mencius said, ". . . What exemplary persons cultivate as their human propensities (*xing*)—that is, their inclinations to act consummately in their roles and relations (*ren*), to act with optimal appropriateness (*yi*), to achieve propriety (*li*), and to act wisely (*zhi*)—are all rooted in their heartmind (*xin*). And the physical complexion that develops in this endeavor first glows radiantly on their faces, is further reflected in their carriage, and then extends throughout their extremities. Without their bodies having to say anything at all, everyone is keenly aware of this personal growth."[54]

In this attempt to understand Mencius on *xing*, it is important to note that he chooses to reserve the use of this term for what is most exclusively and distinctively human:

> The mouth's penchant for taste, the eye's for color, the ear's for sound, the nose's for smell, and the body's for comfort—these are all human propensities (*xing*). And yet because our capacities (*ming*) also have a role in exercising them, exemplary persons are not given to referring to these aptitudes as human propensities (*xing*). A penchant for consummate conduct in the roles of father and son, for appropriateness in the roles of ruler and subject, for ritual propriety in the roles of guest and host, for wisdom in the roles that make persons superior, and for the role that sages have within the way-making of *tian*, are all capacities we have (*ming*). And yet because our human propensities (*xing*) also have a role in exercising them, exemplary persons are not given to referring to such moral habits as mere capacities.[55]

---

54. *Mencius* 7A21: 孟子曰：「。。。君子所性，仁義禮智根於心。其生色也，睟然見於面，盎於背，施於四體，四體不言而喻。」

55. *Mencius* 7B24: 口之於味也，目之於色也，耳之於聲也，鼻之於臭也，四肢之於安佚也，性也，有命焉，君子不謂性也。仁之於父子也，義之於君臣也，禮之於賓主也，智之於賢者也，聖人之於天道也，命也，有性焉，君子不謂命也。

Ming as "capacities" is used here as elsewhere in the *Mencius* to designate those conditions in the life experience over which we have the least influence and control: the various instincts and physiological functions that enable us to sustain life and that in sum, are life itself. *Xing* as "human propensities" by contrast refers to those outcomes in the human roles that carry the strongest human signature: our ability to purposely and deliberately nurture our familial, communal, and ultimately cosmic roles, thereby elevating human experience into an elegant, exemplary narrative. What is distinctive in this discursive process is the cultivation of a critical self-awareness. In rehearsing these roles, Mencius begins radially and expansively from the most basic familial roles to the transformative role the lives of the sages have as epochal meaning makers that extend the cosmic order itself.

Importantly here, however, is that the distinction Mencius chooses to make between our "human propensities" (*xing* 性) and our "capacities" (*ming* 命) must not be reduced to some simple dichotomy between the mental and the physical, the intellectual and the sensual, or the psychical and the somatic. Indeed, as we have seen, the intellectual and physical aspects of our persons are both available to us for cultivation in our best efforts to elevate the human experience. What makes us distinctively human is our propensity for moral growth through concerted effort expressed in our embodied actions' virtuosity. For Mencius, our physicality is certainly a ubiquitous aspect of human activity, but just as with our cognitive and affective competencies, the cultivated transformation of the physical is integral to and reflective of the unremitting effort needed to become consummately human.

Mencius and Intentional Living

For Mencius, the process of habituated growth and the achieved virtuosity initially prompted by our native societal conditions, once stimulated by our heartmind's "four inclinations" and then properly disciplined and directed, suffuse our entire persons to achieve a deliberate and purposeful resolution in our actions. And it is the intentionality and critical self-awareness of our evolving embodied moral habits that serve as the ground of our emerging personal identities:

> Mencius said: ". . . From the age of forty on I have not felt perturbed in my heartmind." . . . It is our intentions (*zhi* 志)

that guide our *qi*, and it is this *qi* that fills up our persons. And it is because our *qi* follows wherever our intentions take us that it is said: Be firm in your intentions and do not distress your *qi*."[56]

We have seen that the character *xing* 性 is composed of *xin* 心, those native social conditions available for growth, and *sheng* 生, the birth, growth, and life of these native social conditions. *Xing* thus understood describes the process through which, with assiduous and unrelenting effort, we can over time become consummately human. As with the character *xing*, the graph for "intending" (*zhi* 志) that is written on the bronzes as *[xx]* combines *xin* 心 as those native social conditions available for growth, with *zhi* interpretable as either 之 or 止, where both graphs mean "going or repairing to."[57] It is thus that *zhi* 志 as 心 + 之 or 止 denotes the activated intentionality as motive force that must attend this vital process of achieving virtuosity in one's conduct. As with the graph for "achieved virtuosity" written alternatively as *de* 德 or *de* 悳, the character for "intending" (*zhi* 志) also means moving straight ahead with determination and resolve (*zhi* 直). Indeed, the character "intending" (*zhi* 志) is defined in the early *Shuowen* lexicon as "purposing" (*yi* 意) and in archaic Chinese, is close in pronunciation to and associated semantically with "knowing" one's way (*shi* 識). We find that this cluster of terms continues the pervasive metaphor of forging ahead with resolution in the "waymaking" (*dao*) that constitutes our shared human narratives.

We might reflect on what seem to be certain suppressed premises in the cosmological and normative language of "virtuosity" that make such virtuosity a specifically human achievement: the achieved quality of coalescence between cultivated persons (*de* 德) and their worlds (*dao* 道) in our role of becoming human. It is significant that the character for *dao* found on the bronzes *[xxi]* is not simply a road—"the Way" as it is conventionally translated. *Dao* is reflexive, including within it a clear graphic representation of persons composed of the human 首 with a full head of hair found as *[xxii]* on the oracle bones and *[xxiii]* on the

---

56. *Mencius* 2A2: 孟子曰:「... 我四十不動心。... 夫志,氣之帥也; 氣, 體之充也。夫志至焉, 氣次焉。故曰:『持其志, 無暴其氣。』」
57. Kwan, "Database," (戰國早期) CHANT 9735.

bronzes.[58] Simply put, *dao* is not *the* Way or *His* Way, as in John 14:6. Rather it is the making of *our* way together, both ancestors and progeny, both whence and whither, as we intentionally and self-consciously forge ahead and strive to be true in our waymaking.

Importantly, this shared road and its trajectory has been constructed by our progenitors. But far from being a finished and predetermined way, it requires our full and deliberate participation in laying the connector to the next generation. The ancestors have provided the coordinates in their passing on of the tradition (*daotong* 道統), but the responsibility of every generation is to "broaden the way" (*hongdao* 弘道) for their own time and place and to provide succeeding generations the benefit of their own extension of this living cultural tradition. And acknowledging the contrapuntal relation between persons and world, *dao* is both waymaking and worldmaking. Given that the word "world" as w(e)oruld (Old English) is etymologically derived from a Germanic compound of *wer* ("man") and *eld* ("age"), it means quite explicitly, "the age or the life of man." This reference to the specifically human sojourn is a warrant for translating *dao* as "worldmaking" to the extent that as a family- rather than God-centered cosmogony, cosmic order is a full collaboration between persons and world.

On the oracle bones, *de* 德 conventionally rendered nominally as "virtue" or "excellence," appears as *[xxiv]*. Similar to the graph for *dao*, it combines the graphs for road, *chi* 彳, and for straight ahead, *zhi* 直, as persons focused on the road ahead walking deliberately forward.[59] On the bronzes, the heartmind (*xin* 心) is added as an additional element in the graph for *de [xxv]*, underscoring the intentionality and self-awareness required to direct the life experience to optimum effect as we extend our way in the world.[60]

[xxiv]

[xxv]

Reinforcing this understanding of *de* as a kind of "conatus"—that is, the purposeful effort of persons striving to make the most of their life experience—is the fact that in several of the recently recovered bamboo texts, the character *de* 德 is written using its graphic variant, 悳. This

---

58. See Kwan, "Database," (西周晚期) CHANT 4469, (甲骨文合集) CHANT 3501C, and (飾奎父鼎西周中期) CHANT 2813.
59. See Kwan, "Database," 殷墟文字甲編 CHANT 2304.
60. See Kwan, "Database," (西周早期) CHANT 2837.

graphic alternative has the heartmind radical *xin* 心 placed beneath the character *zhi* 直 that means "upright," "true," and "moving straight ahead." There is clearly a cognate relationship between these variants for *de* and the character *zhi* 直 meaning "moving straight ahead," and according to the reconstructed archaic language, the two characters *de* and *zhi* were markedly similar in pronunciation, with *zhi* in the 悳 graph being the phonetic signifier as well as having semantic reference.

When we parse this notion of forging "straight ahead" on life's path and reflect upon the normative qualities of action that would follow from it, we find a glossary of related terms: true, direct, proper candid, authentic, rightly positioned, immediate, timely, main, undiluted, deliberate, judicious, decisive, resolute, intense, upright, and so on. Such deliberate, judicious, and disciplined conduct is in sum the meaning of "virtuosity" itself. That is, virtuosity is being true and resolute in optimizing those resources that allow us to find the most productive way forward in our worldmaking together.

In a holographic cosmology, a *this* always entails a *that*. *This focus* always has *that field* implicated within it, and *this* field is always construed from either *that* particular focus or another. With *dao* and *de* as unbounded field and focal center, respectively, there is an immediate graphic resonance between the field of *dao* as an open-ended way that is continuously being extended and its dyadic correlate, the focal *de*, that denotes the insistent particularity of self-conscious human "becomings" living deliberately. Of course, the optimal coalescence between particular persons and the road they are forging together is reflected in the meaning that emerges from the combination of these two terms as the binomial *daode* 道德, which in the modern Chinese language has conventionally come to be translated as "virtue" or "excellence." But this expression *daode* has ancient provenance and early on was used to express the human virtuosity achieved when, through focus and resolution, we achieve an optimal symbiosis within our field of experience. The main theme of the canonical *Daodejing* 道德經, for example, is captured in the *wu*-forms—*wuwei* 無為 (noncoercive acting), *wuzhi* 無知 (unprincipled knowing), *wuyu* 無欲 (objectless desiring), *wushi* 無事 (noninterfering governing), and so on—that in sum constitute the most productive relationships that can be achieved between self-conscious persons and their world. It is for this reason we have been inspired to translate the title of this text, revised according to the recent archaeological finds as the *Dedaojing* 德道經 (literally "the classic of this *de* and its *dao*)," as *Making This Life Significant*.

Returning to this same *Mencius* 2A2 passage cited previously, it continues with Mencius's famous exposition on the purposing of his moral energy—his "flood-like *qi*":

> "Is there some way to cultivate this control over one's anxieties?" . . . "May I dare to ask after your success in this respect, sir?"
> Mencius replied: "I realize what is being said (*zhiyan* 知言), and I am good at nourishing my flood-like *qi* (*haoranzhiqi* 浩然之氣)."
> "May I ask what you mean by 'flood-like *qi*?'"
> Mencius replied: "It is difficult to put into words. It is activating our *qi* to have its most extensive reach and its most intensive resolution. If we nurture it faithfully and without respite, it will fill up all between the heavens and the earth. As the achieved quality of our *qi*, it is of a piece with sustaining optimal appropriateness in our conduct (*yi* 義) and with moving resolutely forward in our way-making (*dao* 道). Without this quality of *qi*, we will starve. Flood-like *qi* is what is born of the cumulative habit of optimally appropriate conduct, and is not something that can be had through merely random acts of appropriateness. If one does anything that would cause disappointment in our heartminding, it starves."[61]

Kwong-loi Shun, in his discussion of the references to *qi* found in the *Mencius*, rehearses passages from the *Zuozhuan* 左傳 and the *Guoyu* 國語, which are classical anthologies of historical stories that expound upon *qi* as the vital energies making up and activating the natural world around us.[62] In the several discourses in which Mencius himself invokes the language of *qi*, he is not, as suggested by some commentators,

---

61. *Mencius* 2A2: 曰："不動心有道乎？"。。。"敢問夫子惡乎長？" 曰："我知言，我善養吾浩然之氣。" "敢問何謂浩然之氣？" 曰："難言也。其為氣也，至大至剛，以直養而無害，則塞于天地之閒。其為氣也，配義與道；無是，餒也。是集義所生者，非義襲而取之也。行有不慊於心，則餒矣。"
62. Kwong-loi Shun, *Mencius and Early Chinese Thought* (Stanford, CA: Stanford University Press, 1997), 67–68.

waxing mystical.⁶³ On the contrary, Mencius is simply making explicit the common sense of his own time and place in Warring States China (475–221 BCE). Indeed, to find our own analogy with this *qi* worldview, we might consider it the classical Chinese counterpart of the now largely unconscious quantitative, genetic, and atomistic assumptions that began for Western culture in classical Greek ontology and that continue to inform our own common sense.

Mencius himself interprets the field of *qi* in terms of specifically moral energy, and in this cited passage he offers advice on the cultivation of human virtuosity.⁶⁴ Again, restated in the cosmological language of focus and field, Mencius attributes his success in achieving resolution in his conduct to two cultivated abilities: "realizing what is being said" (*zhiyan* 知言) and being "good at nourishing my flood-like *qi*." The expression "realizing what is being said" (*zhiyan*) could be an allusion to a passage in the *Analects* wherein Confucius insists that "persons who do not realize what is being said (*bu zhiyan* 不知言) have no way of understanding other people."⁶⁵ This claim serves as an apposite parallel to the phrase "nourishing my flood-like *qi*" in suggesting that we must understand human relations semiotically as a critical and self-conscious "relating to" within the irreducibly social heartminding. In grasping the fundamentally discursive nature of relatedness, we can further come to understand that the quality of those relationships constituting our own particular identities is nothing other than the quality of the sustained conversations we have had with others over time, cultivating in them both a critical self- (and other) awareness. The quality of the persons we are to become is a direct consequence of our ability to communicate effectively and meaningfully within our families and communities.

And this parallel with the second cultivated ability here is clear. That is, Mencius's "flood-like *qi*," like the semiotic and symbolic exchanges needed in understanding others and oneself, is also a modality of discourse. Mencius's claim is that when his *qi* is properly nurtured and

---

63. See Chad Hansen, *A Daoist Theory of Chinese Thought* (Hong Kong: Oxford University Press), 175. Hansen is not alone among scholars who would describe Mencius on *qi* as a "moral mysticism."

64. See Alan K. L. Chan, "A Matter of Taste: *Qi* (Vital Energy) in the Tending of the Heart (*Xin*) in *Mencius* 2A2," in *Mencius: Contexts and Interpretations*, ed. Alan K. L. Chan (Honolulu: University of Hawai'i Press, 2001).

65. *Analects* 20.3: 不知言, 無以知人也。

achieves its most "intensive resolution" (至剛) and self-awareness within his own person, it provides him with the greatest "extensive magnitude" (*zhida* 至大) in the influence he then comes to have on the world. And this same radial and symbiotic "intensive focus" and "extensive field" dynamic is then repeated in the language *dao* 道 and *yi* 義; that is, the reach and influence he is able to acquire (*dao*) is achieved through meaningful resolution in the optimally appropriate relations that constitute his own person (*yi*). For Mencius, to nourish his *qi* most successfully is to achieve the greatest degree of meaningful appropriateness and thus self-conscious resolution within his most extensive field of *qi*. In just this manner, sustained virtuosity in the quality of his conduct (*daode* 道德) is attained as he acquires the greatest degree of potency and effectiveness (*de* 德) in relation to the most far-ranging elements of his various environments (*dao* 道).

Again, to capture this same dynamic between the intensity of focus and the enhanced extension of one's field we might use the familiar language of *jingshen* 精神 that as a binomial is conventionally translated as "spirit, vigor, vitality, drive." *Jing* 精, conventionally translated as "essence," is not some ontological essence to be contrasted with accidents or attributes but is the concentrated source of personal vitality, both physical and intellectual, that is both inherited from parents and acquired from various forms of nourishment. *Jing* is the sap of life, a tangible, life-giving energy with the potency of semen as it is felt self-consciously within one's actions. And *shen* 神, conventionally translated as "spirit," is not the spiritual as opposed to the corporeal but rather this same *jing* vitality as it comes to flow, pervade, and to be manifested through the functional life activities of the mind and the body as a whole. *Shen* is the mystery of how we become "great souled" in our expansive and inspired living. As the *Book of Changes* describes this amorphous energy: "That which cannot be fathomed through effecting a *yinyang* contrast is what is meant by the truly mysterious (*shen*)."[66]

To give a concrete historical example of how the coalescence of focus and field can culminate in such reach and influence, we might say that Confucius's personal virtuosity has held sway for several millennia over the intergenerational transmission of the entire Chinese culture and beyond; this virtuosity has made him one of the most influential persons in human history. It is in this sense that the broad field of Chinese

---

66. *Book of Changes*, "Great Commentary," A5: 陰陽不測之謂神。

culture (*dao*) is implicated in and finds its focus within the continuing, corporate narrative of the historical person Confucius (*de*). Using focus-field language, we can by foregrounding and backgrounding say that holographically the entire field of Chinese culture is adumbrated in the person of Confucius and that the person of Confucius as he lives on in the critical, always self-conscious commentarial literature has brought the entire field of Chinese culture into meaningful focus.

Mencius and the Holography of *Xin* as *Xing*

This focus-field notion of whole persons assumed in this Confucian cosmology stands in contrast to our familiar realist-derived conception of a private inner domain and a shared outer world. The question that Charles Hartshorne has posed is as follows: if we are not externally related in standing "outside" of each other, what then is the nature of our relationship to one another? The focus-field understanding of relationally constituted persons is a Confucian answer to this question, beginning as it does from the doctrine of internal, constitutive relations also previously discussed in some detail. We are cells in an organism, self-conscious organisms within an ecology, and centered ecologies within an unbounded and unsummed galaxy of ecologies. This focus-field model requires a gestalt shift in our understanding of persons in which their particular identities and the unsummed totality—their foregrounded, always unique foci and their overlapping fields—are two holographic and thus mutually entailing ways of perceiving the same phenomenon. Just as each unique note as it is played within the context of a symphony has implicated within it the entire performance and must be evaluated accordingly, so each focal event—that is, the identity expressed through each self-conscious moment in a person's life—has implicated within it this person's entire unbounded narrative field.

In order to fully grasp this holographic understanding of persons, the following oft-cited passage from the *Mencius* might require a more literal reading than it usually receives, since it questions our familiar distinction between an inner self and an outer world:

> Mencius said, "The myriad things of the world are all implicated here in me."[67]

---

67. *Mencius* 7A4: 孟子曰: 萬物皆備於我矣。

To make sense of this Mencian claim, we must appreciate the background cosmological assumptions about the perceived holographic focus and field relationship between particular persons and their experienced world and about the processual nature and the radical contextuality of the human experience. To understand the passage "the myriad things of the world are all implicated here in me" we need to formulate an alternative to our commonsense dualistic understanding of our inner and outer worlds as two separate domains of experience.

Most obviously, as previously noted, it is a commonplace that the Confucian *xin* as "heartminding" serving metonymically for the concept of person does the work of both cognizing and feeling in the life experience, including both felt thoughts and cognitively informed feelings. But as we have noted, with *xin* it is not a matter of getting past one dualism. In this process cosmology, there are no dualisms. There is no strict dichotomy between self and other (*zita* 自他), between subject and object (*zhuke* 主客), between body and mind (*xinshen* 心身), between structure and function (*tiyong* 體用), between thinking and doing (*zhixing* 知行), between inner and outer (*neiwai* 內外), between nature and nurture (*ziran* 自然), and so on.[68] In reconceiving this inner-outer dynamic as a vital, nonanalytic continuity we require an alternative reading of the full range of such distinctions.

To take just one among these dualisms as an example, our common sense prompts us to read subject and object as being dualistic terms that are exclusive of each other. But when we reflect on the Chinese understanding of such distinctions, they have a coterminous relationship as correlative, aspectual categories in which each term is interdependent with and understood in terms of its dyadic relationship. Reflecting on the "objective" and "subjective" dualism, the assumption is that "objectivity" is the presumptive source of fact and truth, not only standing exclusive of "subjectivity" but indeed effectively negating it as offering nothing more than mere opinion. But in the translation of "subjective" and "objective" into the Chinese language as *zhuke* 主客—literally as "host" and "guest"

---

68. The binomial term *ziran* 自然 is usually read as "nature," or more informatively as "self-so-ing," but it can also be read contrastively like these other dyadic pairs as "nature and nurture." We can understand *zi* 自 as both the uniqueness of any particular thing and inclusively as the complete field of relationships that together conspire to sponsor it and provide it with its uniqueness—particular persons, for example. And the *ran* 然 then is the presencing of things each as a particular focus, where their quality as unique persons is a function of the achieved coalescence in their particular fields of relations.

respectively—these two terms stand in an interdependent *yinyang* 陰陽 relationship where the first term is immediately implicated in and can only be understood in its relation with the second. For this process cosmology, nothing can stand independent of its context as either purely objective or purely subjective. Given the wholeness of experience, everything and anything can only be subjective or objective as a matter of degree.

What this means for heartminding (*xin*), of course, is that erstwhile inner and outer domains are irreducibly reflexive, with the objective world always being experienced from one self-conscious perspective or another and the subjective world always having the objective world adumbrated within it. With heartminding (*xin*), these many aspectual rather than dualistic distinctions—structure and function, nature and nurture, and so on—are all nonanalytic and mutually entailing. These distinctions, rather than serving to separate and isolate different components within the "bodyheartminding" experience and thereby fragment the activities that define it, instead reflect the interdependence and interpenetration of the matrix of myriad aspects that function together to constitute the complex human narrative.

We might take our cue from traditional Chinese medicine (TCM) and its understanding of *qi* 氣 as one practical application of this early cosmology. The alternative understanding of the relationship between function and structure in TCM provides us with a significantly different way of understanding Mencius's claim that "the myriad things of the world are all implicated here in me." We must acknowledge that in TCM, there is an inseparability of physiology and anatomy and thus of function and structure. Such mutual implication precludes the formalism and the reification of the anatomical that introduces a doctrine of external relations. Indeed, TCM has a symbiotic understanding of the coterminous relationship between the dynamics of structure and function captured in the expression "forming and functioning" (*tiyong* 體用), which can perhaps be translated more simply and holistically as "trans-*form*-ing." As medical anthropologist Judith Farquhar observes in her attempt to make sense of this Chinese *qi* 氣 cosmology:

> *Qi* is both structural and functional, a unification of material and temporal forms that loses all coherence when reduced to one or the other "aspect."[69]

---

69. Judith Farquhar, *Knowing Practice: The Clinical Encounter of Chinese Medicine* (Boulder, CO: Westview, 1994), 34.

In TCM, systemic physiological functions within an ecology of relations have parity with if not privilege over the more persistent, localized anatomical structures, requiring that diagnostics be holistic and inclusive rather than being overly specific and then, by extension, analytic and exclusive. Remembering the reflexive nature of subjective and objective (*zhuke* 主客) discussed previously, these life functions also have an existential as well as a more objective character. The lived body is experienced self-consciously from the inside as well as being a physical organism to be observed and examined from the outside. The term *zhenmai* 診脈, for example, can certainly be localized as "taking this pulse," but more importantly it is doctor and patient together using tactile sensitivity to feel and interpret the visceral dynamics of the living body holistically—both from within and without. As such, these transactional procedures have synoptic reference not only to the organism as experienced from without but also to the organic, lived relationships this vital organism itself has within its external landscape. Remembering that "patient" comes from the Latin *patiens* from *patior* meaning "to suffer or bear," the TCM patient is not a "patient" in the literal sense of being a passive sufferer. Such a definition of patient is passive both in the sense of having to tolerate with patience the interventions of the outside expert while also bearing whatever suffering is necessary internally. In the case of TCM, however, the erstwhile patient is an active, existentially aware voice in the collaborative process of diagnostics.

Given the holography and focus-field assumptions that ground TCM, in "taking this pulse" (*zhenmai*), the medical practitioner and the patient are by extension collaborating to register the life of the family and community and ultimately to feel the pulse of the living cosmos as expressed through this specific organism. When we use this same language of focus and field to give an account of "bodyheartminding" (*xin*), it is first and foremost an embodied self-conscious center of thinking and feeling that extends out radially to the furthest reaches of an unbounded cosmos via the transactions constituting its physiological, psychological, and sociological narrative. When we read *xin* simply as "the heartmind," we are isolating this one focal aspect as a metonym for the holistic and eventful functions—both physical and psychic, objective and subjective—that in sum constitute a continuing human life in all its dynamic detail and particularity. Indeed, *xin* can only derivatively and abstractly be construed as the discrete physical, vital organ that symbolically represents the full complexity of the interactions and events that are had as experience.

We might cite a second related passage in the *Mencius* that advocates for making the most of our "bodyheartminding" and the symbiotic, expansive phases that follow from it. Such an effort enables us to not only grow our initial conditions in family and community fully but, in the process, also make our own distinctive contribution to the realization of our cosmic context:

> Those who make the most of their "bodyheartminding" (*xin*) realize their natural propensities (*xing*). And those who realize their natural propensities then realize the world around them (*tian*). By consolidating their bodyheartminding and nourishing their natural propensities they do service to the world (*tian*).[70]

Our familiar dualistic separation of inner and outer domains assumes a doctrine of second-order, external relations that obtain among independent things: private, discrete subjects who share an independent, objective world. Such a dualism brings with it the familiar intellectualist exercise called "*intro*-spection," a journey that turns inward away from the objective world to examine the contents of our own private "states of mind." That is, introspection is usually understood as a turning away from our normal outward orientation toward the objective world in order to perform a reflective examination of our own internal mental states and our subjective feelings that mirror that world. Inspired by this Mencian understanding of "bodyheartminding," however, we might want to challenge this assumption about what takes place when we look "inward" by inventing an alternative term—"*intra*-spection"—as being a more appropriate descriptor of an alternative model of self-consciousness. As previously noted, Michael Sandel opts for the search for an "intra-subjective" rather than "intersubjective" conception of self, with the understanding that "intra-" means "on the inside, within" and references internal and constitutive relations as they function within a given entity itself. "Intra-" has organic, ecological implications—an inside without an outside. In this holographic way of thinking, we must resist our default

---

70. *Mencius* 7A1: 盡其心者知其性也。知其性則知天矣。存其心養其性所以事天也。It is important to appreciate the performative implications of the term *zhi* 知—conventionally translated as "knowing." Rather than delimiting this capacity as simply "knowing" something cognitively, we have rendered it here as "realizing" in the performative sense of "making something real."

assumption that organisms are contained within their epidermis and see them instead as interpenetrating entities inhabiting a living ecological field that has neither end nor externality. Thus, *intra*-specting is an existential self-awareness that far from referencing erstwhile separate internal and external domains allows one to register those organic relations that obtain among the things that together constitute a particular entity—in this case, the pattern of relations as they converge to constitute one's own focal identity. The neologism "*intra*-spection" signals the fact that the vital process of self-consciously "*looking into* our own bodyheartminding" is at the same time a *looking outward* into the quality of the coalescence we, in our "bodyheartminding" experience, have achieved within our ecologically contextualizing world. Such an existential "subjective" process parallels the more "objective" orientation in which we expand our reach and influence by functioning like a mirror in our effort to defer fully to our environing others and cultivate optimally productive relations with them. The point is that bodyheartminding is holographic. And indeed since "the myriad things are all implicated here in me" in "making the most of our bodyheartminding," we are literally bringing the entire cosmos into more meaningful focus and resolution from our own self-consciously unique perspectives. In finding such personal resolve, we thus come to function most productively and influentially in our relations with what is happening in the world around us.

To make this point, we might recall a previously cited phrase from *Mencius* and now consider the passage as a whole rather than just the first part. It again expresses this "inner-outer" dynamic in a focus-field and holographic way:

> Mencius said, "Is there any enjoyment greater than, with the myriad things of the world all implicated here in me, to turn personally inward and to thus find resolution with these things. Is there any way of seeking to become consummate in my person more immediate than making every effort to act empathetically by deferring to the interests of others."[71]

Again, in this passage we see that becoming consummate as a human being is a holographic process. The self-awareness of our connectivity's

---

71. *Mencius* 7A4: 孟子曰: 萬物皆備於我矣。反身而誠, 樂莫大焉。強恕而行, 求仁莫近焉。

inner resolution with all of the happenings in the world and the empathetic outer reach and influence we are to have on other things are in fact coterminous and mutually entailing. As I achieve personal resolution, so my reach and influence in the world is extended. There is a symbiosis between self-consciously consolidating my relations within the focus of my own personal identity and deferentially expanding the field of relevance of this focal identity outward, between self-consciously bringing these same relations into meaningful resolution (*cheng* 誠), and deferring to and finding the optimally appropriate fit in the expanding circle of empathetic relations that converge to constitute myself (*shu* 恕). The shift here is between one's person and one's world, between getting and giving, and between foregrounding either the self-conscious resolution of my insistent particularity (*de* 德) or the quality of my life's narrative as it contributes to the unsummed narratives of the totality (*dao* 道). From the former perspective, my unique "subjective" identity is foregrounded as I examine the existential quality of the coalescence I have achieved with my environing others and what they have come to mean as integral to who I am becoming. And in the latter, the extended field of my "objective" world is foregrounded as it is construed and brought into meaningful resolution from my own unique perspective. The quality of resolution in my own identity determines the extent to which I have influence in the world and the extent to which this world is a better one because of me. In this way, not only are the myriad happenings of the world implicated here in me, but more importantly, these same events are made increasingly meaningful by virtue of my capacity to give full resolution to my connectivity with them in my own person. As this symbiosis is described in *Focusing the Familiar*, "Completing oneself is achieving virtuosity in one's roles and relations (*ren* 仁); completing all things is advancing wisdom in the world (*zhi* 知)."[72]

The Narrativity of Human "*Becomings*": A Summary

Bringing Graham's revisionist reading of Mencius on *xing* and our own elaborations on the relationally constituted person discussed in this chapter into summary form, we might begin by observing that *xin* 心 as the "four

---

72. *Zhongyong* 25: 成己, 仁也; 成物, 知也。

inclinations" (*siduan*) references the native physical, social, and cultural conditions of human "becomings" at their incipience as vital manifolds of shared bonds (*renyilizhi* 仁義禮智) that locate these persons within family and community and that incline them toward positive moral growth (*shan* 善) in the discursive roles and relations that constitute them. These native conditions are not only a generic description of the pattern of relations of persons as they are born into, live, and grow within the continuing narrative of a mature culture, they are also normative as a resource for our moral growth in the specific roles that we live. That is, although it is possible through inattention and a lack of effort to lose this capacity for normative growth in our relations, such a native predilection inclines us otherwise; if in fact we commit ourselves with increasing self-awareness to living according to the promptings of these native moral propensities that animate the inchoate pattern of our relations, we acquire increasing moral influence within our families and communities.

Again, we have seen that Mencius's notion of *xin* defies the familiar dichotomies of cognition and affect, body and mind, agent and action, inner and outer, subject and object, nature and nurture, and so on. Thus, as we have observed, if we want to do justice to the complexity of *xin*, rather than translating it simply as "heartmind" that challenges only the first among these many dualisms, we might have to render it as "this particular self-conscious, vital, resolute, and focused bodyheartminding within our field of experience." As such, it denotes a particular focal identity within an extended field of relations and is thus holographic, with "the myriad things of the world all implicated here in me." The living *xin* is a fundamentally relational, existential, and thus vital narrative, and it is only made formal and discrete as a second-order abstraction.

Xing 性, on the other hand, is the human propensity to cultivate our native pattern of relations (*xin*), and when we "make the most" of these initial relations (*jinqixin* 盡其心), we become fully who we are in our roles within family and community. The cultivation of our *qi* 氣 within the context of our discursive relations (*zhiyan* 知言) is what funds such personal growth and conduces to virtuosity in conduct. By cultivating both the self-conscious intensity (*zhigang* 至剛) and the resolution (*cheng* 誠) of this *qi*, the *qi* becomes intentional and deliberate (*zhi* 志). Such *qi* expressed as purposeful actions is animated by our commitment to achieving optimal appropriateness (*yi* 義) in what we do. It is the habituation of optimal appropriateness in our conduct that serves as the most productive disposition we can achieve in our best efforts to make our own surging "flood-like" contribution to the reach and influence (*zhida* 至大) of the proper way (*dao* 道).

The argument then is that the preponderance of the content of what comes to be our "human propensities" (*renxing* 人性) is acquired rather than given as it is expressed in the habitude of "consummatory conduct in roles and relations" (*ren* 仁), "acting optimally appropriate in meaningful relations" (*yi* 義), "realizing propriety in these roles and relations" (*li* 禮), and "acting with intelligence and wisdom" (*zhi* 智). "Natural propensities" (*xing* 性) are no more an essential, inborn given than is "consummatory conduct" (*ren* 仁). Both are a source and a product; that is, *ren* is the assiduous extension of tentative native conditions in an increasingly robust, self-conscious narrative that follows from habituated patterns of consummate conduct. "Acting with intelligence and wisdom" is not applying wisdom to a situation but a condition or quality of acting that arises through the efficacy of one's social actions.

In the absence of those biological, psychological, and metaphysical assumptions that lie behind the notion of the discrete individual, it is the continuing cultivation of unity and resolve in the deliberate purposes of physically and socially diffused and yet resolutely self-conscious persons that become the signature of our unique and coherent personal identities. There is thus an important and repeated distinction that the *Mencius* and other texts make between, on the one hand, simply making retail choices to act according to established conventions and achieving the resolution and focus that consolidates these norms as the structure, unity, and agency of our personal identities on the other. And an achieved propriety in the roles and relations of our narrative identities (*li* 禮) is reflected in an analogous growth and luster of our lived bodies (*ti* 體) that together are simultaneously expressive of this virtuosity. Indeed, just as virtuosity in the roles that we live comes to distinguish us with a self-conscious sense of worth and felt belonging within our families and communities, so the bodily aspect of this virtuosity is manifested in the warm and glowing complexion of our human physicality.

It is only in giving Mencius's notion of *xing* such a reading that we can get past Xunzi's caricature of him as naturalizing morality—that is, asserting that "human nature" is good. And we can thus appreciate the extent to which the insights of Mencius are indeed an extension of the intrepid Confucius, demanding as Mencius does assiduous effort in and full commitment to the project of becoming consummately human.

It is this self-aware, narrative understanding of the Confucian *xing* we can tease out of and reconstruct from Graham's oeuvre that provides us with the focus-field conception of persons. And it is this notion of persons as foci within fields, serving as ground for Confucian role ethics, that provides an alternative conception of persons sufficiently robust to challenge the ideology of a liberal individualism.

Chapter Four

Holography and the Focus-Field Conception of Persons

The Confucian Focus-Field Conception of Persons

In appealing to an understanding of Chinese natural cosmology as the interpretive context for Confucian persons, I want to introduce a language cluster that will distinguish this worldview from the single-ordered and thus reductive teleological model that is pervasive in classical Greek cosmotic ontology and that still significantly informs our common sense. With *eidos* as the principle of individuation in Greek ontology—that is, with some self-same, reduplicated, identical characteristic defining all members of a particular class—the "many" for both persons and world are to be known by the foundational and causal ideal that lying behind, subvenes upon them. In place of this familiar Greek "one-behind-the-many" ontology, we find that early Chinese cosmology has as an alternative, holistic, focus-field model of order that begins from the primacy of vital relationality. That is, if everything is constituted by its relations, and if these relations have no boundary either synchronically or diachronically, then everything is more or less relevant to any other particular thing. The primary consideration is the relative priority given to the environing others within the matrix of relations. This is perhaps the explanation for the primacy of family as a model of order within classical Confucian philosophy, where persons are conceived of as unique foci within their own specific field of family relations.

This holographic sense of order is illustrated rather concisely in the *Expansive Learning* (*Daxue* 大學) included in Zhu Xi's *Four Books* as the *locus classicus* for a succinct statement of the Confucian project:

> The way of becoming expansive in our learning lies in displaying real personal virtuosity, in cherishing the common people, and in dedicating ourselves to doing our very best. Such a regimen for learning can only be set once we have made such a commitment. Only in having set such a regimen are we able to find equilibrium, only in having found equilibrium are we able to be composed, only in being composed are we able to be deliberate in what we do, and only in being deliberate in what we do are we able to get what we are after.[1]

With respect to calibrating and respecting the relative importance of things in our waymaking, the language of the *Expansive Learning* is explicit:

> There is the important and the incidental in things and a beginning and an end in what we do. It is in realizing what should have priority that we close in on the proper way (*dao*).[2]

According to this text, it is collaterality in the project of personal cultivation in all of its complexity that is the source of the kind of expansive learning that will lead to human flourishing. The *Expansive Learning* then goes on to locate such personal cultivation holographically within the process of an expanding cosmic order. Since each person shapes and is shaped by the entire cosmos, the whole cosmos is implicated in each moment of a person's narrative. Such assiduous personal cultivation thus extends outward radially, ripple by ripple, to ultimately contribute its own growth to the attainment of a sustained equanimity in the world:

> The ancients who sought to demonstrate real virtuosity in the world first brought proper order to their states; in seeking to bring proper order to their states, they first set their families right; in seeking to set their families right, they first culti-

---

1. 大學之道，在明明德，在親民，在止於至善。知止而後有定，定而後能靜，靜而後能安，安而後能慮，慮而後能得。
2. 物有本末，事有終始，知所先後，則近道矣。

vated their own persons; in seeking to cultivate their persons, they first knew what is proper in their own heartminding; in seeking to know what is proper in their heartminding, they first became resolved in their purposes; in seeking to become resolved in their purposes, they first sought to extend their wisdom. And the extension of wisdom lay in seeing how things fit together most productively.³

The symbiotic and mutually entailing relationship between accomplished persons and a felicitous context—between the project of personal cultivation and the quality achieved in the social and geopolitical order of the world, between the cultivation of a critical and purposeful self-awareness and the coalescence of a person's relations with their environing others—is made clear as the text reverses the order of the process:

> Once these ancients saw how things fit together most productively, their wisdom reached its utmost; once their wisdom reached its utmost, their thoughts found resolution; once their thoughts found resolution, their heartminds knew what is proper; once their heartminds knew what is proper, their persons were cultivated; once their persons were cultivated, their families were set right; once their families were set right, their state was properly ordered; and once their states were properly ordered, there was peace in the world.⁴

Each person stands as a unique perspective on family, community, polity, and cosmos. And through a dedication to deliberate growth and articulation, everyone has the possibility of bringing resolution—and thus a clearer and more meaningful focus—to the manifold of relationships that locate them within family and community. With the organic, ecological sensibilities of the *Expansive Learning*, there is a symbiotic and holistic focus-field model of order where "learning" itself is nothing other than the cultivation of virtuosity in the transactional events that come to constitute one's narrative, beginning as it does from a growing

---

3. 古之欲明明德於天下者，先治其國；欲治其國者，先齊其家；欲齊其家者，先修其身；欲修其身者，先正其心；欲正其心者，先誠其意；欲誠其意者，先致其知，致知在格物。

4. 物格而後知至，知至而後意誠，意誠而後心正，心正而後身修，身修而後家齊，家齊而後國治，國治而後天下平。

critical and purposeful self-awareness. The meaning of the family is implicated in and dependent upon the productive cultivation of each of its members. And by extension, the meaning of the entire cosmos is in turn implicated in and dependent upon the productive cultivation of each person within family and community. Importantly, while existential narratives themselves are certainly the lived lives of particular persons, they are also unbounded and interpenetrating stories within their natural, social, and cultural ecologies.

Joseph Needham anticipates the focus-field language that gives expression to this holography. He draws heavily upon the work of Marcel Granet in describing the nature of "things" and "persons" within this ecological cosmology, where the identity of any one thing is a function of its location within the dynamic cosmic organism and within the specific matrix of relations that collaborate to give it its resolution.[5] John Henry Clippinger provides us with what might be a more concrete expression of Needham's cosmological observations when he challenges the erstwhile boundaries that separate and delineate persons specifically as individual existents. Clippinger finds that

> there is no such thing as the "individual" independent of the group. We are a crowd of one. There are no sharp dichotomies between species and environment, between one species and another, and between one race or religion and another.[6]

We might appeal to the institution of family, the governing metaphor in Chinese cosmology, as an illustration of the holographic focus and field dynamic described herein. Focus and field language is an apposite vocabulary for expressing the way in which particular family members occupy unique perspectives within this social unit, construing these interpenetrating and mutually constitutive familial relationships from their own particular ecological point of view: grandmothers and grandsons, fathers and daughters. Indeed, the term "focus" is itself etymologically derived from L. *focus* meaning "domestic hearth" or "fireplace," the nucleus around which life in the home has traditionally taken place. From this core idea of hearth and home, focus has come to mean the "locus of divergence and convergence" of persons within a "field"—that

---

5. See Needham, *Science and Civilisation*, 2:280–81.

6. Clippinger, *A Crowd of One*, 179.

is, what the members carry away from the family and what they bring home to it. And "field," too, is another term like "focus" that has a domestic, agrarian reference as the fields that are farmed and grazed and that supply the family with the provisions that are then prepared at the fireplace. I am using "field" here in its extended cosmological and yet still domesticating sense as the unbounded yet graduated sphere of influence of focal persons whose lives are centered in family and extend outward to have cosmic significance. Again, the term *ecology* comes from the Gk. *oikos* "household, dwelling place, habitat" and brings an organic, biological frame of reference to social and political relationships. Perhaps one limitation that this holographic, focus-field language has is that it is perhaps not dynamic enough to capture the ceaseless growth that attends the eventful lives of human "becomings," a continuing and vital process that is always evolving and transforming. Again, our organic metaphor as it is rooted in the classical Greek tradition is heavily freighted with teleological assumptions.

At any given moment, the world is available to each of us for *ars contextualis*, for the art of reconstrual within the context of the human experience. Such reconstrual can be characterized both in terms of the focal identities of persons constituted by the patterns of divergence and convergence that define them as they find resolution in their life narratives and in terms of their narrative fields that are made increasingly meaningful as these divergent and convergent lines extend outward to exercise reach and influence. More simply put, the focus and field holography describes the doings and the undergoings of persons as they shape and are shaped by their vital relations within the imbricated experience of their shared lives. How then can we express this focus-field model in a more concrete way? We might appeal to those exemplary persons whose lives give definition to every cultural tradition and who are remembered by each succeeding generation to tell its story and to galvanize its evolving identity. The more meaningful the lives of these cultural heroes, the greater their imprint on the fabric of their evolving cultural traditions.

We have thus far tried to develop a more nuanced understanding of what the extended and unbounded "field" might mean in a "focus-field" notion of human agency. And we have tried to reconceive the notion of inner life and outer world as holographic, aspectual, and interpenetrating. We now turn to a closer reflection on what the process of "focusing" this field entails and how such language might be useful in expressing a more complex yet perhaps more empirically coherent conception of agency and personal identity. In so doing, we might begin by responding to a concern voiced by philosopher David Wong. While Wong finds it unproblematic to say that "fields take on definition through individuals and their relationships and in that sense are constituted by them," at the same time, he worries that "it is more difficult to say how a field constitutes individuals."[7] We might restate Wong's concern here with specific examples. Wong is saying that it is easier to see how a family takes on its definition by virtue of the members who constitute it than to understand how the family lineage comes to constitute each of its members. Or it is easier to see how history is constituted by a sequence of particular events than to perceive how each event has implicated within it the entire course of history. Or it is easier to understand how a particular person speaks a language than it is to observe how the language speaks the person. What I want to do here in developing this notion of focus-field agency is to try to address this perceived asymmetry between fields being constituted by their foci on the one hand, and the foci being constituted by their fields on the other.

To begin with, just as we would want to distinguish between a leg and walking, we have to avoid the tendency to equivocate on the difference between a body and a person, especially given our habituated language of "nobody," "somebody," and "everybody." Indeed, we must acknowledge that walking, unlike a leg, is a focal, psycho-, and sociosomatic event performed in and with the world. In just this same way, we would do best within this relational cosmology to register a distinction between a body and a person and to think of persons who achieve their transactional and interdependent identities in and with the world as focal narrative events within a continuous history. Still, even as the unbounded totality is present within each eventful person and within each moment of their experience, there is inevitably the matter of graduated and radial degrees of relevance. In the focal identities of family members, for example, immediate and intimate relations are certainly closer to the focal center than distant relatives, and those distant relatives are closer than remote strangers. What is of key significance for persons in shaping the characteristic conduct that constitutes our unique identities is what actually becomes focal, resolute, and habituated. We might want to think of our focal identities as the clines or gradients

---

7. Wong, "Cultivating the Self," 191.

of what becomes most immediately significant for each of us as we try to bring our unique manifold of relationships into its most meaningful resolution. And again, for most of us, what is focal and thus has such privilege is our "embodied living" (*li* 禮) within the continuing narrative of those roles lived in our families and communities. At the same time, our many roles are performed through the always transactional activities we identify with the "living, existential body" (*ti* 體) inherited genealogically through our family lineages.

Indeed, this "narrative" understanding of persons that would allow for the parsing of people as discrete and isolated individuals only as a convenient, functional abstraction provides us with a partial answer to Wong's question about the kind of focal agency we ascribe to Confucian role ethics. I previously cited Wong's description of the *Analects* as "a group with Confucius at the center, engaged in moral cultivation, each with a different configuration of strengths and weaknesses." Wong goes on to make much of the aesthetic dimension of moral conduct within this cultural sensorium:

> The Confucian notion of what it is like to live a fully good life has an aesthetic dimension that might look odd and unfamiliar to a contemporary Western audience. . . . Such stylized action could be said to possess a moral beauty. The moral beauty lies in the gracefulness and spontaneity of what has become a natural respectfulness and considerateness.[8]

Perhaps we can appeal to just this aesthetic sensibility to help clarify how a specific field of relations comes to constitute each person. A Whiteheadian notion of aesthetic order is holistic. It begins from the assumption that all of the concrete and interpenetrating details of this particular painting and its unbounded context are relevant to the totality of the effect. When we move from paintings to persons, we must acknowledge that all of the narrative details—the entire field of events of our lives—are more or less relevant to the emerging identities of whom we are becoming as persons.

Although in his reflections on Confucian ethics Wong moves decisively in the direction of relational persons, he does not seem to

---

8. Wong, "Cultivating the Self," 177.

be willing to take this primacy of relationality as far as we would like. Indeed, beyond the question of determining how the field constitutes the focus, he also asks: who is "in" the relationship? Wong frames his second question thusly: "If I am the sum of my relationships, then who or what is the entity standing in each of these particular relationships?"[9] In asking this question, Wong seems to favor maintaining the primacy of first-order, discrete entities (albeit at first "biological organisms" rather than "persons") over their relations with others and thus to stay with a doctrine of external, second-order relations that would subsequently be established to conjoin such entities. And Wong's own answer to this question, developed in his earlier work and retained in his most recent publications, is the following: "We begin life embodied as biological organisms and become persons by entering into relationship with others of our kind."[10] For Wong, simply put, there must both logically and temporally be two "entities" before there can be a relationship between them. He retains this position in spite of his specific reference to "biological organisms" that would seem by definition to be embedded in and constituted by their vital relations.

Our answer to the question of who is "in" the relationship would be different from Wong's. We would refrain from the abstracting out of ecologically embedded entities that would introduce post hoc divisions into the original experience, and we would simply repeat our answer to Wong's first question. That is, we would claim that focal persons are constituted by their fields of relations. I have never been a critically self-conscious and purposeful "me" without this "me" being this son, this brother, this teacher, this dad, this Canadian and then American, and so on. Quite simply, we are our narratives. And there is no need to reduplicate this intense and habitual focus or center of constitutive relationships by positing an antecedent "substance" within which this field of relationships must inhere. William James challenges such "substance" thinking to be our "inveterate trick" of turning eventful referents into "things":

---

9. Wong, "Cultivating the Self," 192.

10. Wong, "Cultivating the Self," 192. See also his "Relational and Autonomous Selves," *Journal of Chinese Philosophy* 34, no. 4 (December 2004) and "If We Are Not by Ourselves, If We Are Not Strangers," *Polishing the Chinese Mirror: Essays in Honor of Henry Rosemont, Jr.*, eds. Marthe Chandler and Ronnie Littlejohn (New York: Global Scholarly Publications, 2008).

The low thermometer to-day, for instance, is supposed to come from something called the 'climate.' Climate is really only the name for a certain group of days, but it is treated as if it lay *behind* the day, and in general we place the name, as if it were a being, behind the facts it is the name of. But the phenomenal properties of things . . . do not inhere in anything. They adhere, or cohere, rather, with each other, and the notion of a substance inaccessible to us, which we think accounts for such cohesion by supporting it, as cement might support pieces of a mosaic, must be abandoned. The fact of the bare cohesion itself is all the notion of the substance signifies. Behind that fact is nothing.[11]

In order to be clear in formulating our own answer to Wong's question about focus-field agency, we will need to go back to the distinction between the doctrines of external and internal relations we have already discussed in some detail. In spite of our growing awareness of the resolutely ecological nature of experience, the tradition of substance ontology sedimented into our language along with the doctrine of external relations that it entails continues to be our shared and default common sense. This ontology guarantees the primacy and the integrity of the discrete and independent entities Wong is positing when he allows that we as separate organisms "become persons by entering into relationship with others of our kind."

In our earlier efforts, we have tried to build upon the work of scholars such as Marcel Granet, Joseph Needham, Tang Junyi, Fei Xiaotong, and Angus Graham in trying to understand and explain the prominence of analogical thinking as it functions within this early cosmology. Nowhere is such correlative, associative, projective thinking more apparent than in the way in which the fact of associated living produces the categories that define our always transactional experience as living organisms. We shape our environments and are shaped by them. From the outset, our relationality can be fairly described in terms of coming and going, giving and taking, rising and falling, closing and opening, extending and withdrawing, and so on. The doctrine of internal relations that we are ascribing to Confucian persons begins from the primacy of the organic continuity that is constitutive of putative "things." Given the primacy of

---

11. William James, *Pragmatism and Other Writings* (New York: Penguin, 2000), 42.

this vital relationality, both embodied biological relations and higher-order social relations as they are captured in the cognate, aspectual terms of "lived body" and "embodied living"—*ti* 體 and *li* 禮—are organically diffused as those dynamic, interactive, and interpenetrating patterns that make up the narratives of our lives as we live them. Such patterns are initially so weak, tentative, and passive that we may be inclined to describe such infants as "biological organisms," but in so doing, we must refrain from abstracting these same infants from the matrix of relations that locate them within a mature community and culture, taking such an isolated infant as our first-order reality. Such an abstraction would be a clear example of Whitehead's fallacy of misplaced concreteness, which we have previously visited. That is, such infants as organically constituted focal organisms do not terminate at their epidermises but radiate outward within specific patterns of relations that have no end. They are from the outset nested in and informed by the field of familial, communal, and cultural relations within which they continue to evolve. And as these patterns of relations are marked by sustained growth and depth in meaning, such thickening bonds anticipate that such infants are on their way to becoming increasingly unique, self-conscious, and distinctive persons.

But to be clear here, I am claiming that there are no infants as "biological organisms" independent of the web of relationships that constitute them. The argument is that any infant born into the world is not biologically, socially, or culturally a discrete or ready-made entity. Infants are not some exclusive life form with their own initial beginnings or final ends. Rather, on the analogy of such infant life emerging in their mother's womb, they are born in media res as narratives nested within narratives, drawing nourishment through their physical, social, and cultural umbilical cords. Indeed, far from being discrete or isolated, infants are the diffused presencing of physical, social, and cultural fields of radial relationships that extend to the furthest reaches of the cosmos. And with sustained growth and evolving resolution, these infants in time become increasingly self-aware and achieve their distinctive focal identities.

It is a commonplace that newly born infants deprived of family feeling in the first weeks and months of their lives are put at risk in the development of those basic capacities that make us most distinctively human. Indeed, we learn to love by being loved. John Henry Clippinger summarizes recent research on the extreme example of feral children raised in acute isolation and their "psychosocial dwarfism." Not only do these children as aberrant "individuals" fail to "acquire even rudimentary language ability and any sense of self or personal identity," but even their physical growth is stunted to the degree that they have "roughly one-third or less the body weight of a normal child."[12] The conclusion drawn by Clippinger's sources is that

> what it means to be human depends on an intensive and prolonged socialization process. Without that process, the intelligence, language, and social behavior we associate with being human simply do not materialize. . . . These examples of feral children illustrate unequivocally how personal identity is derived from a group identity, and hence, how the one and the crowd are inextricably interdependent.[13]

In making the case that infants cannot be isolated and separated from the activities that make up their lives, we return to our claim that walking as an activity in the world cannot be reduced to the leg that walks. Infants are active, incipiently self-conscious events, not discrete "things." In the same vein, there is an important distinction to be made between the activity of the minds of infants and their brains. The immediate family members who quite literally "mind" the infant communicate and impart their mature culture to this organism and initially serve as the primary resource for an increasingly "mindful" and purposeful child to draw upon in shaping a personal identity. If the phenomenon of infancy teaches us anything, it must be the unequivocal interdependence of our agency. Indeed, from reflection on infancy we should appreciate the always interdependent nature of our relationships not only for the evolving compositing of our identities but perhaps more immediately for our very survival. By thinking back on our early years, we come to understand that "mind" is that social, semiotic ambience that we gradually and quite literally "enroll" in over time. Mind emerges as we embodied organisms through communicating with each other become increasingly self-conscious and transform our merely associated living into our thriving families and communities.

What makes such claims about focal agency counterintuitive for us is the outdated yet persistent pull of our common sense. Indeed, there is

---

12. Clippinger, *A Crowd of One*, 151.
13. Clippinger, *A Crowd of One*, 151.

much in our own contemporary philosophical literature that argues for this same kind of ecological thinking. Early on, John Dewey appealed to the actual situated human experience as we live it to reject the commonsense assumptions about an ostensive autonomous "self" and posited instead persons as habitudes and as organic configurations of relations. What leads us to believe that impulse comes before habit in the growth of human beings is our penchant for isolating such persons and assigning them a beginning and an end. Dewey makes the argument that shared cultural life-forms or "habits" must in fact have priority over instincts, moral or otherwise, by observing that any infant thus isolated from its habitude of dependent relations would quickly become a dead infant. That is, infants left to their own devices without access to or intervention by culturally informed relations could not survive for a single day. Even the meaning of the actions and gestures of infants is derived from the mature communal context within which they reside. Reflecting on the relationship between impulse and habit, Dewey observes that

> the inchoate and scattered impulses of an infant do not coordinate into serviceable powers except through social dependencies and companionships. His impulses are merely starting points for assimilation of the knowledge and skill of the more matured beings upon whom he depends. They are tentacles sent out to gather that nutrition from customs which will in time render the infant capable of independent action. They are agencies for transfer of existing social power into personal ability; they are means of reconstructive growth.[14]

Mark Johnson has more recently done much to argue for the bodily basis of human meaning formation and also for the ultimately aesthetic ground of human flourishing. Johnson maps the way in which the barest of physical image-schemata are extended through the metaphorical projections and elaborations of our imagination to generate complex cognitive and affective patterns of meaning:[15]

---

14. Dewey, *Middle Works*, 14:94.

15. Johnson identifies his basic image-schemata as "containment," "force," "balance," "cycles," "scales," "links," and "center-periphery." In order to make this image-schemata consistent with the primacy of vital relationality in the classical Chinese cosmology, we would be inclined to read these basic images in fundamentally and irreducibly

> Our world radiates out from our bodies as perceptual centers from which we see, hear, touch, taste, and smell our world.[16]

For Johnson, the formal, logical structures of human understanding and the human capacity to produce complex culture is a direct extension of the activities of our lived bodies fashioned through the exercise of our seemingly boundless imagination. In his words, Johnson has urged the view

> that understanding is never merely a matter of holding beliefs, either consciously or unconsciously. More basically, one's understanding is one's way of being in, or having, a world. This is very much a matter of one's embodiment, that is, of perceptual mechanisms, patterns of discrimination, motor programs, and various bodily skills. And it is equally a matter of our embeddedness within culture, language, institutions, and historical traditions.[17]

To give only one example of how higher-order thinking might be the extension of bodily actions, it is not difficult to conceive of how recurrent, habituated physical patterns such as giving and getting, rising and falling, and balancing can be extended, transformed, and metaphorically projected to produce the higher-order economic concepts and values that define a mature culture. We might take a Confucian metaphor and trace this same kind of evolving meaning. In all of the early Confucian writings, the theme perhaps most persistent and pervasive in shaping the philosophical tradition broadly is the project of making our proper "way" in the world through a regimen of personal cultivation in our roles and relations. We previously saw how the earliest form of this character *dao* 道 comprised the coiffured human head (*shou* 首) and the signific that indicates walking (*chuo* 辶), providing a physical portrait of human beings resolutely forging a path forward. We can see further with the linked polysemy of this term *dao* how meaning is extended from our physical to our more complex cognitive experience—that is, from the

---

relational terms describing these always transactional relationships that constitute organisms within their human and natural ecologies.

16. Mark Johnson, *The Body in the Mind: The Bodily Basis of Meaning, Imagination, and Reason* (Chicago: University of Chicago Press, 1987), 124.

17. Johnson, *Body in the Mind*, 137.

physicality of "waymaking" to "showing the way" to the "pathway" we have made, and then on to the cognitively and affectively informed actions of "speaking" and "explaining" that eventuate in proposing a deliberate "method" for doing things. Indeed, this one term takes us from forging a path to extending the cultural center of our human experience, our *daotong* 道統. Our potential as human "becomings" is not a given but rather emerges as a function of our collaboration with the circumstances of our lives that begin from our embeddedness in our bodily experience.

One is Many, Many One

Tang Junyi introduces a cosmological postulate he calls *yiduobufenguan* 一多不分觀 that we might summarize as "one is many, many one." This persistent characteristic of Confucian cosmology provides us with yet another way of conceiving of this dynamic process of personal identity formation. Tang would insist that this protean expression is a distinctive, generic feature of the Chinese processual cosmology locating our persons as vital and specific foci that have implicated within each of us a boundless field of relations. Importantly, *yiduobufen* is another way of describing the doctrine of intrinsic, constitutive relationality we have contrasted previously with external relations. It is, simply put, the assumption that in the compositing of any "one," there is implicated within it the contextualizing "many." This *yiduobufen* proposition can be read in many different ways, as it speaks at once to the following: the inseparability of the one and the many, the continuity between particular identity and context, the copresence of uniqueness and multivalence, the mutuality of continuity and multiplicity, the inclusiveness of integrity and integration, the dynamics of a shared harmony emerging out of relational tensions, the expression of the specific details in the totality of the effect, and so on.[18] It also restates in a different language the focus-field conception of persons: each self-conscious person, as well as each impulse in the life of each person, has implicated within it the boundless "many." This defining feature of Chinese natural cosmology is fundamental to our understanding of the relationally constituted, focus-field conception of persons. Again, as Mencius says, "The myriad things of the world are

---

18. Tang Junyi, *Complete Works*, 11:16–17.

all implicated here in me."[19]

Cosmologically, this proposition of the inseparability of one and many is an alternative principle of individuation that stands in contrast to a classical Greek essentialism, the Platonic one-behind-the-many ontology presupposing that some self-same, reduplicated, identical characteristic defines all members of a particular class. Individuation in Confucian cosmology is effected in a different way. All unique events or foci—particular persons, as an example—are constituted by an unbounded field of more or less relevant relations that collaborate to sponsor them, and they achieve their individuated identities as a function of the quality of coalescence they achieve within these unique fields of relations. That is, moving from description to prescription, a dynamic reading of *yiduobufen* is a summary of the way in which the opportunity is available to each of us to optimize the boundless possibilities that honeycomb the relationships between particular persons and our environing conditions. Tang Junyi's postulate asserts not only that any phenomenon in our field of experience has implicated within it the contextualizing, unbounded many but further that as a unique "one," it can find self-conscious resolution and purpose. But it can also be focused in many different ways according to the multiplicity of roles that come to define its narrative. Importantly, any claim to uniqueness and individuality, far from excluding a person's relations with others, is a function of the quality that this person has been able to achieve within the unique configuration of these same relations.

A version of this same situated and situational dynamic of "individuating" through the one and the many is expressed in the language the Mohists appeal to in explaining the process of individuation. In the later Mohist canons, there is reference to the "unit" or "one" (*ti* 體) and its "complex" or "many" (*jian* 兼), or stated more concisely, some "thing" and its context.[20] But this distinction, far from being simple, makes the point that any fixed and final sense of individuation—of "thing"—is problematic. According to the early *Shuowen* lexicon, *ti* as a "bodily" unit is again divided into the four subcategories of head, trunk, arms, and legs, and each of these units is then divided into three more subcategories for a total of twelve. This fluidity between one and many is consistent with the previously cited observations of Deborah Sommer. Reporting on the

---

19. *Mencius* 7A4: 孟子曰: 萬物皆備於我矣。
20. See A. C. Graham, *Later Mohist Logic, Ethics and Science* (Hong Kong: Chinese University Press, 1978), 265.

occurrence of the tuber or rhizome as a "subterranean body" (*xiati* 下體) in the early literature, Sommer observes that

> when a *ti* body is fragmented into parts (literally or conceptually), each part retains in certain aspects, a kind of wholeness or becomes a simulacra of the larger entity of which it is a constituent."[21]

In this cosmology, there are no assumed ultimate elements or simples. Instead, the formal aspect of *ti* or "unit" emerges according to the functional situation—that is, through the inseparable processes of "forming and functioning" (*tiyong* 體用).

Again, on the bronzes, the character *jian* 兼 appears as two sheaves of grain *[xxvi]*, an ideogram that expresses the idea of "in combination," "together," "simultaneously connected."[22] In this Mohist terminology, the particular unit—that is, what makes the *ti* a "one"—is always a function of how we choose to locate and foreground it. This thumb is a *ti* to this hand that serves as its *jian*, the hand is a *ti* to this arm as its *jian*, this arm is a *ti* to this body as its *jian*, and so on. Something or someone is not "one" in itself but becomes uniquely one by virtue of how it becomes focused in its relations within the dynamic field of others. This thumb is only this thumb by virtue of its location within this hand and by the self-conscious process of extending its context to include this arm, this body, this hitchhiking situation, and so on. That is, the most familiar way of looking at this thumb is to foreground it as an individuated unit, but a more important observation is to see it as being "aspectual" and "functional" by situating it within its relational *and eventful* context not only as an integral feature of this hand but also as being integral to the experience of *what this hand is doing*.

A corollary to the primacy of relationality and its doctrine of internal, constitutive relations is the fact that the field of any particular thing—the thumb in this case—is necessarily unbounded; its web of relations does not terminate anywhere but radiates outward and keeps on going. Hence, all correlations we make between thumb and hand are abstractive rather than final, functional rather than absolute, and narrative rather than essential. This being the case, the thumb is "one" as an

---

21. Sommer, "Boundaries of the *Ti* Body," 294.

22. Kwan, "Database," CHANT 戰國11379.

always fluid center of relationships where, as an aspectual center, it can be self-consciously focused and reconceptualized in many different ways: as a necessary collaborator in finger snaps or *shakas*, as a main actor in the familiar gesture of an emphatic "yes" or (when turned downward) of an equally emphatic "no," or as the responsible digital member for manipulating the spacebar when it is resting on the computer keyboard. And of course, the thumb so described is a simulacrum for persons who are conventionally conceived of as individuals, where such discrete individuality is also abstractive, functional, and ultimately narrative.

John Dewey in *The Public and Its Problems* makes this same point about individuation and the tentative nature of any designated "one." What we might refer to as an "individual" cannot be separated from "its connections and ties" nor from "the consequences with respect to which it acts and moves." Dewey observes that

> we are compelled to say that for some purposes, for some results, the tree is the individual, for others the cell, and for a third, the forest or the landscape. Is a book or a leaf or a folio or a paragraph, or a printer's em *the* individual? Is the binding or the contained thought that which gives individual unity to a book? Or are all of these things definers of an individual according to the consequences which are relevant in a particular situation? Unless we betake ourselves to the stock resort of commonsense, dismissing *all* questions as useless quibbles, it seems as if we could not determine an individual without reference to differences made as well as to antecedent and contemporary connections. If so, an individual, whatever else it is or is not, is not just the spatially isolated thing our imagination inclines to take it to be.[23]

We might invoke Tang Junyi's postulate of *yiduobufen* to respond to a familiar criticism of Confucian role ethics in the Chinese-language literature by some of China's most distinguished philosophers. Guo Qiyong 郭齐勇 and his student Li Lanlan 李兰兰, for example, in a recent article entitled "An Appreciative Critique of Roger T. Ames's Notion of Confucian Role Ethics," provide a detailed, largely accurate, and most generous summary of what I have proposed: the idea that "role ethics"

---

23. Dewey, *Later Works*, 2:352.

is the best way of thinking about Confucian moral philosophy. At the same time, these two scholars are not entirely persuaded by all of my arguments and offer several reservations in the final section of their paper subtitled "The Limitations of the Notion of Confucian Role Ethics." Guo and Li would argue that

> in speaking of Confucian ethics itself, there is no question that it includes a sense of "universalism" (*pubianzhuyi* 普遍主義). As confirmed by many scholars such as Feng Youlan, Tang Junyi, and Zhang Dainian, when Confucianism deploys its social structures, it includes both a concrete dimension and a search for both the "universal" and what is "ultimate" (*zhongjixing* 終極性).[24]

In addition to *pubianzhuyi* 普遍主義 (that I have translated here as "universalism"), Guo and Li and many if not most contemporary Chinese scholars are also comfortable using the Chinese translation of the related English term "transcendence" as *chaoyue* 超越 to describe the important asymmetrical relationship between human beings and *tian* 天. Guo and Li, for example, insist that

> in Confucian conceptual thinking, *tian* has both a "transcendent" (*chaoyue* 超越) reference as well as denoting its relationship to human beings. Revering *tian* in sacrifices to ancestors, and human beings emulating *tian* indicates that for the ancients the transcendent *tian* could descend into the human world.... Terms such as *tian* itself, "the mandate of *tian*" (*tianming* 天命), and "the way of *tian*" (*tiandao* 天道) that serve as ground for Confucian ethics all have a transcendent and ultimate dimension.[25]

---

24. Guo Qiyong 郭齐勇 and Li Lanlan 李兰兰. 安乐哲《儒学角色伦理学》学说的折评 [An appreciative critique of Roger T. Ames's notion of Confucian role ethics] 哲学研究 (*Research in Philosophy*) 47, no. 1 (2015): 從儒家倫理本身來看，無疑包含著普遍主義的情懷，很多學者如馮友蘭、唐君毅、張岱年等都曾指出，儒家建構社會性時有具體的一面，也有普遍性和終極性的追尋。

25. Guo and Li, "An Appreciative Critique," 47–48: 在儒家的思想觀念裡，「天」作為超越的存在與人之間的關聯一直存在，敬天祭祖、人法天等說明古人認為超越性的「天」是可以下貫於人的 . . . 儒家倫理的背後有「天」、「天命」、「天道」的支

I would make three initial responses to the critique of these two philosophers. First, I am keenly aware that the criticisms as they have been formulated here by Guo and Li are shared by many scholars who have voiced the same or similar concerns in their response to the notion of Confucian role ethics. Secondly, I would take what they are calling the "limitations" of my understanding of Confucian ethics as in fact the strength of this vision of the moral life. The language of "universalism" and "transcendence" as it has been expressed in Western philosophy and theology has a long history of being strident, exclusive, oppressive, and condescending. Because claims to universalism do not brook alternatives or exceptions, they have often stood as an uncompromising assertion of unconditional truth. Confucian ethics, on the other hand, grounded as it is in a radical empiricism and the contextualism that comes with it, offers us a more modest and intuitively persuasive way of thinking about how to get the most out the human experience. For Confucian ethics that can be fairly described in the language of "the inseparability of one and many" (*yiduobufen* 一多不分), any generalization must be qualified by its contextualizing conditions. Confucian role ethics begins from an acknowledgment of our interdependence and continuity with each other and with our various environments. Such an ethic is expressed through the deference to others that must follow from such an acknowledgment and through the aspiration made possible by such deference to achieve an optimum symbiosis in our relations.

Thirdly, I believe that the specific disagreements that Guo, Li, and other scholars who have expressed the same concern have with me are, in important measure, a matter of terminology rather than substance. The disagreement is a matter of "sense and reference" that itself requires an appreciation of the narrative context of ideas. I take our seeming disagreement to be a problem of language that arises when, in moving between the process cosmology persistent within Confucian cosmology, on the one hand, and the substance thinking that goes back to the ancient Greeks on the other, we equivocate on our philosophical terms.

While these Chinese terms *pubian* and *chaoyue* have their own limited textual histories, they are first and foremost recent additions to a Chinese academic vocabulary formulated as equivalencies for Western modernity's notions of the "universal" and "transcendent," respectively.[26] To

---

撐,具有超越性、終極性的一面.
26. I would like to thank Lydia H. Liu 劉禾 for helping me think through this issue

the extent we acknowledge that they are translations of the original Greek and now English terms, we encounter a fundamental problem. English terms such as "universal" and "transcendent" are the ground of dualistic thinking. When used in a strict philosophical sense, they carry with them specific ontological distinctions that separate what is real from what is less so and what is the determinative source of things from its creatures. These terms used in this way are grounded in classical Greek metaphysics of "being *per se*" (or "being in itself") and reference an unchanging, intelligible reality that transcends time and space. As unconditional and absolute claims, they stand independent of any particular context. Such notions are the ground of the dualism, objectivism, and foundationalism that has been a signature of much of pre-Darwinian Western philosophy. Indeed, it is precisely this transcendent universal as the single, inviolate, and self-sufficient reality that in the tradition's quest for certainty has promised us an unchanging object of apodictic truth. Such assumptions are again reinforced in the Western narrative when the Church Fathers translate the conceptual structures of Greek philosophy into the language of theology and when the transcendent universal comes to define the singular, independent, and self-sufficient Christian God.

But Guo and Li are reading a Chinese translation of my work on Confucian role ethics and are understanding the terms *pubian* 普遍 and *chaoyue* 超越 not as the translation of the Western terms "universal" and "transcendent" but are making sense of them according to their current use within the Chinese academy. And as long as Guo and Li have this reference—that is, as long as they are reading Chinese and intend the meaning of the Chinese terms as they are understood within the Chinese interpretive context—they are making sense of Confucian cosmology in a way I would endorse without reservation. This is no different from us all agreeing that if *tian* is to be translated as "Heaven," we cannot then equate this Confucian "Heaven" with the Abrahamic conception of God as this notion God has been informed by Greek idealism.

My reading of *pubian* as it would apply to Confucian cosmology is that rather than referencing some independent, originative, determinative, and thus transcendent universal, it describes the overarching, ubiquitous, all-encompassing, and continuous aspect of the human experience that

---

and for the important work she has done in alerting us to the persisting problem of contemporary Asian scholarship using the vocabulary and theoretical framework of Western modernity as its own voice.

complements its concrete, multifarious, and particular characteristics—that is, a complementary relationship that can be expressed in the language of the inseparability of the one and its many (*yiduobufen*). In Confucian cosmology, this complementary, aspectual distinction between one and many is captured in the language of *dao* 道 in its relationship to the myriad things (*wanwu* 萬物) and the "insistent particularity" (*de* 德) of each one of these events. This "one" and "many" distinction is again there in *tian* in its "inseparability" (*heyi* 合一) from the earth (*di* 地) and from the human world (*ren* 人) as well. And further, while terms such as "universal" and "transcendent," taken strictly in their philosophical sense, assert the independence of some ultimate principle from the world of flux and flow, Confucian notions such as *dao* and *tian* are resolutely processual and are invariably construed from one perspective or another. Thus, the continuous aspect that we call *dao* and *tian* as "one" can only be understood by reference to the multifarious and always evolving content of experience as "many." And again, each of the many things that are integral to the overarching *dao* and *tian* are at the same time inseparable from their own unique and ever-evolving contexts.

When *pubian*, *puji* 普及, or *pushi* 普世 are used to describe Confucian values, they quite properly celebrate the wide-ranging and broad application such values have to the human experience in general and might be best translated as "common values" or "shared values." Again, and importantly, what I would take to do the work of erstwhile "ultimacies" (*zhongji* 終極) in Confucian thinking, rather than referencing the boundary conditions of some unchanging ideal, is the shared aspiration within family and community to optimize the creative possibilities available to human "becomings" within their evolving natural, social, and cultural contexts. The aspiration to such "ultimacies" animates the best efforts of persons to achieve and sustain this superlative harmony (*he* 和).

Conversely, were Confucianism to have "universal" values or were *tian* to be "transcendent" in the Greek sense, the categories of explanation in a Confucian philosophy would reside within a two-world cosmogony and would necessarily be dualistic in its separation of reality from appearance and Being from becoming. Rather than the correlative *yinyang* 陰陽 and the inclusive "inseparability" (*heyi* 合一) vocabulary that is in fact ubiquitous in this tradition, we would encounter the familiar dichotomous and exclusionary language of some ontological reality trumping mere appearance. The clear absence of dualistic thinking in Confucian philosophy is a sure sign that transcendental universalism in its classical

Greek visage has little relevance for this cosmology or the philosophical assumptions that follow from it.

Stated positively, I would agree with Guo and Li that Confucian philosophy is fundamentally holistic and thus, by definition, inclusive. It is not relativistic in a fragmenting and pernicious sense. But I would also argue that "if it is not relativism then it must be absolutism" is not the choice we have to make. I would begin from the fact that the kind of absolutism derived from Greek philosophy is now outmoded within its own Western narrative: the assertion that there is a single, final, and unchanging Truth behind the multiplicity of things has been deemed nothing less than fallacious thinking. Confucian philosophy's alternative to a pernicious relativism is not some Confucian variation on this kind of discredited absolutism. Instead, it offers us an inclusive pluralism that is captured in the core value of promoting an achieved diversity: the pursuit of a "superlative and inclusive harmony by activating our differences" (*heerbutong* 和而不同). At the same time, it eschews the kind of "homogenizing uniformity" we would associate with a transcendent universalism in which the "many" reduce to the "one." Simply put, the ontological univocity that comes in the door with universalism is anathema to Confucian pluralism.

As I have suggested, we must be cognizant of the fact that in ascribing such an ontological framework to Confucian cosmology, we are insinuating into this tradition a worldview that has been under assault within the corridors of Western philosophy itself for at least the past century. Indeed, the revolution currently taking place within the Western philosophical community might be fairly described as an attempt to set aside the metaphysics of transcendent universalism, cast off the logic of the changeless that attends it, and repudiate the dualistic assumptions that follow from it. This internal critique that continues to be waged within professional Western philosophy under the many banners of process philosophy, hermeneutics, poststructuralism, postmodernism, pragmatism, neo-Marxism, deconstructionism, feminist philosophy, and so on, takes as a shared target what Robert Solomon has called "the transcendental pretense" in its many iterations: universalism, idealism, rationalism, foundationalism, objectivism, formalism, logocentrism, essentialism, the master narrative, onto-theological thinking, "the myth of the given," and so on. Philosophers today are intent on repudiating these familiar reductionistic "isms" that have emerged over time as putatively novel choices on the merry-go-round of systematic philosophy. In place of a Cartesian rationalism that privileges the precision of clear and distinct ideas in its quest for objective certainty, vocabularies of process, change, particularity, metaphor, creative advance, and indeed productive vagueness have come increasingly into vogue. Simply put, an important direction in contemporary Western philosophy is the attempt to "think process" and to cultivate the practical wisdom needed for philosophy to be relevant to an always changing world order. And the good news for comparative philosophy is that these recent developments in mainstream Anglo-European philosophy are themselves giving rise to an interpretive vocabulary that promises a more productive dialogue with a Chinese philosophical tradition that has never denied change or process.

In addition to using this notion of *yiduobufen*, the inseparability of "one" and "many," to distinguish holistic and inclusive *pubian* thinking from transcendent universalism, I can also respond to another criticism of Confucian role ethics made by Huang Yushun 黃玉順, a contemporary philosopher who is perhaps best known for his consistently innovative work on "Life Confucianism" (生活儒學) and the many issues surrounding social justice. Huang understands the idea of role ethics as advocating for a premodern relational way of life—the kind of Chinese lives lived previously within a shared cultural community with its inclusive relationality. For Huang, the needs of a modern China and modern humanity in general have left this old relational way of thinking behind. In his own words, modernity and its notion of a discrete individualism are necessary conditions for today's new China:

> What we need to pay attention to is that at its several methodological levels, the key idea for role ethics is the contrast between the "individual" or "person" on the one hand, and "relationality" or "correlationality" on the other. Role ethics sees Western philosophy as grounded in individualism and Confucian philosophy in relationalism, sets them up as contrasts, criticizes the former, and attempts to use the latter to solve the problems that come with individualism even to the extent of criticizing the modern concept of human rights. To speak truly, I have real misgivings. Saying nothing about the simplicity of the conclusions or the necessary relationship between modernity and individuality, what I am really concerned about is this: For today's China, with human rights being less rather than more, what can an ethic that gives

highest priority to relations do to protect individual rights? My opinion is that for today's China, what needs to be most severely criticized is precisely the traditional ethic that gives highest priority to relationality.[27]

I am grateful to Huang Yushun for affording me this opportunity to clarify my understanding of Confucian persons and also to raise our shared concern for social justice. First, the contrast developed in Confucian role ethics is not the simple one between individuals and relationality that Huang offers us here. I have tried to address this familiar misreading of role ethics in the distinction I have previously developed between the "discrete individual" and "relationally constituted individuality." When properly conceived, the relational Confucian conception of persons, with its corollary doctrine of internal relations, can be restated in terms of "the inseparability of the uniqueness of particular persons and their constitutive relations" (*yiduobufen*). Confucian persons are not discrete individuals but in their relational individuality are distinctively and self-consciously one and ecologically many at the same time. And the quality of their unique individuality is inclusive of and dependent upon the cultivation of their roles and relations.

With respect to human rights, we can appeal to this same Confucian conception of "one-and-many" persons to reconcile the contradiction I find in the United Nations' Universal Declaration of Human Rights (UDHR).[28] The civil and political rights of individuals articulated in the

---

27. Huang Yushun黄玉顺, 角色"意识:《易传》之"定位"观念与正义问题——角色伦理学与生活儒学比较 [Role consciousness: The concept of "positioning" in the *Commentaries to the Book of Changes* and the problem of justice: A comparison between role ethics and life Confucianism]《齐鲁学刊》[Journal of Qi and Lu] no. 2 (2014): 5. 须注意的是, 角色伦理学在方法论层级上的真正关键概念, 其实是相互对立"个体"(individual或person) 和"关系"(relation或correlation)。角色伦理学把西方哲学归结为个体主义, 而把儒家哲学归结为关系主义, 并将二者对立起来, 批判前者, 试图用后者来解决前者带来的问题, 甚至批判现代的"权利"观念。说实话, 我对此是深表怀疑的。且不说能不能这样简单地归结, 也不谈现代性生存与个体性的内在必然联系, 我所深感忧虑的是: 对于今天的中国来说, 个体权利不是太多了, 而是太少了, 那么, 这种关系至上的伦理如何能够保障个体权利? 我的看法是: 对于今天的中国来说, 亟须批判的正是这种关系至上的传统伦理。

28. See my 儒家的角色倫理學與杜威的實用主義: 對個人主義意識形態的挑戰 [Confucian role ethics and Deweyan pragmatism: A challenge to the ideology of individualism]. 《東嶽論叢》[*Dongyue Tribune*] 總第233期 2013 年第11期). Reprinted in 《

first twenty-one items of the UDHR are often called "first generation" rights. They offer a negative freedom in the sense of protecting the individual's autonomy and sovereignty. These rights are basically entitlements that guarantee freedom *from* encroachments, and in so doing, are designed to secure the integrity of the individual. But in its last six items, the UDHR also lists a number of social, economic, and cultural rights that include the right to security, a job, food, education, health care, decent housing, and much more. What we call "second generation" rights are grounded in our obligations to each other, thereby providing everyone with positive freedom *for* and entitlement *to*—for example, freedom for full participation in communal activities and entitlement to an education. That is, these social and welfare rights are substantial in undergirding a foundation for distributive justice by requiring that persons in degree be responsible for each other and are designed to serve as a necessary check on the excesses of a self-regarding individualism.

Michael Nylan and Thomas Wilson tell the history of the advocacy of these human rights by reference to two of the New Confucians, Zhang Junmai 張君勱 (Carson Chang) and Xu Fuguan 徐復觀, both signatories to the "Manifesto for the Reappraisal of Sinology and a Reconstruction of Chinese Culture" (1958). Another important figure in this story was Zhang Pengchun 張彭春 (Chang Peng Chun) who was himself the single Chinese author among the UDHR team and one of the leading architects of and advocates for the inclusion of the second generation rights.[29] These so-called second generation rights were adopted into the UDHR in the wake of the devastation occasioned by World War II as a way to get national governments to commit themselves to ending poverty within their borders. The advocates of these additional economic, social, and cultural rights would insist that without them all notions of freedom and autonomy are rendered tenuous at best. Such social rights are made necessary because they are concerned with obviating the social and natural impediments to a flourishing society and promoting the full realization of our human capacities within our families and communities. These rights require our active concern as members of the human community in the sense that there are certain things we must do if others are to secure the benefits of these rights; that is, we will at the very least have to pay

---

倫理學》 [*Ethics*] no. 1 (2014).

29. Michael Nylan and Thomas Wilson, *Lives of Confucius: Civilization's Greatest Sage Through the Ages* (New York: Doubleday, 2010), 210.

more taxes and share our personal assets to some degree. Put another way, schools, medicines, jobs, food security, affordable housing, hospitals, and the like do not fall from the sky; they are human creations and come at a cost that we all must share.

Herein lies the fundamental conflict in the contemporary discourse on human rights grounded as it is in the concept of the autonomous individual. To whatever extent we may be seen to be morally responsible for assisting others in the creation and obtaining of those goods that accrue to others by virtue of having second generation rights, to just that extent we cannot be altogether autonomous individuals, enjoying first generation rights, free to rationally decide upon and pursue our own projects rather than having to assist the less fortunate with theirs. These second generation rights are active in the sense that there are certain things I am required to do and certain freedoms I must in degree surrender if you or anyone else is to secure the benefits of these welfare rights. The reconciliation of this UDHR contradiction requires that we reconceive of persons in a way that allows them to retain a robust sense of their own individuality while also acknowledging their responsibility to the many others who constitute their communities. The Tang Junyi postulate of *yiduobufen* that would describe persons as "one and many" also warns against "the perils of abstraction" that we encounter when we ignore context and take what is abstracted from it as fixed and final.

Bringing the discussion of *yiduobufen* back to how Confucian conceptualizes self-conscious and purposeful persons, to know someone is to know their story and to be able to locate them in their continuing and always transactional narrative. It is to know both their whence and their whither. Taking a concrete example, this woman Amy is this father's daughter, this daughter's mother, this husband's wife, this student's teacher, this person's best friend, and so on. Acknowledging the many relations that converge to constitute her focal identity, she is uniquely who she is because of who they are—and who they are for her. On the one hand, she is "one" as a unique, critically self-aware, and persistent personality that becomes increasingly influential to the extent that she is able to bring resolution and meaning to the pattern of specific roles she lives as a caring daughter and a conscientious teacher. And on the other hand, she is "many" with both her immediate family, community, and by extension the entire cosmos with all that is happening, implicated with some greater and lesser degree of resolution in her own intensive and extensive patterns of relationships. The goal for this uniquely individual

Amy in cultivating these many relationships that constitute her as this singular person is to grow and to thus optimize their possibilities—to make the very most of the particular opportunities that her always unique circumstances allow. The greater her self-conscious intensity and resolution, the more sway she has in her world. And by way of contrast, to the extent she is diffused and indefinite and fails to find resolution in her relations, the less she matters.

The meaning of Amy's family, for example, as one locus of resolution, is emergent and constantly being negotiated out of the continuing needs and contributions of the members that constitute it. And its value is disclosed in the quality of meaningful relations they are able to achieve together. The family and the quality of life available to its members is the invariably evolving and provisional consequence of associated living contingent upon the quality of the conduct of those particular persons that come to constitute it. Each of the individual members of the family from his or her own unique perspective expresses the full complement of relations with all of the family members in what they do and who they become. Being neither rigidly linear nor teleologically disciplined toward some given, rationalizing end, this family—and it is always a *this*—is fundamentally and ideally, too, an inclusive, always inimitable, aesthetic achievement.

Paronomasia: A Confucian Way of Making Meaning

The primacy of the inclusive and holistic aesthetic order in the Confucian cosmology is underscored when the distinguished French Sinologist Marcel Granet observes rather starkly that "Chinese wisdom has no need of the idea of God."[30] Two implications of this claim for Confucianism is the absence of some external, objective reality that would promise truth and the absence of the ontological dualism that would convey that truth and make it available. There is little relevance for our familiar and reductive reality and appearance distinction that would rationalize the human experience according to this privileged conception of reality. It is the nature of dualism that when reality, for example, is distinguished from appearance, the first term stands independent of the second and effectively negates its dyadic pair by advancing its superior claim on reality. It is thus that

---

30. Marcel Granet, *La pensée chinoise* (Paris: Editions Albin Michel, 1934), 478.

reason can negate emotion and serve as an engine to find truth on its own without reference to our affective capacities. Again, objectivity will disclose truth, while subjective opinion is not only merely a matter of taste but in fact obscures what is actually true. Indeed, such assumptions are alive and well in our common sense: emotions obstruct rather than reveal truth, and subjective opinion needs to be set aside in the light of objective standards.

In Chinese cosmology, by way of contrast with this dualistic thinking, the changing world as a continuing flow of experience is all real, and both terms in a correlative pair—*yin* 陰 and *yang* 陽, for example—are interdependent and mutually entailing descriptors of some aspect of this real world. Indeed, as we have seen, reason and emotion as thinking and feeling are both equally real functions of Confucian "heartminding" (*xin* 心), and both of them are necessary in our search for what can thus be trusted in our relations: truth as a true friend. Similarly, "objectivity" (*keguan* 客觀) and "subjectivity" (*zhuguan* 主觀) serve today as translations of the dualistic Western language of modernity. But when such terms are understood as integral to Confucian cosmology as "guest" and "host" respectively, they are two aspectual and thus inseparable ways of viewing the same phenomenon, with each of them providing a complementary perspective. The key distinction here is that "dualistic" categories are ontologically distinct from each other with one being more real than the other, and thus they can be distinguished and separated through analysis. "Correlative" categories, on the other hand, are aspectual, with each being equally real and each relying on the other as a necessary complement to what it says about reality.

What follows linguistically from the Confucian primacy of this holistic aesthetic order is the absence of any clear distinction between literal and metaphorical language that such an ontological rationalizing of experience would bring with it. As we saw in *Focusing the Familiar*, there is a seemingly simple and yet profound observation made about the human experience that "since events in the world are never duplicated, their proliferation is beyond comprehension."[31] Such a world being constituted of unique and always particular events precludes the possibility of language being deemed literal as opposed to metaphorical in the sense of referencing some univocal reality as the source of truth. If metaphor can be defined as a figure of speech that describes an object or action

---

31. *Zhongyong* 26: 其為物不貳, 則其生物不測。

in a way that is not *literally* true, then in this Confucian cosmology, all language must be deemed metaphorical. Moreover, it is only such real metaphors producing their productive associations that can function as the ultimate source of meaning.

The Confucian counterpart to the substance ontology and essentialism, which provides the basis for the Aristotelian method of defining things and knowing them, is a paronomastic appreciation of the changing and productive correlations among "events" in the flux and flow of a processual cosmology that enables us to realize a desired world. "Paronomasia" is a technical term for defining and in fact redefining expressions by using words that sound alike or that have a similar meaning.[32] It is thus calling something by another name. Such a strategy for knowing stands in rather clear contrast to Aristotle's taxonomic knowing in which to classify and to thus name something correctly is to know it. For Aristotle, knowledge is acquired through analysis from genus to species. Indeed, given the history of our common sense, we can perhaps better understand this Confucian paronomastic strategy for defining and thus coming to know things by drawing a contrast between it and the way in which Aristotle goes about the business of knowing a world.

Aristotle employs the methods of logic grounded in his ontology as the basic means of articulating the patterns of discourse for all of the sciences that provide us with knowledge. For Aristotle, logic is not simply one among the various ways of knowing but is the tool to be employed as the one source of demonstrable truth by all who would come to know. In addition to Aristotle's attempts to classify the various disciplinary means of coming to know—theoretically, practically, and productively—there were his more "encyclopedic" efforts associated with the organization of the body of the known. The focus in classifying things this way is on articulating the objective description of the "knowable" in relation to the "known." Mary Tiles offers us a summary of this Aristotelian genera and species mode of classification:

---

32. Coming to this issue rather late in the game, J. L. Austin takes on his fellow philosophers with his speech-act theory to make much of the fact that in the ordinary rather than philosophical use of language what we often take to be synonyms—"to look, to seem, to appear," for example—when given closer scrutiny, reveal some very important distinctions. See J. L. Austin, *Sense and Sensibilia*, ed. G. J. Warnock (Oxford: Clarendon, 1962).

The kind of rational structure which is given prominence in Aristotle's works is the structure of a classificatory system—a hierarchy of kinds of things organised successively by kinds (or genera) and forms of those kinds (or species). (In turn species become in effect genera to be divided into [sub] species and genera grouped into more comprehensive genera.) Definitions were not in the first instance thought to be accounts of words but of the "what-it-is-to-be" a thing of that kind, in other words accounts of essence. To define an object—give its name a precise or correct use—was to locate it in a classificatory system.[33]

As we have seen previously, for Aristotle, the most fundamental question philosophy asks is ontological: What is the "*on*" or "being" of something" and the example given in the *Categories*, What is the man in the marketplace? And since the human "being" as subject is its substance (*ousia*), we can ask: what is the substance of something? Substance in its most primary sense describes a thing as an individual (*tode ti*), then by extension as a species (*eidos*), and then as a genus (*genos*). The species tells us more about the substance of a thing than its genus because it is closer to the individual primary substance: the fact that Socrates is a human being tells us more about him than the fact that he is a mammal.

Tiles provides a further account of how the application of Aristotle's classificatory system grounded in this substance ontology is thought to lead to new knowledge:

> This is a hierarchical order based on qualitative similarities and differences. A key assumption underlying such an order is that a thing cannot both have and lack a given quality—the requirement of non-contradiction. Non-contradiction is therefore fundamental to this kind of rational order. . . . Knowledge of definitions (or essences) coupled with the principle of non-contradiction can serve as the foundation for further,

---

33. Mary Tiles, "Idols of the Market Place: Knowledge and Language, unpublished manuscript, (n.d.) 5–6. A revised version is available in Mary Tiles, "Images of Reason in Western Culture," *Alternative Rationalities*, ed. Eliot Deutsch (Honolulu: Society for Asian and Comparative Philosophy, 1992).

rationally demonstrable, knowledge.[34]

Paronomasia as a Confucian strategy for knowing, unlike Aristotle, depends upon neither the identification of essences nor on the principle of noncontradiction. Such ontological and logical assumptions have little relevance for the classical Confucian worldview. In fact, this process and eventful cosmology, in not allowing for any final separation between a putative thing and its context, will not give rise to the principle of noncontradiction that depends on an isolating discreteness. As we will see, paronomasia trades the putative precision that comes with the application of such a principle for an allusive and sometimes productive ambiguity.

As previously observed, paronomasia begins from a redefining of our terms by phonetic and semantic association. This is an appeal to alternative terms that sound alike or that have a similar meaning. Such paronomastic definition is to be found everywhere in the classical Chinese literature. For example, we read in the *Analects*:

> Ji Kangzi asked Confucius about proper governing (*zheng* 政), and Confucius replied to him, "Governing properly (*zheng*) is doing what is proper (*zheng* 正). If you, Sir, lead by doing what is proper, who would dare do otherwise?"[35]

Significantly, in this paronomastic process, the expectation is that we are not just "discovering" definitions about an existing world. Rather, we are actively redefining and delineating an ever-expanding world of meaning, and in so doing, bringing it into being. When we consult traditional dictionaries that chronicle the cultural associations that define this Confucian world—the second-century *Shuowenjiezi* lexicon 說文解字, for example—we discover that many of its entries are not as much defined analytically and etymologically by appeal to some putatively essential, literal, historical "root" meaning, as they are generally explained metaphorically or paronomastically by semantic and phonetic associations. The term "exemplary persons" (*jun* 君), for example, is defined by the cognate and phonetically similar character "gathering" (*qun* 群), an association that arises between these two words not only phonetically but because of the underlying assumption that people will gather around and defer to exemplary persons.

---

34. Tiles, "Images of Reason in Western Culture," 7–8.
35. *Analects* 12.17: 季康子問政於孔子。孔子對曰:「政者, 正也。子帥以正, 孰敢不正?」

As we read in the *Analects*: "Virtuosic persons do not dwell alone; they are sure to have neighbors."³⁶ The term "mirror" (*jing* 鏡 or *jian* 鑒) is defined as "shining radiantly" (*jing* 景) or "looking into, overseeing" (*jian* 監), respectively, indicating that a mirror is a source of illumination and information. "Battle formation" (*zhen* 陣) is defined as "displaying" (*chen* 陳), suggesting that the most important function of carrying a sword and scabbard, or parading in battle formation, is making an overt display of prowess that will effectively deter an enemy. A "ghost" or "spirit" (*gui* 鬼) is defined as "returning" (*gui* 歸), referencing the belief that the *qi* of deceased persons disperses and finds its way back to a more primordial condition as well as to the ancestral home. "Waymaking" (*dao* 道) is understood as "treading" (*dao* 蹈), prompting the *Zhuangzi* to say so eloquently, "The way is made in the walking."³⁷ "King" (*wang* 王) is defined as "repairing to" or "moving toward" (*wang* 往), suggesting that the people will always repair to the True King. Such examples of definition by phonetic and semantic association are legion.

As is clear from the examples cited, a discernible pattern in this paronomastic mode of definition is that erstwhile "nouns" default to "gerunds"—for example, the term "exemplary persons" (*jun*) defaults to "gathering" (*qun*) and "king" (*wang*) to "repairing to" (*wang*)—thereby underscoring the primacy of process over form as a grounding presupposition in this "eventful" cosmology. What is also remarkable about this Chinese paronomastic way of generating meaning is that a word is defined nonreferentially by mining relevant and even seemingly random associations implicated phonetically or semantically in the term itself. The success of the allusion and the quantum of meaning produced by it, therefore, is dictated by the degree of relevance to a particular situation, with some protean associations being more thought provoking and generative of meaning than others.

Such paronomastic tropes are not unheard of in our own cultural narrative, particularly as a device in the literary counterculture that resists foundationalism. Certainly, for the likes of the antinomian maverick, William Blake, for example, wit *is* indeed wisdom, and rhyme *is* reason. And in the pre-Latinized and heroic Anglo-Saxon language, the trope of "kenning" is used to "name and make things known" by correlating and thus compounding terms. Kenning expands meaning by creating

---

36. *Analects* 4.25:「德不孤，必有鄰。」
37. *Zhuangzi* 4/2/33: 道行之而成。

memorable images: for example, a dictionary is a "word-hoard" or a "word-pantry"; an ocean is the "whales' bath," the "foaming fields," or the "sea-street"; the king is the "keeper of rings," the "land-guardian," or "the securer of glory," and so on. And we continue such practices in our vernacular language today with our "bean-counters," "show-stoppers," and "tree-huggers." Kenning is thus to conjure forth imagistic metaphors and to generate associations that expand the horizons of our knowledge, and in so doing, to lift us beyond our ken.

To appreciate the pervasiveness of paronomastic knowing in Confucian philosophy, we might also look at some of the familiar grammatical structures we find in the ancient Chinese texts. What is the value of the grammatical particle *ye* 也, for example? In the absence of the copula verb in classical Chinese, it is appropriate that students of the classical Chinese language are told expressly that *ye* in its usual role of marking noun predication is not the copula "to be."[38] Even so, the particle is often schematized in just this way: AB也 : 'A is B.'[39] And *ye* is usually translated as "is," as we find in the *Analects* passages, "to know what you know and know what you do not know—this then *is* wisdom" (知之為知之, 不知為不知, 是知也).[40] I would argue that *ye* 也 as it is appears in the classical language is not entirely divorced from its usage in modern Chinese, where *ye* as "also" or "too" adds information to a given topic: "She too is English" (*ta ye shi yingguoren* 她也是英國人) or "It is also the same the other way round" (*fanguolai ye yiyang* 反過來也一樣). We can describe *ye* as a "paronomastic" particle marking a perceived association between a particular thing and some other thing, attribute, or quality. In a passage from the *Analects*, for example, *ye* introduces a metaphorical association: "The missteps of exemplary persons are like an eclipse of the sun or moon" (君子的過也如日月之食焉).[41] *Ye* is not asserting strict identity here but rather introduces a comment on a topic: an additional quantum of information that we might glean about the subject through extending its range of associations.

A closer look at "paronomasia" as "knowing more fully by tracing

---

38. Edwin Pulleyblank, *Outline of Classical Chinese Grammar* (Vancouver: University of British Columbia Press, 1995), 20.
39. Pulleyblank, *Classical Chinese Grammar*, 16.
40. *Analects* 6.19 and 2.17.
41. *Analects* 19.21.

out patterns of relevant associations" provides us with a key for unlocking an understanding of how Confucius would propose that we as persons lead significant lives. After all, as we have seen, the Chinese vocabulary for "knowing," far from suggesting the analytical recovery of the real substance behind appearances (as implied by epistemic terms such as "getting," "grasping," "comprehending," "understanding"), is a language of mapping out one's way in the world: "finding our way" (*zhidao* 知道), "unraveling the patterns within the context" (*lijie* 理解), "seeing with full clarity" (*liaojie* 瞭解), "getting through with facility" (*tongda* 通達), and so on. I want to explore how in this Confucian sensibility the paronomastic strategy for defining and redefining our terms of discourse serves as a device for knowledge production. Indeed, I will argue that paronomasia, far from being merely a literary trope, is integral to the analogical or correlative thinking that is a defining feature of the Confucian project in which one makes this particular life meaningful through achieving "correlational" virtuosity.

But first we need to gain a better understanding of the familiar practice of making "correlations" in our experience of the world around us. What exactly do we mean by "relation," and what then does "relational virtuosity" mean in this context? What is the actual "content" of personal relations, and how do relations themselves produce meaning? As we have seen, there is a vital difference of expectation between perceiving individuals as "having" relationships and seeing such persons as actually achieving their individuality through the cultivation of those shared relationships that constitute them. Said another way, associated living and the personal collaboration such individuality entails do not bring discrete people together in relationships but rather make increasingly generative what is already constitutively related. This, then, is to invoke the distinction between a doctrine of conjoined external relations on the one hand and a doctrine of generative, intrinsic, constitutive relations on the other.

The primary gerundive meaning of "relations" is "relating," "reciting," "rehearsing," "telling," "giving a detailed account of a situation or series of events." As I have suggested before, such "relatings" are not only discursive but also become constitutive of who we are becoming. We are, by virtue of the wholeness of our experience, inextricably embedded within a pattern of genealogical, communal, and cultural relationships—our physical, social, and cultural DNA that in sum constitutes our unique genomes. Our incipient relations then grow in value through various modes of associative discourse as they serve to make us at once distinctive and like-minded: for example, language, music, ritualized conduct, body, gifting, food, and so on. Increasingly self-consciously resolute individuals are constituted as distinctive persons through the expanding patterns of deference that locate them in a communicating community, while at the same time the shared communal mind itself is produced through effective "relatings" by the consociation of its members.

Confucius is himself keenly aware of the performative and perlocutionary "ontology" of "relatings" or discourse—that is, the power that language (*ming* 名) in the broadest sense has to shape the community and to command a desired world into being (*ming* 命). For Confucius, "knowing" a world, far from being just cognitive, is to realize it in the sense of "making it real." Confucius is expounding upon precisely this point when he explains to his protégé Zilu what he means by the central Confucian precept "using language properly" (*zhengming* 正名).[42] In this exposition, Confucius uses "names" as "pragmatics" to do the work of an expanding range of different yet organically related modes of discourse on which the flourishing of communal life depends, from language itself to the functioning of the institutions of law and governance. Most importantly, for Confucius, the function of "naming," far from being primarily abstract, theoretical, and referential, has immediate, practical consequences for the quality achieved in the always changing life of the community:

---

42. Zilu was one of Confucius's best-known and favorite protégés. Confucius's feelings for Zilu were mixed. On the one hand, he was constantly critical of Zilu's rashness and immodesty and was impatient with his seeming indifference to book learning. On the other hand, Confucius appreciated Zilu's unswerving loyalty and directness—a person who never hesitated in fulfilling his commitments. He was a person of courage and action who was sometimes upbraided by Confucius for being too bold and impetuous. But being nearer Confucius in age, Zilu with his military temper was not one to take criticism without giving it back. When he asked Confucius if courage was indeed the highest virtue, Confucius tried to rein him in by replying that a person who has courage without a sense of appropriateness would be a troublemaker, and a lesser person would be a thief. On several occasions, especially in the apocryphal literature, Zilu challenges Confucius's judgment. When Confucius associates with political figures of questionable character and immodest reputation—the wife of Duke Ling of Wei, for example—Confucius is left defending himself to Zilu. But with all such complexities and complications considered, Confucius's enormous affection for the irrepressible Zilu still shines throughout the text.

"Were the Lord of Wey to turn the administration of his state over to you, what would be your first priority?" asked Zilu.

"Without question it would be to ensure that names are used properly (*zhengming*)," replied the Master.

"Really? That is so pedantic." responded Zilu. "What does it mean to use names properly anyway?"

"How can you be so obtuse!" replied Confucius. "Exemplary persons defer on matters they do not understand. When names are not used properly, language will not be used effectively; when language is not used effectively, matters will not be taken care of; when matters are not taken care of, propriety in roles and relations and in the playing of music will not be achieved; when propriety in roles and relations and in the playing of music is not achieved, the application of laws and punishments will not be on the mark; when the application of laws and punishments is not on the mark, the people will not know what to do with themselves. Thus, when exemplary persons put a name to something, it can certainly be spoken, and when spoken it can certainly be acted upon. There is nothing careless in the attitude of exemplary persons toward what is said."[43]

The expression *zhengming* has conventionally and perhaps unfortunately been translated as "the *rectification* of names." For Confucius, language is certainly retrospective in the sense that effective discourse requires the use of language according to received, stipulated definitions—for example, the deployment of proper titles and respect for the entitlements that accompany rank. In the literature, Confucius has a strong commitment to such conventions, and to this extent, the idea of "rectification" certainly does part of the job. Simply put, established conventions provide stability and reinforce the hard-won values that define a cultural identity. The past is importantly with us prospectively as guidance for new experience. But because prospective, novel experience is always underdetermined and must

---

43. *Analects* 13.3: 子路曰:「衛君待子而為政, 子將奚先?」子曰;「必也正名乎!」子路曰:「有是哉, 子之迂也! 奚其正?」子曰:「野哉由也! 君子於其所不知, 蓋闕如也。名不正, 則言不順; 言不順, 則事不成; 事不成, 則禮樂不興; 禮樂不興, 則刑罰不中; 刑罰不中, 則民無所措手足。故君子名之必可言也, 言之必可行也。君子於其言, 無所苟而已矣。」

literally be taken on its own terms, the translation of this expression as "rectification of names" is inadequate at best and misleading at worst.

To understand language as only retrospective reduces it to a symbolic and representational means of mapping an already existing world—that is, knowing the world is finding the right name. But language is much more. When used properly, it is the engine that sustains, revitalizes, and amplifies appropriate relations. *Zhengming* as it is explained in this passage should certainly be understood as remembering and applying standards inherited from the past. But for Confucius, language is also importantly prospective and performative. There is the need for the community, grounded in the gravitas of its traditions, to continue to make productive adjustments and novel correlations within the evolving social and political structures. A thriving community must continuously reform, reconfigure, and reauthorize its institutions. The proper use of language is a continuing redefining of our terms of understanding, explanation, and performance through those semantic and phonetic associations that would enable us to make the most of our always changing world.

The fertility of language, like the fecundity of *dao* that means both "waymaking" and "speaking," lies in activating the indeterminacies that are always available and in allowing for *ars contextualis*: the omnipresent opportunity for artful recontextualizing. As we have seen, this correlating process can be understood as "paronomasia"—a prospective reconstruing of the contextualizing conditions of any situation that would allow something to be called by "another name" and in so doing, to produce additional meaning. This liquid called "water," for example, certainly irrigates plants and produces life and, as hydropower, has been used as a traditional source of energy. But with further ingenuity could we not transform it through controlled fusion into a resource that will drive our cars and fly our planes? This amplificatory process certainly begins from a careful mapping out of names as they have been used—that is, a retrospective "rectification of names." But it also requires the imagination to use language and make correlations that will produce novel meaning in an ever-changing world.

Confucius is trying to make several points in defining *zhengming* that in degree confound our expectations. That is, with our common sense being shaped by Aristotle, we are inclined to respect fundamental distinctions that inform our conception of agency. We are inclined to separate "acting" (*prattein*) from "producing" (*poietin*) and an efficient cause or agent (*kinoun*) that initiates change from the material, formal, and final causes that define the outcome of change. As we have seen, Confucius does not begin from such assumptions about discrete agency and agent-centered, productive activity. Rather, his starting point is the importance of the proper and productive use of language within the human community as it provides ambience for the ordinary affairs of the day.

This is a now familiar insight for us in the work of Ludwig Wittgenstein. Indeed, Wittgenstein's understanding of how language functions resonates with the prospective expectations expressed by Confucius in this passage. Introducing his notions of "language games" and "family resemblances," Wittgenstein like Confucius is keenly aware that language and life are two aspects of the same experience. He challenges realist assumptions that language is somehow separate and that by mapping it onto the world it comes to "correspond" to reality in some referential and representational way. Wittgenstein uses the term "language-games" to highlight "the fact that the speaking of language is part of an activity, or a form of life," where such games consist "of language and the actions into which it is woven."[44] And Wittgenstein has a keen awareness of the underdeterminedness of language, allowing room for the prospective activation of the ambiguities and equivocations that are always present to increase its meaning and effect. He argues that concepts do not need to be clearly defined to be meaningful and to precipitate change in the world. Wittgenstein uses the analogy of "family resemblances" to describe how the same word is used in many different ways without any ultimately final or essential meaning and to underscore the lack of any formal boundaries or precision in the different application of one and the same concept. Such an understanding of language highlights the allusiveness and the productive ambiguity that attend the imaginative use of language.

John Dewey also invests enormously in the centrality of language and other modes of communicative discourse (including signs, symbols, gestures, and social institutions) in explaining how the community grows its persons:

> Through speech a person dramatically identifies himself with potential acts and deeds; he plays many roles, not in successive stages of life but in a contemporaneously enacted drama.

---

44. Wittgenstein, *Philosophical Investigations*, 23; Wittgenstein, *Philosophical Investigations*, 7.

Thus mind emerges.[45]

For Dewey, mind is "an added property assumed by a feeling creature, when it reaches that organized interaction with other living creatures which is language, communication."[46] For Dewey, then, what we might call "heartminding" is self-consciously being created in the process of realizing a world. Heartminding, like the world, is *becoming* rather than *being*, and the challenge before us is always how much shared meaning and enjoyment can be generated in its operations. The way in which heartminding and world are changed is not simply in terms of human perception but in their substantial growth and productivity and in the efficiency and pleasure that attends this process. The alternative—that is, for a community to fail to communicate effectively—is for the community to wither, leaving it vulnerable to the "mindless" violence and "heartless" atrocities of shameless creatures who have failed to become human.

This understanding of the generative function of language is further developed in the work of Charles Taylor. Taking discourse as one of the necessary sources of our personal identities, Taylor states the following:

> One cannot be a self on one's own. I can only be a self in my relation to certain interlocutors. . . . A self only exists within what I call "webs of interlocutions."[47]

The range of meaning-making activities described in this *Analects* passage are irreducibly social and situational; persons, families, and communities become what they are discursively through what they say and do in their roles and relations, through what Taylor refers to as "our webs of interlocutions."

In this Confucian model of constitutive "correlatings," then, we are not individuals who associate in community, but rather because we associate effectively in community we become distinguished as unique individuals. We do not have minds and therefore speak with one another, but rather because we speak effectively with one another, we become like-minded with shared life-forms and values. It is not that we have

---

45. Dewey, *Later Works*, 1:135.
46. Dewey, *Later Works*, 1:198.
47. Taylor, *Sources of the Self*, 36.

hearts and are therefore empathetic with one another; but because we feel effective empathy with one another we become wholehearted as a community. Indeed, paronomasia understood as defining a world through associated living within a communicating community is the Confucian way of making meaning.

In Confucian role ethics, the source of personal growth is effective communication and its production of meaning. As we have seen, paronomasia is literally to come to "know" something by another name through extended semantic and phonetic associations. This woman Amy is a unique person, and as we get to know her *paronomastically*—that is, by "another name" in her various roles as "daughter," "mother," "wife," "teacher," "best friend," and so on—our knowledge of her increases proportionately. In this Confucian cosmology, meaning in the world is produced locally and analogically. In our coming to know Amy, we begin from the fact that a meaningful life unfolds in the conduct that defines the various roles she lives. This is the source of meaning Confucius is referencing when he says: "Correlating my conduct with those near at hand can be said to be the method of becoming consummate in my person."[48] Confucius is saying that persons become consummate as they relate effectively in the increasingly meaningful relations they have with those persons who populate their own immediate narratives.

To say that persons become consummate paronomastically by correlating their conduct with those close at hand is to say that they "appreciate" others as others "appreciate" them. To appreciate is certainly to recognize the magnitude and the complexity of other human beings, and in so doing, to strive to be responsive to the needs and aspirations of their fellows. But there is another important sense of "appreciating" that we need to acknowledge here. In pursuing this kind of transformative intimacy, persons in their relationships quite literally "appreciate" each other in the sense that they accrue a dividend of significance from their meaningful relationships, thus making each other more valuable as human beings. Such thick and robust relations are the source of growth in the world, enriching the family, the community, and the cosmos.

In the repeated contrast between "small persons" (*xiaoren* 小人) and "exemplary persons" (*junzi* 君子) that is ubiquitous throughout the *Analects*, such small persons are not only socially and morally retarded individuals, but their selfish conduct makes them a continuing source of

---

48. *Analects* 6.30: 能近取譬, 可謂仁之方也已.

communal divisiveness and distress. Small persons are properly described as "small" in that they are aberrantly discrete "individuals" who have failed to participate in family and community relations and thus have not grown self-consciously as persons: they are stunted and devoid of meaningful relations. By contrast, the text repeatedly invokes "making good on your word" or "living up to your word" (*xin* 信) as the fiduciary activity out of which rewarding friendships develop. In fact, all social and moral growth is fundamentally discursive as the source of a critical self-awareness as well as robust relations with others. And thus, good friendships can only be "made" through effective communication that is grounded in the relations of mutual trust and credibility.[49]

Standing in stark contrast to the inertia of "small persons," sages (*sheng* 聖) are defined by their discursive virtuosity. The earliest form of the character for the term "sage," *sheng* 聖, as it is found on the oracle bones, is composed of the combination of the graph for "ear" (*er* 耳) and for "mouth" (*kou* 口) *[xxvii]*, suggesting that at least one characteristic held in common by the always unique members of this highest order of humanity, in all of their hearing and saying, is their shared virtuosity as self-conscious communicators.[50] Sages are able to hear what is to be heard, and when they speak, they change the world.

[xxvii]

Given the central role of the communicating family and community as the locus of personal growth, in our reading of the *Analects* we find that a pervasive concern throughout this most seminal of the Confucian texts is sensitivity to the proper use of language. In the *Analects*, we are told explicitly that

> the Master said, "Someone who does not understand the propensity of circumstances (*ming* 命) has no way of becoming an exemplary person (*junzi* 君子); someone who does not understand the achievement of propriety in our roles and relations (*li* 禮) has no way of knowing where to stand; someone who does not understand what is said (*yan* 言) has no way of knowing other people (*ren* 人)."[51]

---

49. For a fuller discussion of Confucian friendship, see Hall and Ames, *Thinking from the Han*, 254–269. See also Ames, *Confucian Role Ethics*, 114–121.

50. Kwan, "Database," 甲骨文合集 CHANT 0693.

51. *Analects* 20.3: 子曰:「不知命, 無以為君子也。不知禮, 無以立也。不知言, 無以知人也。」

246 | Human Becomings

In fact, according to the *Analects*, discourse is so fundamental to our flourishing communal life that we are exhorted by Zigong, the most eloquent of Confucius's students, to realize the high stakes involved in the self-conscious choice of each and every word and how a single word can lead to a person's ruin:

> Exemplary persons must be ever so careful about what they say. On the strength of a single word others can deem them either wise (*zhi* 知) or foolish.[52]

Given the perceived power of language, Zigong is thus prompted to ask the Master if there is a single word that can be practiced with profit until the end of one's days.[53] And Confucius replies emphatically that it must be the word "deference" (*shu* 恕) in the sense of deferring action until one can exercise one's imagination in rehearsing options that would allow for the most meaningful response in that particular situation.[54] For Confucius, this one protean word captures everything he has been trying to convey to his students about becoming consummate in their conduct (*ren*): exercising their educated imagination and correlating those relations close at hand with a critical self-awareness to optimize the meaning in their relations with others.

Confucius is able to make much out of the intimate association he perceives between careful attention to what one says (*ren* 認) and

---

52. *Analects* 19.25: 君子一言以為知，一言以為不知，言不可不慎也。See also 1.6, 1.14, and 2.18.

53. Zigong excelled as a statesman and merchant and was perhaps second only to Yan Hui in Confucius's affections. Confucius was respectful of Zigong's abilities—and in particular, his intellect—but was less impressed with his use of this intellect to amass personal wealth. Coming from a wealthy, educated home, Zigong was well spoken, and as such, Confucius's most persistent criticism of him is that his deeds could not keep pace with his words. Putting the many references to Zigong together, it is clear that Confucius was not entirely comfortable with Zigong's lack of commitment to the well-being of others, choosing to increase his own riches rather than taking on the responsibilities of government office. It is true that Zigong was aloof and not a generous spirit. And in his readiness to pass judgment on others, he sometimes acted superior. Even so, much of the flattering profile of Confucius collected in the *Analects* is cast in the words of the eloquent Zigong.

54. *Analects* 15.24 子貢問曰：「有一言而可以終身行之者乎？」子曰：「其恕乎！己所不欲，勿施於人。」

the cultivation of consummate conduct (*ren* 仁). Indeed, the central Confucian moral sensibility of aspiring to become consummate in one's roles and relations (*ren* 仁) is defined unambiguously as "speaking with circumspection" (*ren* 訒), a term that has both phonetic and semantic associations. As we have seen, defining terms paronomastically is a familiar characteristic of the early philosophical literature broadly and of the *Analects* specifically:

> Sima Niu inquired about consummate conduct (*ren* 仁). The Master replied, "Consummate persons are circumspect in what they say (*ren* 訒)." "Does just being circumspect in what you say make you consummate?" he asked. The Master replied, "When things are difficult to accomplish, how can you be but circumspect in what you have to say?"[55]

According to historian Sima Qian 司馬遷, among Confucius's students, Sima Niu had the distinction of being garrulous and impulsive. Confucius is speaking to Sima Niu's limited self-awareness in his seemingly impatient response and is thereby criticizing specifically those like him who fail to treat their words as having the force of action. There is much to be made of the claim in this passage that for Confucius not only are "saying" and "doing" inseparable, but further, the more difficult the task at hand, the more care we must exercise in the self-conscious and critical use of our language. It is the centrality of effective communication in effecting growth in relations that has led us to identify "paronomasia" and the effective correlations it produces as the ultimate source of meaning for Confucian role ethics.

Could Socrates and Confucius Be Friends?

In this Confucian tradition in which the production of meaning itself is the product of increasingly robust relations, we are quite literally in the business of "making" our friends and our friends in the making of us. Friendship is a relationship that is constituted by the persons involved,

---

55. *Analects* 12.3: 司馬牛問仁。子曰：「仁者其言也訒。」曰：「其言也訒，斯謂之仁已乎？」子曰：「為之難，言之得無訒乎？」See Sima Qian 司馬遷, *Shiji* 史記 [Records of the grand historian] (Beijing: Zhonghua shuju, 1959), 2214–2215.

where the continuity of a truly meaningful friendship is a matter of vibrant disclosure in which the friends "change each other's minds" in the most literal, concrete, and transformative sense of this expression. Importantly, the realization of this vital relationship is not at the expense of their personal uniqueness. On the contrary, such friendships are both the source and the consequence of the integrity they acquire as distinctive persons. Their personal integrity is expressed as both the persistent and always evolving uniqueness of each friend and the integrative "becoming one together" that is the substance of real friendship. This understanding of relations among friends as intrinsic and constitutive is best described as productive of an "aesthetic order" in the sense that aesthetic achievements can be described fairly as the aspiration to realize the fullest disclosure of the particular details in the totality of the achieved effect. Such significant relations accrue dividends through the fullest "connectivity" and coalescence within the various activities of the friendship itself.

On this topic of friendship, commentators have often puzzled over what Confucius means when he cautions not once but on two occasions: "Do not befriend anyone who is not as good as you are."[56] The logic that seems to follow from this advice is that while the friends of an exemplary person will be precious few, the friends of a scoundrel will be legion. The simple point Confucius is making here, however, is that since self-conscious personal growth is the outcome of our relating effectively in our relationships, it is only through a regimen of personal cultivation in the most productive of these relationships that we have the opportunity to grow from some inchoate relational beginnings into distinguished and efficacious persons (*daren* 大人 or *shanren* 善人 or *chengren* 成人). Such growth is purposeful; it starts here and goes there. As Confucius himself opines, this project of personal cultivation "is self-originating—how could it originate with others?"[57] But while it is self-originating and reflects purpose, such personal cultivation is by no means a solitary affair; it can only be pursued by nurturing the fecund relations that locate us within our everyday roles of family and community. As we have seen, it is for this reason that the vocabulary of personal cultivation in Confucian philosophy is described in terms that frequently and specifically reference growth and extension from "small persons" to those who, having been nourished through moral conduct, have much added consequence.

---

56. *Analects* 1.8 and 9.25: 毋友不如己者.
57. *Analects* 12.1: 為仁由己, 而由人乎哉?

This declaration to seek friendships only among the very best of persons is a clear acknowledgment that Confucius understands both personal growth and diminution as a function of associated living. And it prompts us to ask: for Confucius, where does meaning come from in a "meaningful" friendship? In a Platonic world wherein meaning has a transcendent reference, friendship is instrumentalized as a commitment to a common end. The conclusion of the reflection on friendship in the *Phaedrus*, for example, is that friends hold all things in common. And when what they hold in common is an *eros* directed toward the transcendent Good, they are *true* friends. Similarly, for the Christian, *philia* as the love among friends and family members is subordinated to *agapē*, the love of a transcendent God channeled through His creatures as their love for one another.

For Plato's remarkable student Aristotle, commonality is also the basis for friendship. While there are lower levels of incidental, contingent friendships that seek utility and pleasure, *true* friends by contrast are described as "another self" or "a second self." Such "friends in virtue" mirror one's own character as it is grounded in constant virtues and in the intellectual activity of *nous*, which is identical in all people. Indeed, Aristotle appeals to the mirror metaphor to illustrate how the real friend in being similarly virtuous is a source of self-knowledge and corroboration.[58] He allows that "contemplative friendships" are higher than the practical kind and that such friendships are rare; they are only available to an elite circle of equally virtuous people.[59] There is a superiority of the theoretical life over the practical and of the speculative vision over daily moral activities. Thus, for Aristotle, the eternal truth that can be grasped by *nous* must be given priority over friendship, even when it means turning away from his own mentor—in his case, Plato: "While both are dear, piety requires us to honor truth above our friends."[60]

For Confucius, like his Greek cousins, friendships can also be described in some ways as a matter of common cause, even while the substance of consummate conduct is always a unique achievement:

---

58. Aristotle, *Complete Works*, 1213a20–26. See Jiyuan Yu, *The Ethics of Confucius and Aristotle: Mirrors of Virtue* (New York: Routledge, 2007), 4.

59. Aristotle, *Complete Works*, 1157b5–1158b11. See Jiyuan Yu, *Ethics of Confucius and Aristotle*, 214.

60. Aristotle, *Complete Works*, 1096a11–16.

> Master Zeng said, "Exemplary persons attract friends through their refinement, and through their friends, promote consummate conduct (*ren*)."[61]

May Sim has identified many resonances between the Confucian and Aristotelian models of friendship, taking careful account of their important similarities.[62] But beyond these commonalities, it must also be allowed that there is a significant distance between the accounts of friendship we find in Aristotle and Confucius. We must consider the metaphysical and biological uniformities in Aristotle's foundational individualism, the self-sufficiency of final and unchanging first principles that are the object of contemplation, the constancy of the regimen of virtues, and the centrality of rationality as primary in making moral decisions.

For Confucius, contra Plato and Aristotle, the ultimate source of meaning is not external but emerges through the nurturing self-conscious process of the friendship itself. And it is the ways in which friends are qualitatively superior to and different from each other that provides the opportunity for a collaborative growth and advancement. Friendship is a classic illustration of the Confucian mantra: "Exemplary persons seek harmony not uniformity."[63] Importantly, it seems that the resources for productive friendships tend to be dispersed among people rather than belonging exclusively to particular paragons. By way of example, when Zigong was asked who Confucius's teacher was, his reply is inclusive in the sense that everyone can, in greater or lesser degree, be a source of personal growth:

> The moral vision (*dao*) of Kings Wen and Wu has not collapsed utterly—it lives on in the people. Those of superior character have grasped the greater part, while those of lesser quality have grasped a bit of it. Everyone has something of Wen and Wu's way in them. Who then did the Master not

---

61. *Analects* 12.24: 君子以文會友，以友輔仁。What makes common cause here "uncommon" is the fact that consummate conduct will always have a different referent for different persons, given the uniqueness of their narratives.

62. See May Sim, *Remastering Morals with Aristotle and Confucius* (Cambridge: Cambridge University Press, 2007), chap. 7.

63. *Analects* 13.23: 君子和而不同。

learn from? Again, how could there have been a single constant teacher for him?⁶⁴

The message here is that because each person is different, Confucius has something—sometimes more, sometimes less—to learn from everyone. This generous appreciation of both the positive and negative possibilities that most relations with other people provide for us in our moral development is made abundantly clear when Confucius famously observes:

> In strolling together with just two other persons, I am bound to find a teacher in their company. Identifying their strengths, I follow them, and identifying their weaknesses, I reform myself accordingly.⁶⁵

Personal growth is the direct result of the quality of the specific productive relations achieved among family and friends. But friendship is different from family. In seeking out and developing meaningful friendships, these critical and self-conscious relations provide a latitude and a degree of freedom not usually characteristic of our relations with blood relatives. This prompts Confucius to observe:

> Persons who are critical and demanding, yet amicable and accommodating can be called a scholar-officials. They need to be critical and demanding with their friends, and amicable and accommodating with their brothers.⁶⁶

Confucius is keenly aware that freely chosen and expansive friendships bring with them significant differences that in some important degree compensate for more homogeneous family relations and, in many ways, can serve as an opportunity for quantum personal growth.

But of course, not all erstwhile friendships are equally fertile. Indeed, our relations with others are not always benign. While our associations

---

64. *Analects* 19.22: 衛公孫朝問於子貢曰："仲尼焉學？" 子貢曰："文武之道，未墜於地，在人。賢者識其大者，不賢者識其小者，莫不有文武之道焉。夫子焉不學？ 而亦何常師之有？"
65. *Analects* 7.22: 三人行，必有我師焉。擇其善者而從之，其不善者而改之。
66. *Analects* 13.28:「切切、偲偲、怡怡如也，可謂士矣。朋友切切、偲偲，兄弟怡怡。」

are certainly an opportunity for growth, Confucius is keenly aware that they can also be a source of personal attenuation:

> Having three kinds of friends will be a source of personal growth; having three other kinds of "friends" will be a source of personal diminution. One stands to be improved by friends who are true, who make good on their word, and who are broadly informed; one stands to be injured by "friends" who are ingratiating, who feign compliance, and who are glib talkers.[67]

Confucius's point here is that a porous border exists around the institution of family that provides additional ground for a more deliberate and purposeful cultivation of friendships and hence one's own individuality as a person. Friends can differ from family in having the potential to provide a degree of growth and complexity that can often go beyond our more formal family bonds. These voluntarily chosen relations, as they develop, come in the door in the sense that close friends frequently become part of extended families and are customarily referred to in family terms: brothers and sisters, uncles and aunties.

The Person of Confucius as a Model of Focus-Field Agency

One of the concerns often expressed about the relationally constituted conception of persons that grounds role ethics, especially when contrasted with the autonomous, self-choosing model of person assumed in liberal individualism, are questions surrounding identity and agency. Does this focus-field conception of persons provide a sufficiently clear account of personal identity, unity, or autonomy? One way of responding to this concern might be to reflect on how personal identity and agency are portrayed in the Confucian texts and more specifically in the person of Confucius himself. In so doing, perhaps a way to get past our inveterate "thing" pattern of thinking is to return to the distinction between a leg and walking and between a body and embodied living. We need to distinguish between a conception of individual agency that locates

---

67. *Analects* 16.4: 益者三友，損者三友。友直，友諒，友多聞，益矣。友便辟，友善柔，友便佞，損矣。

intentionality within each person as a motive force directing their activities as discrete persons and a notion of agency as it is entwined within and motivates diffused yet resolutely focused "activities" or "events" of persons in the world. Just as walking happens as an eventful collaboration between legs and the world, and it cannot be conceived of as being some "thing" discrete and independent of context, persons as events are in the world, and the notion of agency must have the complexity to reflect this fact.

As previously stated, the middle chapters of the *Analects* provide a series of concrete images in the life of Confucius—how he ate, drank, sat, dressed, and engaged different people under different circumstances. These passages provide the images and the anecdotes that brought this exemplary teacher to life for his immediate protégés and for the numerous generations of students that have followed his model down to the present day. It is within these core chapters that the person of Confucius is described as having four things he could not personally countenance—four abstentions that reveal much about Confucius's self-understanding and his own values:

> There were four things the Master abstained from entirely: He would not conjecture, he would not claim or demand certainty, he was not inflexible, and he was not self-absorbed.[68]

The positive implication of these four abstentions taken in sum is that for Confucius, living an ethical life is much more than subscribing to a moral catechism or complying with some predetermined set of imperatives. From these strictures, we can infer an overarching, self-aware, and hermeneutical disposition in his own desired habits of action. We can tell that he has a commitment to pragmatic engagement rather than abstract speculation, an attitude of openness and accommodation rather than a need for finality, a willingness to be flexible rather than any intransigence or obstinacy, and a sensitivity and deference to the needs of others rather than an inordinate concern for his own personal advantage. This habituated, self-conscious disposition is therefore what motivates the virtuosic if not indeed sagacious conduct we associate with the person of Confucius, someone who has served as the role model for an entire cultural tradition.

---

68. *Analects* 9.4: 子絕四: 毋意, 毋必, 毋固, 毋我。

In the Confucian process cosmology that eschews any strong sense of teleology or idealism, the focus is heavily weighted on making the most of the "very now." The underlying assumption is that the best way to take care of tomorrow is by taking care of right now. As a personal regimen, these abstentions locate conduct relationally in what is most immediate in the human experience and focus on shaping a habitual disposition that is most effective in responding concretely to ever-changing circumstances. While we might allow that these four abstentions are of a piece, each being entailed by the others, we might also ask the following: what can we infer about Confucius's self-conscious moral agency from each of these abstentions when they are analyzed individually?

In the first abstention, Confucius is described as refraining from conjecture, speculation, or surmise (*wuyi* 毋意). And this is indeed the portrait of Confucius we find in the *Analects*. Confucius is not a person of principle; that is, we do not find him acting upon broad, theoretical assumptions determined by principles ostensibly existing prior to and informing any particular situation. Instead, he is a person whose agency seems diffused within and responsive to the here-and-now events of a particular human narrative and the theorizing of practice to produce more intelligent outcomes. Most of the language that expresses his moral vision is modal rather than referencing specific actions, exhorting a particular attitude in action rather than any specific rules of conduct. We should act with self-conscious resolve (*cheng* 誠) in our actions and be conscientious (*zhong* 忠) in what we do; we should be assiduous in our studies (*haoxue* 好學) and credible (*xin* 信) in our relations with others. Such an emphasis on modality rather than content reflects the fact that most of our actions are a function of existential commitment in our roles and relations rather than being determined seriatim by a series of fragmented choices, and again the very complexity of life itself requires that optimal moral actions will necessarily be a matter of responding efficaciously to specific circumstances rather than being determined in advance.

From the textual tradition that remembers his life, we witness a Confucius who is not given to habits of thinking and acting that depend upon the seeming clarity provided by remote, theoretical abstractions, but who rather relies pragmatically upon more immediately accessible, demonstrable information. He seems focused upon weighing up and acting upon the untidy, concrete possibilities readily available in the complex roles and events of our lives. The structure and rhythm of his narrative emerges from his best efforts to pursue and sustain propriety within his sanctified roles and relations (*li* 禮).

In resisting conjecture with respect to his understanding of persons, Confucius offers us a wholly naturalistic vision of agency that makes no appeal to a metaphysics of self or to any unifying substratum such as soul, mind, nature, or character. His interpretation of persons (*ren* 人) as "consummate conduct" (*ren* 仁) locates a critically aware, self-conscious agency within activity rather than prior to it and within relations rather than external to them. In resisting speculation with respect to his understanding of the world of experience, he returns us to the ordinary events of the day from which we are to seek the warrant and the justification for our conduct. We are offered a notion of agency that does not appeal to some simple, isolatable, and superordinate unity but rather might best be described as self-conscious resolution in the episodes of a life brought into focus through the patterns of deference shown to Confucius by those colleagues, students, and friends who share in the events of his narrative. Personal resolve (*cheng* 誠) within these relations seems to do most of the work of choice, and rather than imposing his will overtly on others, his agency seems to be driven more by his deference and acquiescence to the needs of those around him whose own actions are being shaped by his model.

The conventional way of understanding personal autonomy is to be self-legislating: persons exercise freedom and control in their actions to the extent that they are governed by their own individual wills. In the more technical Kantian sense, autonomy is defined by persons subjecting their will freely to a universal moral law as it is determined by impersonal reason. In contrast with such assumptions, for relationally constituted rather than discrete persons, the absence of coercion in their relations might be another way to begin to think about this alternative understanding of autonomy. For Confucius, autonomy seems to be expressed as persons with self-conscious resolution in their roles and conduct having full creative participation in the events of their lives. They act through negotiated patterns of deference in which they are able to find the satisfaction of their own needs while respecting the interests of others and to achieve a quality of coalescence in their relations with their fellows that leaves them uncoerced in what they do. Such autonomy is expressed as a complex coherence in one's actions and as described in the *Mencius*, "is of a piece with sustaining optimal appropriateness in our conduct (*yi* 義) and with moving resolutely forward in our way-making (*dao* 道)."[69]

This absence of speculation is immediately evidenced in the family- rather than God-centered conception of religiousness that stands as one

---

69. *Mencius* 2A2: 配義與道.

of the hallmarks of this Confucian tradition. When Fan Chi asks about "wisdom," Confucius does not attempt to formulate the kind of generic, formal definition of such virtues that are familiar to us from the Platonic dialogues. He rather exhorts Fan Chi as this particular person Fan Chi to address his own problem of getting his priorities right:[70]

> To devote yourself to what is most appropriate (*yi*) for the people, and to show respect for the ghosts and spirits while keeping them at a distance can be called wisdom.[71]

Given the speculative assumptions that have become commonplace in our own religious beliefs, this counsel to pursue a practical efficacy in one's relations with others while keeping ghosts and spirits at a distance has persuaded many commentators that Confucius has a lack of interest in, if not an aversion to, the demands of a cultivated religiousness. For such interpreters, Confucius's reticence in seeking intimacy with the spiritual world is a clear indication of his commitment to a kind of secular humanism. This humanistic reading is reinforced by a second passage in the *Analects* that describes the content of Confucius's curriculum. Perhaps even more importantly, this passage stipulates what his teaching regimen excludes. We are told that while Confucius is glad to impart his insights into the received and evolving human culture, he is unwilling to posit what the future might hold for human beings and how the cosmos might continue to unfold:

> Zigong said, "We can learn from the Master's cultural refinements, but will not hear him discourse on subjects such as 'realizing our natural propensities' (*xing*) and 'the way of *tian*.'"[72]

---

70. Fan Chi comes across as an avid enquirer, questioning Confucius on consummate conduct and wisdom in other passages as well: 12.22 and 13.19. He does not seem to be a quick study, repeatedly asking what Confucius means by the answers he is given. On the occasion when Fan Chi asks Confucius how to grow a garden (13.4), Confucius expresses both bewilderment and real impatience with someone who seems unable to establish the proper priorities for the project of becoming consummate as a person.

71. *Analects* 6.22: 務民之義，敬鬼神而遠之，可謂知矣。

72. *Analects* 5.13: 子貢曰: 夫子之文章，可得而聞也; 夫子之言性與天道，不可得而聞也。

Confucius focuses on who we are and what we have achieved as our cultural accomplishments but seems reluctant to speculate upon what we and our world might become.

In interpreting these passages, while some would ascribe to Confucius a disenchanted humanism, we might also look for another reading more consistent with his own family-centered religious assumptions. We might conclude, for example, that for Confucius, real religiousness, rather than being based on reverence for and supplication to remote supernatural entities, is to be found in cultivating bonds much nearer to home. Such an alternative religiousness is manifested as a shared, family-centered spirituality to be achieved in aspiring to live inspired lives within our families and communities. We have seen that for Confucius, growth is centered in a commitment to personal cultivation within intimate family and community relations that then extends outward radially and reflexively to the cosmic totality. There is an interpenetrating center and periphery, where what is most self-consciously intensive has the greatest extended reach and influence and where what is most extensive is reflected back to fortify what is most intensive. More concretely, we might infer that Confucius believes there is a direct and inseparable link between the self-conscious deference, veneration, and gratitude expressed within the moral life at home and the quiet, reassuring spirituality we associate with the expression of reverence for the ancestors and a natural piety. Or said more simply, such Confucian religiousness is nothing other than the sense of cosmic belonging that is inspired by our achieved sense of felt worth within our most immediate and intimate relations.

As we have suggested, if the etymology of religion (L. *religare*) does actually mean "to bind tightly," then *li* 禮 would seem to be the key term for understanding such family-centered religiousness as it serves as the social grammar that produces meaningful bonds and reinforces tenacity within the social fabric. *Li* begins from a ritualized devotion to the family and lineage and then extends to sacralize our roles and relations in community more broadly. On such a reading, the traditional Spring Festival that is alive and well today should be understood as a profoundly religious event. This is the largest regularized migration of any population in human history, and in it we witness a phenomenon wherein the predominantly immigrant urban centers disgorge their populations. Almost every person in the country using any manner of transport available returns to their native place for an extended period of serious moral "re-creation." This recreation is engaged in by a population who, through a lifetime of moral education, have had reverence for family, elders, teachers, and communities inculcated into them, and who take their "native place" (*laojia* 老家) as a prime defining factor in their personal identity. Acting upon this family reverence, they return to their roots to renew their most intimate relations, thereby generating the tensile strength to return to the cities several weeks later and carry on for another year.

A generalization Tang Junyi makes about early Chinese cosmology that captures this family- rather than God-centered religiousness is expressed in his postulate that "the realization of our own natural propensities is nothing other than the unfolding of the natural and cultural processes themselves" (*xing ji tiandao guan* 性即天道觀). This claim acknowledges the fact that who we are becoming is radically embedded in our unbounded narratives and thus can only be understood holographically by considering the full compass of our contextualizing relations. This understanding of focus-field agency requires that persons be brought into focus from the farthest reaches toward the center, from the totality to the particular, and from the most remote factors to our most relevant details. It describes the self-conscious awareness of one's own person as an emerging center of more or less meaningful resolution within the totality. Confucius himself so conceived is a narrative field of events made available to his descendants in those episodes recounted in the *Analects* and elsewhere in the canonical literature. As Confucius's cultural progeny draw inspiration from his story in crafting their own unique persons and habits of conduct, they make his narrative integral to their own lives.

The second abstention in this description of Confucius is his reluctance to claim or demand certainty. Such reticence to invoke the fixed and final as imperatives or universal laws is based upon his fundamental respect for change and novelty. It reflects an awareness of the open-ended complexities of lives lived within a cosmology of "ceaseless procreation in the very 'now,'" a profound sense of ongoing and ineluctable transformation captured in the *Book of Changes* mantra: *shengsheng buyi* 生生不已. And this process of generative procreation is made normative in a complementary passage in the same text: "The greatest virtuosity of the cosmos lies in its life-force."[73] This passage asserts that we are born into, grow together with, and live on within our contextualizing and always evolving natural, social, and cultural relations and that self-conscious growth itself within this context is the substance of cosmic morality.

---

73. 天地之大德曰生。

The sense of agency within this process first and foremost emerges out of a purposeful devotion to the vital, always collaborative roles we live in our continuing personal narratives. This defining feature of focus-field agency requires of us not only our unrelenting attention to continuing growth in these roles but also sufficient moral imagination to be aware of and responsive to our always shifting circumstances. Irreducibly complex persons are vital and inherently active, and in their continuing deference to and collaboration with others, they must necessarily remain provisional, revisionist, and accommodating in all they do. There is, for them, neither finality nor closure.

Confucius's third and closely related commitment is to a flexibility in his actions that follows from this abjuring of certainty. Such flexibility is required from reflexive persons who, being keenly aware of the transactional and associated nature of the human experience, acknowledge their own imbricated identities as variable and yet resolute foci within the contextualizing fields of their environing others. Such focus-field agents have to be understood as irreducibly transactional, consciously shaping and being shaped in their vital patterns of relations. Ultimately, such agency can only be negotiated through established habits of commitment and deference. That is, while such agency is necessarily passive in the archaic sense of invariably "suffering" the actions of others, it must at the same time find the right balance in also being self-conscious, animated, purposeful, and projective. Simply put, morally responsible lives can only be lived through a flexible responsiveness in the activities that come to define our identities.

And the final abstention for Confucius is refraining from being self-absorbed. Critically self-aware agency that is irreducibly social cannot afford to be egoistic or self-obsessed. As they become increasing enculturated through the semiotic processes and symbolic competencies that shape them in their associations, such focus-field agents develop their own inflected and reflexive sense of themselves out of their intra-subjective relations with others. Such hylozoistic agents—at once psychic and profoundly physical—certainly live their many roles through their discursive, vital, and carnal bodies. But as they strive to achieve personal coherence in the changing configuration of their equally organic physical and social relations, such bodies have a porous membrane that is continually embodying their experience as integral to their evolving identities. Such focus-field agents must exercise their cultivated capacity to be responsive to their environments while exhibiting that relationally defined autonomy that comes with the absence of coercion in the activities they share with others. Such an autonomy is the direct consequence of collaborative relations within these environments in which the values and purposes of a web of collaborators become coincident with one's own.

Dewey's Notion of "Individuality": An Associative Analogy

In thinking through the Confucian notion of radically embedded, relationally constituted, and always emergent persons, we might do well to explore Dewey's notion of "individuality" I have alluded to before as a potentially productive example of an associative analogy. Classical pragmatism's innovative turn in the way of thinking about persons within the Western narrative might be helpful in bringing the Confucian version of relationally constituted persons into clearer resolution and for thinking through alternative notions of agency, autonomy, and choice.

In his phenomenology of human conduct, Dewey merges the process psychology of William James and the social psychology of George Herbert Mead to locate the habitudes that constitute persons within their natural and social relations. Mead was a contemporary of Dewey early in his career at the University of Michigan who then joined him on faculty when Dewey was invited to chair the department at Chicago. As Mead insists, "self" is coterminous with the world:

> The self cannot arise in experience except as there are others there. The child experiences sounds, etc., before it has experience of its own body; there is nothing in the child that arises as his own experience and then is referred to the outside things. . . . Only a superficial philosophy demands the old view that we start with ourselves. . . . There is no self before there is a world, and no world before the self. The process of the formation of the self is social.[74]

Using Dewey's own language, this unique relational individuality stands in contrast to what he refers to as an "old psychology" based upon

---

74. George Herbert Mead, *The Individual and the Social Self: Unpublished Work of George Herbert Mead*, ed. David L. Miller (Chicago: University of Chicago Press, 1982), 156.

the assumed presence of some superordinate "soul" or "mind" or "self" as its principle of individuation:

> The traditional psychology of the original separate soul, mind or consciousness is in truth a reflex of conditions which cut human nature off from its natural objective relations. It implies first the severance of man from nature and then of each man from his fellows.[75]

As his radical alternative to what has become our commonsense understanding of the discrete person, Dewey argues that

> only the hold of a traditional conception of the singleness and simplicity of soul and self blinds us to perceiving what they mean: the relative fluidity and diversity of the constituents of selfhood. There is no one ready-made self behind activities. There are complex, unstable, opposing attitudes, habits, impulses, which gradually come to terms with one another, and assume a certain consistency of configuration. [76]

William James was for Dewey nothing less than a mentor and philosophical inspiration. Even so, Dewey was uncomfortable with some of the internal inconsistencies that remained in James's groundbreaking *Principles of Psychology* as it attempts to articulate and endorse a notion of a decidedly individual person described as a stream of consciousness. In a thinly veiled criticism, Dewey insists that

> the doctrine of a single, simple and indissoluble soul was the cause and the effect of a failure to recognize that concrete habits are the means of knowledge and thought. Many who think themselves scientifically emancipated and who freely advertise the soul for a superstition, perpetuate a false notion of what knows, that is of a separate knower. Nowadays they usually fix upon consciousness in general, as a stream or process or entity.[77]

---

75. Dewey, *Middle Works*, 14:60.
76. Dewey, *Middle Works*, 14:96.
77. Dewey, *Middle Works*, 14:123.

Dewey instead, in a different language but still analogous in many ways with the Confucian notion of the roles lived by relationally constituted persons, arrives at an understanding of persons as dynamic, organically situated, focal systems of associated habits and impulses:

> Now it is dogmatically stated that no such conceptions of the seat, agent or vehicle will go psychologically at the present time. Concrete habits do all the perceiving, recognizing, imagining, recalling, judging, conceiving and reasoning that is done. "Consciousness," whether as a stream or as special sensations and images, expresses the functions of habits, phenomena of their formation, operation, their interruption and reorganization. . . . A certain delicate combination of habit and impulse is requisite for observation, memory and judgment.[78]

Dewey appeals to the actual situated human experience as we live it in rejecting the priority of an ostensive autonomous "self" over that of an organic configuration of relations, and in questioning the priority of instincts to shared cultural life-forms. He insists upon the primacy of the relationally constituted, concrete situation as the garden of a self-aware social intelligence and the locus for the pursuit of the consummate life. The optimally appropriate response to our ever-present uncertainties, and any confident resolution of these uncertainties, can only be negotiated within the actual circumstances themselves, with any claims to discrete agency itself being an abstraction from them.

As previously mentioned, Dewey created the neologism "individuality" when he encountered the transition from the ideal of relationally constituted "individualities" to the notion of discrete pecuniary individuals in an increasingly capitalist society. In Dewey's own language, he reviles what he calls the decadent "new" mercantile individualism while also advocating for the return to a robust, "old" individualism that promised us a real kind of personal distinctiveness available through the activation of our substantial differences.

The English word "existence" is derived from its Latin root that means "standing apart from." For Dewey, the cosmology that lies behind

---

78. Dewey, *Middle Works*, 14:124.

his conception of an achieved individuality is an expression of this resolute particularity in its most positive sense, claiming as it does

> that every existence deserving the name of existence has something unique and irreplaceable about it, that it does not exist to illustrate a principle, to realize a universal, or to embody a kind or class. . . . It means that no matter how great the quantitative differences of ability, strength, position, wealth, such differences are negligible in comparison with something else—the fact of individuality, the manifestation of something irreplaceable. It means, in short, a world in which an existence must be reckoned with on its own account, not as something capable of equation with and transformation into something else.[79]

For Dewey, individuality is the antithesis of the putative uniformity that would define us as a natural kind. It is the realization of what each of us specifically can become as distinct from other people, a realization that can only take place within the context of a flourishing communal life. Such exceptionality arises qualitatively through distinctive service to one's community that is a contribution uniquely one's own. "Individuality cannot be opposed to association." says Dewey. "It is through association that man has acquired his individuality, and it is through association that he exercises it."[80] An individual so construed is not a "thing" but a "patterned event" describable first in the language of relationality and social activity and then in terms of uniqueness, self-conscious growth, purpose, and qualitative achievement.

It is in this context that Dewey, in formulating his own irreducibly social conception of person, uses "individuality" consistently to refer to the habitudes of unique, relationally constituted human events. Dewey describes the "individuality" of Abraham Lincoln, for example, as

> an extensive event; or, if you prefer, it is a course of events each of which takes up into itself something of what went before and leads on to that which comes after. The skill, the

---

79. Dewey, *Middle Works*, 11:32.
80. Dewey, *Lectures* (2nd release), 1:122.

art, of the biographer is displayed in his ability to discover and portray the subtle ways, hidden often from the individual himself, in which one event grows out of those which preceded and enters into those which follow.[81]

It is by invoking this kind of vital, eventful language that Dewey is able to appropriately express his notion of individuality. Dewey continues:

> *Individuality is the uniqueness of the history*, of the *career*, not something given once for all at the beginning which then proceeds to unroll as a ball of yarn may be unwound. Lincoln made history. But it is just as true that he made himself as an individual in the history he made.[82]

For Dewey, what is put at risk by the foundational and isolating individualism of liberal democracy is what he celebrates as our socially achieved uniqueness and individuality. He has a harsh opinion of the kind of individualism that would treat human beings as discrete and self-sufficient existents. The problem with such thinking is that

> it ignores the fact that the mental and moral structure of individuals, the pattern of their desires and purposes, change with every great change in social constitution. Individuals who are not bound together in associations, whether domestic, economic, religious, political, artistic or educational, are monstrosities. It is absurd to suppose that the ties which hold them together are merely external and do not react into mentality and character, producing the framework of personal disposition.[83]

Dewey introduces his notion of an emergent "individuality" in his resistance to this foundational, discrete individualism, declaring that individual autonomy so conceived is a bald fiction. For Dewey, it is association that is a fact, and we can use the distinction he develops between

---

81. Dewey, *Middle Works*, 14:103.
82. Dewey, *Middle Works*, 14:103.
83. Dewey, *Later Works*, 5:80.

"individualism" and "individuality" to bring further clarity to this social construction of the person. In Dewey's own language:

> There is no mystery about the fact of association, of interconnected action which affects the activity of singular elements. There is no sense in asking how individuals come to be associated. They exist and operate in association. . . . Thus man is not merely *de facto* associated; but he *becomes* a social animal in the make-up of his ideas, sentiments and deliberate behavior. *What* he believes, hopes for and aims at is the outcome of association and intercourse.[84]

For Dewey, "individuality" is neither a presocial potential nor the kind of isolating discreteness we generally associate with a Lockean individualism. Indeed, he argues that the phenomenon of such an aberrant individualism is realized only under the worst possible circumstances in the numbing monotony of the assembly line in an industrialist society in which workers are reduced to generic automatons:

> The subordination of the enterprises to pecuniary profit reacts to make the workers "hands" only. Their hearts and brains are not engaged. . . . The philosopher's idea of a complete separation of mind and body is realized in thousands of industrial workers, and the result is a depressed body and an empty and distorted mind.[85]

In a way that resonates with Confucian role ethics, Dewey particularizes the fact of associated living and valorizes it by developing a vision of the interpenetrating habitudes of unique, diffused, relationally constituted human beings. In explanation of this notion of "individuality," he develops a distinctive, if not idiosyncratic, language of "habits" to describe the various modalities of association that enable human beings to add value to their activities and to transform what are mere relations into a communicating community. In Dewey's defense of why he would choose a term such as "habit," which brings with it some

---

84. Dewey, *Later Works*, 2:250.
85. Dewey, *Later Works*, 5:104.

negative connotations, rather than invoking more familiar expressions such as attitude or disposition, he argues that

> we need a word to express that kind of human activity which is influenced by prior activity and in that sense acquired; which contains within itself a certain ordering or systematization of minor elements of action; which is projective, dynamic in quality, ready for overt manifestation; and which is operative in some subdued subordinate form even when not obviously dominating activity.[86]

In rehabilitating the term "habits," Dewey further elaborates on the perceived intimate connection between the efforts of sustained human learning and the irreducibly social yet personal habitudes that emerge from it:

> The influence of habit is decisive because all distinctively human action has to be learned, and the very heart, blood, and sinews of learning is the creation of habitudes. . . . Habit does not preclude the use of thought, but it determines the channels within which it operates.[87]

For Dewey, the all too familiar contrast made between erstwhile discrete individuals and the society in which they live is a persistent fiction, with the error lying in the assumption that persons *are* individuals as opposed to understanding on the contrary that their individuality is a social achievement won through the quality of their associated lives together. The quest for greater individual freedom, for example, does not require persons to somehow liberate themselves from the pattern of existing relations and assert their independence from them. Rather, such persons must in fact attempt to change their current configuration of social relations for a better configuration that permits a greater degree of participation in the activities that constitute their communities. We are always and irreducibly persons-in-our-relations and never just persons.

Whatever we have as the initial conditions situating us within community, these conditions must be attended by a substantial process of nurturance and growth for us to achieve our individualities. Like Dewey's unconventional understanding of "experience," another example

---

86. Dewey, *Middle Works*, 14:31.
87. Dewey, *Later Works*, 2:335.

of his use of ordinary language in an extraordinary way is this notion of "individuality." Far from being a ready-made given, "individuality" is a social product—the fruit of effective associated living—that arises qualitatively out of ordinary human experience. Individuality is a "becoming distinguished" that can only take place within the context of a flourishing communal life. "Individuality," like the less felicitous term "character," is an accomplishment. And since this term emerges relationally out of associated living, far from being bounded and discrete, it has implicated within it a "field of selves." Persons so construed are not "things" but vital, patterned "events," describable certainly in the stable language of uniqueness and qualitative achievement but also more dynamically in terms of a self-conscious virtuosic relationality and the expanding patterns of deference such virtuosity elicits from their neighbors.

Dewey insists that "we are born organic beings associated with others, but we are not born members of a community."[88] For Dewey, our "individuality" is initially qualitative and only then becomes quantitative as we achieve our distinctiveness. Our individualities can only emerge through sustained collaboration with others within the context of a flourishing communal life. But as our individuality comes to define us as how we differ in our habitudes from other people, it then becomes quantitative in singling us out as the unique, distinctive persons we have become. A distinctive or even distinguished individual so construed is not a discrete "thing" but a patterned, situated event describable in the language of uniqueness, integrity, social activity, relationality, and qualitative achievement. Dewey is radical in this social construction of the person, rejecting out of hand the idea that human beings are in any way complete outside of the associations they live together with other people. Indeed, he asserts quite boldly that for the human being, "apart from the ties which bind him to others, he is nothing."[89]

Resonances between Confucian Focus-Field Persons and Classical Pragmatism

We have found analogy between the Confucian conception of focus-field persons and the notion of relational "individuality" that evolved out of John Dewey's work and that of the other classical pragmatists. In so

---

88. Dewey, *Later Works*, 2:331.
89. Dewey, *Later Works*, 7:323.

doing, I hope to have not only clarified this alternative conception of relationally constituted persons but also to have deexoticized it. We have seen that, like Dewey, the Confucian focus-field alternative to locating personal identity in some superordinate soul or self or mind is instead to find this same focal coherence in media res as it appeals to a continuing process of habituated coordination and integration within one's embodied roles and relations. We are each holographic as foci of the lived roles and relations that in sum make up our narratives. We might take this analogy one step further in our efforts to get clearer on this more holistic understanding of our focal identities by exploring how the classical pragmatists, themselves process thinkers and advocates of a relationally constituted conception of persons, searched for a language through which to express the holography of our actions. How can the specific acts that come to constitute our unique identities be best described as they occur within an unbounded "field" of activity?

We might begin again from George Herbert Mead. Mead had studied under William James at Harvard before going to Leipzig to finish his education with Wilhelm Wundt, a distinguished psychologist well known in his time for his concept of "the gesture." Mead as a social psychologist was critical of Wundt's separation of the gestures of organisms and their respondents, and he complained that

> Wundt presupposes selves as antecedent to the social process in order to explain communication within that process, whereas, on the contrary, selves must be accounted for in terms of the social process, and in terms of communication; and individuals must be brought into essential relation within that process before communication, or the contact between the minds of different individuals, becomes possible.[90]

For Mead, the problem is an inversion in the actual rhythm of life, making individuals prior to their relations, and making mind, which is in fact the outcome of a process, antecedent to that process. The continuing social experience with its symbolic interactionalism is the ambience in which persons as "selves" take shape and achieve their distinctiveness. In Mead's words, "The body is not a self, as such; it becomes a self only

---

90. George Herbert Mead, *Mind, Self, and Society*, ed. Charles W. Morris, vol. 1 (Chicago: University of Chicago Press, 1934), 49.

when it has developed a mind within the context of social experience."[91] Mead goes on to define "mind" not as an entity but as an irreducibly social process. We do not first have minds and thereby communicate with each other. Rather, because we are engaged in constant communication, we mind each other and become like-minded in doing so. Mead uses his teacher Wundt and the individualistic "old psychology" as his foil:

> For if as Wundt does, you presuppose the existence of mind at the start, as explaining or making possible the social process of experience, then the origin of minds and the interaction among minds become mysteries. But if, on the other hand, you regard the social process of experience as prior (in a rudimentary form) to the existence of mind and explain the origin of minds in terms of the interaction among individuals within that process, then not only the origin of minds, but also the interaction among minds (which is thus seen to be internal to their very nature and presupposed by their existence or development at all) cease to seem mysterious or miraculous. Mind arises through communication by a conversation of gestures in a social process or context of experience—not communication through mind.

True to the contextualism that is the defining feature of classical pragmatism, Mead understands the development of mind in terms of the reflexiveness of personal experience within the continuing social process:

> The evolutionary appearance of mind or intelligence takes place when the whole social process of experience and behavior is brought within the experience of any one of the separate individuals implicated therein, and when the individual's adjustment to the process is modified and refined by the awareness or consciousness which he thus has of it. It is by means of reflexiveness—the turning-back of the experience of the individual upon himself—that the whole social process is thus brought into the experience of the individuals involved in it; it is by such means, which enable the individual to take the attitude of the other toward himself, that the individual

---

91. Mead, *Mind, Self, and Society*, 1:49.

is able consciously to adjust himself to that process, and to modify the resultant of that process in any given social act in terms of his adjustment to it.[92]

In a complementary but somewhat different language, the first point Dewey would make about the irreducibly social construction of persons is that we need to get past our commonsense assumption that we live our lives inside our skins and recognize the extent to which life is "out there" in a way that is organic, interactive, and fully collaborative with the changing world:

> The thing essential to bear in mind is that living as an empirical affair is not something which goes on below the skin-surface of an organism: it is always an inclusive affair involving connection, interaction of what is within the organic body and what lies outside in space and time, and with higher organisms, far outside.[93]

On this basis, Dewey offers us a societal, dynamic, and interactive conception of how mind itself comes into being, where it is "located" in "the qualities of organic action," and how it functions as "a characteristic way of inter-activity." This Deweyan conception of "mind" as a dynamic, extended habitude resonates interestingly with the Mencian notion of a diffused yet centered process of "bodyheartminding" as described previously. In trying to find a way to talk about such a socially located "mind," Dewey wants to get past the isolating "where" question:

> Domination by spatial considerations leads some thinkers to ask *where* mind is. . . . [A]ccepting for the moment the standpoint of the questioner (which ignores the locus of discourse, institutions, and social arts), limiting the question to the organic individual, we may say that the 'seat' or locus of mind—its static phase—is the qualities of organic action, as far as these qualities have been conditioned by language and its consequences.[94]

---

92. Mead, *Mind, Self, and Society*, 1:134.
93. Dewey, *Later Works*, 1:215.
94. Dewey, *Later Works*, 1:221–22.

Dewey then tries to break away from our culturally specific, ontological prejudices that would isolate ecologically embedded entities by separating structure from function and things from what they do:

> But the organism is not just a structure; it is a characteristic way of inter-activity which is not simultaneous, all at once, but serial. It is a way impossible without structure for its mechanism, but it differs from structure as walking differs from legs or breathing from lungs.[95]

Dewey's point is that "mind" is both focused as a locus of persistent habits and again diffused as a field of psychophysical activities being carried out locally in the unbounded world of experience. This participatory, eventful understanding of mind can for Dewey be further clarified in the idiomatic, nondoctrinal, and organismic way that we are given to using the word "soul":

> To say emphatically of a particular person that he has soul or a great soul . . . expresses the conviction that the man or woman in question has in marked degree qualities of sensitive, rich and coordinated participation in all situations of life. . . . To see the organism *in* nature . . . will be seen to be *in*, not as marbles are in a box but as events are in history, in a moving, growing never finished process.[96]

And Dewey provides an ecological and organic image that illustrates how the holographic focus of our habitual behaviors in having both "everything" and "all the time" as their penumbra is thus a construal of the synchronic and diachronic totality from one particular perspective:

> We find also in all these higher organisms that what is done is conditioned by consequences of prior activities; we find the fact of learning or habit-formation. . . . Thus an environment both extensive and enduring is immediately implicated in present behavior. Operatively speaking, the remote and the past are 'in' behavior making it what it is. The action called

---

95. Dewey, *Later Works*, 1:221–22.
96. Dewey, *Later Works*, 1:213.

'organic' is not just that of internal structures; it is an integration of organic-environmental connections.⁹⁷

In whatever way we choose to go about explaining the phenomenon we call "thinking," it is clear to Dewey that each moment in this continuing process, far from being isolatable or discrete, has implicated within it an often unclear but always unbounded field of experience:

> It may be a mystery that there should be thinking but it is no mystery that if there is thinking it should contain in a 'present' phase, affairs remote in space and in time, even to geologic ages, future eclipses and far away stellar systems. It is only a question of how far what is "in" its actual experience is extricated and becomes focal.⁹⁸

In his *Pluralistic Universe*, William James uses a phenomenology of consciousness to reflect on and vividly express what he calls "the pulse of inner life," a pulsation that in being at once holistic and specific requires that we abandon any notion of "inner" and "outer" as exclusive domains. As we have seen in reference to the Mencian notion of *xin* and *haoranzhiqi* 浩然之气, we must reconceive the relationship between the erstwhile "inner" and "outer" in focus-field, holographic terms where they are simply two ways of foregrounding and emphasizing different aspects of the same phenomenon: or more concretely, our focal personal identities within our complex narratives as their field. "Inner" is the question of how self-consciously the quality of my relations makes a difference in my field of experience; "outer" is the question of how in my deferring to the contextualizing others the outside comes "in" to constitute me:

> In the pulse of inner life immediately present now in each of us is a little past, a little future, a little awareness of our own body, of each other's persons, of these sublimities we are trying to talk about, of the earth's geography and the direction of history, of truth and error, of good and bad, and of who knows how much more? Feeling, however dimly

---

97. Dewey, *Later Works*, 1:213.
98. Dewey, *Later Works*, 1:213.

and subconsciously, all these things, your pulse of inner life is continuous with them, belongs to them and they to it.[99]

In this same passage, James (as only he can do) goes on to appeal explicitly to a rather inspired and inspiring language of focal centers and extended fields as his way of getting past the intellectualist habit of dirempting our experience into separate things:

> The real units of our immediately felt life are unlike the units that intellectualist logic holds to and makes its calculations with. They are not separate from their own others, and you have to take them at widely separated dates to find any two of them that seem unblent . . . my present field of consciousness is a centre surrounded by a fringe that shades insensibly into a subconscious more. . . . Which part of it properly is in my consciousness, which out? If I name what is out, it already has come in. The centre works in one way while the margins work in another, and presently overpower the centre and are central themselves. What we conceptually identify ourselves with and say we are thinking of at any time is the centre; but our full self is the whole field, with all those indefinitely radiating subconscious possibilities of increase.[100]

It is clear that in passages such as these, Dewey and James are both offering us a focus-field conception of persons that is radically disjunctive within their own philosophical narratives. Such a challenge to old ways of thinking is perhaps an important reason for the time that has had to elapse before these early pragmatists would be recognized by the mainstream discipline of philosophy as the original and important philosophers they are.

---

99. William James, *A Pluralistic Universe* (New York: Longmans, Green, 1912), 286.
100. James, *A Pluralistic Universe*, 286–288.

Chapter Five

Relational Autonomy and Thick Choices

Taking Stock

Peter Hershock, in his *Valuing Diversity*, observes: "Something that is good for each of us, considered individually, may not be good for all of us."[1] If individual autonomy and equality as conventionally conceived are high values within the virtue ethics discourse—values that necessarily bring with them corollaries such as individuality, rationality, freedom, rights, and personal choice—the counterpart to these values in Confucian role ethics would be what Hershock terms "relational equity" and "an achieved diversity." Drawing upon Buddhist values and practices, Hershock is able to formulate an alternative to the liberal "hypergoods" of autonomy and equality, defining relational *equity* as the heightened realization of dynamically shared well-being and achieved *diversity* as the conserving and coordinating of differences for the full appreciation of the creative possibilities of any situation.[2]

Hershock's reasoning is as follows. Both autonomy and equality are grounded in a doctrine of external relations that subordinates our relations

---

1. Hershock, *Valuing Diversity*, 133.

2. "Hypergoods" is a useful neologism introduced by Charles Taylor in his *Sources of the Self*, 62–63: "Most of us not only live with many goods but find that we have to rank them, and in some cases, this ranking makes one of them of supreme importance relative to the others. . . . Let me call higher-order goods of this kind 'hypergoods,' i.e. goods which not only are incomparably more important than others but provide the standpoint from which these must be weighed, judged, decided about."

with others to our individual selves. A doctrine of external relations prioritizes our personal integrity over our interdependence with each other and the ostensive sameness that obtains among us—our "equality"—over our many differences. Thus, the notions of autonomy and equality as they apply to individuals give us a sense of personal differences as mere "variety"—differences that do not make a difference. That is, we certainly have differences among us that we try to register and tolerate, but such differences are to some important degree mitigated by the assumption that we as individuals are still to be treated as equals. And as persons who would assert their individual autonomy, the relations they enter into remain external and contingent rather than intrinsic and constitutive.

While comparative equality and individual autonomy guarantees that difference can only be variations among basically similar people (variety), the pursuit of relational equity and an achieved diversity allows for the continuing diversification of qualities and propensities that grow our differences into resources for mutual enrichment (diversity). Variety among equals stands in contrast to the diversity that can only be achieved by fully activating and appreciating the important differences we have. That is, we need to acknowledge not only that we differ *from* each other (variety) but also actively differ *for* each other, and in so doing, allow our differences to really make a difference (diversity).

There are two important corollaries to the valorization of equity and diversity that we might note. First, equity and diversity cannot be engineered by individual agents (who do not exist) but must emerge as a function of the coordinated activity among relationally constituted members of family and community. And secondly, the values of equity and diversity extend beyond our human parameters to guarantee the mutual implication and inseparability of ethical, economic, and ecological considerations.

One way of bringing further focus to Hershock's distinction between equity and diversity on the one hand, and individual autonomy and equality on the other, might be to join him in an appreciative critique of Nobel Laureate Amartya Sen who in the mid-1980s began to develop what he has called the "capabilities approach" to the economics of welfare. In his monograph *The Idea of Justice* Sen has also tried (like Kupperman) to marshal all the king's men to put Humpty-Dumpty together again by offering a sustained critique of the "transcendental" theorizing of his teacher, John Rawls, and by trying to reinstate the continuities between theory and practice in a range of different ways. When it comes to the issue of "choice," for example, in service to his strong commitment to liberty, Sen argues for capacity-based reasoning that for particular persons allows for those personal differences in what they would choose. And Sen, rather than simply registering the punctuating decisions or "culminations" that would fragment our judgments, further insists on including the *process* of choice as being integral to any and all of the comprehensive outcomes.[3]

Sen proposes a new method for evaluating human development, for judging the quality of life of a society, and—importantly—for assessing both justice and injustice. In his capabilities approach, he directs our attention to those substantive human freedoms that he calls "capabilities." He takes these freedoms to be alternatives to the familiar utilitarian concern for happiness or pleasure; the resource-based approaches that look to income, wealth, and mental satisfaction; or the libertarian focus on the fairness of the process. And Sen argues for a broad view of freedom—for a full recognition of the heterogeneity of distinctive components of freedom that encompasses our personal differences, the specific opportunities to pursue our objectives, and the process entailed in making choices.

Sen's capabilities approach, grounded as it is in substantive human freedom, is an attempt to go beyond calculations based on some abstract notion of generic individuals by considering what specific individuals under specific conditions are actually able to do. The capabilities approach can perhaps be fairly described by developing a clear understanding of the organic relationship that obtains among a cluster of four key terms Sen advances in explanation of this instrument for measuring human advantage: functionings, capabilities, agency, and individual freedom.

Sen takes what he calls *functionings*, which define a person's life experience—the specific combination of "beings and doings" or "states and activities"—as a central consideration for his capabilities approach. For example, "being" happy and healthy and "doing" the tasks necessary for maintaining a decent occupation are specific functionings. Freedom is a key consideration, since it is clear that the more freedom we have, the more opportunity there is to do and get what we want. To take an example, the functionings of fasting, dieting, anorexia, and starving, while seemingly similar, are not the same because they are distinguished by the presence and the absence of free choice among options. In the first two

---

3. Amartya Sen, *The Idea of Justice* (Cambridge, MA: Harvard University Press, 2009).

cases, we freely achieve what we value, although for different reasons; in the second two instances there is little or no freedom of choice.

How then is a person's overall advantage to be measured? The *capabilities* register the relevant personal qualities and the external conditions that in combination provide the ability, on the one hand, and the opportunity on the other to get what one values. They answer the question of what is possible. Absent the relevant ability, there is no real opportunity, and without opportunity, ability is wasted. But what a person is capable of doing is not simply a matter of weighing up what one actually achieves. It also requires a careful consideration of what persons are free to achieve—that is, a calculation of the options available to them in getting what they value. As in the previously given example of distinguishing between fasting and starving, one's capability—one's freedom and one's opportunity to acquire the food one needs—is a central consideration in measuring one's personal advantage.

Key to what one is or has is how one's situation came to be. One's *agency*, then, is defined as personally choosing as one's goals and objectives the combination of functionings that one values most. Such freedom of choice does not always and need not necessarily conduce to one's optimal well-being. Importantly, although agency is to be assessed primarily in terms of individual freedom, for Sen it also has a social aspect. Successful agency takes place within society and entails free participation in the economic, social, and political life of the community without constraint or coercion. An implication of agency is that freedom to participate fully in the social and political life of society that expands the reach and influence of one's agency, and the reach and influence of one's agency is, in turn, a measure of the quality of one's freedom.

With his appreciation of the importance of differences and of participation in communal life-forms, Sen has taken the notion of agency in a felicitous direction. But clearly at the heart of Sen's capabilities approach is still the strong commitment to personal autonomy that he shares with Rawls—that is, to *individual* freedom. He endorses the freedom one has as an individual to choose one's goals and objectives without coercion or interference. He offers us a nuanced and robust conception of freedom that encompasses what he takes to be the complementary features of capability: the absence of dependence and the absence of external interference. The claim one has on society is this freedom of opportunity and choice. As Sen puts it:

The importance of capability, reflecting opportunity and choice, rather than the celebration of some particular lifestyle, irrespective of preference or choice, is central to the point at issue.[4]

The attention that the introduction of the capabilities approach has attracted from both theorists and policymakers is perhaps an indication of a general dissatisfaction with the remote and abstract discourse that has heretofore attended attempts to theorize justice as the measure of welfare. And Sen's introduction of the capabilities approach has certainly been celebrated as a significant step forward in economic welfare theory. Clearly the most important considerations for Sen in formulating this theory are individual differences, alternative conceptions of happiness, nonmaterialistic factors in the pursuit of happiness, differentials in opportunity, and above all, real freedom.

Sen appeals to the language of the Indian tradition in challenging an abstract, principled approach to justice—what is known as *niti*—on the grounds that the mechanical application of justice as an abstract principle is insufficiently informed by the particular lived circumstances of real people—that is, by *nyaya*. Sen wants to avoid the separation and elevation of institutions from real-life narratives by retaining the continuity between abstract generalities and the concrete detail of lives lived, and to this end, seeks to formulate an "idea" of justice that takes as its warrant achieved equity in the lives of real people.

With his capabilities approach, Sen also acknowledges the need to treat persons as particular individuals with different values and aspirations: in doing this, Sen makes a substantial move to understand justice in a more concrete and inclusive way. Sen particularizes individuals and their circumstances, pluralizes notions of freedom and public reasoning, and even brings in the "comparative questions" to allow for cultural differences. So far so good. Although Hershock and I share an appreciation for the direction that Sen has set for us, we would both still argue that he does not go far enough.

Sen's capabilities approach is certainly an effort to both contextualize and particularize the notion of human agency, locating personal activity within the states and activities of the ordinary human experience. But

---

4. Sen, *Idea of Justice*, 238.

how successful is he in overcoming what Whitehead has called "the perils of abstraction"?[5] Although Sen rejects what he calls "transcendental institutionalism" and argues for a more comprehensive, pluralistic, and pragmatic understanding of social welfare and justice, he still shares some of the basic assumptions of the theorists he is arguing against. Most fundamentally, he wants to frame his "idea" of justice by appeal to the same vocabulary that is invoked to define the liberal conception of the autonomous individual. For Sen as for these other theorists, persons as the subjects of justice are to be characterized in variations on the familiar language of discrete individuality: autonomy, freedom and choice, rationality, equality, and objectivity (or impartiality).

Hershock identifies Sen's capabilities approach as a case where the continuing commitment to the notions of individual autonomy and equality sets real limits on the opportunity for mutual appreciation that equity and diversity would encourage. Hershock observes that

> while Sen (1985) is entirely correct in calling attention to a detrimental bias in much of GCs [Global Commons] and GPGs [Global Public Goods] discourses toward focusing on resources rather than freedoms, it is crucial to resist understanding freedom either as an achieved state of affairs or (as Sen does) as an achieved set of capabilities for exercising real choices in pursuit of one's own, individual interest. If . . . dynamic equity is a function of attenuating self-other and individual-collective polarizations of interest, the extent to which freedom can be affirmed . . . is the extent to which it connotes demonstrating contributory and appreciative virtuosity, not the dualistic, self- and other-reifying exercise of choice."[6]

Hershock is arguing that Sen still retains in important degree the default liberal notion of the discrete and autonomous individual as the subject of justice. Sen defines this autonomous individual in terms of choice, freedom, and rationality without sufficient appreciation of the irreducibly relational nature of personal and situational differences in the lives of real people. Such individuals understood as independent actors giving

---

5. Whitehead, *Modes of Thought*, 58.
6. Hershock, *Valuing Diversity*, 239.

their reasons for exercising autonomy in making their own choices are still deracinated abstractions from what are in fact relationally constituted persons radically embedded in organically interdependent situations. While Sen rejects the abstract principle of justice as being insufficiently robust to deliver justice in the real world, he is still relying upon an abstracted, liberal conception of person that I would argue is both conceptually anemic and empirically false. Indeed, in this respect, I would suggest that while we might celebrate Sen's attempt to respect the importance of the concrete context, his position is still fair evidence of our claim that the ideology of individualism is so ensconced in our thinking that even those contemporary intellectuals committed to a more capacious way of thinking about human morality have difficulty formulating an alternative to this default individualism. As a consequence, these intellectuals ironically reinforce the libertarian values they would erstwhile critique.

Let us recall the argument for why autonomous individuality continues to trump a social, relational conception of person as a viable alternative. Political theorists dating back to the classical Greeks have certainly acknowledged that we are all social creatures strongly influenced by those we interact with and allow that we are deeply influenced by the different cultures within which we live our lives. As Aristotle remarked, a person who could live apart from society might be a beast or a god but not a human being.[7] But this sociocultural dimension of individuals has rarely been regarded as defining our humanity at the moral, political, biological, and metaphysical level. The reasoning is that within our personal narratives our socially defined selves cannot be regarded as being of compelling worth because we have had little control over the contingencies out of which the concrete circumstances of our lives have emerged: our time and place, ethnicity, family lineage, gender, and so on. Consequently, on this individualistic view, what must determine the primary worth of human beings, and thus what must command the respect of all—their dignity, integrity, and ultimate value—is the capacity of individuals to act purposively and to be self-determining: in other words, their *autonomy*. And, of course, in order to be autonomous, individual human beings must not be governed by instinct or passion but rather must be *free* and *rational* in the choices they make.

I want to argue that when Sen retains the abstract notion of the discrete and autonomous individual as the subject of justice rather than

---

7. Aristotle, *Complete Works*, 1253a.

starting from and ending with the shared lives of ordinary people as they are embedded in the roles and relations of family and community, he importantly vitiates his own deliberate strategy to achieve a more comprehensive model of justice. Said succinctly, persons as autonomous subjects like principles as putatively independent, antecedent standards, are simply second-order abstractions from lived relations.

Let's take just two examples of how a default individualism confounds the continuity Sen is seeking between persons and context in his reformulation of the idea of justice. In Sen's discussion of rational choice theory—that is, the theory that people choose rationally if and only if they intelligently pursue their own self-interest—he wants to argue the following:

> The insistence of so-called rational choice theory on defining rationality simply as intelligent promotion of personal self-interest sells human reasoning extremely short. . . . However, while rationality of choice can easily allow non-self-interested motivations, rationality does not on its own demand this. While there is nothing odd or irrational about someone being moved by concern for others, it would be harder to argue that there is some necessity or obligation to have such concern on grounds of rationality alone. . . . Rationality as a characteristic of choice behaviour rules out neither the dedicated altruist, nor the reasoned seeker of personal gain."[8]

For Sen, the putative "self" of both the self-abnegating altruist and the self-interested egoist can be acting "rationally" while having no regard for the consequences their conduct has for other people or for the quality of their relations with those people. Non-self-interested motivations are not necessary in acting rationally. The issue here of course is this: what do we mean by this reified "self"? As Hershock has observed in defining the doctrine of internal relations, if we as persons are in fact constituted by our relations, then the relationships themselves are primary, and we as individual persons or discrete "selves" are secondary abstractions from these relations. This being the case, we need to understand persons by virtue of their interdependent relationships with one another rather than by isolating them as individuals. Selves are inclusive rather than exclusive

---

8. Sen, *Idea of Justice*, 194–95.

of their relations with others. And given such relational interdependence, our always transactional conduct either benefits both parties who constitute the relationship or neither party.

Of course, the irony is that if in fact we are relationally constituted persons rather than discrete selves, self-interested egoists who ignore their own relations with others do not really benefit themselves, and altruists who would sacrifice themselves utterly for someone else contribute nothing to the real benefit of the object of their largesse.[9] Further, since Sen himself chooses to define rationality as choices based upon sustainable reasons, we must ask the question: if the behavior of egoists and altruists benefits neither themselves nor others respectively, can such conduct be considered rational according to Sen's own standard?[10] Indeed, Sen himself seems to doubt his ability to sustain his own reasons behind this claim when, as an aside, he questions "whether advantage-seeking, in either a direct or an indirect form, provides the only robust basis of reasonable behaviour in society." And as he continues rather pointedly: "A related question is whether mutual benefit and reciprocity must be the foundations of all political reasonableness."[11] Although Sen demurs at answering these questions himself, I would contend that because we are relational selves, mutual benefit must be fundamental to all reasonable conduct in every dimension of the human experience: personal, social, and political.

There is a second example in which I would contend Sen's commitment to foundational individualism leads him astray. The problem arises when he wants to explain the Buddha's understanding of the motivation of a mother in helping her child by reference to power and obligation:

> The mother's reason for helping the child, in this line of thinking, is not guided by the rewards of cooperation, but precisely from her recognition that she can, asymmetrically, do things for the child that will make a huge difference to the child's life and which the child itself cannot do. The mother does not have to seek any mutual benefit—real or imagined—nor

---

9. Sen is not oblivious to this problem when he observes that "Paul would have to take note, among other considerations, of the fact that a no-nonsense pursuit of self-love may adversely affect his relations with others, which could be a loss even for self-interested reasons." See Sen, *The Idea of Justice*, 195.

10. Sen, *Idea of Justice*, 180–81.

11. Sen, *Idea of Justice*, 205.

seek any "as if" contract to understand her obligation to the child. That is the point Gautama was making.[12]

Sen is certainly right in dismissing contractarian thinking as being too gross to have any relevance for conventional family relations as they obtain in this example of mother and child. But does any mother really think of her parenting as Sen would suggest in terms of power and obligation? When Sen insinuates a liberal conception of the discrete individual and a doctrine of external relations into the mother-child relationship that effectively separates mother as benefactor and the child as beneficiary, I would argue that his interpretation of the Buddha's words becomes implausible.

If Sen were instead to appeal to the Buddhist relational understanding of persons implicit in the same *Sutta-Nipata* sutra from which he draws his example, he would find that such persons are to be defined in terms of *anattā*, a doctrine of "no-self" in the sense of no permanent, autonomous agency. Further, such relational persons are located in a cosmology of *pratītyasamutpāda*, or dependent coarising, wherein persons are motivated by *karuṇā* and *mettā*—the desire to remove harm and suffering and to bring about well-being and happiness, respectively. In such a Buddhist world, the mother's "reason" (or perhaps better, motivation) for helping her child would be the motherly love that has mutual benefit in enriching not only the lives of both mother and child but the lives of everyone. Indeed, the *Sutta-Nipata* sutra that Sen is referencing here takes the mother-child relation as a natural locus of love that requires no rational or theoretical justification and that teaches an intuitive ideal that should be extended to the world broadly:

> Just as a mother would protect her only child at the risk of her own life, even so, let him cultivate a boundless heart towards all beings. Let his thought of boundless love pervade the whole world: above, below and across without any obstruction, without any hatred, without any enmity.[13]

If, however improbably, the mother was asked why she helped her child, she would likely answer "because she is my daughter," and the sutra's

---

12. Sen, *Idea of Justice*, 205–6.
13. *Sutta-Nipata*, 16.

message is that just such compassion should be extended to everyone. Indeed, an important consideration here is the inadequacy of Sen's reliance upon "reasons" alone to account for or to justify the mother's conduct. A mother might well reason about *how* to best benefit her child, but her motherly feelings would dispose her in any case to act without having to find reasons for doing so.

Bernard Williams, who I have appealed to previously, is helpful in making this same point. In insisting that roles and relations be adequately considered, he is properly concerned that moral problems be couched in concepts thick enough to apply to real features of the world so they can be resolved objectively. Indeed, when it comes to giving reasons for justifying actions that entail intimate family members, Williams gives us the example of a man who, involved in a desperate rescue situation, is required by circumstance to choose between two people who are drowning, in this case a stranger and his wife. Williams observes that

> it might have been hoped by some people (for instance, by his wife) that his motivating thought, fully spelled out, would be the thought that it was his wife, not that it was his wife and that in situations of this kind it is permissible to save one's wife.[14]

Williams is suggesting that any system of morality that insists on some impersonal and impartial standard—some "reasons"—to justify a husband saving his wife is guilty of asking the husband to have "one thought too many." That is, in the real world the husband's action is motivated and justified by appeal to the intimate, meaningful, and complex relationship he shares with this particular woman—quite simply, he loves her—and has nothing at all to do with a second-order need to deliberate upon and formulate some general and reasoned principle of moral obligation.

For Confucian role ethics, dynamic equity as differing *for* each other begins from the fact that mothers and daughters, husbands and wives, and teachers and students emerge together, or not at all. Such interdependence in our lived roles precludes familiar assumptions about individual autonomy and subordinates personal choice to our self-conscious resolve and our continuing and unrelenting commitment (*cheng* 誠) within such lived roles to be the best mothers, husbands, and teachers that we can

---

14. Williams, *Moral Luck*, 18.

be. Relational equity emerges with mutual appreciation and contribution. A good teacher produces a good student, and a good student produces a good teacher; the better the student, the better the teacher, and vice versa. Those who are otherwise good persons might have a wayward child, but a truly good mother does not become such a mother by having a bad daughter. And given the focus-field conception of person—that is, the entire family is implicated within each of its members—we as family members are ultimately what we mean in our relations to, with, and for each other. The strong family prospers because one member is a virtuosic violinist, another is a forceful politician, and yet another is a highly respected scholar: each member is enhanced by the quality of their intimate relations and the growth in value that emerges from mutual appreciation. Where putative equality as it is usually conceived would subordinate if not ultimately disrespect our differences, a productive diversity is achieved only when such differences make a difference for all concerned, and the greater the difference they make, the higher the intensity and quality of the diversity.

Reconceiving Autonomy and Choice in a Focus-Field Notion of Agency

We have rehearsed the attempt by Amartya Sen to provide a more capacious idea of justice that consciously resists the abstractions, decontextualizations, and fragmentations of his teacher, John Rawls. Even so, Sen still defaults to a liberal conception of person and defines this autonomous individual in terms of choice, freedom, and rationality without sufficient appreciation of the irreducibly relational nature of personal and situational differences in the lives of real people. In doing comparative philosophy and thus moving between traditions as Sen attempts to do, we are often given the option of either abandoning our familiar philosophical vocabulary or rehabilitating and extending these same terms to accommodate an alternative, non-Western narrative. In the case of China, for example, since it does not offer a "metaphysics" or "ontology" in the classical Greek sense, or a "religion" in the Abrahamic sense, we could dispose of these terms altogether and simply speak Chinese using its own vocabulary to speak its own worldview. Alternatively, we can try to retrofit this same familiar vocabulary in such a way as to accommodate the uncommon assumptions that would give China its difference and that would also give the discipline of philosophy a more capacious understanding of such terms.

Thus, even though Confucian role ethics is a sui generis vision of the moral life with its own specific technical vocabulary, another way of coming to understand this tradition better within our own philosophical milieu and communicating it more effectively to contemporary Western philosophers might be to ask the following question: how can our familiar terms of art in the contemporary ethical discourse—terms such as "autonomy" and "choice," for example—be reconfigured to be made useful in explaining Confucian role ethics?

Autonomy in the individualistic sense is "Gk *autós*, "self" + Gk *nomos*, "law," and means literally "one who gives law to oneself," or "one who is self-legislating." As we have seen, in Confucian role ethics, terms such as "autonomous persons" and their "choices" require such persons be understood as something other than independent, rational actors and their choices to be something other than such single actors choosing freely in the events that make up their days. In this Confucian case, autonomous actors making choices must reference relationally constituted and radically embedded persons who express their predilections largely through the quality of their personal commitment to the roles they live within their specific narrative events. What we might term "relational autonomy" thus understood does not reference individuals who have control over their specific independent actions but rather refers to self-conscious yet irreducibly social agents who through mutual accommodation in their continuing transactional activities are able to act without raising the specter of coercion. And what we might call "thick choices" do not reference the fragmented, big-moment decision making of discrete individuals who in exercising this freedom hold at bay the influence and interests of others; again, the term "thick choices" refers to irreducibly social agents who with critical self-awareness evidence a sustained commitment over time to a certain pattern of conduct in their roles and relations.

Conventionally "autonomy" in liberal theory suggests independence in the sense of self-governance, beginning from a self that is deemed discrete and exclusive. It can be argued that this conception of personal discreteness is merely a functional abstraction and that the strict autonomy sometimes claimed for it is simply a misleading and yet still powerful fiction. Indeed, if associated living is a fact, our ostensive discreteness is neither an initial condition nor exclusive of others. On the contrary, we become distinctive and even distinguished as the immediate product of the quality of the relations we have been able to effect with others. This Confucian notion of persons provides us with an alternative, gerundive notion of unique and interdependent persons for whom relationality, particularity, and sociality are the source and expression of their individuation and for whom such individuation—their distinctiveness and resolve—far from excluding relationships with others, is to be measured by the virtuosity they are able to achieve in the patterns of relations that come to constitute them. A self-conscious, relational autonomy describes purposeful, noncoercive activities as they achieve consummation in our roles and relations. And the thick choices of irreducibly social agents with critical self-awareness describe the resolution and commitment that such agents have in the roles they live.

Since the relationally constituted person is interdependent with others without specific boundaries, self-governance in any particular situation entails a personal identity that is focal yet in degree diffused and that as transactional must take the relevant interests of all concerned as being integral to the quality of the autonomy achieved. The relational autonomy of such interdependent selves is a function of what they mean for each other as their particular differences are coordinated to optimize a meaningful diversity in shared, intelligent practices. Relational autonomy under such a definition, far from being the expression of some ostensibly independent choice, is a function of qualifying our legitimate purposes with a willing deference to the interests of others, thereby mitigating coercion in our always shared activities. Indeed, those who are deemed exemplary as persons are more autonomous than others: as role models that inspire others, they draw the crowd, and their values inform and shape communal behavior through communal patterns of deference. The exemplary narratives of a Lincoln, a Gandhi, a Martin Luther King, or a Mandela, for example, have this kind of relational autonomy. And through their function as role models, they have effectively inspired populations over generations and have generated a continuing sea change in the values that define our times. Through deference to what they stand for and emulation of their values, we all become implicated in each of their corporate identities.

The point to be made here is that a doctrine of constitutive relations does not deprive persons so described of either their agency or their preferences; it rather requires that we reimagine such familiar terms as "autonomy" and "choice" in a way consistent with the empirical fact of associated living. Given the draw of our default, commonsense commitment to foundational individualism, to speak of a relationally constituted conception of persons is often misunderstood as offering us a much-diluted sense of personal identity. However, as I have previously argued, a strong case can be made that the relational conception of persons, far from compromising the unique identity so highly valued as an expression of personal autonomy, in fact enhances it. Personal identity within the Greek idealist paradigm of human "beings," for example, is a model of externally related, discrete individuals each endowed with some self-same identical characteristic. In such a paradigm, human beings are conceived of as essentially identical and only incidentally different. In this idealist model, personal identity can only carry with it a relatively truncated sense of uniqueness. By comparison, a doctrine of constitutive relations in its assumption that each of us as a person is a singular, inimitable, and nonfungible matrix of relations that is us and only us all the way down, is a model of radically embedded persons that in comparison magnifies the particularity and uniqueness that can be ascribed to them.

In addition, role ethics, by locating persons within the events of their lives, provides an empirically more persuasive notion of human agency by allowing that personal identity is self-conscious, focused, purposeful, and resolute—yet at the same time it is to an important degree diffused in our relationality. While the distinctiveness of our focal identity is guaranteed by such resolution, it is a distinctiveness that is continuous with and dependent upon what we mean for others. In my role of son to this mother, my continuing identity and conduct is necessarily shaped by deference to the feelings of my dear old mum. Personal identity is certainly particular and unique, and yet at the same time it is also multivalent, having imbricated within it a manifold of relations that includes rather than excludes our environing others. And our role identity so construed, while certainly persistent, is also constantly changing; and while it is certainly self-consciously purposive, our identity is also inclusive and accommodating, projectively motivated, yet also deferential and other regarding.

Looking to the Confucian texts to corroborate this understanding of relational rather than individual autonomy and thick rather than fragmented choices, we might take a passage that David Wong cites from the *Analects* as an example he gives in developing his own nuanced conception of what he takes to be "relational and autonomous selves":

The Master wanted to go and live amongst the nine clans of the Eastern Yi barbarians. Someone said to him, "What would you do about their baseness?" The Master replied, "Were exemplary persons to live among them, what baseness could there be?"[15]

Wong's interpretation of this passage is that the Master is more "autonomous" than most people because as an exemplary person, he is the sole author of his own actions in being able to uphold an ideal global trait—that is, "rightness"—without being influenced by those over whom he has gained sway. Such a demonstrated sense of rightness enables him to rise above those context-specific traits triggered by specific persons in specific circumstances. In Wong's own words: "It seems that part of the achievement of noblepersons is this ability to retain ethical excellence and exert influence over others wherever they go and with whomever they live."[16]

And textual evidence from the *Analects* that would seem to support Wong's interpretation comes immediately to mind:

> Ji Kangzi asked Confucius about governing effectively, saying, "What if I were to kill those who have abandoned the proper way in order to attract those who are in fact following it?"
>
> "If you govern effectively," Confucius replied, "what need is there for any killing? If you strive to be truly good in what you do, the people will also be good. The virtuosity of exemplary persons is the wind, while that of petty persons is the grass. As the wind blows, the grass is sure to bend."[17]

The analogy we might draw from this passage that would seem relevant for Wong's interpretation is that Confucius is the exemplary person who understands what is right, and the Eastern Yi barbarians are the base and petty persons who do not know what is right. Such persons will passively bend to the rightness of his proper influence.

---

15. *Analects* 9.14: 子欲居九夷。或曰:「陋,如之何!」子曰:「君子居之,何陋之有?」
16. Wong, "Relational and Autonomous Selves," 425.
17. *Analects* 12.19: 季康子問政於孔子曰:「如殺無道,以就有道,何如?」孔子對曰:「子為政,焉用殺? 子欲善,而民善矣。君子之德風,小人之德草。草上之風,必偃。」

What is Confucius's actual point in this exchange? To begin with, Ji Kangzi as prime minister and head of the Three Families, was seen by Confucius as a usurper of royal power in the state of Lu, and from this and other passages, we know that Confucius saw this interloper as someone who was not capable of proper governance. The fact that Ji Kangzi would posit killing some of his own people as an option in governing them is thus met with Confucius's rebuke. For Confucius, governing effectively depends upon the extent to which rulers are exemplars of the values they would inculcate in their people. But what is the source of these values? As I have previously argued, the term *shan* 善, translated in this passage as the ruler striving to be truly "good" in what he does, is not referring to some qualitatively superior character trait derived from some prior and higher virtue of "goodness" that inheres "in" a person. Nor is it some general principle of "goodness" that informs and supervenes on an action as it is "done" by a person. That is, "good" in the sense of moral growth begins from discursive relational activities within the continuing narrative, and only then can it serve as a general description of a person or action. *Shan* is the gregarious activity of growing our relations and making them "meaningful" by "relating" to each other and communicating effectively. Being truly good in what we do, and such actions being good for whom we do them with, requires deference and respect.

The irreducibly relational nature of all conduct, and the idea that "good" as a quality is understood to be achieved in the relations themselves rather than as a trait belonging to the exemplary person, is made clear in a related passage where the distinction between a civilized population and barbarians is irrelevant to the quality of conduct required of persons who would behave consummately. Regardless whether one is dealing with family, the public, or erstwhile "barbarians," consummate conduct requires sincere deference, respect, and conscientiousness:

> Fan Chi inquired about the conduct of the consummate person (*ren* 仁), and the Master replied, "At home be deferential, in handling public affairs be respectful, and do your utmost (*zhong* 忠) in your relationships with others. Even if you were to go and live among the Yi or Di barbarians, you could not do without such conduct."[18]

---

18. *Analects* 13.19 樊遲問仁。子曰:「居處恭, 執事敬, 與人忠。雖之夷狄, 不可棄也。」

This same *Analects* passage with the metaphor of the wind and grass previously cited is repeated in the *Mencius*. In offering his counsel to a crown prince on the death of his father, Mencius advises the prince to follow the dictates of Confucius in setting a new three-year standard in mourning practices for his court. Again, the message herein is certainly that rulers must be exemplars to effect change in their people. But the important point being made is that the influence of exemplary persons comes from deference and respect in their dealings with others as other-regarding attitudes that are themselves the source of doing both what is "good" (*shan*) and what is "optimally appropriate in the situation" (*yi*).

Mencius's advice to this particular crown prince begins from the self-conscious recognition on the prince's part that he is not held in high regard by his court or his kinsmen because of a lack of seriousness in his past studies. As a consequence of this failure, he as the newly anointed king will have difficulty securing their support in the affairs of state. In following this advice to look to the quality of his own person, the Crown Prince is able to elevate and refine his behavior and give his people a model to emulate. In so doing, he earns the respect of his court and is thus able to effect a change in their conduct. The change is thus collateral: the Crown Prince is improved because of the expectations of his people, and his people are transformed by his now exemplary conduct.[19]

---

19. *Mencius* 3A2: 谓然友曰："吾他日未尝学问，好驰马试剑。今也父兄百官不我足也，恐其不能尽于大事，子为我问孟子。"然友复之邹问孟子。孟子曰："然。不可以他求者也。孔子曰：'君薨，听于冢宰。歠粥，面深墨。即位而哭，百官有司，莫敢不哀，先之也。'上有好者，下必有甚焉者矣。'君子之德，风也；小人之德，草也。草尚之风必偃。'是在世子。"然友反命。世子曰："然。是诚在我。"五月居庐，未有命戒。百官族人可谓曰知。及至葬，四方来观之，颜色之戚，哭泣之哀，吊者大悦。The Crown Prince said to Ranyou, "In the past I have not given myself to my studies, being fonder of horses and swordsmanship. I am afraid that my older relatives and our ministers do not hold me in high regard, and will not give me their utmost in the affairs of state. Please go and consult with Mencius for me."

Ranyou again went to Zou to ask Mencius his advice.

"I understand," said Mencius, "But the Crown Prince cannot get the answer from others in this matter. Confucius said, 'When the ruler died, the Crown Prince would have all of the various officials place themselves under the command of the prime minister. He would eat only thin gruel, his face would turn ink-black, and taking his proper place, he would weep. That none of the various ministers and officers of the court would dare but grieve was because he has set this example. When a superior shows a passion for something, those below are sure to be even

I would read the *Analects* passage about Confucius wanting to live among the Eastern Yi barbarians along the same lines as this *Mencius* passage. For Confucius, "rightness" (*yi* 義) in the sense of "doing what is optimally appropriate" is certainly the standard he would invoke as the ultimate determining factor in this situation or any other. But for him, the idea of rightness is again not some remote, antecedent principle that by virtue of its ostensive objectivity and universality can be applied globally to all cases. Instead, Confucius is suggesting that in living among the "barbarians," both those persons who would aspire to be exemplary and the barbarians, through a process of mutual accommodation and the pursuit of optimal appropriateness in their relations, would become increasingly "significant" (*yi*) for each other. And in this shared narrative, the identities of both Confucius and the "barbarians" would be importantly transformed. Given the relationally constituted person, what is doing the work of Wong's "ideal global trait" would be the interests of the many becoming implicated in the conduct of the one exemplary person. The consequent "optimizing appropriateness" (*yi*) in his actions would serve the interests of all concerned, Confucius as well as the barbarians. And it is this shared harmony that is achieved amid diversity—the inseparability of the one and the many—that would come to constitute Confucius's relational autonomy. The barbarians, being inspired to learn from Confucius and to emulate him as their role model, would certainly be transformative of their conduct, enabling them to rise above any habitual baseness. At the same time, Confucius would also expand in compass to have implicated in him the now virtuosic and yet still resolutely unique conduct of the Eastern Yi barbarians. Importantly, far from this passage anticipating the unilateral imposition of a given standard on the Eastern Yi, Confucius

---

more zealous. 'The excellence of the exemplary person is the wind, while that of the petty person is the grass. As the wind blows, the grass is sure to bend.' This matter lies with the Crown Prince alone."

Ranyou returned and reported his conversation to the Crown Prince.

"Of course, he is right," said the Crown Prince. "This matter really does lie with me and only me."

For five months, the Crown Prince stayed in the mourning shed, and issued no orders or proscriptions. All of his ministers and clansmen praised him and said of him that he understood the observance of ritual propriety. When the time came for the burial ceremony, people came from all over to observe the it. The agony shown in his countenance and the anguish felt through his tears moved all of the mourners deeply.

and the Eastern Yi must have a collateral relationship that in working together allows for mutual accommodation and shared growth.

From Confucius's perspective, his sense of what is appropriate and meaningful (*yi*) would become more capacious by having been exposed to and learning from an alternative cultural source. Indeed, the stature and the influence of Confucius himself would appreciate in value to the extent that his teachings would be adopted by and adapted to the different ways of thinking and living of a new population. Models certainly inspire those who would emulate them, but they cannot become exemplary models absent such emulation, and such deference shown to such role models effects important changes in them as well.

As a concrete way of understanding this passage, we might think of the historical extension of Confucian culture to the "Eastern Yi" as a marker for the East Asian peoples of Korea, Japan, and Vietnam. The values and institutions of this Confucian culture were not imposed on the other East Asian countries through force or occupation. Confucian culture in different ways and in different degrees has over the centuries been appropriated voluntarily by these alternative populations and in the process has been transformative of not just three but indeed all four of these Sinitic cultural traditions, including China itself. The unique cultures of Korea, Japan, and Vietnam—along with the substance of Chinese Confucian culture itself—have all been made richer because of this holographic focus-field process wherein each cultural site has come to be implicated in the others. Autonomy, on this model, is not one exemplar with "rightness" holding sway over others by rising unilaterally above their cultural influence and imposing order upon them. Rather, relational autonomy requires a combination of noncoercive resolution and responsive deference. It is the opportunity for all parties within their relationships to contribute in their own unique ways to an evolving tradition that is one and many at the same time, and in so doing, contribute to the transformation of all parties in this multilateral process.

These four distinctively Confucian traditions of China, Korea, Japan, and Vietnam are seemingly in ascent in our own historical moment. And given the Confucian values they espouse, each of these countries should increasingly become a substantial resource for a changing world cultural order. Unfortunately, these different East Asian Confucian cultures themselves in recent decades have failed to live up to their own values of accommodation, mutual respect, and shared diversity—and consequently have become fragmented and conflicted. To the extent that their own relations have weakened, their potential influence on a new world cultural order has been significantly diminished.

A brief and perhaps salutary aside we might entertain here is the possibility that were these Confucian cultures to achieve a relational autonomy among themselves, they might have a similar transformative effect on the *Western* Yi "barbarians." To date, an obstacle to any such transformation of the Western Yi arises from the persistent, uncritical eliding of modernity and Westernization within the Western cultures themselves. Given the role of universalism as a prominent and persistent ethnocentrism in the evolution of these Western traditions, they have developed an enduring self-understanding of self-sufficiency that has precluded any really significant influence by the emerging Confucian cultures—an attitude that Clifford Geertz has described fairly as "saving the world for condescension." With the exponential rise of East Asia in our own historical moment effecting a sea change in the economic and political order of the world, we can only hope that the relations among the four Confucian cultures themselves might change for the better. And perhaps the elitist and exclusionary self-understanding of the Western Yi might be tempered by the newly emerging hydraulics of world power in all of its guises.

The intimate and inseparable relationship between teaching and learning at issue in anticipating the role Western and Confucian cultures should have in a changing world cultural order provides us with another way of thinking through the notion of relational autonomy. The Chinese character *xue* 學, conventionally understood and translated as "studying" or "learning" in the modern language, in fact originally means "teaching and learning" and suggests the perceived inseparability of these two activities. The term *xue* 學 denotes the ancient and continuous national academy or *taixue* 太學 that dates far back into the mists of history. It appears on the oracle bones as *[xxviii]*, and originally meant "the site and situation of teaching and learning" that we associate with this institution.[20] The Qing dynasty scholar Duan Yucai 段玉裁, among other commentators on the ancient *Shuowen* lexicon entry for *xue*, explains that teaching and learning were thus originally expressed with the same character as institutionalized education itself, a character that only later becomes bifurcated graphically (but remains very close phonetically in the ancient pronunciation) as "teaching" (*xiao/jiao* 斅/教) and "learning" (*xue* 學).

[xxviii]

---

20. Kwan, "Database," 京津4836.

When we reflect on Confucian education under the categories of capacity, opportunity, and effort, the occupations of teaching and learning are coterminous and mutually entailing. Indeed, we will miss the dividends we might accrue and the deficits we might avoid if we treat them separately. When in the *Analects* Confucius is remembered as claiming that "human beings are similar in their natural capacities, but vary greatly by virtue of their habits," he is emphasizing the transformative possibility of education.[21] As Tang Junyi observes:

> This passage does not mean Confucius is asserting that human nature is something fixed and given, but rather implies that "similar in natural propensities" is the human capacity for personal growth and transformation without any fixed limit to its possibilities.[22]

By "similar in natural propensities" (*xingxiangjin* 性相近), Confucius means that human beings are alike in having the capacity for applying themselves to the project of personal cultivation and articulation (*haoxue* 好學). We humans are alike in being educable, and in fact, the wide-ranging variance each of us is able to develop through personal application and habituation is a function of the complexity of our shared, unbounded capacity for education. In this sense, productive habits (*xi* 習), far from being divergent dispositions that contrast with some ostensibly shared, fixed nature, are in fact the expression and realization of this shared yet always particular capacity for creative change.

It is because *xue* means both "teaching and learning" that the ever-modest Confucius, while inclined to self-deprecation when describing his own native capacities, unabashedly prides himself on his love of teaching and on his personal eagerness to learn.[23] These propensities for teaching and learning are captured in his description of himself as *haoxue* 好學—that is, as someone who cherishes education.[24] At the same time, considering the high expectations he has for his students and the

---

21. *Analects* 17.2: 性相近也習相遠也。
22. Tang Junyi, *Complete Works*, 13:32: 此即孔子不重人性之為固定之性之旨，而隱含一相近之人性，為能自生長而變化，而具無定限之可能之旨者也。
23. *Analects* 5.9, 7.1, 7.20.
24. *Analects* 5.28, 7.3, 7.19, 7.34, 7.2.

sometimes harsh judgments he is wont to make on their progress, it is clear that he takes motivation and assiduous effort as his foremost criteria.[25] Regardless of social status or personal means, Confucius exhibits an unwavering commitment to provide able students with their best opportunity for education.[26] Confucius describes his favorite protégé, Yan Hui, in the following terms:

> A person of real character is this Yan Hui! He has a bowl of rice to eat, a gourd of water to drink, and a dirty little hovel in which to live. Other people would not be able to endure his many hardships, yet for Hui they have no effect on the enjoyment he gets out of life. A person of real character is this Yan Hui.[27]

And Yan Hui in return expresses his deepest respect for Confucius and the methods he uses to draw his students forward on the pathway of learning one step at a time:

> Yan Hui, with a deep sigh, said, "The more I look up at it, the higher it soars; the more I penetrate into it, the harder it becomes. I am looking at it in front of me, and suddenly it is behind me. The Master is good at drawing me forward a step at a time; he broadens me with culture and disciplines my behavior through the observance of ritual propriety. Even if I wanted to quit, I could not. And when I have exhausted my abilities, it is though something rises up right in front of me, and even though I want to follow it, there is no road to take."[28]

Not only is Confucius glad to have Yan Hui as his apprentice, but he goes on to describe this one young man alone among all of his

---

25. *Analects* 7.8, 8.12, 8.17, 14.24.

26. *Analects* 7.7.

27. *Analects* 6.11: 賢哉回也! 一簞食, 一瓢飲, 在陋巷。人不堪其憂, 回也不改其樂。賢哉回也。

28. *Analects* 9.11: 顏淵喟然歎曰:「仰之彌高, 鑽之彌堅; 瞻之在前, 忽焉在後。夫子循循然善誘人, 博我以文, 約我以禮。欲罷不能, 既竭吾才, 如有所立卓爾。雖欲從之, 末由也已。」

students in the same terms as he describes himself—that is, as being singularly motivated in his commitment to education (*haoxue*).[29] Indeed, Confucius ascribes to Yan Hui abilities that not only go far beyond those of his other students but also far beyond his own as well.[30] In fact, in the student-teacher relationship between Confucius and Yan Hui, it is not always entirely clear who is the teacher and who is the student.[31]

It is precisely the mutually transformative relationship between Confucius and Yan Hui that provides an image of how real autonomy is not the teacher rising above the students to instruct them morally as to what is right and wrong but rather the noncoercive growth that teachers, as the most advanced learners in the classroom and in their collaborative interactions with their students, are able to experience in their shared relationship. Most educators have had a similar learning experience in teaching their best students. And in our classrooms as we share purposive growth together with these students, we become keenly aware of this kind "relational autonomy" as the motive force that animates our relationally constituted persons as teacher-learners.

Again, there is another warrant for reading the character *xue* 學 as the situated process of "teaching and learning" that might challenge the notion of discrete and autonomous agency and the dichotomous and condescending teacher-culture posture that seems to follow from it. This justification derives from an appreciation of certain cosmological presuppositions sedimented into the classical Chinese language itself. That is, in this process cosmology in which our vital relationality cannot be separated from our uniqueness as persons, the gerundive language that provides an account of the human experience reflects a commitment to the primacy of relationships over agency. Such language tends to describe relationally constituted situations such as "teaching and learning" rather than the actions of specific agents either teaching or learning. Focus-field agency is irreducibly transactional rather than unilateral.[32] The term *xin* 信, for example, means both "credibility" and "trust," which suggests a fiduciary, noncoercive situation that characterizes the collaborative relationship between benefactor and beneficiary. The character *shou* 受 is initially

---

29. *Analects* 6.3, 9.20,11.7.

30. *Analects* 5.9, 6.11, 11.19.

31. *Analects* 2.9, 6.11, 9.21.

32. See Ames, *Confucian Role Ethics*, ch. 2.

"the situation of giving and getting" and then is only later discriminated graphically (but not phonetically) to include agency as "giving" (*shou* 授) and "getting" (*shou* 受). *Ming* 明 means "brilliance" transactionally as both the brilliance of something and the penetrating perspicacity of the person who perceives this brilliance fully. And the language is replete with just such examples. In each case, given that agency within this kind of associated conduct is always in varying degrees bilateral, this situated language suggests that we must accommodate the more inclusive sense of relational autonomy.

Turning from "relational autonomy" to reflect again on the "choices" made by autonomous subjects, the exercise of choice is conventionally understood as a function of deliberative, practical reasoning requiring several steps. A particular person must consider each of the many actions within one's power to perform that will achieve a desired consequence and then determine the extent to which each of them would contribute to the achievement of the appropriate goal or end. Following upon such circumspection, this person must make a deliberate choice to act in the way that best fits that end and then voluntarily engage in the action itself. Individual autonomy is thus expressed as particular persons making their own particular choices.

We have previously encountered Joel Kupperman, who wants to understand moral conduct in a vital and more holistic way by reinstating to a significant degree the processive nature of the moral conduct that leads to character development: the always specific context, the particularity of persons and circumstances, and the growth entailed by such conduct. Kupperman has formulated his doctrine of "character ethics" and sees in the Confucian emphasis on personal cultivation a close analog to his long-term concern with character development. In seeking to replace virtue ethics with character ethics, Kupperman is doing his best to put the Humpty-Dumpty of ethical philosophy back together again. That is, he challenges what he calls the "big moment" ethics we associate with philosophers such as Kant, Bentham, and Mill. He again questions the "snapshot" view of ethical decision making often found in virtue ethics.[33] For Kupperman, this familiar but indeed fragmenting approach to our understanding of ethics—what Dewey calls "ethical atomism"—has introduced a plethora of fractures and fault lines into what Kupperman takes

---

33. "Big moment" is Kupperman's own term. See Joel J. Kupperman, *Learning from Asian Philosophy* (New York and Oxford: Oxford University Press, 1999), 169.

to be a relatively seamless process of developing the qualities of character that enable us to express moral competence in the normal activities of our daily lives. Kupperman resists thinking in terms of decision trees and isolated choices. In formulating his character ethics, one singularly important contribution Kupperman makes that seems more consistent with our actual experience is his more organic and more integrated understanding of how choices actually come about.[34] For Kupperman, the diremption and post hoc compartmentalizing that takes place in much of ethical theorizing, while certainly functional in referencing relevant issues, seems to also disjoin and decontextualize these same concerns.

Kupperman's robust conception of character development is more personal and complex than isolated virtue traits and provides an active, continuous, and particularizing understanding of persons that both unifies and stabilizes lives through time. Consistent with the continuities and context that Kupperman is able to recover with this processual understanding of the growth of character, he challenges atomistic views of choice that would reduce this activity to serial, discrete, arbitrary, and often impersonal decisions "in a way which ignores or slights the moral importance of continuity of commitment." For Kupperman:

> Many of the most crucial "choices" in our lives turn out to be clusters of an indeterminate number of choices, most or all of which point in the same direction, which are such that many are not reflective or explicit. Any model of choice in human life must take account of this.[35]

Kupperman sees choice itself as located within a thick dispositional process in which the continuing momentum provided by commitment and responsibility pays erstwhile "choices" forward to make of ostensive moral judgments a continuous and seamless habit of conduct.

These familiar liberal terms such as "autonomy" and "choice"—and "agency" and "identity" as well—can certainly be adapted and used in role ethics. But ultimately they must be reconceived as instances of foregrounding, abstracting, and focusing particular yet interpenetrating phases in social and ethical activities that remain organically related to and informed by the entire narratives within which they occur. Relational autonomy is a

---

34. Kupperman. *Character*, 108–9.
35. Kupperman, *Character*, 70 and 74.

quality of irreducibly social conduct, and by virtue of shared purpose that precludes coercion, this autonomy unites us in our families, classrooms, and communities. And our "thick choices" reflect a continuing and unwavering commitment to our roles as mothers, teachers, and neighbors.

Sagely Autonomy as the Deep Coalescence (*du* 度) of Human "Becomings" and Their Worlds

In trying to think through an alternative relational conception of autonomy, we had the occasion to survey the specific model of conduct we find in the portrayal of Confucius himself. In so doing, we reflected upon Confucius's fourth abstention—refraining from being self-absorbed. In the Buddhist literature previously cited, we also had occasion to reference the concept of *anattā*, a doctrine of "no-self" in the sense of no permanent autonomous agency. This doctrine of no-self is integral to the cosmology of *pratītyasamutpāda*, or dependent coarising, wherein persons are motivated by *karuṇā* and *mettā*—the compassion needed to remove harm and suffering in an effort to bring about well-being and happiness for all. Such reticence on the part of Confucius, as tradition remembers him, to assert both his individual autonomy and those values that again begin from the interdependence of all things, sets up a contrast with the liberal understanding of individual autonomy that moves us in the opposite direction toward the possibility of "autonomous" sages legislating for all. The Confucian and Buddhist cosmology that begins from the interdependence of all things offers us a conception of autonomy not as the self-legislating of discrete individuals but as the relational autonomy of exemplary persons who, through achieved coercion-free patterns of deference, legislate on behalf of an evolving cosmic order. Taking Confucius as our example, he not only abstains from egoism but introduces a notion of family-centered religiousness that aspires to the optimal coordination of social, political, and indeed cosmic relations—an alternative conception of religiousness that is expressed as a flourishing world. For Confucius, human sagacity has implicated within it the deepest coalescence (*du* 度) of human becomings and their worlds, thus allowing sages as the highest order of human virtuosity to collaborate fully with the heavens and the earth in guiding human flourishing within a flourishing cosmos.

As we have seen, a tradition that begins from an entrenched foundational individualism offers us a conception of autonomy characterized by freedom from external control or influence. Such personal sovereignty that follows from this freedom allows for the exercise of our own independent will in pursuing our freely determined choices. But in the Confucian cosmology that serves as our interpretive context here, autonomy does not mean the exclusion of others but is, on the contrary, an irreducibly social achievement in which familial and social nexuses are legislating for a broader spectrum of persons. Such a relational autonomy is thus the cultivation of optimum coalescence in the roles and relationships that define us, with different members of the family and community coordinating their different resources in shared resolve. But we must be careful here. Rather than thinking of such relational autonomy as bringing the will of separate agents into accord, it is better conceived as a deepening of coalescence within the complexity of those already existing fiduciary roles and relations that give them shared purpose. Relational autonomy with such shared purpose certainly precludes the diminution of energy and creative possibilities occasioned by deflationary coercion. But further, as the collaborative product of assiduous cultivation, with all of its tensions and differences, achieves a complex harmony, such relational autonomy is the expression of the optimal meaning in these same relations. Relational autonomy is simply the personal achievement of optimally meaningful relations that begins from the center of healthy family relations and extends out symbiotically to community, polity, and cosmos. Indeed, autonomy so conceived, far from being an exercise of individual will, is the flower of social and political flourishing made possible by shared patterns of deference to the conduct of the most exemplary people. And as such, relational autonomy conduces to a kind of Confucian religiousness—a distinctively human- and family-centered religiousness that provides a liberating alternative to obedience to God.

We might begin from the fact that the very definition of "religion" in our best English-language dictionaries usually takes some concept of a transcendent deity as its point of departure. The *Oxford English Dictionary*, for example, defines religion as "the belief in and worship of a superhuman controlling power, especially a personal God or gods." Such an understanding of religion propelled Western missionaries to search the Chinese canons for analogs they could borrow to insinuate their own Abrahamic idea of God into the Chinese language. With this uncritical assumption that religion must begin from God, many if not most scholars concerned with defining Confucian religiousness continue along this same path, beginning their foray into Chinese religiousness by appealing to some variation on the rather opaque Shang and Zhou dynasty notions of *shangdi* 上帝 and *tian* 天, respectively. In so doing, these exegetes beg the question of how to understand Confucian religiousness by having already transplanted a conception of "God" into a cosmology that as I have previously argued is fundamentally "a-theistic."

And in advancing this "a-theistic" argument, I have been in good company. I have remarked upon Marcel Granet's claim that "Chinese wisdom has no need for the idea of God,"[36] a characterization of Confucianism endorsed by many of our best Sinologists, Chinese and Western alike.[37] While such a description of a nontheistic "Chinese wisdom" might for some churchmen lower the bar and render any association of this tradition with religion or religiousness questionable, I would insist that Confucianism has its own alternative, family-centered understanding of religiousness that requires an importantly different cluster of terms to give it expression. I have suggested that a key term needed to explain such a Confucian religiousness is the socio-religious idea of *li* 禮: "the achievement of propriety in one's roles and relations." Again, I would argue that the persistently vague and thus protean term *tian* 天, denoting something very different from a transcendent and thus independent "Godhead," also has an important role to play in how family-centered Confucian religiousness comes to be articulated.

Although clearly having a formal, ceremonial reference, the preponderant significance of *li* in defining family and communal life lies in those personal, informal, and particular discursive activities that conduce to and are indeed necessary for religious experience. As we have seen, *li* 禮 as a cognate with the character for "body or embodying," (*ti* 體) has a profoundly somatic dimension where body is often just as effective a language as speech in the discourse necessary to strengthen the bonds among those participating in our various life-forms. The *li* also have an affective aspect wherein feelings suffuse and fortify all of our relational activities, providing the communal fabric with a tensile strength that resists the inevitable strains and ruptures that attend associated living. *Li* is a process of personal articulation in the roles and relations one lives. Refinement through the performance of *li* must be understood in light of the uniqueness of each participant engaged in the profoundly aesthetic

---

36. Granet, *La pensée Chinoise*, 478.
37. See Ames, *Confucian Role Ethics*, ch. 5 for this argument.

project of cultivating themselves to become this always unique person. It is what I have described as the growth and disclosure of an elegant disposition: an attitude, a posture, a signature style, and ultimately a persistent identity.

It is within the context of *li* as this achieved propriety in roles and relations that the ancestral/numinous/cultural/natural notion of *tian* 天 makes its contribution to our understanding of a Confucian family-centered religiousness. *Tian* that we associate with Zhou dynasty religiousness occurs in the oracle bones as the graph *[xxix]*  and as *[xxx]*  that scholars have read as an ideogram depicting what stretches "above" the human head, certainly referencing the pedestrian sky but also perhaps pointing more importantly to the splendor of that sky writ large as the humbling and unfathomable firmament. In a human world prior to the light pollution that has robbed us of this almost daily event, it was this awesome, celestial vault that inspired everything from religion to science and poetry to geometry. On the Zhou bronzes, the graph *tian* is somewhat more stylized and closer to the modern character: *[xxxi]*.[38]  The *Shuowen* lexicon bears out the speculations that would define *tian* in relationship to the human world by glossing *tian* paronomastically as *dian* 顛 meaning "top of the head" and then defining it in terms of the graphic components from which the character is constructed: the combination of the number "one" (*yi* 一) and the character for "greatest" (*da* 大) mean "the singularly vast, the grandest."

As we have seen, the graph depicting *tian* provides little semantic information other than an association with what lies over and above the human head. To cite philosopher Zhang Dongsun 张东荪:

> The Chinese attitude toward the demands of *tian* 天 are simply the desire to know its purposes in order to secure good fortune and avoid misfortune. As to what kind of "thing" *tian* is, they are indifferent. This is because the Chinese people do not consider *tian* to be the ontological ground of the myriad things, and thus do not apply the category of ontology to it.[39]

---

38. Kwan, "Database," 甲骨文合集 CHANT 0198A, 0201B, and 西周中期 CHANT 10175.

39. Zhang Dongsun 張東蓀, 知識與文化: 張東蓀文化論著輯要 [Knowledge and culture: The essential writings of Zhang Dongsun on culture], ed. Zhang Yaonan 張耀南 (Beijing: Zhongguo Guangbo dianshi chubanshe, 1995), 373–74.

It is certainly the case that a philosophical notion such as *tian* is profoundly recondite in the Chinese classics, with language such as "distant" (*yuan* 遠) and "dark" (*xuan* 玄) being invoked to describe it. The fact that the Chinese tradition itself has not pursued any real precision in its understanding of the vocabulary of Chinese religiousness has facilitated a sustained misreading of its general import by many Western interpreters. Indeed "religion" as it is understood among contemporary scholars broadly is a conception of Western "religion" that either collapses the Confucianism into its ranks as in the 1893 World Parliament of Religions or ignores the Confucian alternative altogether. If, for example, we consult the Chinese search engine Baidu for its entry on "religion," we find religion (*zongjiao* 宗教) defined in the following terms:

> Religion is simply a doctrine of the worship of a socially recognized supreme power together with its cultural forms. Religion is a kind socio-historical phenomenon, with most religions being the belief in and reverence for a supernatural force, a creator and controller of the cosmos. It is a system that gives humans a belief in a soul that continues on beyond death.[40]

Such a definition is a good example of how China continues to be theorized according to a Western conceptual structure, having everything to do with Abrahamic religion and very little indeed to do with China's own Confucian religiousness—or even with its institutionalized religions of Daoism and Buddhism.

It has become a commonplace to acknowledge that many unannounced Western assumptions, in the process of Western translators attempting to make sense of the classical Chinese philosophical literature, have been inadvertently insinuated into the understanding of these texts and have colored the vocabulary through which this understanding has been articulated. This phenomenon is nowhere truer than in the language appealed to in interpreting Chinese religiousness and especially in the eliding of the distinction between *tian* translated conventionally as "Heaven" and a Western conception of God.

---

40. 百度: 宗教只是一种对社群所认知的主宰的崇拜和文化风俗的教化。宗教是一种社会历史现象，多数宗教是对超自然力量、宇宙创造者和控制者的相信或尊敬，它给人以灵魂并延续至死后的信仰体系。

But *tian*, far from requiring what Friedrich Schleiermacher describes in *The Christian Faith* as "absolute dependence"—a self-abnegating deference to a self-sufficient, independent deity—is instead an invitation for human collaboration with and contribution to the numinous aspect of our experience.[41] Indeed, the familiar mantra invoked to describe Confucian religiousness, *tianren heyi* 天人合一, describes "the inseparability of the cosmic and human order." It announces the continuity between the drama of human thinking and living and the cosmic context within which this spectacle takes place. The *heyi* relation is a *yinyang* contrastive yet mutually entailing first-order relationship of two inseparable, "aspectual" features of experience that can only be understood in terms of each other. Just as with dyadic pairs such as "up and down" (*shangxia* 上下) and "the heavens and the earth" (*tiandi* 天地), the expression "the cosmic and the human" (*tianren* 天人) denotes a relationship that is one and two at the same time: two complementary aspects of the same phenomenon that cannot be fairly conceived of without reference to each other.

Importantly then, given the resolutely inseparable *heyi* relation between humans and their context, we must resist interpreting this expression as a "putting together" of what were two originally separate things and instead read it in terms of their mutuality in difference. The concern is with the "depth of coalescence" (*du* 度) that can be cultivated and achieved in their first-order relationality. And in this dyadic yet resolutely constitutive relationship, *tian* together with human beings is to be understood as mutually doing and undergoing, both shaping and being shaped by each other. It is thus that a correlative expression such as *tianren* is not simply descriptive but is also prescriptive as an aspiration toward an increasingly meaningful relationship.

Alluding to a complementary and generative relationship between human beings and the way (*dao*), Confucius in the *Analects* asserts that "it is persons who are able to broaden the way (*dao*)," and the *Zhuangzi* also avers that "the way (*dao*) is made in the walking."[42] Analogously, the relationship between *tian* and the human world is fecund and generative, with the challenge for these "two" aspectual worlds to work together collaboratively in building the connector for their own time and place and to thus broaden and extend the cosmic order. It is clear that human beings in this relationship derive much benefit from the ancestral/numi-

---

41. Friedrich D. E. Schleiermacher, *The Christian Faith*, eds. H. R. Mackintosh and J. S. Stewart (London: T & T Clark, 1999), 132.

42. *Analects* 15.29: 人能弘道, *Zhuangzi* 2: 道行之而成.

nous/cultural/natural resources denoted by *tian*. *Tian* certainly provides us with the various environing contexts needed for human flourishing and serves us as an object of cosmic numinosity to revere and emulate. And we must acknowledge that as with most Chinese correlative binomials, the first member of the dyad is hierarchically superior—that is, *tian* ranks above the human being in terms of its meaning and status. But even so, since the relationship between *tian* and human beings is irreducibly collateral, we have to ask: What through personal cultivation can be made of this *tianren* relationship? And more specifically, what does *tian* get in this relationship from human beings?

In our response to these questions, we might appeal to the extensive work of the contemporary philosopher Tang Yijie 湯一介 and his astute reflections over the years on this notion of *tianren heyi*. For Tang, "Confucius is saying that only the capacities of human beings are able to advance and promote the magnificence of the way-making of *tian*."[43] Tang then remarks further that "human beings cannot be separated from *tian* because if they could be, they could not continue to exist, and *tian* cannot be separated from humans because if it could be, there would be no way for its animation and vitality to be made manifest."[44]

Given the doctrine of constitutive, internal, and organic relations that Tang Yijie would assign to this Confucian worldview, we must allow that just as humans are importantly shaped by *tian*, *tian* is in turn shaped in some degree by human beings. How and to what extent is *tian* itself enhanced by the human contribution to cosmic order? Tang allows that *tian* and human beings share the same "heartminding" (*xin* 心), where the notion of being "true" (*zhen* 真) in this relation means "truing"—that is, the deepening congruence that assiduous personal cultivation is able to effect in the relationship between the two. But how is the *tian* aspect of this shared heartminding itself changed and made deeper because of the human role in the extension of cosmic order? And how is this human transformation of *tian* itself expressed in the canonical texts?

This for me becomes a vitally important question because it is in this respect that the Chinese conception of *tian* and the religiosity it entails stands in greatest contrast to the asymmetry between human beings and

---

43. Tang Yijie, *Tang Yijie zhexue jinghua bian* 湯一介哲學精華編 [The essential philosophy of Tang Yijie] (Beijing: Beijing United, 2016), 420: 孔子說: 只有人才可以使《天道》發揚光大。

44. Tang Yijie, *Tang Yijie zhexue jinghua bian*, 424: 《人》離不開《天》, 離開天則《人》無法生存; 《天》離不開《人》, 離開《人》則《天》的活潑潑的氣象無法彰顯。

their God in the Abrahamic religions. The aseity or self-sufficiency of a perfect and thus unchanging Abrahamic God can be read as meaning that human morality is entirely derivative of God and that human beings do not make a difference in themselves. On such a reading, God is everything; human beings are nothing. For example, the theologian Schleiermacher, previously cited in this chapter, celebrates such religiousness as a doctrine of "absolute dependence":

> The feeling of absolute dependence, accordingly, is not to be explained as an awareness of the world's existence, but only as an awareness of the existence of God, as the absolute undivided unity.[45]

Our human role is thus simply to worship and to obey. Contrary to Schleiermacher, who finds peace and solace in this claim of absolute dependence, I find such a doctrine morally demeaning if not repugnant. My understanding of the liberating humanism of the European Renaissance is that it was a direct challenge to such an oppressive religiousness with thinkers such as Voltaire insisting upon the opposite extreme: the intrinsic worth of the world of human beings in themselves without reference to a transcendent and independent Other.[46] It is the collaborative, mutually generative relationship between *tian* and human beings that provides such a stark contrast with the Abrahamic traditions understood in this way. Indeed, the need to cultivate a "depth of coalescence" (*du* 度) in this *tianren* relationship can be brought to bear on how we might think about *tianren heyi* and the human transformation of *tian*.

The *Five Modes of Virtuosic Conduct* (*Wuxingpian* 五行篇) is an ancient but only recently recovered document that might help us think through how the human contribution might in fact profoundly affect *tian*.

---

45. Schleiermacher, *The Christian Faith*, 132.

46. Sinophile Voltaire, for example, who throughout his works heaps praise on a Confucianism that he reads as a kind of rational deism, addresses the King of Prussia on the topic of the Christian Church (and elsewhere expresses similar sentiments about Judaism and Islam), observing that "our religion is assuredly the most ridiculous, the most absurd and the most bloody religion which has ever infected this world. Your Majesty will do the human race an eternal service by extirpating this infamous superstition . . . among honest people, among men who think, among those who wish to think." See Voltaire to Frederick II, King of Prussia, January 5, 1767, in *Oeuvres complètes de Voltaire, 1869* (Texte établi par Louis Moland, Garnier, 1883), 184.

In 1973 at Mawangdui, and again in 1993 at Guodian, two different versions of this text were recovered from two separate archaeological sites having been buried at significantly different times: 168 BCE and ca. 300 BCE respectively.[47] This important document is in the same lineage as *Focusing the Familiar*, which as we have seen argues that human beings through personal cultivation have both the capacity and the responsibility to serve as cocreators with the heavens and the earth.

The opening chapter of *Five Modes of Virtuosic Conduct* explains how a person's conduct becomes habituated as characteristic, identity-forming patterns of moral virtuosity and how this continuing cultivation first produces efficacy (*shan* 善) in human relations and then culminates in a world-changing moral virtuosity (*de* 德):

> Consummatory conduct in roles and relations (*ren* 仁) taking shape within is called moral virtuosity (*de* 德); where it does not take shape within, it is called merely doing what is deemed consummate. Appropriate acting (*yi* 義) taking shape within is called moral virtuosity (*de*); where it does not take shape within, it is called merely doing what is deemed appropriate. An achieved ritual propriety in roles and relations (*li* 禮) taking shape within is called moral virtuosity (*de*); where it does not take shape within, it is called merely doing what is deemed proper. Wisdom (*zhi* 智) taking shape within is called moral virtuosity (*de*); where it does not take shape within, it is called merely doing what is deemed wise. Sagacity (*sheng* 聖) taking shape within is called moral virtuosity (*de*); where it does not take shape within, it is called merely doing what is deemed sagacious.[48]

---

47. Two versions of this text belonging to the Zisizi-Mengzi lineage (SiMengpai 思孟派) have been recovered in archaeological finds, first on a silk text at Mawangdui (1973) dating to 168 BCE, and then the Guodian text (1993) on bamboo strips dating from ca. 300 BCE. The fact that redactions of the same text have been found at such a physical and temporal distance from each other speaks to the perceived importance of the document in its own time.

48. 五行篇1: 仁形於內謂之德之行, 不形於內謂之行。義形於內謂之德之行, 不形於內謂之行。禮形於內謂之德之行, 不形於內謂之行。智形於內謂之德之行, 不形於內謂之行。聖形於內謂之德之行, 不形於內謂之行。德之行五, 和謂之德, 四行和謂之善。善人道也, 德天道也。

This passage makes the same distinction we found in Mencius between (1) doing something that is prompted by the anticipated approbation of others and (2) acting consistently and instinctively out of a cultivated moral virtuosity (*de*), a self-conscious moral virtuosity that in having been habituated has become who you are. There are persons who are merely able to follow conventional values in acting in a way deemed proper by the community; there are also those who through an assiduous personal regimen are able to establish consummatory habits of conduct in their roles and relations and act out of this moral virtuosity.[49]

How then does this cultivated moral virtuosity "take shape within" to become habituated conduct? In interpreting this passage, we can appeal to the familiar Confucian expression *shenqidu* 慎其獨 to shed light on the way in which such conduct is set and consolidated "within." We encountered the expression *shenqidu* earlier in our analysis of the first chapter of *Focusing the Familiar* where I interpreted it as the process of exemplary persons consolidating their virtuosic habits as a resolute disposition for action. The interlinear commentary included in the Mawangdui version of this *Five Modes of Virtuosic Conduct* document offers its explanation of this same expression *shenqidu*. This commentary is explicit in referencing *xin* or "heartminding" as the personal identity that is produced when these five patterns are set as the root of virtuosic conduct. The commentary reads:

> The expression "*shenqidu*" means accommodating these five modes of virtuosic conduct within and focusing them carefully in one's heartminding. Having consolidated these five modes of conduct, they become as one. And this 'one' then refers to the five modes of virtuosic conduct that, having been consolidated as the [one] heartminding, is then taken as one's personal identity.[50]

The meaning of this expression *shenqidu* found in the *Expansive Learning* (*Daxue*) has much the same import as when it occurs here in *Five Modes of Virtuosic Conduct*. It is defined as "becoming resolute in one's thoughts

---

49. It should be noted that education itself is in degree a modeling of what others do and thus introduces some complexity into this distinction.

50. 慎其獨也者，言舍夫五而慎其心之謂也。獨然後一，一也者，夫五為□（一）心也，然後得之。

and feelings" (*chengqiyi* 誠其意), that is, internalizing and consolidating a habitual disposition of conduct to be expressed consistently as one's moral virtuosity.

Having made this important distinction between mere conduct and habituated moral virtuosity, this opening passage of *Five Modes of Virtuosic Conduct* then concludes by offering the reader a distinction between efficacy (*shan* 善) as the waymaking of the human being, and moral virtuosity (*de* 德) as the waymaking of *tian*:

> When harmony (*he* 和) is achieved among these five modes of virtuosic conduct, it is called moral virtuosity (*de* 德), while achieving harmony only among the first four of them is called efficacy (*shan* 善). Efficacy is human way-making (*rendao* 人道), while moral virtuosity is the way-making of *tian* (*tiandao* 天道).[51]

This distinction here between human waymaking and the waymaking of *tian* that assigns "moral virtuosity" (*de*) to *tian* is made curious by the fact that the text has up to this point used the same term, "moral virtuosity," (*de*) to describe the quality of human conduct achieved when it has been internalized by human beings as their habitual way of behaving. In this first chapter, then, moral virtuosity (*de*) is described both as the waymaking of *tian* and as the waymaking of consummate human beings.

To appreciate what is meant here by the distinction between "human waymaking" and "the waymaking of *tian*" we need first to suspend our uncritical yet default Abrahamic theological assumptions and thus resist the temptation to think it is referencing two exclusive domains. As Tang Yijie has repeatedly averred, the human-*tian* collaboration in waymaking is an emergent, increasingly inspired way of being in the world that always has both a human and a cosmic aspect. Here the text states that a harmonious integration of the first four modes of virtuosic conduct as moral virtuosity (*de* 德) produces human efficacy (*shan* 善). But when the fifth mode of virtuosic conduct is added to this harmony—that is, the sagacity of human beings (*sheng* 聖)—it produces a moral virtuosity (*de*) that is to be associated with *tian*.

In this text then, moral virtuosity (*de*), far from being described as the exclusive waymaking of *tian*, stands and is expressed as a collaboration

---

51. 德之行五,和謂之德,四行和謂之善。善人道也,德天道也。

between *tian* and the waymaking of the highest order of humanity: the sages. Given that the sages are the paramount exemplars of what is humanly possible, this moral virtuosity is manifested in the world as the consummate expression of the operations of both sagacious human beings and the contextualizing *tian* as they deepen their relationship in their collaborative activities. Not only is such sagacity to be understood as the human being achieving the reach and the influence of *tian*, but moreover we must allow that *tian* itself is deepened and extended by this compounding human sagacity. This shared virtuosic conduct not only underscores the primacy of the *tianren* relationship over the secondary distinction between *tian* and human beings but also makes the important point that human beings in their role as sages can continue and extend the work of *tian*.

This insight into the mutuality of the waymaking of human beings and *tian* expressed through sagacious conduct is further strengthened when we reflect on the four inclinations (*siduan* 四端) of "heartminding" (*xin* 心) that for Mencius define the native conditions that locate the human being within family and community and that are thus available for personal cultivation. Of course, as we have seen in this *Five Modes of Virtuosic Conduct* chapter, these first four modes of virtuosic conduct *renyilizhi* 仁義禮智 are identical with the "four inclinations" (*siduan*) of the Mencian heartminding. As we have also found in *Mencius*, "those who make the most of their 'heartminding' (*xin*) realize their natural propensities (*xing*). And again, those who realize their natural propensities then realize *tian*."⁵² What is clear here is that such moral virtuosity, rather than being some characteristic pattern of behavior established by complying with external, antecedent principles—or from the reduplication of an erstwhile internal and innate human nature—is the product of a collaboration between persons and their worlds. Again, these four inclinations are not only productive of a cultivated human efficacy (*shan*) but also provide the ground for the Mencian claim that everyone, given these initial conditions, can aspire to behave sagaciously in their conduct.

But we need a clarification here. The Mencian claim is not that each human being has some innate potential that can be actualized to make everyone a sage; rather it is the collaboration between our initial inclinations and our world that can produce sagacious conduct. There is

---

52. *Mencius* 7A1: 盡其心者知其性也。知其性則知天矣。

an important difference between saying that everyone has some inherent potential of becoming a sage and that everyone who behaves like a sage *is* a sage. The potential for becoming a sage only emerges pari passu in the transactional events that constitute the substance of a human life. Mencius makes this point explicitly:

> Cao Jiao inquired: "Is it the case that we can all become Yao's and Shun's?"
> Mencius replied: ". . . The way-making of Yao and Shun was nothing but family reverence (*xiao*) and fraternal deference (*ti*). If you wear Yao's clothes, speak his words, and do what he does, then you *are* a Yao."[53]

Mencius's point here is that it is sagacious conduct that makes someone a sage. Indeed, it is behaving sagaciously that stands as the ultimate "depth of coalescence" (*du* 度) in the *tianren* relationship. It is also important to realize that such sagacity is the ultimate expression of human autonomy in the sense that it is a quality of human virtuosity allowing for the full collaboration of exemplary human beings in preserving a flourishing cosmos.

There is much textual evidence that sagacity is the ultimate coalescence in the first-order *tianren* relationship. As we witness throughout the canonical Confucian texts, the vague notion of *tian* takes on a particular human visage as the texts repeatedly correlate these always unique sages with *tian* by characterizing them metaphorically in grand, celestial terms. In the Guodian version of *Five Modes of Virtuosic Conduct*, for example, a common celestial vocabulary is used to correlate the excellence of the sage-king Wen (literally, King "Culture") as the paragon of human culture, with the way of *tian*:

> Sagacity and wisdom are whence propriety and music arise, [and are what bring harmony to the five modes of virtuosic conduct]. When the five modes of virtuosic conduct are in harmony there is happiness; where there is happiness, there is moral virtuosity; where there is moral virtuosity, the nation

---

53. *Mencius* 6B2: 曹交問曰：" 人皆可以為堯舜，有諸？" 曰："... 堯舜之道，孝弟而已矣。子服堯之服，誦堯之言，行堯之行，是堯而已矣。"

will flourish. Such was the insight of King Wen. This is what the passage from the *Book of Songs* means in saying "[King Wen presiding above; he shines] in the heavens (*tian*)."[54]

And again, it states quite explicitly in *Focusing the Familiar* that everyone who can conduct themselves as sages can have a transformative effect on *tian*. It is

> only those in the world of utmost resolution who are able to separate out and braid together the many threads on the great loom of the world. Only they set the great root of the world and realize the transforming and nourishing processes of heaven and earth.
> How could there be anything on which they depend?
> So earnest, they are consummate (*ren*);
> So profound, they are a bottomless abyss (*yuan*);
> So pervasive, they are *tian* (*tian*).
> And only those whose own capacities of discernment and sagely wisdom extend to the powers of *tian* could possibly understand them.[55]

In the *Analects*, the same kind of celestial hyperbole is used to describe Confucius specifically:

> Zigong said, ". . . The superior character of other people is like a mound or a hill that can still be scaled, but Confucius is the sun and moon that no one can climb beyond. Were persons to cut themselves off from such illumination, what damage would this do to the sun and moon? It would only demonstrate that such persons do not know their own limits."[56]

---

54. *Book of Songs*, 235; compare Bernhard Karlgren, *The Book of Odes: Text, Transcription, and Translation* (Stockholm: Far Eastern Antiquities, 1950), 185–86. 五行篇 15: 聖知, 禮樂之所由生, 五〔行之所和〕也。和則樂, 樂則有德, 有德則邦家興。文〔王之示也如此。文王在上, 于昭〕于天。此之謂也。

55. *Zhongyong* 32: 唯天下至誠, 為能經綸天下之大經, 立天下之大本, 知天地之化育。夫焉有所倚? 肫肫其仁! 淵淵其淵! 浩浩其天! 苟不固聰明聖知達天德者, 其孰能知之?

56. *Analects* 19.24: 子貢曰:「. . . 他人之賢者, 丘陵也, 猶可逾也; 仲尼, 日月也, 無得而逾焉。人雖欲自絕, 其何傷於日月乎? 多見其不知 量也!」See also *Analects* 19.21 and 25.

Indeed, in this same chapter of the *Analects*, there are several such passages that would associate Confucius directly with *tian*:

> Zigong said, "... The Master cannot be matched just as a ladder cannot be used to climb the sky (*tian*).... How could anyone be his peer?"[57]

Again, in *Focusing the Familiar*, Confucius takes on full cosmic proportions in being identified with the turning of the seasons and the operations of the natural order itself:

> Confucius modeled himself above on the rhythm of the turning seasons (*tian*), and below he was attuned to the patterns of water and earth. He is comparable to the heavens and the earth (*tiandi*), sheltering and supporting everything that is. He is comparable to the progress of the four seasons, and the alternating brightness of the sun and the moon.[58]

For Tang Yijie, who draws upon the cosmology made explicit in the *Book of Changes*, it is in this sense that human "becomings" with their production of human culture are inseparable from the flourishing of nature's sublimities. That is, human beings are nothing less than a cocreative and transformative moral force in the cosmos. My argument here, inspired by Tang's work on the *tianren* relationship, is that in these classical Confucian canons, human sagacity is understood not only as having the capacity to introduce epochal transformations in the human experience but also as having a transformative influence on the quality of *tian* and an amplificatory effect on the moral meaning of the cosmos broadly. Said another way, the relatively vague notion of *tian* as it is expressed in these early texts is brought into focus and made explicit through the specific lives of our human sages. If Confucius can elevate the worth of human "becomings" by insisting that they "are able to broaden the way," (*ren neng hongdao* 人能弘道), we can extend this celebration of humanity by joining Zhu Xi in proclaiming that "the sages

---

57. *Analects* 19.25: 子貢曰: "... 夫子之不可及也, 猶天之不可階而升也。... 如之何其可及也。"
58. *Zhongyong* 30: 仲尼 ... 上律天時, 下襲水土。辟如天地之無不持載, 無不覆幬, 辟如四時之錯行, 如日月之代明。

can continue and carry out the workings of *tian*" (*shengren neng jitian liji* 聖人能繼天立極).[59] The ultimate expression of relational autonomy in the Confucian world is nothing less than the aspiration to achieve a human virtuosity that would enable us as sages to collaborate fully in guiding a flourishing cosmic order. That is to say, the Confucian versions of individual autonomy and choice reconceived as relational autonomy and thick choices combine to provide us with a holistic strategy for optimizing the human experience.

The poetry of these canonical texts is inspirational, quite literally breaking into song in describing the capacity of the highest order of human beings to make a cosmic difference. But now we must turn to the practical, historical question: How have such sagacious persons activated their personal commitment to achieving the deepest coalescence in the relations that constitute them and world? And in so doing, how have they institutionalized and made practicable such aspirations? And from our own vantage point as contemporary human becomings, we must further ask ourselves: what in our own place and time are the practical social and political mechanisms that would be necessary for the elevation and optimization of the human experience?

---

59. See Zhu Xi's 朱熹 preface to his commentary on the *Zhongyong* 中庸章句集注 in his commentary on the *Four Books* 四書集注.

Chapter Six

Holism, Democracy, and the Optimizing of the Human Experience

Contextualism: Abjuring "the Perils of Abstraction"

Confucian role ethics is not an alternative ethical theory. It is a holistic vision of the moral life that begins from the primacy of practice and takes theorizing as an intrinsic feature—a nonanalytic aspect—of practical activity. It is grounded in a holographic, focus-field understanding of persons that acknowledges the continuity of immediate experience within our various contexts and then appeals to the situated common sense that emerges when we aspire with imagination to make the most of this experience. Erstwhile theoretical tools arise for philosophers in this tradition in media res—that is, from the need to make our human practices more intelligent and productive within the context of the practices themselves. Such a way of thinking about the moral life attempts to give full measure to the indeterminacy and the open-ended transitivity that attends what are always unique activities. In so doing, in serving as an alternative to abstract theorizing, it necessarily trades off a degree of clarity and rigor that for such theorizing comes at the cost of simplifying what is always more complex.

In this chapter, then, we want to explore the practical matter of how Confucianism has institutionalized its aspiration to optimize the human experience and then reflect on how we might activate these institutions and make them practicable in the concrete social and political lives of ordinary people today. Alfred North Whitehead, worried about the cost of the persisting imbalance that has us relying upon the ostensive clarity of abstract theory at the expense of the more murky and tentative world of practice, is often quoted as saying "we think in generalities, but we live in detail." In rehearsing the history of philosophy, Whitehead accuses Epicurus, Plato, and Aristotle of being "unaware of the perils of abstraction" that render knowledge closed and complete. According to Whitehead, "the history of thought" that he associates with these great men

> is a tragic mixture of vibrant disclosure and of deadening closure. The sense of penetration is lost in the certainty of completed knowledge. This dogmatism is the antichrist of learning.

Whitehead exhorts us to appreciate the processual and open-ended nature of experience and to give full measure to the transitions and conjunctions that are integral to the eventful nature of our lives:

> In the full concrete connection of things, the characters of the things connected enter into the character of the connectivity which joins them. . . . Every example of friendship exhibits the particular character of the two friends. Two other people are inconsistent in respect to that completely defined friendship.[1]

We might want to pay attention to the example of "friendship" Whitehead offers us here to illustrate the prospective "sense of penetration"—what he terms the "creative advance"—that is arrested and compromised by assumptions about the certainty of knowledge. For Whitehead, friendship is the enrichment of the human experience that occurs when two always unique persons are able to pursue and consolidate a continuing pattern of productive relations. Using Whitehead's own language, he insists that anyone other than these two specific persons would be "inconsistent" in this particular relation. For Whitehead, it is the continuing quality of the process of the friendship itself, including both unique, nonsubstitutable friends *and their connectivity*, that is the concrete, nonfungible fact of *this* friendship. Evaluations of the quality of their relationship that would appeal to fixed characteristics such as their obligations to one another, or even the two persons themselves as putative "individuals," must be understood as only second-order abstractions from what is a complex lived reality.

---

1. Whitehead, *Modes of Thought*, 58.

Indeed, as remarked upon previously, at a cosmological level for Whitehead, the very assumption that there are such things as discrete individuals is a prime example of what he calls the "fallacy of simple location." Whitehead rejects the world of "objects" as abstractions from our experience and argues that the fundamental realities of both experience and nature itself are best understood as irreducibly extended and dynamic events.

Sor-hoon Tan, in her argument that the conduct of human beings is irreducibly social and organic, invokes John Dewey's "retrospective fallacy"—a fallacy that resonates with Whitehead's fallacies of "simple location" and "misplaced concreteness"—as a challenge to the isolating reduplication of personal identity that occurs when we abstract persons from the connectivity of their narratives. Tan observes that

> those still preoccupied with *identity* often complain that Dewey's view is that of a "self-in-action without a self." They miss the point of Dewey's protest against traditional conceptions of the self. For Dewey, there could be no self outside of experience, outside of human doing and undergoing. The distinction between "self" and action is "after the fact." Unity precedes distinctions in experience; to think otherwise is to commit the "retrospective fallacy"—to mistake a distinction introduced into experience by later reflections as fully present in the original experience. . . . Selfhood is an eventual function that emerges with complexly organized interactions, organic and social.[2]

In furthering this commitment to concrete context and common sense, I want to abjure the "Euthyphro problem," which would insist that principles of adjudication must be prior to and separate from the objects of our judgment and that something must be determined to be intrinsically good—good in itself—rather than being deemed good as a summary judgment on its always relational narrative. Socrates famously asks Euthyphro: Is something holy because it is loved by the gods? Or is it loved by gods because it is holy? And then answers his own question by insisting on the latter. Continuing in this same dialogue, Socrates

---

2. Sor-hoon Tan, *Confucian Democracy: A Deweyan Reconstruction* (Albany: State University of New York Press, 2003), 27.

makes a further point in support of his answer through a rather convoluted grammatical argument: he claims anything that is loved as holy must itself be both logically and temporally holy prior to its being loved. That is, the thing must have some essential characteristic itself that then induces the state or accident or attribute of its being loved. Simply put, you have to have an "it" before it can be loved.

Of course, the success of such an argument depends upon a logic grounded in a substance ontology that allows for a clear distinction between essences and their attributes—between something and its contextualizing relations. We might recall Aristotle's ontological and thus isolating *what* question that answers what can be said *of* the man in the marketplace, standing in contrast to the subsequent ancillary questions that identify what can be attributed to and thus be *in* the subject once substantially understood. But this same argument falters in an event ontology where the essence-and-attribute dualism has no purchase and where what is putatively "essential" is simply a generalization made from a pattern of evolving relationships within a narrative. That is, something being holy, far from being a quality intrinsic to that thing itself, is a function of what an event means for those persons within its continuing context.

An old church in Wales, for example, made quite holy in its own time, can become someone's house when its congregation has dispersed and faded away. As such, it is only a provisional convenience if not a grammatical nicety for us to describe the church as "being holy" rather than as "holy-ing" under a specific set of conditions. Something being holy is situational and thus a function of having over time become valorized as holy and as continuing to be loved by the gods and anyone else because of the interest invested in it. Further, in this alternative eventful logic, and contra Socrates, the actual content of something that is "holy-ing" or continually "becoming" holy changes over time rather than being some essential and unchanging property that defines it. In other words, what something is, what the thing does, and what it means for other things are no more than aspects of its continuing narrative. Things are what they are because of their place and function in respect to the wholeness of experience.

Perhaps in our own times, "good" might be a more familiar example than "holy" of something deemed to have intrinsic worth independent of its context. Indeed, the protean richness of the Chinese language has always been (and continues to be) a function of the novel contexts that over time lend themselves to being described as some new kind of specific "good." The evolving production of binomials to stipulate different relationally produced "goods" is the underlying secret of how Chinese as a natural language functions in amplifying its powers of description. Such always novel combinations are a clear and persistent example of what we have previously rehearsed as the cosmological postulate that insists on the radical contextualism of things, "the inseparability of one and many" (*yiduo bufen guan* 一多不分觀).

To cite just one example of how the Chinese language itself works to respect context, it can be argued that the graph *mei* 美, often translated as "beauty," is in fact much better rendered "beautiful," where the semantic difference lies in our culturally specific tendency to understand "beauty" as some given and essential quality something "has." "Beautiful" on the other hand is the description of a particular thing or event that is referring to it within its specific context. As the *Zhuangzi* observes, different contexts produce different "beautifuls":

> A gorilla will take a female ape as his mate, an elk will mount his doe, and fish will frolic about with other fish. Mao Qiang and Lady Li were eyed as great beauties by the gentlemen, but when fish see these ladies they dive into the deep, when birds see them they soar into the skies, and when deer see them they bolt for their lives. Who among these four animals knows what is the right source of arousal?[3]

On the oracle bones, the character *mei* 美 written as *[xxxii]* depicts a human being with head ornamentation, sometimes understood as a feathers-and-hair headdress and sometimes as jewelry made from animal horns.[4] Indeed, it is because this same term can be attached to so many different things and situations that it can be parsed to mean everything from fine, handsome, exquisite, elegant, dainty, pleasing, improving, happy, moral, scenic, aesthetic, majestic, magnificent, resplendent, gorgeous, poignant, fertile, rich, delicious, sumptuous, lush, delicate, and sweet, to praises, considerations, kindnesses, fine deeds, and so on.

[xxxii]

---

3. *Zhuangzi* 2/6/68–70: 猨,猵狙以為雌,麋與鹿交,鰌與魚游。毛嬙、麗姬,人之所美也,魚見之深入,鳥見之高飛,麋鹿見之決驟。四者孰知天下之正色哉?
4. Kwan, "Database," 甲骨文合集 CHANT 0210.

Dewey and the Postulate of Immediate Empiricism

John Dewey's contextualism and holism would also assert that "holy" or "good" or "beautiful" is invariably a function of context. Dewey, with some uncharacteristic humor, asserts that perhaps the most pervasive fallacy in our thinking is a kind of unlimited universalism that

> consists in the supposition that whatever is found true under certain conditions may forthwith be asserted universally or without limits and conditions. Because a thirsty man gets satisfaction in drinking water, bliss consists in being drowned.[5]

Dewey would argue that if we want to understand what "good" (or anything else) means, we have to ask the following question: what is it experienced *as*? It is only in thus respecting experience as where we must both begin and end our inquiry that we do justice to the full complexity of "good" and its always provisional nature.

In a seminal essay written very early in his career, Dewey sets a clear trajectory for how his pragmatic philosophy would unfold. In "The Reflex Arch Concept in Psychology," Dewey, inspired by his intellectual mentor, William James, provides a clear example of how the "old psychology" is guilty of what James has called "*the* psychological fallacy" in retrospectively fragmenting, isolating, and separating elements within what is always a continuous experience. At the time of Dewey's essay in 1896, within the fledgling discipline of psychology, the neural circuitry of the reflex arc was informed by the prevailing Cartesian dualism. As such, this arc continued to be misunderstood by separating "stimulus," "idea," and "response" into discrete and independent links in a chain, thus making the former the "cause" and "explanation" of the latter two. Dewey describes the problem in the following terms:

> Instead of interpreting the character of sensation, idea and action from their place and function in the sensory-motor circuit, we still incline to interpret the latter from our preconceived and preformulated ideas of rigid distinctions between sensations, thoughts and acts. The sensory stimulus is one thing, the central activity, standing for the idea, is another

---

5. Dewey, *Middle Works*, 14:123.

Holism, Democracy, and the Optimizing of the Human Experience | 323

thing, and the motor discharge, standing for the act proper, is a third.⁶

And Dewey has on offer a rather straightforward and empirically persuasive solution:

> What is wanted is that sensory stimulus, central connections and motor responses shall be viewed, not as separate and complete entities in themselves, but as divisions of labor, function factors, within the single concrete whole, now designated the reflex arc.⁷

What Dewey is arguing for is the wholeness of experience in which the meaning of the "stimulus," far from being discrete and prior, is in fact informed in its interpretation by the one's entire narrative. In the example he uses, a child is drawn to the light of a candle because of a continuous feed of her associations and memories of tactile knowing, and likewise, her response to the candle is conditioned by habits and values that have evolved within the same narrative. Simply put, stimulus, idea, and action are nonanalytic aspects within a continuing narrative with each of them being implicated in and being the cause and effect of the others, depending upon the perspective one takes. Far from being discrete, external, and causal, stimulus is part of a circuit of continuous and interpenetrating events within the episodes of a life. Dare we say that the focus-field language foregrounding and thus bringing into focus any one aspect within experience, as informed by the entire narrative as its field, would seem to be an apposite vocabulary for capturing Dewey's reflex arc insight.

Further, and building upon the intuitions presented in this "Reflex Arch" essay, Dewey introduces what he calls the "postulate of immediate empiricism" as his further reflection on the nature of the human experience, and "how" it means:

> Immediate empiricism postulates that things—anything, everything, in the ordinary or non-technical use of the term "thing"—

---

6. John Dewey, *The Early Works of John Dewey* (1882–1898), ed. Jo Ann Boydston, vol. 5 (Carbondale: Southern Illinois University Press, 1971), 97.

7. Dewey, *Early Works*, 5:97.

> are what they are experienced as. . . . If *any* experience, then a *determinate* experience; and this determinateness is the only, and is the adequate, principle of control, or "objectivity." . . . If you wish to find out what subjective, objective, physical, mental, cosmic, psychic, cause, substance, purpose, activity, evil, being, quality—any philosophic term, in short—means, go to experience and see what the thing is experienced *as*.[8]

In the interest of clarifying Confucian role ethics, I would like to add principles, values, and virtues to Dewey's list of "subjective," "objective," and the other "philosophic terms" enumerated here. All of these philosophical terms can only be adequately defined by looking at how they are "lived" and what we have experienced them *as*. Again, what Dewey is saying is that all of experience is relevant to any one aspect of it—an insight into the nature of experience we have tried to capture in rehearsing Tang Junyi's cosmological idea of "the inseparability of the one and the many." We might reformulate Tang's ecological assertion rather simply as anything happens only because everything else happens. And again, everything else happens only because any particular thing happens.

Before Dewey formulated his postulate of immediate empiricism, William James had earlier offered his own version of a similar idea that probably inspired Dewey, referring to it as a "radical empiricism":

> To be radical, an empiricism must neither admit into its constructions any element that is not directly experienced, nor exclude from them any element that is directly experienced. For such a philosophy, the relations that connect experiences must themselves be experienced relations, and any kind of relation experienced must be accounted as 'real' as anything else in the system.[9]

And more recently, Hilary Putnam, yet another advocate of a pragmatic approach to philosophy, brings additional clarity to this postulate of imme-

---

8. Dewey, *Middle Works*, 3:158, 164, 165–66.

9. James, *Pragmatism*, 315. Dewey's "refinement" on this idea lies in his insistence that experience is what it is without allowing for any difference between what is known and what is imagined to be. He does not follow James in any qualitative or ontological distinction between primordial experience and more secondary experience.

diate empiricism by not only rejecting "view-from-nowhere" objectivism but by further insisting that the subjective dimension of experience is always integral to what the world really is. Putnam insists that

> elements of what we call "language" or "mind" penetrate so deeply into what we call "reality" that the very project of representing ourselves as being "mapper's" of something "language-independent" is fatally compromised from the start. Like Relativism, but in a different way, Realism is an impossible attempt to view the world from Nowhere.[10]

Putnam will not admit of any understanding of the real world that would separate it from its human participation and does not accept our experience of it as what the world *really* is:

> The heart of pragmatism, it seems to me—of James' and Dewey's pragmatism if not of Peirce's—was the supremacy of the agent point of view. If we find that we must take a certain point of view, use a certain 'conceptual system,' when engaged in a practical activity, in the widest sense of practical activity, then we must not simultaneously advance the claim that it is not really 'the way things are in themselves.'[11]

In arguing for the reality of experience as it is "had," these classical and neopragmatists challenge the familiar equation between knowledge and reality that has grounded classical epistemology as being a fundamental and persistent error: what Dewey distains as "reality as the self-luminous vision of the Absolute."[12] Simply put, experience is what it is, and it is all real: our dreams and misperceptions as much as our most persistent and efficacious insights. And because this experience is continuous, all of it is relevant to the understanding of any one event within it. Again, the focus-field gestalt shift seems to be a felicitous way of construing and correlating the relationship between particular events and the process of experience as a whole.

---

10. Hilary Putnam, *Realism with a Human Face* (Cambridge, MA: Harvard University Press, 1990), 28.
11. Hilary Putnam, *The Many Faces of Realism* (La Salle, IL: Open Court, 1987), 83.
12. Dewey, *Middle Works*, 3:164.

Evaluating Roles in Confucian Role Ethics

I want to argue that the reductionism consequent upon failing to begin from a proper awareness of the wholeness of experience has allowed ethical theorists in the name of rigor and clarity to rationalize ethical conduct, and in so doing, to simplify the complexity of moral deliberation. If, on the contrary, we do accept the postulate of immediate empiricism, we might ask the following questions: What does such holism mean for Confucian role ethics as a vision of the moral life? And how does it factor into the evaluation of roles and their performance?

Steve Angle provides a fair-minded, generous, and yet still critical evaluation of our argument that Confucian role ethics is sufficiently distinctive to resist the current collapsing of it into existing Western moral theories. As Angle surmises, one reason we do emphasize the differences between these familiar moral theories and Confucian role ethics is because of the serious asymmetry that continues to skew comparisons between Confucian ethics and Western ethical theory, with scholars continuing to tailor their interpretations of Confucian ethics to fit the Western templates. We do insist that given the vintage of this tradition, the relatively recent encounter of Confucian role ethics with Western ethical theory cannot be taken as its defining moment. We must allow the Confucian tradition and its texts to speak on their own terms. Our guiding premise, simply put, has been that the interpretive context must be respected in the reading of these Confucian texts. Although Angle does cite some of the secondary literature that would challenge such a premise, he himself ultimately seems to take our side, concluding his own discussion of moral theory in the *Analects* with a cautionary note similar to our own. Speaking for himself, Angle avers there are many "hazards on the way to meaningful comparisons between ancient texts and modern theories" that arise when we forget that "the text has a complex social, conceptual, and historical context of its own."[13]

Our own project has certainly been to remind readers of the Confucian canons to be cognizant of this general problem of interpretive context. But more specifically, as I have noted, it is also clear that the notion of persons in Confucian ethics resists some of our most fundamental and familiar distinctions. For this reason, one prominent blind among these many hazards announced by Angle that might compromise responsible

---

13. Steve Angle, "The *Analects* and Moral Theory," *Dao Companion to the Analects*, ed. Amy Olberding (Dordrecht, The Netherlands: Springer, 2014), 252.

cultural comparisons is a failure to appreciate this alternative, focus-field notion of person and its holographic understanding of the relationship between inner self and outer world.

Angle does allow that when Rosemont and I insist Confucian role ethics is a sui generis vision of the moral life, we "are not claiming that Confucian role ethics is incommensurable with Western moral theories."[14] On the one hand, we certainly do attempt to articulate what we take to be the profound depth of the different cultural and cosmological assumptions that have occasioned the current asymmetry in comparative philosophy: a prime example being the radically different conception of persons that grounds Confucian role ethics. But this effort should not be taken to preclude the possibility of any productive, mutually edifying dialogue with Western ethical theories. In fact, both Rosemont and I in our published work have been explicit on the desirability of having just such a conversation, and indeed, it is this perceived need that inspired my earlier volume and this present sequel as well.[15] And beyond our own work, our graduate students, as part of the next generation of comparative philosophers, continue to write dissertations, academic papers, and monographs that make productive comparisons between Confucian role ethics, feminist care ethics, and Deweyan social ethics, as well as with many more mainstream moral theories.

The most substantial philosophical concern that Angle expresses about our position on Confucian role ethics is perhaps captured in the following question:

---

14. Angle, "The *Analects* and Moral Theory," 245.

15. From early on, Rosemont has consistently anticipated this second step of bringing role ethics and Western ethical theory into conversation: "I do not wish to imply that the early Confucian writings are the be-all and end-all for finding answers to the multiplicity of questions I have posed. . . . Some Western philosophical concepts will, and should remain with us, some others will have to be stretched, bent, and/or extended significantly in order to represent accurately non-Western concepts and concept clusters." See Rosemont, "Rights-Bearing and Role-Bearing Persons," 92, 94.

And while wanting to allow the vocabulary of Confucian role ethics to speak for itself, I have also been explicit on this further challenge: "The next stage in the effort to give full expression to role ethics as a new and compelling vision of the ethical life will require a sustained conversation between Confucian philosophy and existing Western ethical theories that is able to draw creatively upon these very different ways of thinking about the refinement and evaluation of human conduct." See Ames, *Confucian Role Ethics*, xvii.

> The *Analects* clearly sees the need for critical evaluation of the ways that roles are inhabited by particular people. Does "Confucian role ethics" provide adequate critical purchase for such an assessment? . . . If we need to be able to talk about good parents and bad, . . . the question then becomes in what terms we judge or articulate such goodness.[16]

It would seem that for Angle, if we are going to judge whether a person is living a particular role in a normatively justifiable way, the standard of evaluation must precede and be external to the role itself. "Good" has to have some higher-order value than just pointing at a "good parent." One cannot simply assert that "I am a good parent" without further justification. As one of his examples, Angle cites A. T. Nuyen's version of Confucian role ethics as allowing that "the distinction between a good and bad occupier of a role is determined by how well a given individual fulfills the obligations associated with the given role"—obligations that as standards presumably exist independent of the role itself.[17] Angle believes that if we were to make a similar claim to be normatively committed to a general vision of interdependence and relationality as a preexisting standard, then we would end up with "virtuosity ethics" as opposed to "virtue ethics," where the quality of intimacy and mutuality provided by appeal to such a standard would do the work of the specific virtues. Such a position in fact would not be role dependent at all and could presumably have a productive conversation with virtue ethics.

Angle advocates for a separation between "virtues" and "roles" and then treats such virtues as higher-order standards that can be used to evaluate and justify roles. We on the other hand insist that roles and the virtuosity expressed in the conduct that defines them are inseparable. Again, it is the relations and their quality that are first order, while abstracted "objects"—either putative individuals or their ostensive virtues—are

---

16. Angle, "The *Analects* and Moral Theory," 246–47.

17. Angle, "The *Analects* and Moral Theory," 248, note 42. One problem with an appeal to generic "obligations" that define roles is again that it focuses on abstract individuals and their abstract obligations rather than on the lived roles of persons in their relations. To begin with, since fiduciary roles have to be defined in terms of both trust and credibility simultaneously, they require reference to an appropriate balance between privilege and obligation in the relationship. And then there are the particularities of the circumstances that must be considered as well.

second order. The content of erstwhile virtues, values, and principles is abstracted from the concrete conduct that constitutes lived roles, and then lived roles in turn, and to some degree, come to be guided by such fluid and always tentative abstractions. Importantly, we must be alert to the fact that as our roles change, the content of our moral categories changes along with them. Indeed, one important contribution that role ethics makes to the discourse is to alert us to the always particularist, processual, provisional, and revisionist status of our moral vocabulary.

Confucian role ethics is grounded in a radical empiricism that rules out the possibility of logically and temporally prior criteria being sufficient in themselves for adjudicating conduct. As an empiricism, it insists on the primacy of practice and the evolving and particular nature of our norms as they continue to theorize our practices. There are expressed concerns that this kind of evolutionary ethics does not have the theoretical elegance of being able to find our best answers by appealing to fixed, complete, and univocal criteria. For example, the anthropologist R. R. Marett says of philosopher Cook Wilson that "all of this evolutionary stuff about ethics seemed rather pointless to him, as holding that ethical principles were demonstrably 'there,' though mankind might have endulged in all manner of false starts before debouching on the highway of reason."[18] But for Confucian role ethics, theorizing experience is not prior to or independent of our practices; rather, this experience emerges out of and is integral to our practices, evolving with them to provide direction. And as a radical empiricism, Confucian role ethics respects the spontaneous emergence of novelty always present in the lived experience that locates all judgments in media res and precludes any final ends. Our basis for making judgments must be found in the search for the best actions that conduce to optimum growth in roles lived within the unique, always evolving circumstances themselves. I would further contend that Confucian role ethics is most importantly empirical in the sense that it is consistent with what we actually do in making our moral judgments. As I will argue in exploring the key notion of "deference and dramatic rehearsal" (*shu* 恕), our critical self-awareness functions within the roles we live. Who among us in point of fact simply applies fixed criteria to determine the best way forward in responding to our practical moral problems?

Our claim is that in Confucian role ethics, all human relations are ultimately role based, and conduct that conduces to growth in these

---

18. R. R. Marett, *A Jerseyman at Oxford* (Oxford: Oxford University Press, 1941), 118.

relations and to fostering human flourishing is the substance of morality. It is a nonreductionistic prospering of the role itself with all of the complexity that attends it that must produce the proper standards of adjudication. The extent to which parents are deemed "good" parents, far from referencing some personal characteristic that informs their conduct—or compliance in their actions with some antecedent and external norm—can only be judged by the quality of their evolving relationships with their always unique children in their always unique situations. That is, the parents must first be "good with," "good for," "good in," "good to," "good at" and so on, as logically and temporarily prior to any derivative general characterization of their being "good" parents.

Of course, given the focus-field holography that is in play, such judgments about our roles are always informed by generalizations derived from cultural patterns of how such roles have been lived over time. In aspiring to be a good father to my two sons, my role as father can and should be informed by the best models available to me, and I will certainly be a better father as a result. And over time, through success and failure in practice, I have presumably learned something and have developed certain habituated ways of responding to the practical challenges I regularly face. But all such generalizations made from past experience and about good role models, although serving as valuable guidelines, are still inadequate in themselves. In the final analysis, and not incidentally, the analogies I am able to draw upon from prior successes and the role models I choose to emulate must be tailored to the specific roles and circumstances. Ultimately, I must be this particular father to these two very different sons in this particular situation. And I must in every moment continue to learn what this means.

Indeed, we might use the generic term for "good" in classical Chinese—*hao* 好—as a heuristic for making the argument for the assumed priority of relationships in determining what is "good," for allowing the inadequacy of any particular representation of its content, and for accepting an always evolving redefinition of what it means to be "good" in the roles we live. On the oracle bones and the bronzes, this graph is initially inspired by and depicts the specific relationship between a mother and her child *[xxxiii]* reflecting at least one specific kind of "good."[19] But over time and on the record, the application of the character evolves and is extended in different circumstances to describe productive roles more

[xxiii]

---

19. Image taken from Kwan, "Database," 甲骨文合集 CHANT 0460.

broadly. Its original, specific reference to mother and child is both diluted and enriched in finding this broader compass. On the bronzes, for example, a brave and strong male is deemed a "stout fellow" (*haohan* 好漢), and a woman of striking appearance is deemed a "handsome woman" (*haonu* 好女). The content of the moral vocabulary—in this case, "good"—is not one thing; it evolves and is derived over time from the many changing roles and relations that define our unique human narratives. The requisite moral artistry and the aesthetic sensibilities needed to make the most of a specific matrix of relationships—the role of being the best parent to this child in this situation—are in themselves normative.

Just as we argue against beginning from deracinated persons as the subject of moral reflection, we cannot begin from abstract principles or virtues or values as the presumptive determinants of what constitutes moral conduct. Again, just as particular persons embedded in their particular narratives are the proper subjects of evaluation, any standards of evaluation are also ultimately derived from particular instances of human flourishing within our roles and relations and are best applied with such an awareness. Our argument is that critical moral deliberation should begin from and return to the wholeness of experience. And any generic standard of adjudication as a generalization can only be a generalization, and to give it a higher or exclusive value introduces the real danger of compromising the capaciousness required for appropriate moral reflection.

When Angle suggests that interdependence and relationality might serve as preexisting standards for evaluating conduct, these are certainly important factors, but I am concerned that he is not giving sufficient weight to the cosmological assumptions we want to claim as ground for such standards. The primacy of these assumptions locates any particular behavior within a holistic, focus-field framework. We would certainly allow that specific episodes of conduct are focal and must be understood in terms of the interdependence of roles and relations, but we would further insist that such events are also "specious" in the Jamesian sense of having implicated in them not only the entire narratives of the persons involved but also the entire field within which this conduct takes place. And such an acknowledgment means that these standards are still internal rather than external as being implicated within the concrete episodes themselves. The specific narrative certainly has available to it generalizations that can serve as rules of thumb. But the ultimate source of these principles, virtues, and values is itself those compounding human narratives from which such generalizations are drawn. And further, any ostensive empirical generalization that might serve instrumentally as a putative "external" standard must be adapted to the specific conditions of always unique situations.

How then do we specifically and critically assess roles as they are lived? We begin from a sense of what is proper within the roles being performed in a particular situation. We can and do stipulate general features of human flourishing to serve as guidelines and recommendations. But it is important to know where such guidance comes from, since it is ultimately the growth in the specific role itself—my complex relationship with this specific student, for example—that is primary. It is this student in this role that gives the necessary specificity to what the content of such "flourishing" would be and what the best response to any situation would be. When someone takes erstwhile principles to be more than useful generalizations and is then praised as a person of principle, this description should be taken as a criticism rather than a compliment. To begin from abstract principles and then tailor concrete situations to accommodate these same principles is a failure of imagination that not only misses the real challenge virtuosic conduct requires but also perpetuates a real violence. To be sensitive moral actors, we must exercise the cultivated moral imagination necessary to adapt those analogically available generalizations to the specifics of always novel situations.

To return to the question of "good" as an example of a possible preexisting norm or standard, we can no more provide a formula for the good teacher than we can for a work of art. We have all had good teachers, and we would not assume that some set of general characteristics that defines the teacher-student relationship can do justice to the phenomenon. In fact, there are congeries of differences among all such relationships. The role itself as it is lived between this teacher and this student has its own normative force that resists our generic reductions. Good teachers serve as exemplary models rather than as a source of abstract principles that can be articulated and followed, and as I have previously observed, they are usually invoked anecdotally rather than by appeal to generic character traits. For me to assert that "I am her teacher" is itself a normative injunction, referring others analogically to their own concrete past exemplars for adjudication. In addition, invoking this role is more helpful to me in determining what I should do, and more useful to others in making a moral evaluation, than any list conjured forth of abstract virtues or vices.

Perhaps another way of responding to Angle's need for an independent standard would be to argue that these Confucian texts give primacy to the thick notion of "achieving propriety in one's lived roles and relations" (*li* 禮) as its primary criteria for moral judgment that by definition must take the specific relevant interests of all parties into account (*yi* 義). And while Confucians certainly regard abstractions such as the rule of law and the application of punishments as necessary social institutions, they also construe this recourse to law not only as an unfortunate (although sometimes necessary) intervention but also as a clear admission of communal failure. We read in the *Analects*:

> If you lead the people with policy and effect social order with punishments, they will avoid wrongdoing, but will not develop an appropriate sense of shame (*chi* 恥). If you lead the people by modeling virtuosity in your conduct (*de* 德) and effect social order by encouraging propriety in roles and relations (*li* 禮), the people will not only develop a sense of shame, but will also order themselves.[20]

Serving as a basis for critical assessment is the moral virtuosity displayed in the role modeling of rulers, the proper functioning of familial and social roles, and the commensurate sense of shame that develops within ritually choreographed yet also specific family and community relations. While the dynamics of *li*-structured family lineages provide a concrete normative pattern of relations for a thriving community, abstract precepts such as the application of laws or policies, or the attendant threat of punishment, are at best only secondary injunctions.

I do take Angle's question about whether "Confucian role ethics" provides adequate critical purchase to assess the quality of moral conduct most seriously. Indeed, this objection is perhaps the most persistent reservation that has been expressed with respect to our concept of role ethics. Daniel Bell, for example, first voices a concern with the claim that we are constituted by our relations. He suggests that relations are of different kinds. While some of them might indeed be "constitutive" (our immediate family relations, for example), others are better described as "contingent" (second cousins and shopkeepers).[21] I am assuming that

---

20. *Analects* 2.3: 道之以政, 齊之以刑, 民免而無恥; 道之以德, 齊之以禮, 有恥且格。

21. Daniel A. Bell, "Roles, Community, and Morality: Comment on *Confucian Role Ethics*," in *Appreciating the Chinese Difference: Engaging Roger T. Ames on Methods, Issues, and Roles*, ed. Jim Behuniak (Albany: State University of New York Press, 2018), 205–6.

Bell's distinction makes the point that some relations are more essential to our identity than others. As I have argued, while all of our roles are constitutive of who we become (those important family relations we have little control over, as well as those that are incidental and that we might choose quite arbitrarily), I would certainly agree that some of these roles are more important and thus define personal identity more than others.

But Bell's main concern has to do with his worry over the perceived relationship between role ethics and moral obligation. He distinguishes between two claims: "the strong claim that the (constitutive) roles we occupy determine (or are the main source of) the content of our moral obligations and the weaker claim that our (constitutive) roles set constraints upon what we ought to do." He rightly associates my position with the former, stronger claim, while he himself wants to advocate for the latter. Bell's position in sum is again that if "role ethics is to provide morally-informed practical guidance, it needs to be constrained by moral standards external to the roles."[22]

David Elstein also joins ranks with Angle and Bell to formulate a similar complaint about role ethics. Elstein worries that role ethics leads us into a kind of cultural relativism because, in demurring on essential standards of adjudication, there is no basis for critical reflection and informed judgment when operating within a particular community—or when we move from one community to the next. The example Elstein gives is that of a traditional Chinese upper-class woman who is expected to find her contentment in living the domestic roles of an exemplary wife and mother. Indeed, "should she have wanted a life engaging in wider society outside the home she could be justly criticized." The problem is that "Ames does not explain how family roles come to be defined, or whether there is any way to criticize them in the particular historical context in which they are dominant."[23]

I would respond to Elstein by insisting that role ethics does provide us with general standards of adjudication, beginning with the critical question of how we foster optimal growth in this particular historical context in the specific roles that define us. The point would be that any general standard would have to be only the starting point that we would then have to make specific to the case. And again, role ethics concerns

---

22. Bell, "Roles, Community, and Morality," 209.
23. Elstein, "Contemporary Confucianism," 244.

itself not only with personal growth but also about whether on balance in this context everyone's interests are being taken fully into account (*yi* 義). That is, in role ethics, the measure of morality is quite simply the quality of meaningful growth in the relationships that come to constitute our identities. What is being described as "relativism" is the fact that role ethics is particularistic, pluralistic, inclusive, and falliblist in the sense of always being open to revision.

In the case of the upper-class woman, for example, one can certainly argue that the routinized domestication as wife and mother that precludes her from access to those roles in public life necessary to grow herself socially and politically can fairly be judged to be a diminution in the possibilities of growth not only for herself but also for the other various members of her family and for her community as well. And to cross cultural lines, such concerns could equally be invoked and judgments made on a woman locked within a world of Victorian values as well. How do we arrive at such a determination? As our criteria of judgment, we invoke the "idea" of optimizing growth in these roles and relationships and the corollary concern that the interests of all concerned must be properly considered. We can further argue that the kind of violences perpetrated by racism, misogyny, and slavery are all clearly a diminution in the possibilities for growth in any community and for the entire community, including the perpetrators. Clearly because the interests of some are being attenuated to serve the misconceived interests of others in such cases, general standards of adjudication can and should be made.

But for role ethics, beyond invoking such generalizations that are ultimately derived from roles themselves, what standards can be applied to take the proper measure of this growth in relations? To answer this question, virtue ethicists' identification of their essential standards for critical reflection and judgment might invoke inborn and thus universalizable virtues. Deontologists might appeal to a priori and thus universalizable autonomous moral feelings that determine our duties and obligations. And utilitarians might claim that we have the innate and thus universalizable capacity in our moral reasoning to calculate the optimum utility derivable from human actions. In these cases, they assert standards that are ostensibly objective by virtue of their independence of particular roles and relations.

Role ethics as a holistic vision of the moral life, as with virtue ethics, is certainly concerned with the approbation or denunciation of our fellows and also with amplifying our positive influence in the world.

Like deontic ethics, role ethics is also concerned with our motivations and the fulfilling of our obligations to others, and in so doing, striving to do what is right. And as with utilitarian ethics, role ethics is concerned about the consequences of our actions and the socially redeeming goods they are able to produce. But for role ethics, there is the need in the complexity of the human experience to avoid fragmenting the process of moral deliberation by separating agents from their actions, persons from our communities, our motivations from our actions and their consequences, and the theoretical from our concrete practices. Neither the general standard nor the theory in itself is sufficient to do justice to the job.

Where role ethics departs from these familiar ethical theories is in its insistence that we begin and end in the everyday practical activities that are expressed through the roles we live. First, we must recognize that the source and the substance of our erstwhile standards of adjudication, whether we call them principles, values, or virtues, are perhaps less tidy but wholly empirical generalizations abstracted from the complexity of roles themselves as they are being lived within concrete human narratives. And again, the deployment of these norms must consider the specific narratives to which they are to be applied. Role ethics seeks to take all of the desiderata of our ethical theories into account and reconcile their conflicts by negotiating the optimum balance among them in the concrete circumstances of actual practice.

Role ethics is grounded in a holistic, ecological sensibility that resists treating abstractions, be they putatively generic virtues, innate moral feelings, or our faculty of moral reasoning, as either our first-order realities or as our final ends. To accommodate the full spectrum of different human interests and needs, we need to keep the aspirational "idea" of optimal growth in our roles and relations that must always be determined within the changing contours of particular, concrete situations, functional in qualifying any abstract and thus ostensibly complete social or political institutions, or any set of fixed principles or values. At the same time, we must seek out those social and political institutions flexible enough to provide the beginning and the pliant structure necessary for pursing intelligent growth and refinement in our roles and relations.

What is the alternative in role ethics to a reliance on abstract principles in determining the most appropriate conduct? What is our decision procedure? And how in fact did we move historically from the role of the upper-class woman in Chinese and Western Victorian conceptions of the family institution to our present always evolving reconfigurations of such a role? If we reflect on how we actually go about finding our way in our moral quandaries, we will find that Confucian role ethics and its advocacy of critically self-conscious dramatic rehearsal in our roles and relations seem to be consistent with not only our best intuitions as to what we should do, but more importantly, with what we usually do.

Scenario Rehearsal (*shu* 恕) as Method for Determining Consummate Conduct (*ren* 仁)

The commitment in Confucian role ethics to a radical empiricism is evidenced in recommending the evaluative process of *shu* 恕 as the pathway to consummate conduct (*ren*). *Shu* is a critical and experimental method in which we rehearse the different possible dramatic scenarios in our roles and relations in our search for the best one among them. There have been many different interpretations of this term *shu* in the literature as scholars have puzzled over its import for ethical decision making and its implications. This perplexity is reflected in the various ways in which *shu* has been translated in the philosophical literature: as "altruism" (Wing-tsit Chan), as "reciprocity" (Tu Wei-ming, Raymond Dawson, and Ni Peimin), as "consideration" (Waley), as "mutuality in human relations" (Fingarette), and as "understanding" (Slingerland). I think D. C. Lau has the best grasp of the meaning and function of *shu* when he interprets it as the method of "using oneself as a measure in gauging the wishes of others" and thereby determining how to become consummatory in our conduct (*ren* 仁).[24] To use the term "method" rather than "methodology" is purposeful, resisting as it does the separation of the theoretical from the practical and ends from means. Ni Peimin

---

24. Wing-tsit Chan, *A Source Book in Chinese Philosophy* (Princeton, NJ: Princeton University Press, 1963), 44; Tu Wei-ming, *Centrality and Commonality: An Essay on Confucian Religiousness* (Albany: State University of New York Press, 1989), 34–36; Raymond Dawson, *Confucius* (New York: Hill and Wang, 1981), 41; Arthur Waley, *The Analects of Confucius* (London: George Allen and Unwin, 1938), 105; Herbert Fingarette, *Confucius: The Secular as Sacred* (New York: Harper and Row, 1972), 55; Edward Slingerland, trans., *Confucius: Analects with Selections from Traditional Commentaries* (Indianapolis: Hackett, 2003), 242; and D. C. Lau, *Confucius: The Analects* (*Lunyu*), Hong Kong: Chinese University of Hong Kong Press, 1992), xv–xvi.

insists that *shu* as a productive method must be distinguished from any simple application of rules:

> A method is different from a rule in that a method is *recommended* to *enable* a person to live better, whereas a rule is *imposed* on a person to *limit* what one can do.[25]

Shu 恕 requires imaginative analogical projection in the service of an inclusive moral generosity. Said simply, *shu* is a kind of deference. This understanding is borne out by the etymology of the graph, constituted by the cognate character, *ru* 如, that means "as to, like, as if, resembling, can be compared with, supposing, the same as" and *xin* 心, "heartminding." This character *ru* 如 occurs in the oracle bones as *[xxxiv]*, interpreted by commentators as one person inquiring of another.[26] Indeed, this notion of analogical deference is also suggested by the cognate character *ru* 汝 that means "you"—that is, taking the "other" into full account in what we do. Putting these ideas together, *shu* is activating the moral imagination of our thoughts and feelings necessary to conjure forth the best possibilities available and arrive at and act upon those moral judgments that register fully the needs and interests of everyone. That is, *shu* is consideration: a thoughtful and heartfelt deference to others in what we determine it is best to do.

There can be no question of the central importance this *shu* method of "putting yourself in the other's place" has in the Confucian moral vocabulary. When Confucius insists "his proper way" (*dao*)—his moral vision—is bound together with a single, continuous thread," one of his senior protégés, Master Zeng, explains to the other students what Confucius means by such a declaration: "The moral vision of the Master is nothing more than doing your utmost (*zhong* 忠) after having put yourself in the other's place (*shu* 恕)."[27] Lau makes the compelling argument that *zhong* and *shu* can be fairly described as "one" continuous thread because they are in fact two aspects integral to the same decision-making process. *Shu* is the imaginative reflection within a process of scenario rehearsal

---

25. Ni Peimin, *Understanding the* Analects *of Confucius: A New Translation of* Lunyu *with Annotations* (Albany: State University of New York Press, 2017), 67.

26. Kwan, "Database," 甲骨文合集 CHANT 0470.

27. *Analects* 4.15: 子曰:「參乎! 吾道一以貫之。」. . . 曾子曰:「夫子之道, 忠恕而已矣。」

whereby one tries to determine the best thing to do, and *zhong* is then the commitment to do one's best in accomplishing the best outcome of such a determination.[28]

On another occasion, Confucius again makes *shu* a primary strategy for determining conduct when he responds to Zigong's question: "Is there one term that can be acted upon until the end of one's days?" Confucius says categorically that "indeed, it is *shu*."[29] The process of *shu* begins from moral perplexity, requires a critical self-awareness and the imagination necessary for a creative search for the most appropriate response by rehearsing alternative scenarios and their outcomes, and then culminates in investing the assiduous effort necessary to realize what has been determined to be the best course of action. It is not surprising that *shu* in the classical texts and in the *Shuowen* lexicon is frequently associated with *ren* 仁 as the desired consequence of this method of deliberation; that is, *shu* is the method whereby one achieves what is consummate in one's roles and relations. Just as *shu* is a matter of reflectively coordinating one's own conduct with the behavior of others to optimum effect, *ren* is also the product of such analogical deliberation and growth. Importantly, *shu* as a method of deliberation and *ren* as consummate conduct are at once means and ends. One deliberates in order to be deliberate, and one aspires to act consummately in order to be consummate. We have seen this process captured in the *Analects* when it refers to this same *shu* method of deliberation only in a different language: "Correlating one's conduct with those near at hand can be said to be the way of becoming consummate in one's conduct (*ren*)."[30]

We can say that *shu* is the moral application of correlative or analogical thinking. The centrality given to *shu* respects the unparalleled importance that self-awareness and imagination play in correlating one's conduct with others and in refining our moral judgment through deliberation. Moral imagination is not invoked as supplemental, subsidiary, or remedial to a critical self-awareness but as necessary for the continuous education and refinement of our empathetic capacity for understanding and responding effectively to the interests of others. As in any aesthetic judgment, imagination is the motive effort to correlate each of the

---

28. See Lau, *Confucius*, 16.
29. *Analects* 15.24: 子貢問曰:「有一言而可以終身行之者乎?」子曰:「其恕乎! 己所不欲, 勿施於人。」Compare *Analects* 5.12 and 12.2.
30. *Analects* 6.30: 能近取譬, 可謂仁之方也已。

specific details within the entire picture of what is occurring, and in so doing, to broaden the context of moral consideration and the quality of one's response.

Shu is a fundamentally aesthetic disposition initially shaped within family bonds where one's "person" emerges in the process of striving to optimize the concrete roles and relations one lives. *Shu* is this grandson responding to this grandmother, taking her both as an object of his deference and as a resource for his own personal growth in his relations to others. In the fullness of time, *shu* is then extended as a quality of responsiveness in shaping and deepening relations outside of the home. "Putting yourself in the other's place" (*shu*) is thus an omnipresent and indispensable disposition for living life deliberately and responsively. It requires a critical self-awareness, a keen memory that recalls analogous situations, a creative imagination that can provide a serial rehearsal of possible scenarios in anticipation of their consequences, an empathetic understanding of the other, a penetrating intelligence that can discern the best course forward, and an assiduous resolve that is able to make the most of felicitous correlations.

And *shu* contrasts sharply with the assumption that more abstract and calculative analytic or theoretical strategies are sufficient in themselves for determining moral conduct. Understood as "putting yourself in the other's place," it is the most fundamental gesture of a concrete, contextualizing moral disposition. It entails a recognition of the importance of "deference" both in the sense of fully considering the interests of others and in the sense of deferring action until we can overcome uncertainty through sound deliberation in our moral inquiry. There is certainly a significant role for cognition and deliberation in *shu*, but we do not want to overly rationalize this process. *Shu* requires a holistic responsiveness. With *shu* there is perhaps an even more central role for affective inquiry to complement the cognitive in an epistemology of feeling that weighs up the circumstances with full empathy and concern. Just as a critical skepticism can become a matter of intelligent habit, so too an empathetic responsiveness to others results in a routinized disposition for compassionate concern. In fact, the evolution of a *shu* habitude lies in its growth from what is at first a more deliberative exercise to become a kind of extemporaneous, unselfconscious moral artistry in one's interpersonal activities. As Ni Peimin argues, such refinement in one's dispositions is not only morally empowering but liberating by expanding one's range of options for intervention:

Once a person becomes a master artist, he or she would be able to use discretion and respond appropriately even when the situation demands deviation from well-established protocols.[31]

There is a further point with regard to deference that can be inferred from the *Analects*, where *shu* as "putting yourself in the other's place" is given an alternative characterization. *Shu* in this text is also defined negatively as "do not impose on others what you yourself do not want."

This "negative" version of the Golden Rule is negative because it does not begin from the assumption that there is some objective and universal standard that can serve as warrant for "doing unto others as you would have them do to you." Indeed, to begin from the presumption that there is such a standard and that one has privileged access to it—and furthermore on that basis to assume one knows the right thing to do to someone else—is at least condescending if not disrespectful. Instead, by assuming the negative version of the Golden Rule, the task remains open and provisional, allowing that deliberation on how to best grow the relationship with this person can only be pursued through a careful consideration of the needs of this specific person within the possibilities of these specific circumstances.

In using the critically reflective and reflexive process of scenario rehearsal as the basis for determining what would be the best course of action, an obvious principle of exclusion is to avoid doing to others what we ourselves do not like. In our reflections on what is best to do, doing to someone else what we ourselves do not want done to us would at the very least contaminate our motives. Indeed, the starting point for "putting yourself in the other's place" is the awareness that there are indeed other places. A good beginning in the inquiry, then, would be to discount those actions that we find undesirable. But more important, beyond this rather obvious beginning, we must be fully cognizant that there is a world of contingencies that require thoughtful and imaginative exploration.

Previously we had recourse to rehearse Amartya Sen's capabilities approach to developmental theory, a method that resonates in degree with *shu*. The capabilities approach is Sen's attempt to go beyond calculations based on some abstract notion of generic individuals by considering what specific individuals under specific conditions want to do and what they are actually able to do. Impatient with the minimalist standards provided

---

31. Ni, *Understanding the* Analects, 67. Ni refers the reader to *Analects* 9.30.

by principled and rule-based moralities, Sen is also keen to respect the concrete, the processual, and the optimal range of differing needs and values that together make up richly different visions of the good life.

If we return to the examples of the upper-class woman in traditional Chinese or Victorian society, we can as a generalization from our own historical moment certainly critique these visions of the moral life as being limiting and oppressive for women. But lest we get too smug in our efforts toward a more enlightened alternative, we should perhaps remain aware that a hundred years hence, in reflecting back on the configuration of gender relations in our own time, our progeny will be wondering what we were thinking. Nietzsche famously decries the arrogance of the "modern man" who out of self-interest is given to naturalizing existing conditions to constitute what then becomes a lacerating herd morality intolerant of deviations or differences. For Nietzsche, it was this same modern man who was mad enough to advocate for the unnatural Christian values that he himself despises and to then take these same values to be the end of history.[32]

Indeed, the more we insist on essential standards of adjudication, the less likely we will be aware of their limits and their need to change. That is, there seems to be an inverse ratio between the weight we might invest in erstwhile antecedent and complete principles we can base our judgments on and the extent to which we must necessarily concern ourselves not only about the tyranny of the majority but also about the ineluctable evolution in any table of values. We might begin prospectively from an appreciation of differences that obtain among persons themselves as they shape and are being shaped in a radically changing world. Such evolving differences require a necessary porousness in any organizing categories we might impose upon them, be they biological, social, ethical, or political. This being the case, should we uncritically embrace the assumption that some final and complete articulation of human morality is either a welcome or a necessary possibility? From the perspective of an always evolving Confucian role ethics, a basic assumption would be that what seems desirable today is likely to be oppressive tomorrow if it does not change.

---

32. Friedrich Nietzsche, *The Gay Science*, trans. Walter Kaufmann (New York: Random House, 1991).

John Dewey and the "Idea" of Democracy

What these reflections on holism and contextualism mean for the project of theorizing the conception of persons for Confucian role ethics—of human becomings—is that particular persons can only be understood by virtue of their place and function within the process of experience as a whole. We have seen that the narrative, focus-field conception of persons begins from the fact of associated living: in other words, from the fact that we as persons are irreducibly social and that we shape and are shaped by the transactions that constitute the roles and relations that define our lives. And normativity in these same roles arises from becoming a good daughter and a good neighbor—that is, an achieved efficacy in the cultivation of these discursive roles within the context of family and community.

We now turn to the various arguments made in the works of John Dewey, A. N. Whitehead, and Tang Junyi that would not only confirm the premise of the associated nature of human experience but also from their different perspectives would stipulate the ideal social and political conditions conducive to such personal cultivation. Indeed, these three contemporary philosophers offer us a cosmologically justified vision of how this very fact of association can be transformed into the flourishing community as the highest expression of our mutuality and interdependence. Each of them in their own language argues that what they are calling "democracy" is not one political form among many but is in fact precisely the never-to-be realized ideal of associated living. An excursus here into this cosmological understanding of democracy as a social, political, and ultimately religious ideal provides one more perspective on how to theorize the Confucian conception of persons for Confucian role ethics and its goal of optimizing the human experience.

In his own time, Dewey invoked a cosmological understanding of the "idea" of democracy to use as a touchstone to resist what he perceived to be an unfortunate tendency in the evolution of the American liberal democracy to drift away from the secure moorings of its defining premises; this drift has become increasingly pronounced since Dewey's death. To this end, Dewey introduces an important distinction between the "idea" (and sometimes "ideal") of democracy and democracy as a political form. In *The Public and Its Problems*, Dewey is holistic in looking for the real substance of democracy in the informal, the concrete, and the everyday—that is, in the lives and relationships of particular people in their own particular communities. He defines "the democratic idea in its generic social sense" in the following specific terms:

> From the standpoint of the individual, it consists in having a responsible share according to capacity in forming and directing the activities of the groups to which one belongs and in participating according to need in the values which the groups sustain. From the standpoint of the groups, it demands liberation of the potentialities of members of a group in harmony with the interests and goods which are common.[33]

We must be careful because a misunderstanding of Dewey's language here (and it frequently has been misunderstood) could undermine his deeper meanings. For Dewey, the "individual" and the "group" referenced here are neither separate nor separable entities. On the contrary, given Dewey's commitment to the wholeness of experience as the starting point of all reflection, lives lived together have priority over discrete individuals, and concrete situations have priority over the abstraction of single agency. As we have seen, friendships in which we are embedded are the first-order reality; the friends within these relations, when lifted out of their relations as discrete individuals, are only second-order abstractions from the concrete friendship. The real "individuality" of these friends—the term that Dewey coins to establish a distinction between discrete, independent "individuals" and unique, relationally constituted persons—is constituted by their relational habitudes. Said another way, individuals and groups are to be understood holographically as focus and field rather than as part and whole, wherein the totality is implicated within each particular, and each particular construes the totality from its own perspective. Each person is a particular configuration of social relations, and each group or community is an ecology constituted by uniquely particular participants.

But how extreme is Dewey in advancing this fundamentally social construction of the person? As we have seen with Dewey's notion of emergent "individuality," to say that persons are irreducibly social is not to deny the integrity, uniqueness, and diversity of human beings; on the contrary, it is precisely to affirm and endorse these conditions as the achievements that determine them as particular persons. They are not

---

33. Dewey, *Later Works*, 2:327.

"autonomous" in the sense of being discrete, self-legislating individuals. Rather, they are unique persons constituted by their own inimitable field of relations—someone's spouse and someone else's friend, someone's teacher and someone else's colleague—who, to the extent that these relations are not compromised by coercion, have a relational autonomy.

Dewey's insight is simple: association is a fact. We do not come into relationships but begin from being radically situated in and constituted by our relations. For Dewey, the "idea" of democracy, therefore, is a social, political, and religious ideal in the sense of providing the conditions for taking full advantage of the opportunity that human life provides us. The "idea" of democracy is the cosmological answer to the following questions: How do we grow initially inchoate, constitutive relations of persons-in-community to make them optimally productive? And in growing such relations, how can we optimize the possibilities of the human experience? The idea of democracy is thus both aesthetic and normative. It is the aesthetic of optimizing the creative possibilities of the communicating community and thus getting the most value and meaning out of the human experience. And it is normative in providing a concrete strategy for cultivating our interpersonal relations and maximizing their growth. For Dewey, the "doings and undergoings" of each and every person in this "Great Community" is the source and substance of real democracy—the optimal and virtuosic relationality of focal, holographic "individuals" as each of us uniquely and cooperatively shapes and is shaped by the emerging and shared communities to which we belong.

There is for Dewey a logic here. It begins from the observation that we are constituted by our relations, and so it follows that if our neighbors do better, we do better. Positively stated, the idea of democracy is a strategy for getting the most out of the relations that constitute a community; negatively stated, it is a clear acknowledgment that any coercion in these roles and relationships is a diminution in the creative possibilities of the community. To be clear, Dewey's "idea" of democracy is not one possible option for associated living that exists among other alternatives, nor is it simply one political system among many. It is rather the necessary but always less than successful aspiration after the completed or perfected ideal of consummate relatedness. As Dewey insists, the "idea" of democracy is nothing less than "the idea of community life itself."[34]

---

34. Dewey, *Later Works*, 2:328.

On Dewey's understanding, the "idea" of democracy begins from an acknowledgment of the uniqueness of each person and each situation and requires accordingly that any political form be open to the requisite reformulation and adjustment that must accommodate the continuing emergence of personal differences. Such an understanding of democracy acknowledges an Apollonian and Dionysian tension between form and the vital fluidity of life itself. Political form is after all by its very nature conservative, and its "re-form" must wait upon the living and liberating "idea" of democracy to serve it as the antidote to all entrenched formal structures as it circulates through the institutions of the thriving community.

The familiar institutionalized "forms" of democracy—a constitution, the office of president, the polling station, the ballot box, and so on—cannot guarantee political flourishing. If left unreformed by frequent appeal to the "idea" of democracy, these forms can, on the contrary, become a source of oppression, violence, and coercion. Witness the constitution of the former Soviet Union or the Jim Crow laws of the American South as formal iterations of democracy that had little to do with the animating "idea" of democracy. Formal institutions, while certainly necessary, are often historical carryovers from dynastic forms of government endorsed by traditions that had not only failed to embody the "idea" of democracy in their own hour but in their inertia risk the danger of over time retarding if not threatening the fluid "idea" of democracy itself.

A constitution, for example, in a revolutionary America two hundred years ago might quite reasonably guarantee the right of individuals to bear arms as members of a "well-regulated militia"—a musket over the fireplace is perhaps necessary to defend a now free state were the British overlords to return. But an argument can be made that this now formally ensconced and yet anachronistic right, unreformed and thus not "well-regulated," has become a source of mindless aggression in our very different contemporary setting. Far from serving the "idea" of democracy, the Second Amendment has become institutionalized to enable an invincibly entrenched and frightening culture of antisocial violence. This erstwhile right marks America as by far the most violent society among the developed nations and to some degree encourages a callousness that compromises our community's ability to flourish. It is often said that the cure for the ills of democracy is more democracy. Dewey would agree. But he would refine this claim by insisting that "more democracy" can only be achieved by a democratic society constantly returning to the "idea" of democracy to challenge and restructure its recalcitrant political forms.

Whitehead and the Cosmological Ground of Democracy

If we need further corroboration for the intimate relationship between what Dewey has identified as the "idea" of democracy and its cosmological justification, Whitehead in his own theoretical language (but similar to Dewey in spirit) describes the cosmological "ideal" of democracy as an aesthetic and moral achievement that enables us to optimize the creative possibilities of the human condition. Whitehead observes that

> the basis of democracy is the common fact of value experience, as constituting the essential nature of each pulsation of actuality. Everything has some value for itself, for others, and for the whole. This characterizes the meaning of actuality. By reason of this character, constituting reality, the conception of morals arises . . . Existence, in its own nature, is the upholding of value intensity. Also no unit can separate itself from the others, and from the whole. And yet each unit exists in its own right. It upholds value intensity for itself, and this involves sharing value intensity with the universe. Everything that in any sense exists has two sides, namely, its individual self and its signification in the universe. Also either of these aspects is a factor in the other.[35]

Translating this philosophically abstract description into concrete communal terms, Whitehead is asserting that unique persons certainly have their own integrity, but it is an integrity that has its moral meaning and aesthetic value not exclusive of their relations but only by virtue of what these same persons as constituted by these relations mean for each other and for the community as a whole.

In *Process and Reality*, Whitehead allows that his "philosophy of organism seems to approximate more to some strains of . . . Chinese

---

35. Whitehead, *Modes of Thought*, 111.

thought."³⁶ This is certainly the case here, where Whitehead, using his own terminology, offers us an alternative vocabulary resonating rather closely with the language I have appealed to in expressing the cosmology that serves as the interpretive context for the growth of Confucian persons. What Whitehead calls the "two sides" of everything—the "individual self" and "signification for the universe"—is what I have referred to as the focus-field, holographic nature of things, including persons, of course. And with these two "aspects" of any particular thing, it means that the totality is implicated in each particular—*dao* 道 as field is implicated in each insistent particular focus as *de* 德. The language that is used to describe such a cosmos is "aspectual" rather than analytical in referencing as it does different perspectives on the same phenomenon rather than separate elements within it. Persons and communities, for example, far from standing opposed to each other, are two ways of entertaining the same event as configurations of relations that either foreground the focal person or foreground the communal field, each with their respective points of view. As with Dewey, Whitehead is interpreting democracy here as a religious ideal where each person has their own unique integrity; at the same time, he makes this same "value intensity" available to the cosmos as a source of shared, diversified meaning. This sense of personal contribution, felt worth, and the profound sense of belonging that follows from it, is precisely religiousness as *religare* and the "binding tightly" it implies, when Whitehead proclaims:

> This doctrine is the direct negation of the theory that religion is primarily a social fact. . . . Religion is what the individual does with his own solitariness. . . . and if you are never solitary, you are never religious. Collective enthusiasms, revivals, institutions, churches, rituals, bibles, codes of behaviour, are the trappings of religion, its passing forms. . . . Accordingly, what should emerge from religion is individual worth of character.³⁷

Whitehead's language of "solitariness" is often misunderstood. In suggesting that real religiousness is each of us making the most of who we can become, he is echoing Dewey's distinction between the "idea"

---

36. Whitehead, *Process and Reality*, 7.
37. A. N. Whitehead, *Religion in the Making* (New York: Fordham University Press, 1996), 16–17.

of democracy and its political forms and between an achieved, unique "individuality" and the deracinated, discrete individual.

Tang Junyi's "Idea" of Confucianism as Optimizing the Human Experience

Tang Junyi, like Dewey and Whitehead, provides us with a cosmological understanding of what we might call the "idea" of Confucianism that resonates closely with the "idea" of democracy as it has been previously discussed. Tang's elaboration on this "idea" enables us to identify the Confucian core values that would provide the optimal conditions for personal realization. Tang also takes this holographic, interdependent, and productive relationship between "particular" and "totality"—a relationship perhaps better described as "focus" and "field," or ecologically situated "events" and their "environments"—as *the* distinguishing feature and most crucial contribution of Chinese culture broadly. Tang sees in this relationship

> the spirit of symbiosis and mutuality of particular and totality. From the perspective of coming to know something, this means an unwillingness to isolate the particular from the totality (this is most evident in the cosmology of the Chinese people), and from the perspective of ties of feeling and affection, it means the commitment of the particular to do its best to realize the totality (this is most evident in the attitude of the Chinese people toward daily life).[38]

While Tang is rather abstract in this observation, we can make it more concrete by identifying this mutuality and interdependence of particulars and totality that grounds Chinese cosmology with the key role that

---

38. Tang Junyi, *Complete Works*, 1:8: . . . 將部分與全體交融互攝 之精神; 自認識上言之, 即不自全體中劃出部分之精神 (此自中國人之宇宙觀中最可見之); 自情意上言之, 即努力以部分實現全體之精神 (此自中國人之人生態度中可見之)。This focus-field rather than part-whole language is an expression of the correlativity ubiquitous in Chinese cosmology. This correlativity, in some of its most abstract and ancient iterations, is captured in the expressions: "the inseparability of one and many" (*yiduobufen* 一多不分) within "this focus and its field" (*daode* 道德), "changing and persisting" (*biantong* 變通), and "reforming and functioning" (*tiyong* 體用) cosmology.

personal cultivation must have in the flourishing of the cosmos. What Tang is offering us here is nothing other than a summary statement of the focus-field holography outlined in the *Expansive Learning* and a reiteration of the central theme of *Focusing the Familiar* explored in some detail previously: the capacity and the responsibility that always unique human beings have to be cocreators for a flourishing cosmos. In the symbiotic relationship between cultivated persons and a flourishing cosmos, this "spirit" of Confucian culture becomes the perceived value of inclusive, consensual, and optimally productive cooperation in our families and in our social and political institutions. The cultivation of personal worth is the source of human culture, and it is this human culture in turn that as a compounding cosmic resource provides the most felicitous context for personal cultivation. Through patterns of deference to our environing others, the creative possibilities for our narrative transactions and the resources we can draw upon for our own self-reconstrual are proportionately magnified and extended.

Tang Junyi, with his own critical assessment of the strengths and weaknesses of Confucianism, repeatedly insists that any historical connection Confucianism has had with the failed political forms of feudalism, monarchism, and patriarchalism is accidental and transient rather than essential. For Tang, what might be called the persistent "idea" of Confucianism is not to be recovered from some potted ideology, or some set of hoary imperial institutions, or from access to some privileged religious revelation. In taking the holographic, interdependent, and productive dynamic between "part" and "whole" as *the* distinguishing feature and most distinctive contribution of Confucian culture broadly, Tang is relying heavily upon the cosmology of the *Yijing* 易經 or *Book of Changes* and the possibilities of the human experience together in his description of the underlying transactional dynamics of Chinese culture. And I suggest that it is this cosmological "idea" of Confucianism rather than any of the superficial liberal claims about egalitarianism that Tang would deem immediately relevant to the path that its own process of democratization must follow to be true to its Confucian premises.

To recover fully what Tang Junyi takes to be the realization of the Confucian ideal, we must square Confucianism's social and political philosophy with what he understands to be these cosmological assumptions that ground traditional Chinese culture. When this holographic interpenetration and symbiosis of particulars and totality is translated into the more concrete social and political arena of the human community, it becomes the value of inclusive, consensual, and optimally productive cooperation among persons to optimize their then shared vision of the good—a social and political aspiration that we can associate immediately with the definitions of real democracy that have been articulated by Dewey and Whitehead.

The "Idea" of Confucianism and the Quest for Its Regulative "Forms"

With Tang Junyi's "idea" of Confucianism and its "focus-field" or "narrative" conception of human "becomings" in hand, we can now turn to the following question: what is the Confucian regulative "idea"—what Charles Taylor calls the "hypergoods"—that would guide our conduct and anticipate the realization of the distinctively human possibility of superlative harmony? Given the primacy of an unbounded, vital relationality, the emergent identity of always unique persons is going to be a function of what they mean for the full, unbounded complement of all other things that give them context. As we have seen, the "one" and the "many"—the one, boundless *dao* as the continuous yet unsummed totality of all of the contents of our experience, and the many of the myriad of unique things or events that in their totality constitute it—are simply two "aspectual" ways of parsing the same experience.

It is in this sense, as a corollary to the primacy of vital relationality, that this early Chinese cosmology—which serves as the evolving interpretive context for the Confucian tradition—is an aestheticism in which each person is a specific focus within which the unbounded field of experience is implicated. What in Whiteheadian terms makes this Confucian cosmology an aesthetic order rather than reductionistic rational order is that it is holistic, unbounded, inclusive, and resolutely anarchic.[39] This is but to say that in the patterned order of the cosmos, one in which no single privileged order predominates, all things not only have their own unique role in aspiring to make the most of themselves; but by participating fully in this process of identity formation itself, they become collaborators in the production of the contrapuntal harmony of the social, natural, and cosmic orders.

---

39. For the distinction between an aesthetic and logical or rational order, see Whitehead, *Modes of Thought*, 58–63.

Tang Junyi has provided us with a cosmological understanding of the "idea" or "ideal" of Confucianism that might enable us to anticipate the trajectory of the continuing process of what will be a distinctively "Confucian" version of democratization. In the human world, this cosmology is captured in the way in which an achieved propriety in our roles and relations (*li* 禮) brings full resolution to and thus aestheticizes the human experience. Given the relational, focus-field nature of persons, it is the Confucian formula of everyone-in-community aspiring to achieve this optimal propriety in their roles and relations that resonates immediately with Dewey and Whitehead's assumptions about the grounding premises of real democracy. For both Dewey and Whitehead, as we have seen, democracy is nothing less than a social, political, and ultimately cosmological mode of association that enables each unique person to get the most out of the human experience and that allows the community and cosmos to take full advantage of the optimal contributions of its many.

Just as Dewey's "idea" of democracy is his vision of the flourishing communal life made possible by optimizing the "individuality" of the uniquely distinguished persons that constitute it, Tang Junyi's Confucianism is also directed at achieving the highest integrated cultural, moral, and spiritual growth for individuals-in-family-and-community. What makes the distinctively Confucian "values" ideal is that each one of them—"family reverence" (*xiao* 孝), "fraternal deference" (*ti* 悌), "aspiring to propriety in one's roles and relations" (*li* 禮) "personal cultivation and consummation in one's roles and relations" (*ren* 仁), "waymaking" (*dao* 道) by means of "virtuosic habits of conduct" (*de* 德), and so on—functions within this aestheticism to optimize the creative possibilities that are available in the evolving culture.

Where the Confucian ideal clearly differs from Dewey and Whitehead, and it is a profoundly significant difference, is in the central role it assigns to the institution of family as the entry point for pursuing this aspiration for human flourishing. This is no small matter, particularly for Dewey. For Dewey to ignore the family as what is most "familiar" (both terms having the same root L. *familia*) would seem to vitiate his own insistence that philosophy must be immediately empirical. Again, Dewey's "reconstruction in philosophy" is an exhortation to philosophers to give up the technical problems unique to their professional discipline in order to address the pressing issues of the day, issues that for most people necessarily begin from family life.

For Tang Junyi, Chinese culture begins from and always returns to the everyday lives of the people and the natural patterns of deference that give cadence to family living. The natural deference that pervades family life is certainly the entry point for developing moral artistry.[40] The meaning and value produced by family relations lived properly is not simply the primary ground for social and political order; full participation in *li* has cosmological and religious implications as well. Family bonds properly nurtured are the point of departure for understanding we have a moral responsibility for cultivating the expanding web of relations that reach far beyond our own localized selves.[41] The institution of family is for each of us the center of cosmic order. As we see in the *Expansive Learning*, all symbiotic order ripples out in concentric circles from personal cultivation in family and community, only to return reflexively as a cosmic surge that comes back to nourish this primary source. In *Focusing the Familiar* we are told explicitly that family feeling is the source of the civility fostered by our ritualized roles and institutions:

> Aspiring to act consummately in your roles and relations (*ren* 仁) is becoming a person (*ren* 人); and loving your family is what is of greatest consequence. Optimal appropriateness (*yi* 義) means doing what is most fitting (*yi* 宜), wherein esteeming those of superior character is most important.[42] The degree of devotion due different kin and the degree of esteem accorded those who are different in the quality of their conduct is what gives rise to the observance of ritual propriety (*li* 禮).[43]

By contrast, within the broad sweep of Western philosophy and culture, "family" as an institution has not served as a significant inspiration for social and political order. We would be hard-pressed to find any family-centered philosophical notion comparable to the vital importance

---

40. Tang Junyi, *Complete Works*, 4:219–302.
41. Tang Junyi, *Complete Works*, 4:210–15.
42. *Zhongyong* 20: 仁者人也, 親親為大; 義者宜也, 尊賢為大. Note the paronomastic nature of the definitions for *ren* and *yi* here, that is, definition by semantic and phonetic association.
43. *Zhongyong* 20: 仁者人也, 親親為大; 義者宜也, 尊賢為大. 親親之殺, 尊賢之等, 禮所生也.

that "familial reverence" (*xiao* 孝) has had for Confucian philosophy as its prime moral imperative. If we rehearse the contributions of the mainstream philosophers within the Western narrative, few indeed invoke family as a productive model for organizing the human experience. Plato's abolition of the guardian family in the *Republic* and Aristotle's denigration of the private "household" (*oikos*) as a source of "privation" are fairly representative. Even Dewey, who would allow that democracy "accords with the historic spirit of the Chinese race," is true to the mainstream of his own tradition when it comes to the institution of family, not only ignoring it as a model of organization but going on to question its value.[44] On the one hand, Dewey does seem to be keenly aware of the organic and irreducibly relational nature of the family and that the meaning of its members arises out of their mutual associations:

> The family . . . is something other than one person, plus another, plus another. It is an enduring form of association in which the members of the group stand from the beginning in relations to one another, and in which each member gets direction for his conduct by thinking of the whole group and his place in it, rather than by an adjustment of egoism and altruism.[45]

Even so, Dewey perhaps with additional encouragement from the May Fourth reformers of his time, avers that China's historical investment in the family as the central institution appealed to in structuring the human experience will have to be abandoned as a precondition for its modernization and democratization:

> The notion that, by the mere introduction of western economy, China can be "saved," while it retains the old morality, the old set of ideas, the old Confucianism—or what genuine Confucianism had been petrified into—and the old family system, is the most utopian of sentimental idealisms. Economic and financial reform, unless it is accompanied by the growth of new ideals of culture, ethics and family life (which constitute the real meaning of the so-called student movement of

---

44. Dewey, *Middle Works*, 11:197.
45. Dewey, *Later Works*, 7:299.

today), will merely shift the sore spots. It will remedy some evils and create others.[46]

Within the Western narrative, going back to Plato, objectivity has always served as a pervasive value among those philosophers who would look to shared moral reasoning and categorical imperatives as the ultimate source of moral order. It might be that in this Western tradition, the sustained lack of interest in the always partial relations that emerge from family feeling is due to the almost uncritical importance invested in objectivity and impartiality as a necessary condition for ethical conduct. Such reticence to see family as a model, measure, or precondition for social and political order among our best thinkers contrasts starkly with the Confucian worldview in which family is *the* governing metaphor and in which *all* relationships are ultimately perceived as familial. We can fairly claim that the signature of the Confucian tradition has been that human morality is an expression of immediate family feeling and an extension of these same feelings to the world more broadly.

But not all contemporary Confucian philosophers, perhaps heavily influenced by liberal values, agree with this traditional commitment. Huang Yushun is not atypical of contemporary Chinese scholars who express real reservations about the centrality of the model of family and family roles in Confucian ethics. Huang would argue that

> while in recent years, many Confucians put special emphasis on family to the extent that they take family to be the special feature of Confucianism and the signature of Chinese culture, this is not necessarily so.[47]

For Huang, family and the roles that define it are variables that have continued to evolve across history. For him, we have to look elsewhere for the grounding values of Confucian morality:

> Family is a concept that has changed with history. We had a clan-based family in the antique times of regency, a family-lineage family in ancient and the more recent imperial times,

---

46. Dewey, *Middle Works*, 13:103 and 230.
47. Huang Yushun 黄玉顺, 角色意识 [Role consciousness], 8: 近年来，有不少儒者特别强调家庭，甚至认为家庭伦理才是儒学的特色、中国文化的特征。其实未必如此。

and a nuclear conception of family in modern times, as well as complex family models such as single parent families and legalized same-sex families. These different models of families in different times had different family ethics, different codes of propriety, different arrangements of hierarchies, and different fixed roles. For this reason, the root question of Confucianism does not lie with roles. Roles are stipulated according to propriety and status, and propriety and status are determined by the standards of consummate conduct (*ren*) and optimal appropriateness (*yi*). This is the kind of role awareness we should bear in mind today.[48]

I would argue contra Huang that the underlying wisdom in this Confucian tradition is its appeal to the model of the family. If superlative harmony and an optimizing symbiosis is in fact the goal of the human experience, then family is the single human institution to which persons are most inclined to fully commit themselves. While Dewey and Whitehead demand this same optimizing of human resources from their cosmological understanding of "democracy" as a social, political, and religious ideal, Confucianism would assert that the institution of family must serve as the necessary ground of such a "democracy" if it is to be deployed in this Deweyan and Whiteheadian sense. To transform the world into a family, according to this Confucian sensibility, is to promote the model that will best accomplish the goal of getting the most out of each of our narratives as human "becomings." With "family reverence" (*xiao*) as the governing moral imperative, the values of "consummate conduct" (*ren*) and "optimal appropriateness" (*yi*) that Huang Yushun takes as more basic than family, are in fact themselves rooted in family as this most basic of human institutions. At the very beginning of the *Analects* we read the following:

---

48. Huang Yushun 黃玉順, 角色意識 [Role consciousness], 8: 家庭本身就是一個歷史地變動的概念；我們曾經有上古王權時代的宗族家庭；曾經有中古皇權時代的家族家庭；還有現代的核心家庭，以及諸如合法的單親家庭、乃至合法的同性戀家庭等複雜的家庭形式。這些不同時代的家庭形式具有不同的家庭倫理，不同的「禮」的制度、不同的「位」的安排、不同的「角色」定位。就此而論，「角色」問題並非儒學的根本所在；角色是由「禮」、「位」規定的，而「禮」、「位」又是由「仁」、「義」導出的。這是我們今天所應具有的一種「角色」意識。

It is a rare thing for someone who has a sense of family reverence and fraternal deference (*xiaoti* 孝弟) to have a taste for defying authority. And it is unheard of for those who have no taste for defying authority to be keen on initiating rebellion. Exemplary persons concentrate their efforts on the root, for the root having been properly set, the way will grow therefrom. As for family reverence and fraternal deference, they are I suspect, the root of consummate conduct (*ren* 仁).[49]

As Huang reports, there is no question that the institution of family has changed over time, and the challenge of liberal values has certainly reconfigured old ways of thinking about life within the extended family. We must allow that in their modern guise, family and family feeling have to a degree been redistributed to fund surrogate relationships. However, the distinctively Chinese phenomenon of the annual Spring Festival migration and the profoundly religious nature of returning home to renew family and communal bonds suggest that the cultural impulse of family feeling continues unabated.

We certainly must agree with Huang Yushun and the earlier May Fourth reformers as well that the Confucian appeal to family as its organizing metaphor for the human experience has not been altogether benign. While it can be fairly argued that such an appeal is the most profound insight of this Confucian tradition for rethinking the ground of real democracy, the manipulation of the intimate kinds of relations we associate with family have, in our time, also been the source of an endemic culture of corruption that continues to be China's main obstacle along the road to democratization.

For Dewey, we have seen that in his time the primary problem he addresses by invoking the "idea" of democracy is his attempt to overcome the entrenched inertia of political "form," which if left unreformed will stifle the life of a truly democratic community. If the goal to be realized for contemporary China is a Confucian democracy, the problem the "idea" of Confucianism faces is precisely the opposite from that of its Western counterpart. That is, with so much investment in informal, intimate familial relationships, the Confucian tradition has been slow to produce the formal, more "objective" institutions and regulations necessary to

---

49. *Analects* 1.2: 有子曰: 其為人也孝弟, 而好犯上者, 鮮矣; 不好犯上, 而好作亂者, 未之有也。君子務本, 本立而道生。孝弟也者, 其為仁之本與。

sustain its own Confucian version of "democracy." To the extent that it has produced these regulatory structures, these same formal institutions are often compromised and eroded by an excess of attention paid to personal as opposed to civic relationships. Indeed, as its own Confucian "forms" of democracy continue to emerge in China, we are bearing witness to the fact that the cure for the ills of a Confucian democracy is the establishment of those formal civic institutions of democracy that preclude corruption and the transparent and effective appeal to rule of law that will contain the excesses of intimate family feelings.

The kind of governance most appropriate to the rapidly ascending China is one that will embody the persistent and distinctive values of its own antique tradition. It is one that must acknowledge the holistic, ecological nature of the human experience, the *yinyang* interdependence of all things within their environing contexts, and the always provisional, emergent nature of natural, social, political, and cosmic order without any anticipated fixity or finality. Such governance will have to give high valorization to integration and inclusiveness and to aspire to maximize difference within an achieved harmony and shared diversity. These values being fundamentally holistic, China will need to achieve and sustain a proper balance between the formal rigors needed for structure and refinement and the continuing respect for the informal particularities that are essential for any real human flourishing.

Chapter Seven

From Human *"Becomings"* to a Process Cosmology

Interpretive Assumptions

I began my monograph *Confucian Role Ethics* by arguing that we must allow this Confucian tradition to have its own voice and to speak on its own terms; hence, the importance of the subtitle of this book, *A Vocabulary*—that is, Confucianism's own vocabulary. My objective was to respect the linguistic and historical conditions under which Confucian ethics has evolved and let a respect for context serve as the basis for my best interpretative efforts. My strategy was to try to excavate the assumptions that are distinctive to early Chinese cosmology and then attempt to formulate the Confucian moral vision as it evolved within this always changing yet persistent worldview. But such an approach that begins from cosmological assumptions and then locates the human experience within them might in fact reverse the way in which our human cosmologies are usually developed and expressed. That is, human beings do not first grasp the principles underlying cosmic order and then seek to discipline our human experience by adopting these regularities. Rather, it would seem that the cosmological assumptions distinctive to any tradition are importantly a projection onto the world from our most fundamental life conditions: birth and death, love and strife, crime and punishment, toolmaking and applications, music and art, and so on.

In China, the patterns of correlative thinking that date back at least to the Shang dynasty reveal a modality of thinking with its own dyadic associations, novel metaphors, suggestive images, and evocative iconography that structures the ordinary affairs of the day. In the *Book of Changes*, it rehearses the history of how human technologies such as housing, farming, transportation, and writing were derived from the inspiration human sages took from the most basic environmental operations captured in the images (*xiang* 象) and systematized in the hexagrams (*gua* 卦). It would seem that human values, at once generic and unique, have over time been correlated with the rhythms of the natural environment to constitute the assumed ordering structure of the cosmos.

The satirist Xenophanes, impatient with the Olympian pantheon of anthropomorphic gods, famously observed that Ethiopians see their gods as black and snub nosed and that Thracians envision blue-eyed and red-haired gods. Xenophanes then extended this same thought to how oxen, horses, and lions would likely conceive of their deities, with the idea that we make gods in our image.[1] The point is that a worldview and its common sense is negotiated over time by coordinating the particular values and metaphors that inform the everyday experience of a particular population and the world that gives this experience its context.

In this final chapter, then, having attempted to bring some clarity to the focus-field narrative conception of human becomings from which the Confucian project begins, I now turn to the task of trying to articulate more fully the process cosmology that has evolved in its relation to the assumptions about persons and the human experience and has served as the interpretive context for reading canonical texts and their commentaries. Fortunately, there is a lineage of earlier philosophers of culture who have recognized the necessity of excavating these uncommon assumptions in their best efforts to give this tradition its differences. My contribution, then, will be to try to say again what these precursors have already said in a way made clearer by having taken the Confucian focus-field conception of persons as a good starting point: as the source of our cosmic speculations. Remembering Xenophanes and his claim that we are wont to analogize our gods from our own personal experience, the question we must address here is what then does the "cosmos" of Confucian focus-field persons look like, and what is the language we need to give it expression?

Important scholarship has been undertaken over recent decades that rehearses the evolution of various correlative cosmological schemes

---

1. Xenophanes, Fragments B15 and B16.

in China between the fall of the Western Zhou in ca. 770 BCE and the emergence of a systematic cosmology in the third century BCE. A survey of the more important contributions that tells the story of this development in both Chinese and Western scholarship is available in Wang Aihe's *Cosmology and Political Culture in Early China*. In particular, Wang emphasizes the symbiotic relationship between changes in the political order of the day and the evolving cosmological sensibilities, as well as changes in the relationship between the human world and the perceived cosmic regularities. With respect to this emerging cosmology, Nathan Sivin has observed that "man's prodigious creativity seems to be based on the permutations and recastings of a rather small stock of ideas."[2] I will argue that the correlative thinking first described by Marcel Granet as "la pensée chinoise" or "Chinese thinking" seems to belong to this small but fertile inventory and that it has had a long history in shaping the contours of the Chinese cultural tradition, paralleling in some ways the defining force of metaphysical realism in molding the categories and the grammar of the Western philosophical narrative. Wang Aihe appeals to prominent contemporary scholars such as Li Ling (1991, 1993), Robin Yates (1994), and Mark Lewis (1990) who argue that these correlative cosmologies, far from being of a marginal, esoteric interest to a few court adepts, in fact constituted a shared symbolic discourse through which "both intellectuals and ordinary people spoke and thought."[3] Certainly, the recent Warring States archaeological discoveries reinforce this judgment, demonstrating as they do the pervasiveness of correlative cosmological presuppositions entailed in the mantic practices that directed the daily lives of the people.

What then is the persistent yet always evolving "common sense"—the deep cultural stratum, the uncommon assumptions—of the ancient Chinese worldview that has its beginnings in the self-understanding of the human experience? David Keightley with his lifetime study of Shang dynasty divination practices claims that "the origins of much that is thought to be characteristically Chinese may be identified in the ethos and world view of its Bronze Age diviners."[4] Indeed, Keightley believes that

---

2. Nathan Sivin, foreword to *The Theoretical Foundations of Chinese Medicine* by Manfred Porkert (Cambridge, MA: MIT Press, 1974), xi.

3. Wang Aihe, *Cosmology and Political Culture*, 76.

4. Keightley, "Shang Divination and Metaphysics," *Philosophy East and West* 38 (1988): 389. Keightley here is positing a position shared by several of our most distinguished

it is possible for the modern historian to infer from the archaeological, artistic, and written records of the Shang some of the theoretical strategies and presuppositions by which the Bronze Age elite of the closing centuries of the second millennium BC ordered their existence.[5]

From his research on the oracle bone inscriptions, the earliest extant form of Chinese writing, Keightley has concluded that certain presuppositions of the early Shang culture evolved to become further articulated in what we take to be the formative period of classical Chinese philosophy:

> The glimpse that the oracle-bones inscriptions afford us of metaphysical conceptions in the eleventh and tenth centuries B.C. suggests that the philosophical tensions that we associate primarily with the Taoism [Daoism] and Confucianism of Eastern Chou [Zhou] had already appeared, in different form, in the intellectual history of China, half a millennium earlier.[6]

Keightley allows the grammatical structure of the language itself can serve as an important resource that can be quarried to reveal a thick vein of cultural assumptions:

> Without necessarily invoking the Sapir-Whorf hypothesis of linguistic relativity, one can still imagine that the grammar of the Shang inscriptions has much to tell us about Shang conceptions of reality, particularly about the forces of nature.[7]

What specifically then are these underlying assumptions that Keightley believes he has unearthed and recovered in his archaeology of

---

interpreters of the Shang dynasty, including Kwang-chih Chang, "Some Dualistic Phenomena in Shang Society," *Journal of Asian Studies* 24, no. 1 (November), 1964; and Marcel Granet, "Right and Left in China," *Right and Left: Essays on Dual Symbolic Classification*, ed. Rodney Needham (Chicago: University of Chicago Press, 1977). For Keightley's collected papers in which he elaborates on these arguments, see David N. Keightley, *These Bones Shall Rise Again*, ed. Henry Rosemont Jr. (Albany: State University of New York Press, 2014).

5. Keightley, "Shang Divination and Metaphysics," 367.
6. Keightley, "Shang Divination and Metaphysics," 388.
7. Keightley, "Shang Divination and Metaphysics," 389, note 1.

Shang dynasty culture? Keightley sketches a classical Greek worldview in which human moral failures stand in stark contrast to the permanent, ideal reality that its metaphysical transcendentalism guarantees:

> Put crudely, we find in classical Greece a Platonic metaphysics of certainties, ideal forms, and right answers, accompanied by complex, tragic, and insoluble tensions in the realm of ethics. The metaphysical foundations being firm, the moral problems were intensely real, and as inexplicable as reality itself.[8]

If, as the dominant classical Greek metaphysical views would have it, unity and permanence are fundamental, then the disappointing phenomenal world experienced by us as mere persistence, tainted as it is by a continuing stream of flux, cannot be finally real. In this classical Greek worldview, of which Plato is a fair proponent, "reality" must refer to that which *grounds* the world of appearances, while changing phenomena as *mere appearances* are at best misleading and illusory.[9] It is this classical Greek assumption that we can make an object of the world and thereby decontextualize ourselves from it that allows us as detached spectators to entertain an erstwhile view from nowhere. And it is indeed this same putative "view from nowhere" that stands as guarantor for the possibility of objective truth and certainty. Keightley then contrasts the familiar dualistic tensions between the ideal and the real that are so pervasive in classical Greek thinking to the ecological process cosmology he has discovered already extant in his Shang dynasty remnant sources. Keightley asserts that there is no detectable recourse to this pervasive, reality-appearance, "two-world" distinction in classical Chinese thought and nothing of the dualistic categories and modality of thinking that

---

8. Keightley, "Shang Divination and Metaphysics," 376.

9. Much good work is being done to rescue the artist Plato from the received idealist Plato, dominated as this latter interpretation has been by systematic metaphysics. In his *Eros and Irony: A Prelude to Philosophical Anarchism* (Albany: State University of New York Press, 1983), my collaborator David Hall argued for an erotic and ironic Plato whose philosophy is best understood as a continuing reflective process rather than as some final answer. But even while agreeing with Hall that this is a much more interesting Plato truer to the documents that define him, we still must acknowledge that it is this received idealist Plato filtered through the Church Fathers and twentieth-century scientism that has exercised such a fundamental and enduring influence on the evolution of the Western cultural narrative.

follows from it.¹⁰ As Keightley has opined, the early Chinese thinkers were not interested in the search for some unchanging ontological ground for the phenomenal world. Rather, they wanted to figure out how to coordinate and correlate the happenings of their always changing world to get the most out of the human experience:

> To the early Chinese . . . if reality was forever changeable, man could not assume a position of tragic grandeur and maintain his footing for long. The moral heroism of the Confucians of Eastern Chou [Zhou] was not articulated in terms of any tragic flaw in the nature of the world or man. This lack of articulation, I believe, may be related to a significant indifference to the metaphysical foundation of Confucian ethics.¹¹

Keightley argues that in early China, absent the foundational assumptions of Greek idealism, lives were lived in which human success or failure depended on making the most of the changing phenomenal world around them. He ascribes to these early Chinese divinatory sources what is today being described by interpreters of the classical period as a distinctively Chinese mode of correlative thinking through dyadic *yinyang* "aspectual" categories. This mode stands in stark contrast to Greek rationalism and its resolutely dualistic vocabulary. According to Keightley's reading, oracle-bone divination subscribed to

> a theology and metaphysics that conceived of a world of alternating modes, pessimistic at times, optimistic at others, but with the germs of one mode always inherent in the other. Shang metaphysics, at least as revealed in the complementary forms of the Wu Ting [Ding] inscriptions, was a metaphysics of yin and yang.¹²

---

10. For a detailed discussion of this issue, see the "Cultural Requisites for a Theory of Truth" chapter of Hall and Ames, *Thinking from the Han*. Nathan Sivin, a most cautious interpreter of the classical Chinese world who is most reluctant to advance "either-or" comparisons, states unequivocally that the "fundamental claim, which we usually refer to as appearance vs. reality, has no counterpart in China." See Nathan Sivin, *Medicine, Philosophy and Religion in Ancient China: Researches and Reflections* (Aldershot, UK: Variorum, 1995), 3.

11. Keightley, "Shang Divination and Metaphysics," 376.

12. Keightley, "Shang Divination and Metaphysics," 377.

This "correlative" *yinyang* thinking, purported here to date back at least to the Shang dynasty, is a modality of reflection that advances in both complexity and explanatory force through the proliferation and accumulation of productive dyadic associations, persistent images, and evocative metaphors: all of which are weighed, measured, and tested in ordinary experience. This correlative *qi* cosmology that is an omnipresent background in the later philosophical dialectic and cultural practices of Warring States China was evolving pari passu with the increasingly complex life-forms of the ancient period.

In their collaborative comparisons of Greek and Chinese philosophy and science, Geoffrey Lloyd and Nathan Sivin add their authority to a contrast in Greek and Chinese modes of inquiry between the Greek pursuit of a fixed object of knowledge, and the Chinese search for correlations that can be productively drawn from the contents of experience. While there is a proclivity among the early Greeks to engage in an exclusive dialectic in their quest for apodictic truth, the classical Chinese sources reveal a continuing search for a relationally constituted and inclusive harmony and consensus:

> The dominant, but not the only, Greek way was through the search for foundations, the demand for demonstration, for incontrovertibility. Its great strengths lay in the ideals of clarity and deductive rigor. Its corresponding weaknesses were a zest for disagreement that inhibited even the beginnings of a consensus, and a habit of casting doubt on every preconception. The principal (though not the sole) Chinese approach was to find and explore correspondences, resonances, interconnections. Such an approach favored the formation of syntheses unifying widely divergent fields of inquiry. Conversely, it inspired a reluctance to confront established positions with radical alternatives.[13]

Lloyd and Sivin underscore the primacy and dominance of assumptions about relationality and synthetic growth in this classical Chinese worldview as producing the predominance of a distinctive mode of inquiry. Such a claim about growth through productive correlations reinforces Fei Xiaotong's argument we have previously rehearsed: that an emphasis on

---

13. Geoffrey Lloyd and Nathan Sivin, *The Way and the Word: Science and Medicine in Early China and Greece* (New Haven, CT: Yale University Press, 2002), 250.

hierarchical kinship relations within the human experience also produces a distinctive kind of morality—a family-centered relational conception of moral competence we have termed "Confucian role ethics."

These insights into the differences between our early cosmologies proffered by some of our most distinguished scholars give rise to my argument on behalf of thick generalizations. That is, to explore the central issues and arguments of the early Confucian texts within the framework of its own cosmology makes available to us appropriate access to their own philosophical import, while a failure to correlate the content of the philosophical corpus with this evolving yet persistent worldview by default locates the early developments of Chinese philosophy within a way of thinking not its own. It is for this reason that I would contest a resistance among some contemporary Sinologists to thick cultural generalizations. I would insist that our complex and always changing cultural milieus are themselves rooted in and grow out of a deep and relatively stable soil of unannounced assumptions sedimented over generations into the language, customs, and life-forms of a living tradition. I would argue that to fail to acknowledge this fundamental character of cultural difference as a quixotic safeguard against the sins of either "essentialism" or "relativism" is not innocent. Indeed, like the preacher who on Monday commits the very sins he railed against the day before, this antagonism to cultural generalizations leads to the uncritical naturalizing of one's own contingent cultural assumptions and to the insinuating of them into our interpretations of other traditions.

Indeed, one might argue that the bugbear of "essentialism" is itself a culturally specific worry. Essentialism arises from familiar classical Greek assumptions about ontology as "the science of being" and from the application of strict identity (or "essences") as the principle of individuation that follows from such an ontology. I would embrace the basic idea that culture is an ongoing evolving process that entails novelty and persistence, crises and continuities, idealities and realities, and transformation and resistance. And at the very least, we must strive with imagination to take other cultures on their own terms if our comparative studies of them are to provide the mutual enrichment that they promise.

A. N. Whitehead, in service to thick generalizations, famously claims that "the safest general characterization of the European philosophical tradition is that it consists of a series of footnotes to Plato."[14] Although

---

14. Whitehead, *Process and Reality*, 39.

this statement illustrates all too well what John Dewey has impatiently criticized as Whitehead's "excessive piety toward those historic philosophers from whom he has derived valuable suggestions,"[15] still Whitehead's basic point is well made: the ideas of Plato were formative, persistent, and indeed continue to have real relevance in understanding the trajectory of contemporary Western culture. While we can certainly argue that the post-Darwinian internal critique within the Western philosophical narrative has for a century and a half been a sustained revolution against persisting Platonic assumptions, we would have to allow that such a turn in the tradition is still dialectically coupled with Plato as an argument against his basic tenets. And again, at our present juncture after philosophers for 150 years have done their utmost to root out what they now take to be fallacious ways of thinking, Platonic realism still remains largely intact as our cultural common sense.

A Thick Generalization: Distinguishing "Events" from "Objects"

The irrelevance for classical China of the familiar ontological reality-appearance dichotomy in its various forms that would separate the objective from what is subjective has broad consequences for the way in which the human experience has been understood and the manner in which the Confucian cultural sensibility has been shaped. The notion of the "real" as what is *objective*—that is, the "object" of true knowledge—is one immediate implication of the reality-appearance distinction and the dualistic worldview that issues from it. Joseph Needham disassociates early Chinese cosmology from such familiar assumptions freighted in our own narrative about some external and thus objective source of cosmic order when he claims that

> Chinese ideals involved neither God nor Law. . . . Thus the mechanical and the quantitative, the forced and the externally imposed, were all absent. The notion of Order excluded the notion of Law.[16]

---

15. Paul Schlipp, *The Philosophy of Alfred North Whitehead* (New York: Tudor, 1941), 659–60.

16. Needham, *Science and Civilisation in China*, 2:290.

The most fundamental difference between these two contrasting classical cosmologies is thus the prominence of "substance" as ontological ground in the classical Greek tradition and the fluid "process" orientation of the classical Chinese narrative, defining us as either discrete human "beings" or as eventful human "becomings," respectively. A corollary to the privileging of a formal, unchanging reality over the flux of appearances in the dominant classical Western worldview is the tendency to privilege the discrete and quantitative over the continuous and qualitative.[17] The identity of "things" or persons tends to be atomistic: a function of quantitative discreteness that parses identity in terms of essential and accidental properties. Wholes are constructed out of discrete yet coherent parts. Families and communities are collections of individual persons, each of whom has their own integrity. This priority of discreteness and quantity is entailed in the priority of stasis and permanence and of the substantial over the processual. Each person in the community defined by some self-same identical characteristic has some presocial, precultural, and enduring warrant for their membership. Further, this priority given to discreteness and quantity in turn disposes toward a concern for the clarity of formally defined concepts and the necessity of unchanging truths—both of which are more congenial to a quantitatively discrete and measurable world.[18]

What Tang Junyi in describing Chinese cosmology refers to as the "world as such," is a unique and boundless "world-ing," and we observers always live our lives within it. Without a standpoint for asserting objective truths about the world, persons are always reflexively implicated in the way in which they understand and organize their experience of it. The values of the always interested viewer are necessarily implicated in any observation. As a consequence, saying something about the world is always a matter of selected interest that says something about one's own person

---

17. Jean-Paul Reding, "Words for Atoms, Atoms for Words—Comparative Considerations on the Origins of Atomism in Ancient Greece and the Absence of Atomism in Ancient China," *Comparative Essays in Greek and Chinese Rational Thinking* (Aldershot, UK: Ashgate). See also Sivin, *Medicine, Philosophy and Religion*, 2–3.

18. It is the priority given to the quantitatively discrete that is the target of William James when, in the *Principles of Psychology*, he argues for the equal reality of "conjunctions and transitions" in the stream of consciousness. See *William James: The Essential Writings*, ed. Bruce W. Wilshire (Albany: State University of New York Press, 1984), 47–81.

and perspective. The absence of a basis for making objective statements about our experience means that erstwhile objective definition and simple description are problematic, making fact and value interdependent and mutually entailing. Thus, any severe line that would purport to divide and then elevate science from culture, chemistry from alchemy, astronomy from astrology, geology from geomancy, and psychology from physiognomy, would be tenuous. Indeed, the distance between description and prescription is ultimately dependent upon the degree of self-consciousness in what is done, where a greater awareness of who one is and what one brings to the experience would presumably reduce one's own footprint. William James offers some insight here on the inescapability of the subjective point of view. As a starting point for reflection, James offers us the following holistic definition of a "fact":

> A conscious field *plus* its object as felt or thought of *plus* an attitude towards the object *plus* the sense of self to whom the attitude belongs . . . is a *full* fact, even though it be an insignificant fact; it is of the *kind* to which all realities whatsoever must belong.[19]

In the early Confucian cosmology, absent this assumed notion of *objectivity*, there can only be the flux of passing circumstances. Without *objectivity*, erstwhile objects dissolve into the flux and flow—into the changefulness of their surround. Indeed, they are not "objects" as such, but *events*, continuous with all other events. What are perceived as persistent "things" that sustain an identity across time from birth, maturation, and eventual decline are in fact horizons of relationships that have relative yet transitory stability within a manifold of constant change. The identity of any "thing" thus conceived, though persistent, is analogic in the sense of

---

19. William James, *Varieties of Religious Experience: A Study in Human Nature* (New York: Penguin, 1981), 499. One unresolved incoherence in James is that he wants to hold on to this understanding of experience and at the same time, as a scientist, to assert the possibility and desirability of pure description—of descriptive neutrality. Perhaps one way of resolving this issue would be to distinguish phenomenal description from interpretive description. What does it mean to give a good account of something? For James, genius lies with what Emerson called "seeing-into" things and taking them all in—being a good visualizer. Again, perhaps for James it is just a matter of psychological animation—it makes a difference for us to try to be neutral in our descriptions because we then get more out of things.

being constituted by and a function of its range of dynamic associations. It is what it is by virtue of its location and role within a boundless pattern of vital relations. The language of process is an eventful discourse without objects or erstwhile facts, and to speak and hear this language is to experience and be inspired by the flow of things.

As human beings, the notion of the real as *objective* gives privilege to the analytic and dialectical mode of engagement by promising a single truth that allows discrete parties to "protest" in the sense of first standing apart from, "objecting" to, and thus dissenting on behalf of, this single truth. An alternative mode of discourse to this exclusionary dialectic that is available for human becomings is captured in the positive sense of "protest" that we find in the common expression, "I protest my innocence." To protest thusly, far from taking exception and objecting to something, is "to testify on behalf of" and to thus affirm with solemnity one's allegiance to a particular situation. Here the guiding assumption is an awareness that our transactions are always relational and reflexive, implicating us in one way or another in whatever depositions we might choose to make.

A Thick Generalization: Distinguishing "Phases" from "Elements"

This distinction between human beings and human becomings is brought further into focus by another contrast we find between substance ontology and process cosmology. Elemental theory is a prominent theme in classical Greek thought paradigmatic of substance ontology in privileging both discreteness and quantity. According to Nathan Sivin, such elemental theories "claim that things are made up of minute ultimate parts that usually do not look like the parts that are big enough for us to see."[20] Early on, the Chinese *wuxing* 五行 were in fact translated as "the five elements," associating this cosmology with the various Greek elemental theories. But several prominent scholars such as Sivin himself, Angus Graham, and John Major have, in their interpretive studies, sought to correct this earlier misleading understanding of the *wuxing* 五行 cosmology. According to Major:

---

20. Sivin, *Medicine, Philosophy and Religion*, 2–3.

The problem with "five elements" is that the Chinese concept of *wu-hsing* [*wuxing*] . . . has none of the sense of "basic ingredient" or "irreducible essence" of the Latin *elementum* nor of that term's various Greek conceptual ancestors. . . . In contrast, the translation Five Phases, which now is rapidly gaining acceptance, clearly has connotations of change consistent with the Chinese concept of cyclical transformation.[21]

Wang Aihe has provided a cogent summary of this Sinological debate about the proper translation of this term, *wuxing*:

The traditional translation is "Five Elements," a term most convenient for comparative studies of Chinese thought and thought in other civilizations. Yet "elements" does not fully represent the Chinese term *Wuxing*, which literally five "goings," "conducts," or "doings," nor does it convey the basic nature of *Wuxing* as a cosmology of interaction and change. Many scholars have proposed alternatives, including five forces, agents, entities, activities, or stages of change. Of these, "Five Phases" has acquired a wide acceptance among specialists.[22]

These recent elucidations of *wuxing* as "five phases" have permitted a much more productive approach to the important and pervasive notion of *qi* 氣 that becomes explicit among cosmologists in the late fourth and early third centuries BCE.

The Greek elemental theories are one familiar version of the reality-appearance distinction that is markedly absent in Chinese cosmological explanations. That is, in the Chinese sensibility, there is no putative Being behind the beings, no unchanging formal aspect behind the changing world, no One behind the many, no atomic level where unchanging "real"

---

21. John Major, "A Note on the Translation of Two Technical Terms in Chinese Science: *Wu-Hsing* and *Hsiu*," *Early China* 2 (1976), 1–2. I would, however, disassociate myself from Major's initial claim that "the Chinese concept *wu-hsing* is one of function rather than constituent matter." In a subsequent exchange with Richard Kunst, Major then clarifies what he means by "function" as "categories of relations." See his "Reply to Richard Kunst's Comments on *Hsiu* and *Wu Hsing*," *Early China* 3 (1977): 69–70. My understanding is that *wuxing*, like *qi* or *dao* or *yinyang*, would resist any severe function-structure distinction and that the relations are themselves constitutive.

22. Wang Aihe, *Cosmology and Political Culture*, 3.

atoms rearrange themselves to constitute an apparent world. The Chinese counterpart to Greek "elemental" theories that was initially confused with them is the phasal understanding of the animated, autogenerative process of *qi* transformation: the *yinyang* 陰陽 variations that occur in *qi* and the "five phases" (*wuxing*). *Qi* is both *what* experience is and *how* it is, as it persists and yet is constantly changing in its formal aspect. The five phases are quite literally a "functional" equivalent of the Greek elements: rather than referring to ultimate "parts," they reference both the functioning and the reforming of the various phases of the changing world itself as such transformation is captured in the metaphorical language of "shade and light" (*yinyang*) and of metal, wood, water, fire, and earth (*jinmushuihuotu* 金木水火土). The bipolar opposition symbolized by *yinyang* forces generates a dynamic tension that drives the ongoing processes of change. These creative processes are parsed into the distinct although continuous transitional five phases that provide an account of continuity and flux, persistence and change, similarities and differences, associations and contrasts. Just as spring becomes summer, and summer becomes autumn, so wood "becomes" water, and water becomes fire. It is the application of the notion of "phases" to the manifold of processes that allows for these processes to be parsed into distinctive, consummatory "events." Even though summer is a transition between spring and autumn, we can still treat it as a distinctive period in any given year. And although persons are transitional between progenitor and progeny, they are also uniquely particular persons. Such distinct "events"—narratives nested within narratives—then serve conceptually as the functional and structural equivalent of the quantitatively discrete "things" that we find in a substance ontology.

In Wang Aihe's work on the relationship between this evolving cosmology and political change, she cautions us that such *wuxing* "theorizing" has to be understood within the holistic process cosmology. This cosmology begins from the primacy of practice and takes theorizing as an intrinsic feature of practical activity itself that tries to make practices more productive and intelligent within the context of the practices themselves. Such theorizing is an effort to influence the always evolving circumstances to their best advantage:

> *Wuxing* is not simply a set of concepts, a school of philosophy, a mode of thinking, or a commonly agreed-upon representation; instead, it is a cultural phenomenon that changes

through history, a discourse for political argument and power struggle, and above all, an art of action in a world of conflict and change.[23]

This inseparability of the theoretical and the practical, the functional and the structural that defines this cosmology reflects a profoundly different way of thinking about what things are and how they arise in the human experience.

A Chinese Cosmology with "Its Own Causality and Its Own Logic"

Marcel Granet, in his study of the early Chinese canons, finds what he takes to be just such a distinctive way of thinking—what some Sinologists and comparative philosophers have come to call variously "correlative," "analogical," "associative," or "coordinative" thinking. Joseph Needham, much influenced by what he defers to as the "genius" of Granet, takes the organic wholeness and ecological nature of experience, and the correlative way of thinking of "human becomings" that attends it, to be a persistent and defining presupposition in the process cosmology of classical China.[24] I cite Needham here, relying heavily as he does upon Granet, to provide us with an entry point for a sustained reflection on what this notion of "correlative thinking" might mean:

> A number of modern students—H. Wilhelm, Eberhard, Jablonski, and above all, Granet—have named the kind of thinking

---

23. Wang Aihe, *Cosmology and Political Change*, 3.
24. Although Needham takes Marcel Granet's *La pensée chinoise* to be "a work of genius," he criticizes Granet along with other major commentators on Chinese cosmology such as Alfred Forke and H. G. Creel for having "the serious defect of assuming that the cosmism and phenomenalism of the Han was ancient." The scientist Needham chooses instead to attribute the emergence of this correlative worldview to the School of Naturalists—Zou Yan 鄒衍 (305–240 BCE) and the Yinyang lineage 陰陽家—a special company of thinkers who had the marked advantage of having "a mind trained in the natural sciences." See Needham, *Science and Civilisation*, 2:216–17. On this matter, as previously rehearsed, I side with scholars such as David Keightley who in his many publications wants to ascribe correlative thinking as a characteristic pattern of thinking, to intellectuals as far back as the Shang dynasty.

with which we have here to do, "coordinative thinking" or "associative thinking." This intuitive-associative system has its own causality and its own logic. It is not either superstition or primitive superstition, but a characteristic thought-form of its own. H. Wilhelm contrasts it with the "subordinative" thinking characteristic of European science, which laid such emphasis on external causation. In coordinative thinking, conceptions are not subsumed under one another, but placed side by side in a pattern, and things influence one another not by acts of mechanical causation, but by a kind of "inductance."[25]

Needham describes this correlative thinking as having "its own causality and its own logic" and as being "a characteristic thought-form of its own."[26] On this basis Needham invites us through a portal that would seem to take us, like Alice, to the other side of the looking glass where he shares with us his encounter with a somewhat wonky world that has left the reassuring stability of our own rational structures behind:

> The key-word in Chinese thought is *Order* and above all *Pattern* (and if I may whisper it for the first time, *Organism*). The symbolic correlations or correspondences all formed part of one colossal pattern. Things behaved in particular ways not necessarily because of prior actions or impulses of other things, but because their position in the ever-moving cyclical universe was such that they were endowed with intrinsic

---

25. Needham, *Science and Civilisation*, 2:280.

26. In a chapter I wrote on "methodology" in Chinese philosophy, I tried to temper the claim by Granet and Needham about the uniqueness of this associative way of thinking, and in so doing, to demystify this putatively other world by building on the notion of "abductive reasoning" as a more familiar form of correlative thinking developed by C. S. Peirce, the reputed founder of American pragmatism. Indeed, when his fellow pragmatist William James characterizes the pragmatic method as simply asking, "What difference does it make?" he is requiring that "doing philosophy" be an imaginative and experimental way of thinking directed at enhancing the human experience through the production of the capacity to live life intelligently—a demand that resonates immediately with these Chinese canons. See Roger T. Ames, "Philosophizing with Canonical Chinese Texts: Seeking an Interpretive Context," in *Research Handbook on Methodology in Chinese Philosophy*, ed. Sor-hoon Tan (London: Bloomsbury, 2016).

natures which made their behaviour inevitable for them. If they did not behave in those particular ways they would lose their relational position in the whole (which made them what they were), and turn into something other than themselves. They were thus parts in existential dependence upon the whole world-organism. And they reacted upon one another not so much by mechanical impulsion or causation as by a kind of mysterious resonance.[27]

Needham again draws on Granet to provide what is a vivid description of the unfamiliar cosmological vision we need as our interpretive context for understanding the Confucian notion of person, alerting us not only to what this cosmology is, but perhaps more importantly, to what it is not:

> Social and world order rested, not on an ideal of authority, but on a conception of rotational responsibility. The Tao [*dao*] was the all-inclusive name for this order, an efficacious sum-total, a reactive neural medium; it was not a creator, for nothing is created in the world, and the world was not created. The sum of wisdom consisted in adding to the number of intuited analogical correspondences in the repertory of correlations. Chinese ideals involved neither God nor Law. The uncreated universal organism, whose every part, by a compulsion internal to itself and arising out of its own nature, willingly performed its functions in the cyclical recurrences of the whole, was mirrored in human society by a universal ideal of mutual good understanding, a supple regime of interdependences and solidarities which could never be based on unconditional ordinances, in other words, on laws.[28]

Needham says in explanation of *dao*, "the universal uncreated organism" often described as the "source" of all things, that it "was not a creator, for nothing is created in the world, and the world was not created." What he means here is that this cosmology brings with it an alternative understanding of creativity: that creativity as a generative

---

27. Needham, *Science and Civilisation*, 2:280–81.
28. Needham, *Science and Civilisation*, 2:290.

procreativity and a continuing in situ or "situated" increase in meaning that would defy any ex nihilo separation between creator and creature. The furniture of the world is not created in the sense of emerging out of nothing, and it does not suffer annihilation in the sense of returning to nothing. *Dao* and the myriad things (*wanwu*), rather than referencing distinct and independent realities, are two aspectual ways of looking at the same always transforming phenomenal world and our continuing experience within it.

Granet appeals to this language of "aspect" to express the way in which erstwhile "things" are in fact dynamic matrices of productive relations that constitute continuous, extended events:

> Instead of observing successions of phenomena, the Chinese registered alternations of aspects. If two aspects seemed to them to be connected, it was not by means of a cause and effect relationship, but rather "paired" like the obverse and converse of something, or to use a metaphor from the *Book of Changes*, like echo and sound, or shadow and light.[29]

Granet is here reflecting on the resonant "pairing" among alternations of aspects defining all events denoted by the familiar dyadic vocabulary of the *yinyang* tension (陰陽), "field" and "focus" (*daode* 道德), "determinacy" and "indeterminacy" (*youwu* 有無), "change" and "continuity" (*biantong* 變通), "the heavens" and "the earth" (*tiandi* 天地), "the world" and "the human experience" (*tianren* 天人), "forming" and "functioning" (*tiyong* 體用), "the social grammar" and its "musicality" (*liyue* 禮樂), "heartminding" and "spirituality" (*xinshen* 心神), "intensity" and "extensiveness" (*jingshen* 精神), "the lived body" and "heartminding" (*shenxin* 身心), "the consummatory" and "the optimally appropriate" (*renyi* 仁義), and so on. To take "determinacy" and "indeterminacy" (有無) as an example, these terms are a nonanalytic, explanatory vocabulary of "aspects" that we must appeal to in giving a fair account of the ceaseless emergence of any of the things and events that come to constitute the continuing human experience. And such an ineluctable process of transformation requires a gerundive, explanatory language such as "forming (*ti* 體) and "functioning" (*yong* 用) to report on the mutuality of structure and performance as the world turns.

---

29. Cited in Needham, *Science and Civilisation*, 2:290–91.

In understanding what Needham means here by "rotational responsibility" with each thing having "a compulsion internal to itself," we will have to recollect the doctrine of internal relations previously rehearsed and the alternative, holistic "causality" it entails. In this classical cosmology, the animating and transforming *qi* 氣 is conceptualized in terms of what in modern parlance we might call a "vital energy field" in which "things" are sometimes more and sometimes less persistent perturbations or foci in this field. Having arisen, these intertwined "events" continue in the fullness of time to transform into other things. The vital field is not only pervasive as a condition of all things but also consistent with Needham's description of this field as "a reactive neural medium"; it is also the "neural," existential medium through which all situated things emerge in their relations to constitute what they are becoming. There is neither animating *qi* without structuring form, nor form without animating *qi*. Indeed, as we have seen, "form" and "animating *qi*" are two nonanalytic aspects of the same transforming reality, where "transitivity" and "form" are both implicit ways of understanding the transformative "functioning and forming" (*tiyong* 體用) process. As such, "animating *qi*" and the various ways we have of saying "forming" are an explanatory rather than an ontological vocabulary; we need both terms to give an adequate account of what we experience.

The focus-field cosmology that Granet and Needham are ascribing to this Chinese worldview and the aspectual language needed to give it voice are revealing of what Needham is referring to as "the universal uncreated organism" with "its own causality and its own logic." With respect to causality then, given the vital, internal, and constitutive nature of the relations that underlies the focus-field holography, causality does not reference some agency outside and temporally prior to the perceived configuration of the things happening but rather speaks to the creative, interdependent, and causal nature of the relations themselves.

When we ask, "Which comes first, the chicken or the egg?" we have to allow that they must both evolve together or not at all. From the perspective of classical Western metaphysics, we might say this Chinese cosmology shaves with Ockham's razor not once, but twice. Chinese cosmology begins from what is happening within the autogenerative world itself (*ziran* 自然) rather than appealing to the notion of a transcendent and independent First Mover as the cause and architect of the world. And with respect to persons, Chinese cosmology begins from a phenomenology of what unfolds and compounds as moral habits within the human narrative itself rather than appealing to an independent and reduplicative nature or soul as the source of human conduct.

If, as Peter Hershock has observed, we see "relationality as first order (or ultimate) reality and all individual actors as (conventionally) abstracted or derived from them," then we must understand causality in a cosmos described as autogenerative (*ziran*) to be the backgrounding or foregrounding of particular foci and their unbounded fields, where anything is the cause of everything, and everything is the cause of anything. The *ziran* causality means that the "self" (*zi* 自) in the "self-so-ing" process is certainly uniquely what it is, but it is also inclusive of all of the extended relations of any particular thing or event as this manifold of relations conspires and gives life to the unique conatus (*ran* 然) that makes this thing insistently so. Said simply, everything causes anything, and thus any particular thing is both the cause and the effect of everything else.

Shi 勢: An Aesthetic Alternative to the Logic of "Things" and to an "External Causality"

There is another complex term that might be helpful in thinking through a cosmology described by Needham as having "its own causality and its own logic," a claim that "human becomings" think in an importantly different way from a "human being." *Shi* 勢 is a generic term that expresses the complex, holistic, and dynamic process of "trans-*form*-ing" (*tiyong* 體用) as it occurs within the evolution and consummation of any particular "thing" or situation. There is the aesthetic of the cultivating and refining of things that is captured in the etymology of *shi* as "sowing and cultivating" (*yi* 蓺) with its cognate term, the "performing arts" (*yi* 藝). Such associations suggest that situations do not just happen; they emerge in their complexity as a growing pattern of changing relations that are vital and that display the possibilities of incremental design as well as an achieved, aesthetic virtuosity. At the same time, situations by definition are "situated" and as such, have a formal morphology or "habituated" aspect—a localized "taking place" with its insistent particularity and its own persistent yet always changing configuration.

We might be initially overwhelmed when we rehearse what is in fact a nonexhaustive list of the possible English translations for this term *shi*. But we might also look for an organizational logic in this glossary of terms by subsuming this list of various translations under four rubrics selected from among these possible equivalencies:

Relationality: leverage, differential, advantage, purchase
Vitality: potential, momentum, timing, tendency, propensity
Virtuosity: influence, power, force, style, dignity, status
Embodiment: terrain, configuration, situation, circumstances, disposition, shape, appearance

Such a range of renderings used to translate *shi* as it is found in different contexts is revealing of the extraordinarily broad compass of meaning implicated in this one term. On reflection and with imagination, we can recover a perhaps unfamiliar, alternative logic and a sense of causality from a survey of these seemingly disparate meanings. We might observe that *shi* is holistic, denoting "thing," "action," "attribute," and "modality" all at once. Hence, it is translated in different contexts as a noun, a verb, an adjective, and an adverb. In lifting coherence out of this pattern of seemingly disjunctive associations, we might begin from the matrix of relations that constitutes any particular situation and registers the vital and thus changing pattern or structure that emerges from them. This dynamic structure—from its first-order relationality and vitality to its achieved virtuosity as it bodies forth—can be drawn upon to answer some of our basic cosmological questions.

First, this reflection on *shi* provides an alternative vocabulary for thinking through the dynamics of our field of continuing experience and the multiplicity of its content. *Shi* provides a centered, "from-field-to-focus" conception of the principle of how we come to individuate things and set horizons upon them. That is, beginning from the wholeness of experience, we divide up, conceptualize, foreground, and thus make determinate an eventful "thing" within an otherwise continuous flow of relations by bringing focus and meaningful resolution to its horizons as it is entertained from one perspective or another. The primacy of vital relations means that situation will always have priority over agency and that no putative agent does anything by itself.

An ostensive "thing" is first a specific focus, matrix, or configuration within an expansive context of always changing, constitutive relations. Importantly, it can be cultivated and shaped to achieve insistent focus and resolution in its interdependent relations with the "other" things that constitute it. The dynamics of *shi* explains what it means for something that is at once unique and yet continuous with other things to act and to move—and to be acted upon and to be moved—where its shaping and being shaped is one continuous process.

Shi as thus one and many, as unique foci within their respective fields, provides some insight into the logic of a more fluid sense of continuity within diversity and of an internal and spontaneous *ziran* causality in which everything "causes" anything, and anything is a cause of everything. Indeed, the inseparability of continuity and diversity guarantees the uniqueness of each situation and means at the very least there can be no single dominant order but only many interdependent and interpenetrating sites of order.

When this term *shi* with its alternative logic and causality is used to reflect on the human condition specifically, it explains the emerging individuality of unique, potentially consummate "persons" situated within the evolving circumstances of their extended families and communities, as well as within the changing conditions of their natural and cultural environments. *Shi* suggests how the persisting habits and the specific habitudes that constitute human identities are shaped from originating impulses into the definite and significant activities of always unique persons. Such persons are irreducibly transactional, ingesting and embodying their environs as uniquely focused fields of roles and relations. The cultivated distinctiveness of such persons, far from being exclusive of their relationships, is rather the immediate product of the quality that is being achieved in them. To the extent that we are able to thrive within productive relations, we can emerge as distinctive and sometimes even distinguished persons, thereby bringing distinction to the nexus of relations to which we belong. The holographic reversibility of inner and outer means that in searching inwardly for a unique, lived identity we are in fact exploring the web of outward relations that make us who we are. And in projecting outward to register most fully the unbounded web of relations that give us context, we are reflexively discovering our innermost selves.

Since the entire world is implicated within each of us as persons, it is only appropriate that we regard ourselves with the same esteem that we would extend to the world. Or said more simply: to love ourselves is to love the world. It is only those who by fully realizing this interpenetration between world and things, and the interpenetration among things themselves, can extend themselves to the full compass of experience as a precondition for making their own distinctive contribution to it and exercising their influence within it.

The *Book of Changes* 易經: A Cosmological Vocabulary

Previously I have suggested that our cosmologies are commonly projections onto the cosmos that have their origins in assumptions about our own persons and the ways in which we live our lives. What canonical resources should we appeal to within this classical Confucian tradition then, for correlating the notions of cosmos, persons, and the human experience broadly, in order to make the thick generalizations needed to provide the interpretive context for taking this tradition on its own terms? As important as the Daoist and Confucian canons have been in the articulation of Chinese intellectual history, and as much as they can be appealed to as textual evidence for claims about early Chinese cosmology, perhaps no single text can compete with the *Yijing* 易經 or *Book of Changes* in terms of the sustained interest it has garnered from succeeding generations of China's lettered classes and the influence it has had on Confucian self-understanding. The *Book of Changes* has been and still remains, in every sense, the first among the Confucian canons. Indeed, it is this open-ended classic with its centuries of accruing commentaries that has set the terms of art for the evolving Confucian cosmology.

The *Book of Changes* is a complex text that includes both a manual used as a heuristic and a later set of seven appended commentaries for "figuring out" the human experience. That is, the commentaries provide a vocabulary of complex images and pursue correlations (*xiang* 象) about the way things work in the relationship between the human world and its cosmic context.[30] The commentaries are themselves composite and sometimes fragmentary, and they are certainly subsequent to the manual itself, in some cases dating to as late as the early Han dynasty. Even so, portions of them are hugely important as a summary of early Chinese cosmology that has had an abiding influence on the Chinese sense of its world. One of these documents, the *Xici* 繫辭, usually called the *Great*

---

30. Since three of these commentaries are divided into two sections each, they are usually referred to collectively as the "Ten Wings." The manual itself, used traditionally as an instrument for pursuing productive correlations, is of a much earlier vintage than the commentaries and has come to be referred to independently as the *Zhouyi* 周易.

Commentary 大傳, is perhaps the most important source we presently have for thinking through the assumptions of early Chinese cosmology. Given that a silk manuscript version of this text dating from 168 BCE was recovered at the Mawangdui archaeological site in Changsha in 1973, we have at least a *terminus ad quem* for its compilation.

David Keightley sees the rhythm of "alternation and transformation" (*bianhua* 變化) in the ceaseless process of change made explicit in this *Great Commentary* fascicle as a later elaboration on a modality of change already recognized in Shang dynasty metaphysics. In order to bring this refinement on the notion of change into sharper focus, we might begin from the observation that our conventional translation of *Yijing* as the "*Book of Changes*" is ambiguous to the extent that there are many different modalities of "change" that are referenced in this early process cosmology. Indeed, there is a rather extensive vocabulary of terms that can and often have been translated as "change": "transforming" *hua* 化, "being in flux" *bian* 變, "removing" *qian* 遷, "replacing" *geng* 更, "taking away" *ti* 替, "transferring, altering" *yi* 移, "reforming" *gai* 改, "exchanging" *huan* 換, "peeling away" *ge* 革, "increasing, adding, profiting" *yi* 益, and many more. The early commentaries parse the specifically *yi* 易 modality of change paronomastically as *yi* 益 "increasing, adding, profiting," a kind of change that is consistent with the declared and self-conscious claim of the text to provide its sagely counsel in making the most of the human experience. The contemporary commentator Guo Moruo 郭沫若 argues that the term *yi* 易 in fact should be read as the ancient abbreviated form of the graph *ci* 賜 meaning "gifting," "transacting," "exchanging." And given that the transactional "ex-changing" modality of "change" is the ultimate source of value and increased meaning in a cosmology that gives primacy to vital relationality, Guo's suggestion is compelling.[31]

In this seminal text, the notion of both cosmic and human change is described in the aspectual and processual language of symbiotic bipolar opposites such as "flux and continuity" (*biantong* 變通), "alternating succession" (*yinyang* 陰陽), and "penetration and receptivity" (*qiankun* 乾坤) within the vital context of "the heavens and the earth" (*tiandi* 天地), which complement each other and that together provide an account of the ongoing process of transformation that continues without respite within an unbounded totality.[32] It is within this flux and flow that the

---

31. See the entry for 易 in Kwan, "Database."
32. Keightley, "Shang Divination and Metaphysics," 374–75.

transactional human life unfolds, with the challenge for human beings to fathom these cosmic operations and correlate the events of their experience to optimum effect.

The intellectual milieu for early Chinese thinkers as it is captured in the vocabulary of the *Great Commentary* was a phenomenal world of process and change construed alternatively as *dao* 道 ("the unfolding of the boundless field of experience") or *wanwu* 萬物 ("the ten thousand processes or events"), or perhaps more simply put, "everything that is happening." A familiar metaphor in the early corpus for the novel arising and subsiding of the always unique phenomena of the world is the "swinging gates of *tian*" (*tianmen* 天門):

> Thus the closing of the swinging gates is called receptivity (*kun* 坤); the opening of the gates is called penetration (*qian* 乾). The ongoing alternation of openings and closings is called flux (*bian* 變), and the inexhaustibility of the comings and goings is called continuity (*tong* 通). When something is manifest, it is called an image (*xiang* 象), and taking on physical form it is called a phenomenon (*qi* 器). To get a grasp of these things and apply them is called emulation (*fa* 法). Putting them to good use so that all of the people can take advantage of them is called insight into the mysteries of the world (*shen* 神).[33]

The process of change imagined here as the opening and closing of the swinging gates—a metaphor that resists our default assumptions about agency—provides us with insight into how change was conceived and the vocabulary used to think about it. As in so many passages in the *Great Commentary*, this text begins with observations about the form and functioning of the natural processes and then concludes with advice on how effective collaboration with this changing world can inspire the human experience:

> Thus, that which goes beyond form is called *dao*; those things that have form are called phenomena. The transforming and tailoring that goes on among things is called their flux, while

---

33. *Great Commentary*: 是故, 闔戶謂之坤; 闢戶謂之乾; 一闔一闢謂之變; 往來不窮謂之通; 見乃謂之象; 形乃謂之器; 制而用之, 謂之法; 利用出入, 民咸用之, 謂之神。

their advance and application is called their continuity. To take up this understanding and bring it into the lives of the common people is called the grand undertaking.[34]

The coordination of the relationship between the changing world and the human experience to optimal effect is the main axis of the *Book of Changes*. The purpose of this text is fundamentally normative and prescriptive. It purports to address what is perhaps life's most pressing question: what kind of human participation in the natural processes can optimize the possibilities of this world in which natural and human events are its two inseparable, mutually shaping aspects?

Where meaning is not available to us from putative metaphysical foundations—what Keightley has described as "a Platonic metaphysics of certainties, ideal forms, and right answers"—then guidance for leading the most meaningful lives must have been formulated and passed on within the continuing historical narrative by the most sagacious of our progenitors to coordinate the human experience with changing cosmic processes. Confucian morality itself is a cosmic phenomenon emerging out of the symbiotic and synergistic transactions that take place between the operations of nature and our concerted human efforts. This *Book of Changes* describes life itself—a generative procreativity—as the most generic characteristic of our experience:

> The greatest capacity (*dade* 大德) of the world around us is its life-force. The greatest treasure of the sages is said to be the attainment of standing (*wei* 位). The means of maintaining standing is aspiring to become consummate in one's conduct (*ren* 仁). The means of attracting and mobilizing others is the use of the available resources. Regulating these resources effectively, insuring that language is used properly, and preventing the people from doing what is undesirable is called optimal appropriateness (*yi* 義).[35]

---

34. *Great Commentary* A12: 是故，形而上者謂之道，形而下者謂之器。化而裁之謂之變，推而行之謂之通，舉而錯之天下之民，謂之事業。
35. *Great Commentary* B1: 天地之大德曰生，聖人之大寶曰位。何以守位曰仁，何以聚人曰財。理財正辭，禁民為非曰義。

Human spirituality as "inspired living" arises from a penetrating understanding of the workings of change and then "aspiring" to a quality of appropriate conduct that such an understanding can occasion. We must read the initial natural conditions while they are still inchoate, anticipate the possibilities of these stirrings, and then aspire to make the most of the productive indeterminancy that is always the penumbra of the phenomenal world. The "intensive" conduct of the exemplary person becomes "extensive" as it serves as a model for and is deferred to by the people:

> Understanding the incipient (*ji* 幾) gives insight into the mysteries of the world (*shen*). That exemplary persons (*junzi*) are not obsequious in dealing with superiors or self-serving in dealing with subordinates is because they understand the incipient. The incipient is a hint of movement from which one can see in advance impending fortune. Exemplary persons having seen the incipient are aroused to action without waiting to see what transpires. . . . Exemplary persons in their understanding of both the inchoate and the obvious, of both the soft and the hard, make such paragons a beacon for the myriad people.[36]

In fact, it is a spirituality emerging from always appropriate and productive conduct that is the highest achievement humanity can aspire to:

> It is because making the most of the mysteries of the world (*shen*) in our understanding of the processes of transformation is the fullness of human virtuosity (*de*) that no one has yet to figure out how to go beyond this.[37]

In telling the story of its own inspired origins, this *Great Commentary* explains how a human responsiveness to context has come to enchant the cosmos. The remote ancestors Fu Xi and Shen Nong established a rhythm in the human experience, enabling them to chime in with the cadence of the "flux and continuity" (*biantong* 變通) that they perceived

---

36. *Great Commentary* B4 知幾其神乎？君子上交不諂，下交不瀆，其知幾乎，幾者動之微，吉之先見者也，君子見幾而作，不俟終日。. . . 君子知微知彰，知柔知剛，萬夫之望。

37. *Great Commentary* B5: 過此以往，未之或知也。窮神知化，德之盛也。

to be enduring characteristics of the world around them. Inspired by the efficacy of their insights into the workings of the cosmos, these early progenitors then represented their interpretation of life in the world in a hexagramic language of images, models, and patterns for the benefit of the generations to come. Importantly, these hoary sages, far from pursuing some disinterested interrogation of nature, were engaged in a project of human articulation, refinement, and enculturation (*wenhua* 文化) that incorporates within it the world around them:

> According to the *Book of Changes*, with everything running its course, there is flux (*bian*), where there is such flux, there is continuity (*tong*), and where there is such continuity, it is enduring.[38]

In their efforts at *ars contextualis*—at "the art of contextualizing"—Fu Xi and Shen Nong sought to effectively coordinate the experience of the human being within the processes of nature, and in so doing, to optimize the creative possibilities of the cosmos. There is a perceived continuity between the human experience and the natural world within which it takes place: between human-inscribed petroglyphs and the natural striations found in stone and between the changing modalities of human thought and the turning array of terrestrial and celestial patterns. The sage kings cultivated a thick continuity between nurture and nature that is expressed in the evocative images that constitute the *Book of Changes*. This continuity is made explicit in expressions such as "the inseparability of the human and cosmic orders" (*tianren heyi* 天人合一)," the "mutual responsiveness of the human and cosmic orders" (*tianren xiangying* 天人相應), and "the resonance between the human and cosmic orders" (*tianren ganying* 天人感應). Importantly, such expressions are not reporting on two originally separate elements being reconciled after the fact but rather on the symbiotic mutuality and interpenetration of these aspectual dimensions of the human experience.

Indeed, this assumed continuity between nature and nurture is reflected in the fact that the same vocabulary is used to express the creative advance in both the human and the natural ecologies. For example, the

---

38. *Great Commentary* B2: 易窮則變，變則通，通則久。

vocabulary of "waymaking" (*dao* 道), "vital energies" (*qi* 氣), "patterned inscribing" (*wen* 文), "patterning" (*li* 理), "alternating" (*yinyang* 陰陽), and the perpetual interface between "flux and continuity" (*biantong* 變通) are all used to reference both the human and the natural worlds. In this cocreative relationship with the world around us, there is no initial or originative *logos*. Language and its significance emerges pari passu with a world that is continually being spoken into being by what Charles Taylor has called "the language animal," with the important qualification that these early progenitors were able to "read" the natural world and discern a shared and evolving cosmic language in the images they captured in the hexagrams. Within this cosmic context, the collaborative process of making meaning was first activated in the imagination of our earliest ancestors and then applied semiotically to "figure out" and give expression to their experience of the world. In the fullness of time, this discursive process has come to configure and express our reality, our cultural imaginary.

Building on this auspicious beginning, the sage kings who were later descendants of Fu Xi and Shen Nong—first the Yellow Emperor, then Yao and Shun—continued to construct human technologies, modes of transportation, social institutions and customs, and the written language inspired by particular hexagrams, with each hexagram providing a dynamic image of some natural process. And the text reports on this continuing symbiotic collaboration:

> The sages had the capacity to see the way the world operates, and perceiving the way things come together and commune, they put into practice their statutes and codes of propriety.[39]

It has been this gradual and ongoing process of structuring and ritualizing the human experience thus remembered in and inspired by the *Great Commentary* that has enchanted life in the world and that continues to produce its mystery and spirituality:

> When Shen Nong had passed, the Yellow Emperor, Yao, and Shun continued his innovations. They fathomed the flux and flow of the world around them and saved the people from

---

39. *Great Commentary* A8: 聖人有以見天下之動，而觀其會通，以行其典禮。

exhaustion. Through spiritual insight (*shen*) they transformed the human experience, and enabled the people to find what was most fitting in their lives.[40]

The productive symbiosis that can be achieved between the human and the natural world is practical inspiration for effective human living, lifting the human experience out of its base animality and elevating it to high culture. Human culture has transformed the markings on the backs of turtles into awe-inspiring calligraphy and pottery designs. Feeding at the trough has been elevated into fine dining and the elegance of the tea house and its rituals. Raw natural ore has been smelted and cast as sanctified bronze ceremonial vessels, and extracted plant matter has been transmuted into exquisite paintings and architectural designs. The cacophony of life has been focused and refined into the magic of sublime music, the animal heat of random copulation has been transformed into the warmth of hearth and home, and mere associations have become the institutions of true fellowship and the flourishing community.

In addition to enabling human beings to live moral and aesthetic lives, this understanding of the processes of change and productivity revealed by the *Book of Changes* has given them access to the very mysteries of the cosmos:

> The Master asked rhetorically, "Does not the person who understands the course of flux and transformation in fact have insight into the mysterious workings of the world?"[41]

Of significance in the nature and function of religiousness in this tradition is that the enchanted, numinous dimension of the human experience and its many mysteries (*shen* 神) does not belong to some other world. Far from it, such spirituality is the inexhaustible product of human efficacy and refinement within this world and the boundless penumbra that emanates from it:

> The *Book of Changes* is the sage's means of probing what is profound to its very limits, and examining thoroughly what

---

40. *Great Commentary* B2: 神農氏沒,黃帝、堯、舜氏作,通其變,使民不倦,神而化之,使民宜之。

41. *Great Commentary* A9: 子曰:「知變化之道者,其知神之所為乎。」

is still incipient (*ji* 幾). It is only through this profundity that the sages can discern the purposes of the world; it is only through the incipient that they can consummate the business of the world; it is only through insight into the mysteries of the world that they can be quick without haste and can arrive without even going.⁴²

In the course of time, such high expectations of the human experience have produced what I have referred to previously as an "a-theistic" religiousness—a religiousness that makes no appeal to an independent, transcendent deity as the source of order. It is this human- and family-centered religiousness that elevates the *cultivated* human experience into what *Focusing the Familiar* describes in cosmic proportions as human beings becoming cocreators with the heavens and the earth. Human beings, without reference to those limiting assumptions about religious transcendentalism and supernaturalism that would set boundaries on their experience, have become a source of profound meaning in their own boundless world: a world that is the only world. Cosmic creativity as described in the *Book of Changes* is fully a collaboration between human beings and their own environing context, positing a natural cosmology that reverses the gravity of theistic religiousness to convey what John Berthrong has called "the world-dependent nature of divine reality."⁴³

Tang Junyi and the *Book of Changes* Cosmology

Tang Junyi derives several organically related and mutually entailing postulates from the *Book of Changes* that can be used to reveal underlying assumptions about the human experience, and more specifically, about how human becomings are to be conceptualized within this process cosmology. The claim that the *Book of Changes* itself explicitly makes is that its way of characterizing the "holographic" cosmos can in turn be used to characterize anything within it—the unbounded totality to be found in every graph:

---

42. *Great Commentary* A10: 夫易, 聖人之所以極深而研幾也。唯深也, 故能通天下之志。唯幾也, 故能成天下之務。唯神也, 故不疾而速, 不行而至。

43. John Berthrong, *Concerning Creativity: A Comparison of Chu Hsi, Whitehead, and Neville* (Albany: State University of New York Press, 1998), 1.

> As a document, the *Book of Changes* is vast and far-ranging, and has everything complete within it. It contains the way of the heavens, the way of human beings, and the way of the earth.[44]

We might, for example, reflect on the last two hexagrams in the *Book of Changes*, *jiji* 既濟 and *weiji* 未濟, that together conjure up the images of first having forded the river and then not yet having gotten across—a pattern of having finished only to begin again. While the penultimate hexagram takes us full cycle and to closure, the last hexagram speaks to the ceaselessness and bottomlessness of the spiraling cosmic processes, precluding the strong "initial beginning and final end" teleological commitments that inform classical Greek thinking.

Such a characterization of the cosmos is consistent with how relationally constituted persons and the possibilities of the human experience have been conceptualized in this Confucian tradition. I have previously recounted how Angus Graham eventually came to his own understanding of the term "human propensities" (*xing* 性) consistent with this open-ended and emergent conception of cosmic order. Rejecting the assumption that *xing* references some predetermined and innate human nature—a "transcendent origin" that would anticipate a "transcendent end"—Graham came to a narrative understanding of *xing* as the capacity of always unique relationally constituted "human becomings" to pursue an optimal symbiosis within their ever-changing world. Such an emergent conception of cosmic order is consistent with the notions of life and death as these events occur and are understood within the context of a continuing family lineage and the intergenerational transmission of culture. Again, there is an understanding of culture that does not require the teleologically informed regulating and stewarding of nature's spontaneous growth; there is instead a contrapuntal responsiveness to nature's bounty that allows human beings to elaborate upon it, elevate it, and (through this collaboration) live a decidedly aesthetic if not profoundly spiritual life.

In his reflections on the cosmology underwritten by the *Book of Changes*, Tang Junyi begins by its affirmation of the reality and sufficiency of our empirical experience without any need to go beyond it. Indeed, with his first proposition, the postulate that "there is no fixed substance"

---

44. *Great Commentary* B8: 《易》之為書也，廣大悉 備，有天道焉，有人道焉，有地道焉。

(*wudingtiguan* 無定體觀), he rejects outright the relevance of any notion of ontological substance or substratum. In Tang's own words:

> The cosmos in the minds of Chinese people has always been nothing more than a continuous stream, a kind of moving flow. All of the things and events of the cosmos are just a continuing process. And beyond this process there is no fixed substratum that supports it.[45]

For the conception of persons, then, this means the irrelevance of a foundational, superordinate notion of self, soul, mind, nature, and so on. With this postulate, Tang is acknowledging both the fluidity and coagulation of *qi* 氣 as it animates the world in its ceaseless flux and flow.[46] The absence of any essentializing substratum—"what-it-means-to-be-this-kind of a thing"—means that experience, rather than being constituted by "things" that can be parsed as indivisibles into a taxonomy of natural kinds, is a flow of resolutely unique perturbations of and transactions among foci of *qi*—"the myriad events" (*wanwu* 萬物) and "all that is happening" (*wanyou* 萬有). Given the intrinsic and constitutive nature of relations, persons are in fact understood to be narrative streams of unique, mutually conditioning events. And the web of always shifting relationships that constitutes each person as an "event"—as *this* particular focus within *this* expansive field of experience—is itself a novel and unique construal of the totality. Entailed by the uniqueness of all persons as matrixes of relations is the absence of any notion of strict fixed identity, or the "law of non-contradiction" logic, that would follow from it. There is no appeal in this cosmology to some self-same shared characteristic that would make any two "different" persons in fact essentially the same.

Another proposition offered by Tang Junyi we have already referenced that is a corollary to the absence of any appeal to substratum is "the inseparability of the one and the many," or stated more elaborately, "the inseparability of uniqueness and multivalence, of continuity and multiplicity, of integrity and integration," and so on (*yiduo bufen guan* 一

---

45. Tang Junyi, *Complete Works*, 11:9: 中國人心目中之宇宙恆只為一種流行，一種動態；一切宇宙中之事物均只為一種過程，此過程以外別無固定之體以為其支持者 (substratum).

46. Tang Junyi, *Complete Works*, 11, 9–11.

多不分觀).⁴⁷ In the *Book of Changes* cosmology, the identity of anything and of everything can only be understood by reference to its context. What Tang means by this claim is that if we begin our reflection on the emergence of cosmic order from the wholeness of lived experience, we can view experience in terms of both its dynamic continuities and its manifold multiplicity, as both a ceaseless processual flow and as distinctive, consummatory events. This postulate is one more example of the mutual implication of binaries that characterizes all phenomena in the natural world—in this case, particularity and the totality, self and other. That is, any particular phenomenon in our field of experience can be focused in different ways: on the one hand, it is a unique and persistent particular, and on the other, since it is constituted by the full complement of its relationships, it has the entire cosmos and all that is happening implicated within it. How this is reflected in the understanding of persons is that they are uniquely who they are as distinct from all others, yet in their magnitude, to give a full account of the social, natural, and cultural relationships that constitute any one of them, we must exhaust the cosmic totality.

A process worldview is one of radical contextuality where the embedded particular and its context are at once continuous and distinct. In the *Book of Changes*, this sense of the mutuality of oneness and manyness is reflected in the image of the four seasons that are certainly distinctive and yet at the same time continuous with, and implicated in, each other:

> In their magnitude and scale, the processes of nature are a counterpart to the heavens and the earth; in their flux (*bian*) and in their continuity (*tong*), they are a counterpart to the four seasons.⁴⁸

This notion of the inseparability of continuity and multiplicity is necessary to understand the familiar claim we find throughout the early philosophical literature about the "oneness" of things, or of humans becoming "one" with all things, often stated as a kind of personal and even religious achievement.

---

47. Tang Junyi, *Complete Works*, 11:16–17.
48. *Great Commentary* A6: 廣大配天地，變通配四時。

That the *Book of Changes* has traditionally been given pride of place as first among the classics is revelatory of the primacy invested in process and change in Chinese cosmology, contrasting rather starkly with the ontological intuition that "only Being is" we find at the core of Parmenides's treatise, *The Way of Truth*. If Greek ontology as its starting point is grounded in an unchanging and self-sufficient "substance" (*ousia*), "being *per se*," the cosmology of the *Changes* takes as the most generic characteristic of experience "the generative procreativity of life itself" (*shengsheng* 生生). Tang Junyi's postulate that acknowledges the fact that the processual flow of experience is without initial beginning or final end is captured in his third postulate: "the unceasingness of procreating" (*shengsheng buyi guan* 生生不已觀) that echoes the observation in the *Book of Changes* that "ceaseless procreating is what is meant by 'change'" (*shengsheng zhi wei yi* 生生之謂易).[49] We might get further clarification on the nature of such "change" by remembering the Guo Moruo commentary that associates the character for "change" (*yi* 易) with its cognate *ci* 賜, "exchanging, transacting, gifting." Cosmic meaning is emergent in the vital transactions and exchanges among the unique events that constitute our world of experience. And experience so understood is continuous, genealogical, and naturalistic in the sense of making no appeal to any metaphysical or supernatural source.

The phenomenal world in classical China is an endless flow, evidencing its formal character only as "trans-*form*-ation" in which the formal aspect, always attended by temporality, is the cadence and (when properly cultivated) the musicality of life. In fact, the *Book of Changes* says explicitly that "the mysteries of the world have no squareness and change has no shape" (*shenwufang er yiwuti* 神無方而易無體).[50] Willard Peterson in interpreting this passage suggests that "to have no 'squareness' is to be not susceptible of being differentiated into parts and to be not adequately delimited by any conceptual bounds."[51] Insight into the mysteries of the world must go beyond all rationalizations because

---

49. Tang Junyi, *Complete Works*, 11:20–22; *Great Commentary* A5.

50. *Great Commentary* A4.

51. Willard J. Peterson, "Making Connections: 'Commentary on the Attached Verbalizations' of the *Book of Change*," *Harvard Journal of Asiatic Studies* 42, no. 1 (1982): 103.

the process of change can never be contained or arrested by any formal structure. Putative "things" are in fact a processive and hence always provisional flux of "events."⁵²

The contemporary philosopher Pang Pu 龐樸 makes an illuminating distinction in explaining "procreating" (*sheng* 生). He contrasts procreating as "derivation" (*paisheng* 派生) in the sense of one thing being the source or origin in giving birth to an independent existent, like a hen producing an egg or an oak tree producing an acorn, with procreating as "transmutation" (*huasheng* 化生), in which one thing continuously transforms into something else: like summer becoming autumn and autumn becoming winter. But these two senses of "procreating" are profoundly asymmetrical. In the *paisheng* "derivative of" modality of growth, it is only the rare egg that is incubated to become another hen, and it is only the rare acorn that takes root to become another oak tree. In the predominant *huasheng* "transmutating into" modality of change, most eggs in fact become omelets and most acorns, squirrels. And even in the rare cases where a hen's egg actually becomes another chicken, the erstwhile discreteness of this "independent existent" is qualified by a genealogical continuity with both its progenitor and its progeny.⁵³

Both of these senses of "procreating"—derivation and transmutation—are relevant to Chinese cosmology. Importantly, as we have seen with the hen and her egg, the discreteness and independence entailed by *paisheng* is qualified by the processual and contextual assumptions of *huasheng*. And the processual continuity of *huasheng* is parsed as unique "events" by the consummatory nature of *paisheng*. Neither uniqueness nor continuity will yield to the other; both are implicated in one another. The notion of intrinsic relationality that allows for the uniqueness and distinctiveness of particular things, on the one hand, and for the continuity that obtains among them on the other, disqualifies part-whole analysis and requires instead a gestalt shift to focus-field thinking in which "part" and "totality"

---

52. In fact, at least as early as the Ming dynasty, the Chinese expression for "thing," *dongxi* 東西, is literally "east-west," referencing the location of town markets and underscoring the relational and contextual understanding that attends Chinese phenomenological perceptions.

53. Pang Pu 龐樸, "Yizhong youji de yuzhou shengcheng tushi: Jieshao Chujian Taiyi shengshui" 一種有機的宇宙成圖式：介紹楚簡《太一生水》, *Daojia wenhua yanjiu* 道家文化研究 17 (1999): 303.

are two nonanalytic foregrounding and backgrounding perspectives on the same phenomenon.

In pursuing this distinction between "derivation" and "transmutation," Pang Pu is alerting us to a further refinement in our understanding of the relationship between what comes before and what follows from in the ongoing cosmological process. Taking the human experience specifically, while we might be inclined to understand the progenitor and progeny genealogy as a series in which there is an independence of the latter from the former, early Chinese cosmology on reflection sees genealogy as clearly a combination of both *paisheng* as "derivative of" and *huasheng* as "transmutating into." *This* progenitor is taken as giving way to *this* unique progeny but also continuing on in the family lineage to live within the same progeny. The child is certainly "independent" of the parents, and yet the parents live on in their child—and in their children's children—in many ways beyond their mere physicality.

In Confucianism, with the emphasis on history, ancestor reverence, intergenerational transmission, and continuing cultural identity, there is traditionally a powerful sense of genealogical continuity where the progeny is to be understood as the foregrounding of this particular person in a continuing lineage. One's family surname (*xing* 姓) is the first and continuing source of identity, while one's given name (*ming* 名) within the course of one's lifetime is complemented by a proliferation of assumed style names (*zi* 字), sobriquets (*hao* 號), and a web of specific family designations such as "uncle number two" (*ershu* 二叔) and "auntie number three" (*sanzhou* 三妯), with a series of professional titles such as "teacher" (*laoshi* 老師) and "director" (*zhuren* 主任), and then, when all is said and done, with a usually celebratory posthumous title (*shi* 諡). Each of these different names, as the roles one lives within a complex narrative, reflects one's unique contribution to the meaning of family and community.

Indeed, this serial sequencing of names is most revealing of a personal narrative. The person we know today as "Sun Yat-sen," for example, has the genealogical name of Sun Deming 孫德明, locating him in the web of the Sun family by sharing the second character *de* with both his brother and his other relatives of the same generation. Born in the Guangdong village of Cuiheng 翠亨, Sun arrives in Hawaii at age thirteen and is known to his family and community by his intimate "nursing name," Sun Dixiang 孫帝象, a name that as "the god's image" remembers and celebrates the local Cuiheng village god, the "God of the North" (*beidi* 北帝). This infant name in its Cantonese pronunciation, Tai Tseong, is found on the ledger of the Punahou School he attended, but because English lacks the Cantonese phoneme "tseong," the name was rendered "Tai Chu," and he was likely called the same by his teachers and classmates. When he is later baptized as a Christian in Hong Kong at age seventeen, he takes the name Sun Rixin 孫日新, or "daily renewing," an expression that alludes to the *Book of Changes*. In the same year, a mentor gives him the name Sun Yixian 孫逸仙, "liberated immortal" (pronounced "Yat-sen" in Cantonese), and from then on this becomes his formal name within the English-speaking world. In any official Chinese documents, however, and in his calligraphy as well, he uses his "big name" (大名), Sun Wen 孫文 as "Sun the cultured." And along the way, he assumes the courtesy name (字), Sun Zaizhi 孫載之, taken from the familiar expression "culture is how way-making is conveyed" 文以載道, as a play on his "big name" "cultured" (*wen* 文). In addition to the Zhongshan county in Guangdong province, every major city in China today remembers Sun Yat-sen with their "Zhongshan" (中山) parks and "Zhongshan" main streets, and the province of Guangzhou has its Zhongshan University 中山大學. But where did this name come from? Sun Zhongshan 孫中山, and more often Dr. Sun Zhongshan 孫中山先生, is taken from his Japanese alias "Nakayama Shō" 中山樵. Sun used this Japanese name while hiding from agents and spies enlisted by the Qing Court who dogged him relentlessly in Japan and around the world as he schemed to foment a revolution that would ultimately topple the Qing dynasty. And finally, in death, Sun Yat-sen has come to be known affectionately by a grateful China as *guofu* 國父 ("the father of our nation") locating this cosmopolitan figure squarely within the continuing genealogy of the Chinese people.

Sun Yat-sen's many names tell his complex story. Philosophically speaking, "meaning" as "sense," or "making sense" of something, requires that we acknowledge the narrative function of language wherein the social and political context is always integral to the meaning of what is being said. The application of such correlative pragmatics that relate persons to the events of their lives and that amplify the meaning of these episodes is not only retrospective but also importantly prospective and programmatic as well, constantly being deployed to anticipate new situations and to extend our complex, continuous, and evolving narratives.

From this excursus on the cosmological postulate of "ceaseless pro-creating," we can see how this description of cosmic order reflects the resolutely familial source of Confucian values, with both its genealogical assumptions and its commitment to the intergenerational transmission of culture. As a corollary to this "ceaseless procreating" and the narrative understanding of persons that follows from it, Tang Junyi's fourth characterization of the *Book of Changes* natural cosmology is "the postulate of non-determinism" (*feidingming guan* 非定命觀).[54] Herewith, Tang is asserting the irrelevance of fatalism for both Confucian cosmology and the human experience. In Tang Junyi's reading of the *Changes* the vitality of "ceaseless procreating" precludes the kind of determinism we associate with strong teleology: for Tang, there can be no real temporality, history, or change in a predetermined universe that has a fixed end. The human experience, then, is the bottomless unfolding of an emergent, contingent narrative according to the rhythm of its own internal creative processes without any fixed or final pattern and without any external guiding hand. Importantly, in this transformative process, a lifetime is understood as inseparable from the quantum of change that attends the underdetermined and emerging narratives of always unique persons. Indeed, genuine change—that is, the spontaneous emergence of novelty in the unique relations that are constitutive of people as events—is just another way of saying "genuine time." Time in the human experience is nothing other than the capacity of persons to change and to be changed in their associations, and as such, describes their propensity for transformation and renewal within their specific family and communal ecologies. In this open-ended cosmology, neither time nor the fecundity of our relationality will be denied.

Tang Junyi also restates this "nondeterministic" characterization of Chinese natural cosmology in a positive way with his fifth postulate: "the notion that there is a continuity and inseparability that obtains between determinacy and indeterminacy, motion and equilibrium, and all other such correlative binomials" (*heyouwu dongjing guan* 合有無動靜 觀).[55] Rather than being driven by any kind of necessary, deterministic teleology, the *Book of Changes* cosmology assumes the possibility of human collaboration in a contingent and negotiated optimizing symbiosis (*he* 和). This is but to say that human flourishing is the consequence of our best attempt to make the most out of the creative possibilities of the human

---

54. Tang Junyi, *Complete Works*, 11:17–19.
55. Tang Junyi, *Complete Works*, 11:11–16.

experience. The penumbra of indeterminacy that honeycombs an always provisional cosmic order means that the erstwhile forms and functions that define the events of our lives are mutually entailing. All form is constantly undergoing adjustment to maintain functional equilibrium and is vulnerable to and ultimately outrun by the process itself. At the same time, all functioning is shaped, refined, and made more efficient by evolving formal structures and is constantly being reformed to meet changing demands. There is nothing and thus no one that does not give way to the process of trans-*form*-ation.

Given that the world is without beginning or end, the goal for human beings in each and every moment is to achieve that kind of productive correlationality that optimizes the creative possibilities of the always unique situation. The achievement of an optimally productive harmony is not driven by some predetermined mechanical process, divine design, or rational blueprint. While the articulation and stabilizing regularity in the narrative of any particular person anticipates the way in which the events will continue to unfold, the indeterminate aspect within this story defeats any notion of formal necessity or absolute predictability. The combination of pattern and uncertainty precludes the possibility of universal claims about the human experience and renders precarious any globalizing generalizations. All we can depend upon is the *relative* stability provided by the confluence of always site-specific and particular expressions of order, with the need for vigilant attention to those variables at every level that might well amplify into larger-scale changes. Order so conceived is thus emergent and unique, and its ultimate source is local.

The omnipresent feature that underscores the contingent nature of any emerging order—human or otherwise—is its underdeterminacy. That is, there is an indeterminate aspect (*ji* 幾) entailed by the uniqueness of each participant that qualifies order, making any pattern of order novel and site specific, irreversible, reflexive, and to an extent, unpredictable. Taking persons as an example, all human beings might be similar enough to justify certain generalizations, yet each person is at the same time a unique, *one* of a kind. It is this uniqueness of each person that precludes the possibility of any logarithmic understanding of human conduct, and that keeps the definition of humanity an open-ended and ongoing proposition.

What follows from this interface between continuity and multiplicity is the cyclical and recursive nature of this processual cosmological order. This feature of the cosmology is described by Tang Junyi with a sixth proposition: "the notion that nothing advances but to return" (*wuwang bufu guan* 無往不復觀). This characteristic in the human experience registers the reflexivity of all conduct as it turns back to reshape its source. Since all participants in any instance of order are correlational, the unique particular cannot be separated from its context—focus cannot be separated from its field. Again, looking at this feature of cosmic order from a human perspective, any personal construal of order is recursive—a coming back upon itself. Personal conduct begins from a cultivated, critical, and purposeful self-awareness; then it shapes the world in what it accomplishes and comes back to bring this personal awareness into clearer resolution. Quite literally, what goes around comes around. To pollute the world is to pollute one's own body. To enchant the world is to enchant one's own life. To serve the best values of one's community is to serve one's own best interests. Great persons produce great worlds. It is this recursion that parses process into episodes, distinguishing and consummating the particular "events" of a life lived within it.

The flowering of this particular orchid is a unique life, while in its withering it produces the compost necessary to nourish the roots of the new life it has invested in its seeds. Such generative procreativity is the observed cadence and regularity of the world around us as it expresses its inherent capacity for self-transformation. The human experience also has its flowering with the turning of the seasons, where sixty years completes one full cycle, from the refulgent spring of life to the depths of winter, only to produce out of itself yet another cycle. Importantly, the "cyclical" process, while passing through familiar phases, is not replication. Each day is a new day. It is the unfolding of an endless spiral that evidences persistent and continuing life patterns on the one hand and novelty on the other, with each moment having its own unique character. The human experience unfolds as always unique persons advance together to shape their shared narratives through the discursive activities that command their specific worlds of meaning into being.

A corollary that follows from this notion of the consummating of particular life stories is that there is a priority of a dynamic, radial center over any putative boundaries. Order begins here and goes there, only to return. Perhaps these several postulates proffered by Tang Junyi can be summed up in the following claim: in Confucian natural cosmology, everything is at once local and global. Hence, we can describe person, family, community, and world in terms of the dynamics of being centrifugal centers that extend outward as radial circles, in degree subjective and objective—and in degree local and global. But these centers radiate outward only to draw back into themselves centripetally an energy that intensifies their own foci by having deferred to and appropriated what is most extended.

Tang Junyi has a final cosmological proposition derived from the *Book of Changes* that again expresses the idea that we are born into and extend out from a particular and specific context: "our natural propensities are in fact the way of *tian* (*xing ji tiandao guan* 性即天道觀)."[56] This claim is really only a more complex way of acknowledging the holographic interpenetration between particular human beings and the cosmos referenced in "the continuity between and inseparability of the human and the cosmic orders" (*tianrenheyi* 天人合一), a continuity that is always centered, genealogical, historicist, and boundless.

As we can see from this set of seven propositions, the cosmology that Tang Junyi derives from the *Book of Changes* and appeals to as the grounds for the "idea" of Confucianism, is resolutely genealogical, meliorative, particularist, and emergent. Tang's Confucianism is a pragmatic naturalism directed at achieving the highest integrated cultural, moral, and spiritual growth for persons-in-family-and-community as they coordinate the human experience with its cosmic context. In Tang's understanding of harmony as an optimizing symbiosis that starts here and goes there, the Confucian sages are no more than ordinary persons who, through commitment and assiduous discipline in cultivating their relations, are able to carry out the most ordinary of things in extraordinary ways. Those persons who in their own lives achieve *real* significance are our sages. And all of us, given the conditions the human experience in its wholeness provides, have the opportunity to live just such significant lives.

---

56. Tang Junyi, *Complete Works*, 11:22.

Epilogue

Why Theorize Confucian Persons for a Changing World Cultural Order?

Now it is a commonplace that Confucianism and East Asian philosophies broadly—Buddhism and Daoism as well—with their shared cosmological assumptions having been made explicit in the *Book of Changes*, begin from the primacy of growth and strengthening of vital relationships we associate with what James Carse has called "infinite games." We have seen that Confucian culture properly understood celebrates the relational values of deference and interdependence; it understands persons as constitutively embedded in and nurtured by unique, transactional patterns of relations. The question is whether a contemporary Confucian ethic that locates moral conduct within a thick and richly textured pattern of family, community, and natural relations can be a force for challenging and possibly changing the world geopolitical and cultural order.

Evidence is that there is at least an active minority in Asia who would answer this question affirmatively and who feel that Confucian culture can contribute significantly to the contemporary project of articulating a new world cultural order. Domestically in China we have over the past several decades witnessed a dramatic rise in "schools of canonical learning" (*guoxueyuan* 國學院) across most of the elite college campuses within China. And many of the best institutions of higher learning around the world have Chinese government-funded "Confucius Institutes" (*Kongzi xueyuan* 孔子學院) as partnerships between Chinese and Western entities; there are now over five hundred such institutes. It is clear that Confucian philosophy and its values are being actively promoted both at home and internationally by a combination of identifiable academic and political forces within China itself.

Another factor that might influence a changing world cultural order is China's "One Belt, One Road" (BRI) initiative that was introduced in late 2013 and is quickly becoming indicative of China's growing influence in the world. This massive strategy comes at a time when populist and nationalist movements within a beleaguered America and Europe are producing governments that are withdrawing from free trade agreements and either contesting or reneging on commitments to address global issues such as nuclear proliferation, mass immigration, environmental degradation, and runaway climate change. Indeed, there seems to be among Western nations an increasing rush to return to the finite games of single actors playing to win. The "One Belt, One Road" alternative being offered by China is a litmus test that will register the extent to which China's resources can be drawn upon to reconfigure the economic, political, and cultural order of the world. If China lives up to the Confucian values I have tried to outline and together with the international community is able to foster a compounding pattern of win-win infinite games, it will become a singularly important player in a new global order. But if China fails to make good on a rhetoric grounded in its own cultural assets of "win-win" (*gongying* 共贏) and "shared future for the human community" (*renleimingyun gongtongti* 人類命運共同體), then its expansionist policies will be a Chinese iteration of the colonization and imperialism unleashed on the world by European and American actors over the past few centuries and that continues unabated in its new economic guise. Under such a failed scenario, this formidable BRI initiative will likely change the winners but will do little more than reinforce those persisting geopolitical and economic inequities that continue to destabilize the world order.

What is the relevance of Confucianism as it has been transmitted through the classical canons for a changing world cultural order? For those who believe that Confucian philosophy has values and institutions that can be of significant benefit to a new world cultural order, important and critical questions need to be asked retrospectively about both the contributions and the failings of Confucianism as a pan-Asian phenomenon over its long history. Prospectively, too, we must ask if the globalization of Confucian values would make a felicitous difference in the contemporary global dynamic, and if so, how the prevailing and impoverishing equation between modernity and Westernization that erases Confucian culture altogether is to be challenged? Perhaps most importantly, how can a global Confucianism be retrofitted to constitute a critical, progressive, evolutionary, and emergent force that will make its own contribution to resolving the pressing issues of our times? What in concrete terms does the Confucian tradition have to offer a changing world cultural order?

As a living cultural tradition, the continuities between contemporary China and its earliest cultural roots are much more evident than the more tenuous links, for example, between ancient Greece and the modern nation-state of Greece, between ancient Rome and what is now modern Italy, or between ancient Egypt and its contemporary state. China provides an inclusive hybrid model of cultural change wherein the heat of contestation over the centuries has fired the furnace of amalgamation and fusion. This is a tradition in which the tides of Western learning, Buddhism, and then its various subsequent waves—from the Jesuits to Protestant educators to the influx of Marxism and down to phenomenology and pragmatism in our own times—have been ingested and internalized to become the evolving Confucian tradition itself. And the enduring momentum of this Confucian tradition comes from the fact that it proceeds from a relatively straightforward account of the actual human experience. Confucianism, rather than relying upon metaphysical presuppositions or supernatural speculations, is a pragmatic naturalism in the sense that it focuses on the possibilities for enhancing personal worth available to us here and now through enchanting the ordinary affairs of the day. Confucianism as a culture is simply the attempt to inspire the most ordinary of things within the human experience to become the most extraordinary of things. In this process of the intergenerational transmission of a living civilization, the cultural genealogy is implicated in and dependent upon the productive cultivation of its participants. And by extension, the meaning of the entire cosmos is implicated in and dependent upon the productive cultivation of persons within their families and communities. Personal worth is the source of human culture, and human culture in turn is the compounding resource that provides the context for each person's cultivation.

In terms of its religious sensibilities, Confucianism offers an alternative "family-centered" rather than "God-centered" religiousness, which unlike the competing Abrahamic traditions is not given to posturing as singular, exclusive, and absolute. Such a human religiousness has not, in the name of some ostensive One Truth, precipitated war and carnage among its adherents. Confucianism is at once "a-theistic" and profoundly religious.[1] It does not appeal to an independent, retrospective, and substantive divine agency as the reality behind appearance and as the source of all cosmic significance. Indeed, it is a religious tradition without a God: a religious sensibility affirming a spirituality that emerges out of the inspired human experience itself. For Confucianism, the world is an autogenerative, "self-so-ing" process—*ziran er ran* 自然而然—that includes the energy of its ongoing transformation as residing within the continuing narrative itself. Its world is an inside without an outside. And human feelings themselves are the motor of religious meaning, understood both retrospectively and prospectively as an unfolding and inclusive spirituality achieved within the qualitatively inspired activities of the family, the community, and the natural world. Human beings are both inspired by and contributors to the numinosity that elevates and refines the human experience within the world in which we live. There is no church (except for the extended family), no altars (except perhaps for the dining room table), and no clergy (except for the exemplary models both past and present who are deferred to as the living center of the community). Confucianism celebrates the way in which the process of human growth and extension is shaped by and contributes to the meaning of the totality—a notion of creatio in situ that stands in stark contrast to the theology of the creatio ex nihilo traditions in which the creator Godhead is everything and His creatures are nothing.

In the absence of eschatology, it seems that the early Confucian thinkers were preoccupied with making the most of the phenomenal world of process and change construed simply as "the unfolding field of experience" (*dao* 道), "the ten thousand processes and events" (*wanwu* 萬物), and when considered together, "everything that is happening." These early Confucian philosophers were less inclined to ask *what* makes something real or *why* things exist and more interested in *how* the complex relationships that obtain among the changing phenomena of their surroundings could be negotiated for optimum productivity and value. It is the pursuit of superlative quality in an achieved personal, social, and ultimately cosmic harmony rather than any theological or

---

1. See Roger T. Ames, "*Li* 禮 and the A-theistic Religiousness of Classical Confucianism," in *Confucian Spirituality*, ed. Tu Wei-ming and Mary Evelyn Tucker, vol. 1 (New York: Crossroads, 2003). A more sustained argument for the profundity and legitimacy of this alternative religiousness is found in Rosemont, *Rationality and Religious Experience*.

teleologically derived assumptions about origins or causal speculations about some grand design that served as a fundamental guiding value for these seminal thinkers.

Confucianism can also contribute to our understanding of social order. Confucian community is grounded in the aspiration for an achieved propriety in human roles and relations (*li* 禮), a way of translating this key philosophical term that is a considered choice. On the formal side, *li* are those meaning-invested roles, relationships, and institutions that facilitate thick communication and that promote the feelings of family and community. All formal conduct constitutes one aspect of *li*—including table manners, patterns of greeting and leave taking, graduations, weddings, funerals, gestures of deference, ancestral sacrifices, and so on. In this formal sense, the *li* constitute a social syntax that in the semiotics of the human experience provides each member with a defined place and status within the family, community, and polity. But the institutional *li* within this process cosmology are rhythm rather than form. The existential aspect of *li* makes them alive, always provisional, and emergent. The pattern of *li* can be fairly described in terms of a cultural hermeneutic as it is transmitted from generation to generation, serving a living civilization as repositories of meaning and enabling persons to appropriate persisting values and to make them appropriate to their own always novel situations. While we perform the *li* in the present, much of their efficacy stems from their being a link to both the past and the future.

In the discursive family and community, social order emerges out of the relational virtuosity made possible by effective communication, and *li* is nothing less than communal "language" in its broadest sense. Certainly, *li* is linguistic, but it is much more than just speaking to each other. It is also the language of body and gesture, music and food, protocols and ceremony, institutions and their functions, and roles and relationships. For Confucius, the "human becoming" as a social achievement is an adaptive success made possible through the applications of the social intelligence perpetuated through *li*. Society is not derivative of individual properties nor is the individual the product of social forces. Associated living and the personal collaboration such individuality entails do not bring discrete people together in relationships but rather makes increasingly productive what is already constitutively related. Confucianism provides a conception of family and community based on the pursuit of a sustained propriety within the roles and relations that bind them together. As what is most fundamental and enduring, *li* nurtures the internal dynamic of social and political order, making the invocation and imposition of the rule of law, while unfortunately necessary at times, always second best and a clear admission of communal failure.

With respect to Confucianism's contribution to human culture as a philosophy of education, we must begin by acknowledging that personal cultivation is certainly the root of Confucian philosophy, and again such personal growth is itself the substance of education. But we must also observe that any root that has not been properly set and that lacks a fertile environment will soon wither and die. To continue this horticultural metaphor, Confucian education must be understood as a process that is "radically" embedded in and grows within the roles and relations that constitute us as persons in the fertile context of our families and communities. The close link between education and Confucian morality lies in the fact that they are both grounded in a sustained growth in our roles and relations. Education so conceived is not instrumental as a means to some desired end but is a process that is an end in itself. We pursue education and thus grow simply to live intelligent lives, and we become moral through this growth in our relations simply to behave as moral human beings.

With "family reverence" (*xiao* 孝) as the governing moral imperative of classical Confucianism, it is clear that any understanding of philosophy of education in this tradition must begin from the primacy of those vital roles and relations that constitute us as persons in family and community. That is, within this interpretive framework, associated, interpersonal living is taken as empirical fact. Every person lives and every event takes place within a vital natural, social, and cultural context. Our lives are lived not beneath our skins but in the world. And no thing does anything by itself. Association being a fact, our different roles lived within family and community are nothing more than the stipulation of specific modes of associated living: mothers and grandsons, teachers and students, and even second cousins and shopkeepers. Many of these designated roles, far from being arbitrary and contingent, can be traced back into the mists of history and the emergence of human beings in their earliest forms as being basic to the human experience of family and community life. The role of mothers and communal elders is integral to the human genealogy. But while we must acknowledge that associated living is a simple fact, the consummate conduct that comes to inspire virtuosity in the roles lived in family, community, and the cultural narrative broadly is normative. What we have come to call "Confucian role ethics" is no more than stipulated kinds of association that register the personal growth of each person in the roles that they live. Confucian role ethics is what human beings, with effort and imagination, are able to make of the fact of association.[2]

With Confucian role ethics as a vision of the moral life, Confucianism offers a win-win or lose-lose alternative to the divisive and deflationary model of winners and losers characteristic of the ideology of liberal individualism. Indeed, when we turn to Confucian role ethics, the specific guidelines offered for consummate conduct, rather than appealing to self-sufficient, abstract principles or values or virtues, look primarily to theorizing practice within the contours of our concrete and existentially more immediate familial and social roles. In contrast to abstract principles, there is a vital sense of propriety in our lived roles and relations that we can feel viscerally—a commitment to what it means to be this son to this mother. And on that basis, role ethics provides the kind of intuitive insight that would suggest to us, quite specifically, what we ought to do next. Role ethics, in offering insight into how to behave most productively in our relations, provides an explanation for proper conduct that does not obscure the inevitable complexity of human activities in service to a simple-minded sense of right and wrong. "Because he is my brother" is both a disarmingly simple and yet a profoundly complex justification for my conduct and is persuasive in a way that other reasons are not.

In summary, then, I believe that this exploration of the Confucian notion of persons is particularly felicitous at a time when a runaway libertarianism claims moral purchase by invoking the unfettered freedom of the autonomous individual as the foundation and ultimate source of social and political justice. On this argument, the libertarian can then reject any conception of justice that retards such freedom as fundamentally immoral. That is, the once benign and productive fiction of a foundational individualism has now become a pernicious default ideology among urbane intellectuals who, in a post-Marxist era, have abandoned any gesture in the direction of what they perceive to be a faceless collectivism.

The single most important common denominator within the various areas of the Confucian cultural sensorium thus rehearsed, from education to ethics, is the relationally constituted conception of persons. In this monograph, then, I have argued that perhaps the most important contribution Confucian philosophy has to offer our times is precisely its own elaborate, sophisticated, and ethically compelling conception

---

2. See Ames, *Confucian Role Ethics*.

of relationally constituted persons that can be drawn upon to critique and challenge the entrenched ideology of foundational individualism. Particularly at a critical time when we can fairly anticipate a quantum transformation in the changing world cultural order, this alternative conception of persons as human becomings should allow Confucianism its rightful place at the table.

The argument in these pages has not been that the Confucian values I am advocating can solve all of the world's problems. Nor has the argument been that the ineluctable forces of Westernization are pernicious and need to be contained. Instead, my attempt to bring attention to the Confucian tradition has been that we would do well to make room for all of the cultural resources available to us at a time in history when the most dramatic changes to the human condition are gathering on the horizon. In many ways, the position advanced herein has been compensatory, trying to overcome the kind of ignorance that comes with the uncritical ignoring of an ancient tradition integral to the identity of a quarter of the world's population. This Confucian cultural tradition is of great value not only as a source of enrichment for world culture but also as a substantial critique of our existing values. We would all do well to know it better.

Bibliography

Ames, Roger T. 安樂哲. "Reconstructing A.C. Graham's Reading of *Mencius* on *Xing* 性: A Coda to 'The Background of the Mencian Theory of Human Nature' (1967)." In *Having a Word with Angus Graham: At Twenty-Five Years into His Immortality*, edited by Carine Defoort and Roger T. Ames. Albany: State University of New York Press, 2018.
———. "Philosophizing with Canonical Chinese Texts: Seeking an Interpretive Context." In *Research Handbook on Methodology in Chinese Philosophy*, edited by Sor-hoon Tan. London: Bloomsbury, 2016.
———. "Classical Daoism in an Age of Globalization: From Abduction to *Ars Contextualis* in Early Daoist Cosmology." *Taiwan Journal of East Asian Studies* 12, no. 2 (December 2015).
———. 儒家的角色倫理學與杜威的實用主義: 對個人主義意識形態的挑戰 [Confucian role ethics and Deweyan pragmatism: A challenge to the ideology of individualism]. 《東嶽論叢》 [Dongyue tribune] 總第233期 (2013): 年第11期). Reprinted in 《倫理學》 (*Ethics*) no. 1 (2014).
———. *Confucian Role Ethics: A Vocabulary*. Hong Kong: Chinese University Press, 2011.
———. "*Li* 禮 and the A-theistic Religiousness of Classical Confucianism." In Vol. 1, *Confucian Spirituality*, edited by Tu Wei-ming and Mary Evelyn Tucker. New York: Crossroads, 2003.
———. "The Meaning of Body in Classical Chinese Philosophy." In *Self as Body in Asian Theory and Practice*, edited by R.T. Ames, W. Dissanayake, and T. Kasulis. Albany: State University of New York Press, 1993.
Ames, Roger T., and David L. Hall. *Making This Life Significant: A Translation and Philosophical Interpretation of the* Daodejing. New York: Ballantine, 2003.
———. *Focusing the Familiar: A Translation and Philosophical Interpretation of the* Zhongyong. Honolulu: University of Hawai'i Press, 2001.
Ames, Roger T., and Henry Rosemont Jr. "From Kupperman's Character Ethics to Confucian Role Ethics: Putting Humpty Together Again." In *Moral

Cultivation and Confucian Character: Engaging Joel J. Kupperman, edited by Li Chenyang and Ni Peimin. Albany: State University of New York Press, 2014.

———. *The Analects of Confucius: A Philosophical Translation*. New York: Ballantine, 1998.

Angle, Steve. "The *Analects* and Moral Theory." In *Dao Companion to the Analects*, edited by Amy Olberding. Dordrecht, The Netherlands: Springer, 2014.

Anscombe, G. E. M. "Modern Moral Philosophy." *Philosophy* 33 (1958).

Aristotle. *The Complete Works of Aristotle. The Revised Oxford Translation*. Edited by Jonathan Barnes. Princeton, NJ: Princeton University Press, 1984.

Austin, J. L. *Sense and Sensibilia*. Edited by G. J. Warnock. Oxford: Clarendon, 1962.

Bagley, Robert. "Shang Archaeology." In *Cambridge History of Ancient China: From the Origin of Civilization to 221 B.C.*, edited by Michael Loewe and Edward L. Shaughnessy. Cambridge: Cambridge University Press, 1999.

Barrett, Timothy. "Chinese Religion in English Guise: The History of an Illusion." *Modern Asian Studies* 39, no. 3 (2005): 509–33.

Bell, Daniel A. "Roles, Community, and Morality: Comment on *Confucian Role Ethics*." In *Appreciating the Chinese Difference: Engaging Roger T. Ames on Methods, Issues, and Roles*, edited by Jim Behuniak. Albany: State University of New York Press, 2018.

Berthrong, John. *Concerning Creativity: A Comparison of Chu Hsi, Whitehead, and Neville*. Albany: State University of New York Press, 1998.

Bloom, Paul. *Just Babies*. New York: Random House, 2014.

Boodberg, Peter A. "The Semasiology of Some Primary Confucian Concepts." *Philosophy East and West* 2, no. 4 (1953).

Campbell, James. *Understanding John Dewey*. La Salle, IL: Open Court, 1995.

Carse, James. *Finite and Infinite Games*. New York: Ballantine, 1987.

Carter, Ian. "Positive and Negative Liberty." In *The Stanford Encyclopedia of Philosophy*. Edited by Edward N. Zalta. Stanford, CA: Stanford University Press, 2016. https://plato.stanford.edu/archives/fall2016/entries/liberty-positive-negative/.

Chan, Alan K. L. "A Matter of Taste: *Qi* (Vital Energy) in the Tending of the Heart (*Xin*) in *Mencius* 2A2." In *Mencius: Contexts and Interpretations*, edited by Alan K. L. Chan. Honolulu: University of Hawai'i Press, 2001.

Chan, Wing-tsit. *A Source Book in Chinese Philosophy*. Princeton, NJ: Princeton University Press, 1963.

———. "The Evolution of the Concept *Jen*." *Philosophy East and West* 4, no. 1 (January 1953).

Chang, Kwang-chih. "Some Dualistic Phenomena in Shang Society." *Journal of Asian Studies* 24, no. 1 (November 1964).

Clippinger, John Henry. *A Crowd of One: The Future of Individual Identity*. New York: PublicAffairs, 2007.
Cohen, Paul A. *Discovering History in China: American Historical Writing on the Recent Chinese Past*. New York: Columbia University Press, 1984.
Dalmiya, Vrinda. "Linguistic Erasures." *Peace Review* 10, no. 4 (1998).
Davis, Sir James F. *The Chinese: A General Description of the Empire of China and Its Inhabitants*. London: Charles Knight, 1836.
Dawson, Raymond. *Confucius*. New York: Hill and Wang, 1981.
Daxue and Zhongyong: Bilingual Edition, edited by Ian Johnston and Wang Ping, Hong Kong: Chinese University Press, 2012.
Dewey, John. *The Correspondence of John Dewey, 1871–2007 (I-IV)*. Vol. 1, 1871–1918, 1871–2007. Charlottesville, VA: IntelLex. The Past Masters Database. http://www.nlx.com/collections/132
———. *The Later Works of John Dewey, 1925–1953*. Edited by Jo Ann Boydston. Carbondale: Southern Illinois University Press, 1985.
———. *The Middle Works of John Dewey, 1899–1924*. Edited by Jo Ann Boydston. Carbondale: Southern Illinois University Press, 1977.
———. *The Early Works of John Dewey, 1882–1898*. Edited by Jo Ann Boydston. Carbondale: Southern Illinois University Press, 1971.
Drabinski, John E. *Diversity, 'Neutrality,' Philosophy* (blog), May 11, 2016. http://jdrabinski.com/2016/05/11/diversity-neutrality-philosophy/.
Elstein, David. "Contemporary Confucianism." In *The Routledge Companion to Virtue Ethics*, edited by Lorraine Besser-Jones and Michael Slote. New York: Routledge, 2015.
Emerson, Ralph Waldo. "American Civilization." *Atlantic Monthly* 9 (1862): 502–11.
Emmet, Dorothy. *Rules, Roles and Relations*. London: Macmillan, 1967.
Farquhar, Judith. *Knowing Practice: The Clinical Encounter of Chinese Medicine*. Boulder, CO: Westview, 1994.
Fei, Xiaotong. *From the Soil: The Foundations of Chinese Society*. Translated by Gary G. Hamilton and Wang Zheng. Berkeley: University of California Press, 1992.
Fingarette, Herbert. "The Music of Humanity in the Conversations of Confucius." *Journal of Chinese Philosophy* 10 (1983).
———. *Confucius: The Secular as Sacred*. New York: Harper and Row, 1972.
Franklin, Ursula. "On Bronze and Other Metals in Early China." In *The Origins of Chinese Civilization*, edited by David N. Keightley. Berkeley: University of California Press, 1983.
Fraser, Chris. "Mohism." In *The Stanford Encyclopedia of Philosophy*. Edited by Edward N. Zalta. Stanford, CA: Stanford University Press, 2012. http://plato.stanford.edu/archives/fall2012/entries/mohism/.

Garfield, Jay, and Bryan Van Norden. *New York Times*, May 11, 2016. http://www.nytimes.com/2016/05/11/opinion/if-philosophy-wont-diversify-lets-call-it-what-it-really-is.html.

Gimello, Robert M. "The Civil Status of *li* in Classical Confucianism." *Philosophy East and West* 22 (1972): 203–11.

Giradot, Norman J. *The Victorian Translation of China: James Legge's Oriental Pilgrimage*. Berkeley: University of California Press, 2002.

Graham, A. C. *Studies in Chinese Philosophy and Philosophical Literature*. Albany: State University of New York Press, 1990. First published by the Institute of East Asian Philosophies, National University of Singapore, 1986.

———. "Replies." In *Chinese Texts and Philosophical Contexts: Essays Dedicated to Angus C. Graham*, edited by Henry Rosemont Jr. La Salle, IL: Open Court, 1991.

———. *Disputers of the Tao*. La Salle, IL: Open Court, 1989.

———. *Later Mohist Logic, Ethics and Science*. Hong Kong: Chinese University Press, 1978.

———. "The Background of the Mencian Theory of Human Nature." *Tsing Hua Journal of Chinese Studies* 6.1–2 (1967).

Granet, Marcel. "Right and Left in China." In *Right and Left: Essays on Dual Symbolic Classification*, edited by Rodney Needham. Chicago: University of Chicago Press, 1977.

———. *La pensée chinoise*. Paris: Editions Albin Michel, 1934.

Guo Qiyong 郭齐勇 and Li Lanlan 李兰兰. 安乐哲《儒学角色伦理学》学说的折评 [An appreciative critique of Roger T. Ames's notion of Confucian role ethics] 哲学研究 [Research in philosophy] no. 1 (2015).

Hall, David L. *Eros and Irony: A Prelude to Philosophical Anarchism*. Albany: State University of New York Press, 1983.

Hall, David L., and Roger T. Ames. *Thinking from the Han: Self, Truth, and Transcendence in Chinese and Western Culture*. Albany: State University of New York, 1998.

Hansen, Chad. *A Daoist Theory of Chinese Thought*. Hong Kong: Oxford University Press, 1992.

Hartshorne, Charles. *A History of Philosophical Systems*. New York: Philosophical Library, 1950.

Hershock, Peter D. *Valuing Diversity: Buddhist Reflection on Realizing a More Equitable Global Future*. Albany: State University of New York Press, 2012.

———. *Buddhism in the Public Sphere: Reorienting Global Interdependence*. New York: Routledge, 2006.

Hou Hanshu 後漢書 [History of the later Han dynasty]. Peking: Zhonghua shuju, 1965.

Hoyt, Sarah F. "The Etymology of Religion." *Journal of the American Oriental Society* 32, no. 2 (1912).

Hsiao, Kung-chuan. *A History of Chinese Political Thought*. Translated by F. W. Mote. Princeton, NJ: Princeton University Press, 1979.

Huang, Yushun 黄玉顺. 角色意识:《易传》之"定位"观念与正义问题——角色伦理学与生活儒学比较 [Role consciousness: The concept of "positioning" in the *Commentaries to the Book of Changes* and the problem of justice: A comparison between role ethics and life Confucianism)《齐鲁学刊》[*Journal of Qi and Lu*] no. 2 (2014).

Ing, Michael David Kaulana. *The Dysfunction of Ritual in Early Confucianism*. Oxford: Oxford University Press, 2012.

James, William. *Pragmatism and Other Writings*. New York: Penguin, 2000.

———. *William James: The Essential Writings*. Edited by Bruce W. Wilshire. Albany: State University of New York Press, 1984.

———. *Varieties of Religious Experience: A Study in Human Nature*. New York: Penguin, 1982.

Johnson, Mark. *The Body in the Mind: The Bodily Basis of Meaning, Imagination, and Reason*. Chicago: University of Chicago Press, 1987.

Kang Yunmei. *Zhongguo gudai siwangguan zhi tanjiu* [An exploration of the ancient Chinese view of death]. Taipei: National Taiwan University History and Chinese Literature Series no. 85, 1994.

Karlgren, Bernhard. *Grammata Serica Recensa*. Stockholm: Museum of Far Eastern Antiquities, 1950.

———, trans. *The Book of Odes*. Stockholm: Bulletin of the Museum for Far Eastern Antiquities, 1950.

Keightley, David N. *These Bones Shall Rise Again*. Edited by Henry Rosemont Jr. Albany: State University of New York Press, 2014.

———. "The Shang: China's First Historical Dynasty." In *Cambridge History of Ancient China: From the Origin of Civilization to 221 B.C.*, edited by Michael Loewe and Edward L. Shaughnessy. Cambridge: Cambridge University Press, 1999.

———. "Shamanism, Death, and the Ancestors: Religious Mediation in Neolithic and Shang China, ca. 5000–1000 B.C." *Asiatische studien* 52 (1998): 763–828.

———. "Early Civilization in China: Reflections on How it Became Chinese." In *Heritage of China: Contemporary Perspectives on Chinese Civilization*, edited by Paul S. Ropp. Berkeley: University of California Press, 1990.

———. "Shang Divination and Metaphysics." *Philosophy East and West* 38 (1988): 367–97.

Kim, Myeong-seok. "Is There No Distinction between Reason and Emotion in *Mengzi*?" *Philosophy East and West* 64, no. 1 (2014).

Kupperman, Joel J. "Tradition and Community in the Formation of Character and Self." In *Confucian Ethics: A Comparative Study of Self, Autonomy, and Community*, edited by Kwong-loi Shun and David B. Wong. Cambridge: Cambridge University Press, 2004.

———. *Learning from Asian Philosophy*. New York and Oxford: Oxford University Press, 1999.

———. *Character*. New York and Oxford: Oxford University Press, 1991.

Kwan, Tze-wan. "Multi-Function Character Database." Research Center for Humanities Computing. http://humanum.arts.cuhk.edu.hk/Lexis/lexi-mf/.

Lai, Karyn. "*Ren* 仁: An Exemplary Life." In *Dao Companion to the Analects*, edited by Amy Olberding. Dordrecht, The Netherlands: Springer, 2014.

Lau, D. C. *Confucius: The Analects (Lunyu)*. Hong Kong: Chinese University of Hong Kong Press, 1992.

———. *Mencius*. Hong Kong: Chinese University Press, 1984.

Lakoff, George, and Mark Johnson. *Metaphors We Live By*. Chicago: University of Chicago Press, 1980.

Legge, James, trans. *The Chinese Classics*. 5 vols. Hong Kong: University of Hong Kong Press, 1960.

Lewis, Mark Edward. *Writing and Authority in Early China*. Albany: State University of New York Press, 1999.

———. *Sanctioned Violence in Early China*. Albany: State University of New York, 1990.

Liji 禮記 [Record of rites]. *A Concordance to the Liji*. Lau, D. C. and Chen Fong Ching. Hong Kong: Commercial, 1992.

Li, Ling 李零. 中國方術考 *Zhongguo fangshu kao*. Beijing: Zhonghua Shuju, 1993.

———. 試圖與中國古代的宇宙模式 "'Shi tu' yu Zhongguo gudai de yuzhou moshi." *Jiuzhou xuekan* 4, nos. 1–2 (1991): 5–53, 49–76.

Li, Zehou. "An Explanation of the Summary Chart on Ethics" 关于"伦理学总览表"的说明. 2018.

———. *The Path of Beauty: A Study of Chinese Aesthetics*. Oxford: Oxford University Press, 1994.

Liang, Tao 梁 涛. "Zhu Xi dui 'shendu' de wudu ji qizijingxue quanshizhong de yiyi 朱熹"慎獨"的誤讀及其在經學詮釋中的意義. *Zhexueyanjiu* 哲学研究 第 3 期 (2004).

Liu, Lydia H. *Translingual Practice: Literature, National Culture, and Translated Modernity—China, 1900–1937*. Stanford, CA: Stanford University Press, 1995.

Lloyd, Geoffrey, and Nathan Sivin. *The Way and the Word: Science and Medicine in Early China and Greece*. New Haven, CT: Yale University Press, 2002.

Loewe, Michael. *Chinese Ideas of Life and Death: Faith, Myth, and Reason in the Han Period (202 BC–220 AD)*. London: Allen and Unwin, 1982.

Major, John. *Heaven and Earth in Early Han Thought*. Albany: State University of New York Press, 1993.

———. "Reply to Richard Kunst's Comments on *Hsiu* and *Wu Hsing*." *Early China* 3 (1977): 69–70.

———. "A Note on the Translation of Two Technical Terms in Chinese Science: *Wu-Hsing* and *Hsiu*." *Early China* 2 (1976): 1–3.

Marett, R. R. *A Jerseyman at Oxford*. Oxford: Oxford University Press, 1941.

Martinez-Robles, David. "The Western Representation of Modern China: Orientalism, Culturalism and Historiographical Criticism." *Digithum* 10 (2008). http://www.uoc.edu/digithum/10/dt/eng/martinez.pdf.

May, Larry. *Sharing Responsibility*. Chicago: University of Chicago Press, 1992.

McLeod, Alex. "*Ren* as a Communal Property in the *Analects*." *Philosophy East and West* 62, no. 4 (October 2012).

Mead, George Herbert. *The Individual and the Social Self: Unpublished Work of George Herbert Mead*. Edited by David L. Miller. Chicago: University of Chicago Press, 1982.

———. *Mind, Self, and Society*. Edited by Charles W. Morris. Chicago: University of Chicago Press, 1934.

Mozi 墨子 Harvard Yenching Sinological Series, Supplement 21. Beijing: Harvard-Yenching Institute, 1948.

Needham, Joseph. *History of Scientific Thought*. Vol. 2 of *Science and Civilisation in China*. Cambridge: Cambridge University Press, 1956.

Neville, Robert Cummings. *Ritual and Deference: Extending Chinese Philosophy in a Comparative Context*. Albany: State University of New York Press, 2008.

Ni, Peimin. *Understanding the* Analects *of Confucius: A New Translation of* Lunyu *with Annotations*, Albany: State University of New York Press, 2017.

Nietzsche, Friedrich. *The Gay Science*. Translated by Walter Kaufmann. New York: Random House, 1991.

———. *Beyond Good and Evil*. Translated by Walter Kaufmann. New York: Vintage, 1966.

Nuyen, A. T. "Confucian Role Ethics." *Comparative and Continental Philosophy* 4, no. 1 (2012): 141–150.

Nylan, Michael. "Boundaries of the Body and Body Politic in Early Confucian Thought." In *Boundaries and Justice*, edited by David Miller and Sohail Hashmi, 112–35. Princeton, NJ: Princeton University Press, 2001. Reprinted in *Confucian Political Ethics*. Edited by Daniel A. Bell. Princeton, NJ: Princeton University Press, 2007.

Nylan, Michael, and Thomas Wilson. *Lives of Confucius: Civilization's Greatest Sage through the Ages*. New York: Doubleday, 2010.

Palsson, Gisli, Bronislaw Szerszynski, Sverker Sorlin, John Marks, Bernard Avril, Carole Crumley, and Heide Hackmann. "Reconceptualizing the 'Anthropos' in the Anthropocene: Integrating the Social Sciences and Humanities in Global Environmental Change Research." *Environmental Science & Policy* 28 (April 2013).

Peterson, Willard J. "Making Connections: 'Commentary on the Attached Verbalizations' of the *Book of Change*." *Harvard Journal of Asiatic Studies* 42, no. 1 (1982).

Pulleyblank, Edwin. *Outline of Classical Chinese Grammar*. Vancouver: University of British Columbia Press, 1995.

Putnam, Hilary. *Realism with a Human Face*. Cambridge, MA: Harvard University Press, 1990.

———. *The Many Faces of Realism*. La Salle, IL: Open Court, 1987.

Reding, Jean-Paul. "Words for Atoms, Atoms for Words—Comparative Considerations on the Origins of Atomism in Ancient Greece and the Absence of Atomism in Ancient China." In *Comparative Essays in Greek and Chinese Rational Thinking*. Aldershot, UK: Ashgate, 2004.

Richards, I. A. *Mencius on the Mind: Experiments in Multiple Definition*. New York: Harcourt, Brace, 1932.

Rosemont, Henry, Jr. *Rationality and Religious Experience*. La Salle, IL: Open Court, 2002.

———, ed. *Chinese Texts and Philosophical Contexts: Essays Dedicated to Angus C. Graham*. La Salle, IL: Open Court, 1991.

———. "Rights-Bearing and Role-Bearing Persons." In *Rules, Rituals, and Responsibility: Essays Dedicated to Herbert Fingarette*, edited by Mary Bockover. La Salle, IL: Open Court, 1991.

Rosemont, Henry, Jr., and Roger T. Ames. *The Chinese Classic of Family Reverence: A Philosophical Translation of the* Xiaojing 孝經. Honolulu: University of Hawai'i Press, 2009.

Ryle, Gilbert. *The Concept of Mind*. New York: Routledge, 2009.

Sandel, Michael J. *Liberalism and the Limits of Justice*. Cambridge: Cambridge University Press, 1982.

Sandel, Michael J., and Paul J. D'Ambrosio, eds. *Encountering China: Michael Sandel and Chinese Philosophy*. Cambridge, MA: Harvard University Press, 2018.

Schleiermacher, Friedrich D. E. *The Christian Faith*. Edited by H. R. Mackintosh and J. S. Stewart. London: T & T Clark, 1999.

Schlipp, Paul, ed. *The Philosophy of Alfred North Whitehead*. New York: Tudor, 1941.

Sen, Amartya. *The Idea of Justice*. Cambridge, MA: Harvard University Press, 2009.

Shun, Kwong-loi. "Studying Confucian and Comparative Ethics: Methodological Reflections." *Journal of Chinese Philosophy* 36, no. 3 (September 2009).

———. *Mencius and Early Chinese Thought*. Stanford, CA: Stanford University Press, 1997.

Shusterman, Richard. *Body Consciousness: A Philosophy of Mindfulness and Somaesthetics*. Cambridge: Cambridge University Press, 2008.
Sim, May. *Remastering Morals with Aristotle and Confucius*. Cambridge: Cambridge University Press, 2007.
Sima Qian 司馬遷. Shiji 史記 [Records of the historian]. Beijing: Zhonghua shuju, 1959.
Sivin, Nathan. *Medicine, Philosophy and Religion in Ancient China: Researches and Reflections*. Aldershot, UK: Variorum, 1995.
———. "State, Cosmos, and Body in the Last Three Centuries B.C." *Harvard Journal of Asiatic Studies* 55, no. 1 (1995): 5–37.
———. Foreword to *The Theoretical Foundations of Chinese Medicine* by Manfred Porkert. Cambridge, MA: MIT Press, 1974.
Slingerland, Edward, trans. *Analects: With Selections from Traditional Commentaries*. Indianapolis: Hackett, 2003.
Smiley, Marion. *Moral Responsibility and the Boundaries of Community*. Chicago: University of Chicago Press, 1992.
Sommer, Deborah. "Boundaries of the *Ti* Body." In *Star Gazing, Fire Phasing, and Healing in China: Essays in Honor of Nathan Sivin,* edited by Michael Nylan, Henry Rosemont Jr., and Li Waiyee. Taipei: Academy Sinica, Institute of Philology, 2008.
Standaert, Nicolas. "The Jesuits did NOT Manufacture "Confucianism." *East Asian Science, Technology and Medicine* 16 (1999): 115–32.
Sutta-Nipata. Translated by H. Saddhatissa. London: Curzon, 1985.
Tan, Sor-hoon. *Confucian Democracy: A Deweyan Reconstruction*. Albany: State University of New York Press, 2003.
Tang Junyi 唐君毅. *Complete Works of Tang Junyi* 唐君毅全集. Taipei: Xuesheng shuju, 1991.
———. "Zhongguo zhexuezhong ziranyuzhouguan zhi tezhi 中國哲學中自然宇宙觀之特質 [The distinctive features of natural cosmology in Chinese philosophy]. *Zhongxi zhexue sixiang zhi bijiao lunwenji* 中西哲學思想之比較論文集 [Collected essays on the comparison between Chinese and Western philosophical thought]. Taipei: Xuesheng shuju, 1988.
Tang Yijie 汤一介. *Tang Yijie zhexue jinghua bian* 汤一介哲学精华编 [The essential philosophy of Tang Yijie]. Beijing: Beijing United, 2016.
Taylor, Charles. *The Language Animal: The Full Shape of the Human Linguistic Capacity*. Cambridge, MA: Harvard University Press, 2016.
———. *Sources of the Self: The Making of the Modern Identity*. Cambridge, MA: Harvard University Press, 1989.
Tiles, Mary. "Images of Reason in Western Culture." In *Alternative Rationalities*, edited by Eliot Deutsch. Honolulu, HI: Society for Asian and Comparative Philosophy, 1992.

———. "Idols of the Market Place: Knowledge and Language." Unpublished manuscript, n.d.

Tu, Wei-ming. *Centrality and Commonality: An Essay on Confucian Religiousness.* Albany: State University of New York Press, 1989.

Voltaire. *Oeuvres complètes de Voltaire, 1869.* Texte établi par Louis Moland, Garnier, 1883.

Wang, Aihe. *Cosmology and Political Culture in Early China.* Cambridge: Cambridge University Press, 2000.

Watson, Burton. *The Complete Works of Chuang Tzu.* New York: Columbia University Press, 1968.

Waley, Arthur. *Three Ways of Thought in Ancient China.* Stanford, CA: Stanford University Press, 1939.

Weissman, David. *A Social Ontology.* New Haven, CT: Yale University Press, 2000.

Wheatley, Paul. *The Pivot of the Four Quarters: A Preliminary Enquiry into the Origins and Character of the Ancient Chinese City.* Chicago: University of Chicago Press, 1971.

Whitehead, A. N. *Religion in the Making.* New York: Fordham University Press, 1996.

———. *Process and Reality: An Essay in Cosmology.* 2nd ed. New York: Free Press, 1979.

———. *Dialogues of Alfred North Whitehead*, edited by Lucien Price. Boston: Little, Brown, 1954.

———. *Modes of Thought.* New York: Free Press, 1938.

Williams, Bernard. *Moral Luck: Philosophical Papers 1973–1980.* New York: Cambridge University Press, 1981.

Williams, Raymond. *Keywords: A Vocabulary of Culture and Society.* New York: Oxford University Press, 1976.

Wittgenstein, Ludwig. *Philosophical Investigations (PI).* Edited by G. E. M. Anscombe and R. Rhees. Translated by G. E. M. Anscombe. Oxford: Blackwell, 1953.

Wong, David B. "Cultivating the Self in Concert with Others." In *Dao Companion to the Analects*, edited by Amy Olberding. Dordrecht, The Netherlands: Springer, 2014.

———. "If We Are Not by Ourselves, If We Are Not Strangers." In *Polishing the Chinese Mirror: Essays in Honor of Henry Rosemont, Jr.*, edited by Marthe Chandler and Ronnie Littlejohn. New York: Global Scholarly Publications, 2018.

———. "Relational and Autonomous Selves." *Journal of Chinese Philosophy* 34, no. 4 (December 2004).

———. "Is There a Distinction Between Reason and Emotion in Mencius?" *Philosophy East and West* 41, no. 1 (1991): 31–44.

Wu, Xiao-ming. "Philosophy, *Philosophia*, and *Zhe-xue*." *Philosophy East and West* 48, no. 3 (1998).
Yates, Robin D. S. "Body, Space, Time and Bureaucracy: Boundary Creation and Control Mechanisms in Early China." In *Boundaries in China*, edited by John Hay. London: Reaktion, 1994.
Yijing (Chou-I). Sinological Index Series Supplement 10. Peking: Harvard-Yenching Institute, 1935.
Yearley, Lee. *Mencius and Aquinas: Theories of Virtue and Conceptions of Courage*. Albany: State University of New York Press, 1990.
Yu, Jiyuan. *The Ethics of Confucius and Aristotle: Mirrors of Virtue*. New York: Routledge, 2007.
Zhang, Dainian 張岱年. 中國哲學大綱 [An outline of Chinese philosophy]. Beijing: Chinese Academy of Social Sciences Press, 1982.
Zhang, Dongsun 張東蓀. 知識與文化: 張東蓀文化論著輯要 [Knowledge and culture: The essential writings of Zhang Dongsun on culture], edited by Zhang Yaonan 張耀南. Beijing: Zhongguo Guangbo dianshi chubanshe, 1995.
Zhang, Yanhua. *Transforming Emotions with Chinese Medicine: An Ethnographic Account from Contemporary China*. Albany: State University of New York Press, 2007.
Zhang, Zailin 張再林. 作爲身體哲學的中國古代哲學 [Traditional Chinese philosophy as the philosophy of body]. Beijing: China Social Science Press, 2008.
Zhao, Tingyang. 趙汀陽, 天下體系: 世界制度哲學導論 [The Tianxia system: An introduction to the philosophy of world institution]. Beijing: Peoples' University Press, 2011.
Zhou, Yiqun. *Festival, Feasts, and Gender Relations in Ancient China and Greece*. New York: Cambridge University Press, 2010.
Zhu Xi 朱熹. *Commentary on the Four Books* 四書集注 *Zhongyong* 中庸章句集注.
Zhuangzi 莊子 Harvard-Yenching Institute Sinological Index Series, Supplement 20. Peking: Harvard-Yenching Institute.
Zuozhuan 左傳 Harvard-Yenching Concordance Series, Supplement 11. Peking: Harvard-Yenching Institute.

Index

abstraction, 32, 45–47, 53, 74, 77, 149, 333, 336; and Amartya Sen's individual, 279–286; the perils of, 317–321
aesthetic order, 105, 111, 115–120, 130–131, 141, 154–159, 211, 216, 231–232, 248, 339–341, 345, 351–352
agency, 76, 20; Aristotle on, 241–242; focus-field conception of, 209–218, 252–260, 286–301, 379; and responsibility, 26–27
an 安 question particle, 50–51
Analects of Confucius, 60–61, 64, 65, 66, 67, 69, 70, 74, 76, 77, 79, 88, 92, 96, 100, 104, 105, 106, 107, 110, 113, 114, 116, 118, 123, 139, 140, 148, 191, 211, 235–241, 253, 289–294, 306, 314, 315, 326, 328, 333, 339, 341, 356–357
Angle, Steve, 326–329
animality, human, 184–185, 388
Anscombe, Elizabeth, 19
Anthropocene epoch, 136
Aquinas, Thomas, 162
Arendt, Hannah, 76
Aristotle, 5, 6, 20, 27, 34–40, 46, 50, 51, 53, 56, 58, 68, 130–131, 148, 165, 241, 281, 320, 354; and friendship, 247–252; and taxonomic knowing, 233–235
ars contextualis (the art of contextualizing), 139, 209, 241, 386
Asad, Talal, 7–8
Asia Pacific Economic Cooperation (APEC), 11
aspectual language. *See* language, aspectual
asymmetry in cultural comparisons, 1–14, 19, 326–327
Austin, J. L., 233
autonomy, 26, 28, 262, 298, 345; and the absence of coercion, 255, 260; defined, 287; and equality, 275–276; individual, 301–302; relational, 275–316, 345; sagely, 301–316

Barrett, Tim, 95
Beethoven, Ludwig, 56–57
Behuniak, Jim, 133
Bell, Daniel A., 333–334
Bentham, Jeremy, 299
Berthrong, John, 389
biantong 變通 (changing and persisting, persistence in change, flux and flow), 58, 102, 158, 349, 376, 382–384, 385–387, 392

421

Blake, William, 236
Bloom, Paul, 174
body, embodying. See *ti* 體
Book of Changes (*Yijing* 易經), 17, 58, 102, 155, 158, 162, 193, 258, 315, 350, 360, 376, 381–400, 401; and the meaning of "change" (*yi* 易), 382; and Tang Junyi's cosmological postuates, 389–400
Book of Songs (*Shijing* 詩經), 50, 87, 110, 123, 138, 144–145
Borges, Jorge Luis, 149
BRI, "one belt one road initiative," 402
bronze inscriptions (*jinwen* 金文), 98
Buddhism, 275, 283–285, 301, 305, 401, 403
Butler, Joseph, 2

capabilities approach, 276–285
Carroll, Lewis, 19
Carse, James P., 13, 401
categories, 18, 219
causality, holistic *ziran* 自然, 373–378; holistic *shi* 勢, 378–381
Chan, Wing-tsit, 67, 337
chaoyue 超越 (transcendence, all-pervading), 221–228
cheng 誠 (sincerity, resolve, resolution), 21, 64, 66, 91, 104, 137, 142–145, 165–167, 200, 201, 254, 255, 285–286
Ch'ien Mu [Qian Mu], ix
Chinese Classic of Family Reverence (*Xiaojing* 孝經), 82, 83, 85, 86, 87, 95, 122, 124
choices, thick, 275–316
Christianity, 3, 8, 32
Clippinger, John Henry, 41–44, 208, 214–215
Cohen, Paul A., 8
concepts, the nature of, 170–171

Confucianism, 9–10; as English translation of *rujia* 儒家 (literati class), 95–97, 100; as a living cultural tradition, 403; as a philosophy of education, 406; as a radical empiricism, 61–62; religiousness, 403–405; and role ethics, 406–407; and social order, 405–406; as state doctrine, 159; Tang Junyi and the "idea" of, 349–358, 400. See also *rujia* 儒家 (literati class) and *ruxue* 儒學 (literati learning)
Confucius, 9–10, 27, 28, 30, 55, 60–62, 64, 66, 70, 81, 82, 86, 93, 94, 95, 96, 101, 102, 103, 104, 110, 112, 113, 114, 124, 139–144, 147, 148, 160, 192, 193, 194, 202, 211, 235–241, 289–294, 306, 314, 315, 338–339 and focus-field agency, 252–260; and the four abstentions (*sijue* 四絕), 253–260, 301; and friendship, 247–252; and ritualized living, 113–119; as *tian*, 314–316
Confucius Institutes, 401
contextualism, 317–325, 343, 391–392. See also *yiduobufenguan* 一多不分觀
correlative thinking, 359–365, 373–378
cosmology, 138, 359–360; Confucian process, 16–17, 33–34, 38–40, 48, 50, 52–54, 57–59, 75, 77, 85, 102, 107, 111, 136–137, 139–145, 152, 164, 166–168, 171, 179, 191–200, 205–218, 218–231, 231–247, 373–378; from human becoming to process, 359–400
creatio in situ (situated creativity), 136, 375–376, 405

creatio ex nihilo (creation out of nothing), 157, 375–376, 405
creativity, 375–376; of God, 157–158; promethean, 157–158
Creel, H. G., 373
critical self-awareness, 63, 65, 66, 70, 75, 76, 82, 118, 143, 148, 155, 158, 187, 192, 199, 201, 203, 207–208, 230, 245–246, 255, 259, 287–288, 329, 339–340
culture, metaphor of, 153–159; as a way of life, 155

D'Ambrosio, Paul, 25
dao 道 (way-making, proper way, field), 20, 52, 55, 71, 79, 87, 95, 110, 133, 135, 140, 142–143, 148, 149, 157, 168–169, 176, 206, 225, 236, 250, 255, 306, 338, 351, 352, 375, 387, 404; definition of, 188–191, 217–218, 241, 383; as field, 348
Daodejing 道德經, and the *wu* 無-forms, 190
daotong 道統 (orthodox cultural lineage), 95, 125, 189, 218
Darwin, Charles, 16, 367
Davis, Sir John Francis, 95
Dawson, Raymond, 337
Daxue 大學. See *Expansive Learning*
Dazhuan 大傳 (*Great Commentary*). See *Great Commentary* (*Dazhuan* 大傳)
de 德 (moral virtuosity), 21, 86, 143, 200, 225, 309–312, 333, 352, 384; definition of, 20, 188–190; and virtue ethics, 20, 68; as *de* 得 (getting and gaining), 64, 141; as focus, 348
democracy, 10, 350–352; Confucian, 357–358; Dewey and the "idea" of, 22, 343–347; and optimizing the human experience, 317–358
Dewey, John, x, 15, 16, 21, 22, 28, 30, 45, 80, 150, 152, 299, 351; and communication, 242–243, 352, 356, 367; and Confucius, 9; on family, 354–355; and focus-field conception of person, 267–273; on habits, 216; on the "idea" of democracy," 343–347, 348–349, 357; on individuality, 260–267; and the postulate of immediate empiricism, 322–325, 326; and the principle of individuation, 221; and the reflex arc, 322–323; and the retrospective fallacy, 319
Drabinski, John E., 4–5
du 度 (achieved coalescence), 64, 108–109, 138; of human becomings and world, 301–316
dualistic thinking, xii, 33, 49, 153, 179, 195, 198, 201, 224–225, 231, 363–364
Duan Yucai 段玉裁, 295

Eberhard, Wolfram, 373
education, moral, 6–7, 60, 63, 92, 112, 124, 132, 147, 155, 207, 258, 296–298, 406
Eichmann, Adolf, 76
eidos. See formal cause
Einstein, Albert, 78
elemental theory, 370–373
Elstein, David, 19, 334–335
Emerson, Ralph Waldo, 22, 47, 124–125
Emmet, Dorothy, 42–45, 91
equity, 130–131, 275–280
epistemology, 48–52; vocabulary of, 51, 238
essentialism, 36, 75, 166, 289, 320, 366

ethics, care, 327
ethics, character, 28–30, 299
ethics, Confucian role, 5, 15, 17–18, 21, 30, 31, 52, 59–145, 180–181, 211, 221–227, 265, 285–287, 317, 335, 343, 359, 366, 406–407; evaluating roles in, 326–337
ethics, deontic, 19–20, 335
ethics, utilitarian, 5, 19–20, 335
ethics, virtue, 5, 17, 19–20, 28–29, 64, 68, 299, 328, 335
Euthyphro problem, the, 319–320
exemplary persons. See *junzi*
Expansive Learning (*Daxue* 大學), 84, 104, 148, 206–208, 310–311, 350, 353

Fairbank, John, 8
family, 80, 89–94, 107–108, 131, 138–139, 205, 208–209, 214, 283–285, 352–358; and friendship, 251–252; as the governing cultural metaphor, 355; lineages, 92, 119, 125, 130–131, 138–141, 333; in the Western philosophical narrative, 353–358
Fan Chi, 69, 256, 291
Farquhar, Judith, 196
feelings, human (*qing* 情), 340; a cosmic force, 136–145
Fei Xiaotong 費孝通, 89–94, 213, 365–356; and differential mode of association (*chaxugeju* 差序格局), 90, 94; and organizational mode of association (*tuantigeju* 團體格局), 90, 94
Feng Youlan 馮友蘭, 222
Fingarette, Herbert, 31, 337
finite games, 13–14, 402
Five Classics, 102
focus-field, conception of agency, 209–218, 258–259, 286–301, 344–345; conception of persons, 205–274, 317, 351, 360; and classical pragmatism, 267–273; defined, 208–209; language of, 20, 38, 43, 48, 69, 84, 105, 122, 136, 190, 193–194, 201, 203, 323, 325, 348, 349–350, 377–380, 391–392, 394, 398
Focusing the Familiar (*Zhongyong* 中庸), 71, 73, 104, 131–145, 148, 158, 166–167, 200, 232, 309–310, 315, 350, 353, 389; and the meaning of *zhongyong* 中庸, 140
Forke, Alfred, 373
formal cause (*eidos*), 18, 34, 46, 51, 154, 166, 169; as the principle of individuation, 205
Foucault, Michel, 7
Four Books, 104, 105, 131, 206
Franklin, Ursula, 99
Fraser, Chris, 133–134
friendship, 245, 247–252, 344; and family, 251–252; Whitehead on, 318
Fu Xi 伏羲, 385–388

Gandhi, Mahatma, 288
Gao, Master, 160–161
Garfield, Jay, 3–5
Geertz, Clifford, 295
generalizations, 149, 151, 330–332, 342, 366, 381, 388; and *yiduobufen* 一多不分 contextualism, 223; distinguishing events from objects, 367–370; distinguishing phases from elements, 370–373
gerund, 54, 63, 169, 171, 179, 236, 288, 298
Gernet, Jacques, 32
God, 2, 78, 134, 157, 176, 188–189, 224, 231, 305, 375, 404; transcendent, 302–303, 378

Goethe, Johann Wolfgang von, 157
Golden Rule, 341
Graham, Angus, 31–40, 45, 53–54, 58, 72, 159, 200, 213, 370, 390; initial developmental model of the Mencian *xing* 性, 164–167; narrative reading of the Mencian *xing* 性, 167–173
Granet, Marcel, 55, 169, 180, 208, 213, 231, 303, 361, 373–378
grammar, philosophy of, 32–33
Great Leaning (*Daxue* 大學). See *Expansive Learning*
Great Commentary (*Dazhuan* 大傳), 17, 381–400
guanxi 關係 (relations, personal connections), 90
Guo Qiyong 郭齊勇, 221–227
Guo Moruo 郭沫若, 382, 393
Guodian bamboo strips, 65, 309, 313
Guoyu 國語, 191

habits, 309–311; Dewey on, 261–270, 344
Hall, David L., 164, 363
hao 好 (good), 332; defined by context, 330–331
harmony, 11
Hartshorne, Charles, 175–176, 194
he 和 (superlative harmony, optimizing symbiosis), 21, 137, 138, 145, 149, 167, 223, 356, 397–398, 400; defined, 128–145; and *li* 禮 (ritual propriety, embodied living), 106–145; and *ti* 體 (body, embodying), 106–145
Heidegger, Martin, 27
Hegel, G. W. F., 4, 8–9, 22, 24, 27, 35, 42, 147
Hershock, Peter D., 39–42, 131, 378; on diversity and equity, 275–280

heyi 合一 relation, defined, 306
holography, 25, 43, 50, 52, 69, 73, 122, 153, 166, 190, 258, 271–273, 294, 348, 377, 389–390; and the focus-field conception of persons, 205–274, 330; of *xin* as *xing* in the Mencius, 194–200, 201
Hou Ji 后稷 (legendary cultural hero), 92
Hsiao Kung-chuan (Xiao Gongquan) 蕭公權, 101
Huang Yushun 黃玉順, 227–230, 355–357
Hui Shi, 49
human "becoming," 147–153, 169–170; narrativity of, 200–203
human "being," 147–153, 169–170; ontological understanding of, 159–163; developmental understanding of, 159–163
human rights, 10, 227–230; first generation, 229–230; second generation, 229–230
Hume, David, 4–5
hunger, world, predicament of, 12–13
hypergoods, 23, 275, 351

idealism, 15, 34, 254, 364
imagination, moral, 60, 158, 332, 338–339, 353
idealism, 150, 162, 169, 224, 289
individualism, x–xii, 13, 20–21, 22, 23, 41, 45–47, 58, 90, 152, 164, 175, 180, 203, 227, 229, 250, 252, 264–266, 289, 301–302, 407–408; Amartya Sen on, 279–286
individuality, 22, 23, 45–47, 238, 380; Dewey on, 260–267, 344, 352

individuation, principle of, 219–221
infinite games, 13–14, 401–402
Ing, Michael, 112–113
inner and outer. See *neiwai* 內外
intentionality, 253. See also *zhi* 志 (intentionality)
interpretive context, 77, 84, 326, 381–400
"intra-" defined, 24–25, 198–199

James, William, 212–213, 260, 261, 331, 368, 369, 374; and focus-field conception of person, 268–273; and *the* psychological fallacy, 322; and radical empiricism, 324
Jaspers, Karl, 27
jian 諫 (remonstrating, remonstrance), 81, 127
jingshen 精神 (vigor, vitality), 376; defined, 193
Johnson, Mark, 21, 153, 170; and physical image-schemata, 216–218
junzi 君子 (exemplary persons), 64, 79, 88–89, 101, 103, 135, 136, 139, 140, 141, 147, 186, 235, 245, 290–295, 385; and *xiaoren* 小人 (petty persons), 244–245
justice, x–xii, 227–229, 277, 279

Kant, Immanuel, 4, 6, 19, 23, 147, 255, 299
Keightley, David, 361–365, 373, 382, 384
kenning, Anglo-Saxon, 236–237
Kim, Jung-Yeup, 84
King, Martin Luther, 288
Kupperman, Joel, x, 28–30, 276; on choice, 299–301
Kwan Tze-wan, 151

Lai, Karyn, 67, 71–72
Lakoff, George, 153, 170

language, analytic 55–58, 232–235; aspectual, 55–58, 68, 77, 85, 106, 145, 167, 174, 185, 195–196, 225, 232, 306, 323, 348, 351, 364, 376–377, 382, 386; metaphorical, 232–233; modal 66, 254
Lau, D. C., 161, 337–339
Lee, Ming-huei, 19
Legge, James, 2–3, 132
Lewis, Mark, 361
li 禮 (ritual propriety, embodied living, social grammar), 21, 76, 90, 100, 103, 145, 149, 160, 202, 211, 214, 245, 254, 303, 309, 333, 352, 353, 405; definition of, 109–110; and Confucius, 113–119; and *he* 和 (superlative harmony, optimizing symbiosis), 106–145; and L. *proprius*, 112; and *ti* 體 (embodying, lived body), 87–88, 106–145
Li Lanlan 李蘭蘭, 221–227
Liang Tao 梁濤, 135
Liji 禮記. See *Record of Rites*
Li Ling 李零, 361
Li Zehou 李澤厚, 97, 147–148
Lincoln, Abraham, 263–264, 288
Liu Xiang 劉向, 157
Liu, Lydia H., 7–8, 18, 223–224
Liu Xie 劉勰, 157
Lloyd, Geoffrey, 365
Locke, John, 4, 265
logic, holistic *shi* 勢, 378–381. See also focus-field language
Loy, Hui-chieh, 133
Lu Xun 魯迅, 129
lun 倫, 18
lunlixue 倫理學, 18

MacIntyre, Alasdair, 19
Major, John, 370–371

Mandela, Nelson, 288
Marett, R. R., 329
May, Larry, 26–27
May Fourth reformers, 10, 354, 357
McLeod, Alex, 67
Mead, George Herbert, 21, 260, 268–269
mei 美 (beautiful), defined, 321
Mencius, 2, 6, 34, 71, 91–92, 104, 121, 126, 142–143, 144, 218–219, 255, 270, 272, 292–293; on becoming a sage, 312–313; on body, 179, 185–187, 310, 312, 313; and the holography of *xin* 心 as *xing* 性; intentional living, 187–194; misreadings of, 173–180; and personal cultivation, 184–194; on *xing* 性, 147–204
Militarists, 159
Mill, John Stuart, 5, 299
Milton, John, 157
mind, 215, 261, 269–270, 391; Dewey on, 242–243, 270–273
ming 命 (force of circumstances, propensity of things), 55
missionaries, 2
modernity, Western, 6–8, 10–14, 155, 223–224, 227, 295, 402
Mohism, 5, 49, 101, 132–134, 143, 159, 219–221
Mou Zongsan 牟宗三, 19
Mount Lu, 50
musicality, cosmic, 57, 111, 129, 393

naming practices, 395–396
Needham, Joseph, 153, 169, 180, 208, 213, 367, 373–378
neiwai 內外 (inner and outer), 194–200
Neville, Robert Cummings, 41
Ni Peimin, 337–338, 340–341
Nietzsche, Friedrich, 32–33, 157, 342

Nuyen, A. T., 23, 328
Nylan, Michael, 16, 229

objective and subjective. See *zhuke* 主客
Okin, Susan Moller, x
ontology, substance, xi, 16, 18, 31–40, 68, 73, 166, 168–169, 212–213, 219, 224–226, 233–235, 286, 304, 320, 366, 367–368, 377, 390–391, 393; and the *what* question, 35–38, 48, 49, 53, 59, 129
oracle bone script (*jiaguwen* 甲骨文), 98

Pang Pu 龐樸, 394–395
Parmenides, 393
paronomasia (definition by phonetic and semantic association), 231–247
Peirce, C. S., 325, 374
persons, focus-field conception of, xii, 52, 194–200, 205–274, 286, 317, 327, 343; intrasubjective conception of, 21; theorizing the, 22–31; narrative conception of, xii, 26, 28, 34–35, 51, 54, 62–65, 73, 76, 77, 80, 147–203
Peterson, Willard, 393
philosophical fallacy, *the*, 80, 150
philosophy, professional discipline of, 3–5, 9
Plato, 16, 148, 149, 354, 363, 366–367, 384; and friendship, 247–252
potential, 39, 84, 152–154, 162, 165–166, 168, 170, 177, 312–313
pubian 普遍 (universal, shared values, common values), 221–228
Putnam, Hilary, 324–325

qi 氣 (vital moral energy, *qi*), in Mencius, 187–194, 196, 201, 272, 371–372, 377, 387, 391
questions, the *what*, 35–38, 47–55, 58, 67, 69–70, 147, 234, 320, 404; the *whence and whither*, 47–56, 58, 70, 148, 230; the *where and when*, 51–52

racism, 27
Ranyou 冉有, 70
Raphael, 148
Rawls, John, x, 23–24, 276, 286
Record of Rites (*Liji* 禮記), 85, 110, 122
Records of the Grand Historian (*Shiji* 史記), 127, 129
rectification of names. See *zhengming* 正名 (using language properly)
relationality, primacy of vital, 73, 77, 86, 105, 192–193, 197, 205, 213–214, 220, 298, 351, 370, 406
relations, definition of, 238–247; doctrine of internal relations, 25, 37–45, 47, 170, 194–200, 213, 218, 220, 228, 238, 282–283, 307, 377–379, 391; doctrine of external, 25, 37–45, 198, 212, 218, 238, 276, 285, 289
religare (binding tightly), 86, 256, 348
religiousness, Confucian, 60, 67, 86, 92–93, 98–100, 106, 109, 122, 138, 255–258, 301–316, 387–389, 403–405; and the Spring Festival, 256–257; and spirituality, 385
remonstrating, remonstrance. See *jian* 諫
ren 仁 (consummate person/conduct), 21, 26, 62, 64, 67, 71, 77, 78–79, 103, 106, 118, 142–143, 148, 149, 166, 174, 200, 202, 250, 255, 291, 309, 352, 353, 356, 357, 384; and family, 80; and scenario rehearsal (*shu* 恕) as method, 337–342; and speaking with circumspection (*ren* 訒), 247; as a way of saying "role ethics," 65–77; "twoness" of, 73–77, 81–82
Richards, I. A., 6, 112, 178
River Elegy (*Heshang* 河殤), 10
Robbins, Dan, 133
role model, 60–62, 64, 71, 74, 95, 113–115, 139, 253–260, 288–301, 330, 333, 404
"root" metaphor, 84–86, 120, 121, 124, 148, 150, 153
Rosemont, Henry, Jr., ix–x, 26, 29, 47, 65, 78, 164, 327, 404
rujia 儒家 (literati class), 94–106, 125; etymology, 96. See also Confucianism
ruxue 儒學 (literati learning), 10, 96, 100. See also Confucianism
Ryle, Gilbert, 76

sacrifice, ancestral, 78, 93, 98, 112, 126, 222
sages (*shengren* 聖人), 140–145, 176–177, 184–186, 253, 301–316, 360, 385–389, 400; defined, 245; and "initiating" (*zuo* 作), 100–101
Saussure, Ferdinand de, 31–32
Sandel, Michael, 21, 23–28, 30, 161, 198
Schleiermacher, Friedrich, 306, 308
School of Names, 159
second amendment, 346
Sen, Amartya, x, and capabilities approach, 276–285, 286, 341–342
Shakespeare, William, 53
shan 善 (good at, efficacy), 291, 292, 309–312; defined 150–151,

183–184; way-making of the human being, 311–312
shame, sense of, 76, 82, 118, 333
Shang dynasty, 109, 111, 359, 361–365, 373, 382; and bronze production, 97–100, 109
shangdi 上帝 (god on high), 303
Shelley, Mary, 157
shen 身 (lived body)
Shen Buhai 申不害, 49
Shen Dao 慎到, 49
Shen Nong 神農, 162, 385–388
shenqidu 慎其獨, 135–136, 310–311
shengshengbuyi 生生不已 (ceaseless procreating), 102, 258, 384, 393–397
shi 勢 (holistic causality), 378–381
shu 恕 (empathetic deference, putting oneself in the other's place, dramatic rehearsal), 64, 75, 149, 246, 329, 337; defined, 337–339; as a method for becoming consummate (ren 仁), 337–342
Shun 舜, (sage-king), 91–92, 104, 126, 184–185, 313, 387
Shun, Kwong-loi, 2, 5–6, 191
Shuowen lexicon, 48, 188, 219, 235, 295, 304, 339
Shusterman, Richard, 120, 185
siduan 四端 (four inclinations), 172, 173–174, 179, 181–183, 184, 187, 200–201, 312
Sima Niu 司馬牛, 69, 247
Sima Qian 司馬遷, 126–129, 247; and a Letter in Reply to Ren An, 127–128
Sima Tan 司馬談, 126
Sivin, Nathan, 16, 361, 364–365, 370
Slingerland, Edward, 101–102, 337
Socrates, 148, 234, 319–320
Solomon, Robert, x, 226

Sommer, Deborah, 121, 219–220
soul, 16, 22, 148, 261, 271, 391
Standaert, Nicolas, 95
Su Shi 蘇軾, 50
Sun Yat-sen, 395–396
Sunzi: The Art of War, 158

Tan, Sor-hoon, 319
Tang Junyi 唐君毅, 52, 57–58, 75, 134, 169, 177–178, 180, 218–219, 222, 230, 258, 296, 324, 343, 368; and Book of Changes cosmology, 389–400; and the "idea" of Confucianism, 349–358; and family, 353
Tang Yijie 湯一介, 307, 311, 315
Taylor, Charles, 21, 23, 28, 30, 183, 243, 275, 351, 387
teleology, 15, 34–36, 51, 84, 129, 145, 149, 150, 152, 162, 166, 168, 205, 254, 390, 397, 405; and culture, 154–159
theorizing practice, xii–xiii, 61, 72, 115, 158, 254, 329, 401–408
ti 體 (embodying, body), 21, 87, 145, 211, 214, 216–218, 259, 303, 380; defined, 118–129; and he 和 (superlative harmony, optimizing symbiosis), 106–145; and li 禮 (ritual propriety, embodied living), 106–145; Mencius on, 179, 185, 186–187, 202; physical and cultural embodiment, 78–79, 86, 87, 95–96, 104, 106–107, 118–129; as unit and combination, 219–221
tian 天 ("Heaven"), 141, 168–169, 198, 224, 303; Confucius as, 314–316; defined, 304–316; the purposes of (tianzhi 天志), 133–134; the way of, 142, 222, 256, 311–312

tianrenheyi 天人合一 ("the inseparability of the human and cosmic orders"), 134–138, 222, 225, 301–316, 386, 400

Tiles, Mary, 233–235

tiyong 體用 (forming and functioning, trans-*form*-ing), 69, 113, 171, 195, 196, 220, 349, 376, 377, 378

traditional Chinese medicine TCM, 196–197

transcendence. See *chaoyue* 超越 (transcendence, all-pervading)

Tu Wei-ming, 72, 337

Turner, Kevin J., 76

universal. See *pubian* 普遍 (universal, shared values, common values)

Universal Declaration of Human Rights (UDHR), 228–230

ultimacies. See *zhongji* 終極 (ultimacies, optimizing harmony)

Van Norden, Bryan, 3–5

Voltaire, 308

Waley, Arthur, 167–168, 337

Wang Aihe, 16–17, 361; on *wuxing* 五行 (five phases), 371–373

Wang Chong 王充, 131

Weisman, David, 37–38

Wen, King 文王 (King "culture"), 87, 103, 104, 250, 313–314

wenhua 文化 ("culture"), 386; compared with "culture," 153–159; and martial force (*wu* 武), 158

Westernization, 10–14

Wheatley, Paul, 98

Whitehead, A. N., 21, 175, 343, 349, 351, 352, 356; on Confucius, 9; and aesthetic order, 130–131, 156, 211, 351, 366–367; and the cosmological ground of democracy, 337–339; and the fallacy of simple location, 175–176, 319; and the fallacy of misplaced concreteness, 175–176, 214, 319; and the perils of abstraction, 280, 317–319; and rational order, 130, 156, 351

Wilhelm, H., 373–374

Williams, Bernard, 59–60, 285

Williams, Raymond, 155

Wilson, Cook, 329

Wilson, Thomas, 229

Wittgenstein, Ludwig, 18, 170–171, 242

Wong, Ben, 133

Wong, David B., 64, 133, 137, 209–214, 289–294

Wu, King 武王, 104, 250

wuxing 五行 (five phases), as a phasal theory, 370–373

Wundt, William, 268–269

Wuxingpian 五行篇, 135, 308–314

Xenophanes, 360

xiao 孝 (family reverence, filiality, intergenerational transmission), 76–77, 102, 104, 116, 122, 124, 126, 127, 128, 131, 149, 258, 352, 406; as a cosmic force, 82; as a way of saying "role ethics," 78–94; and paterfamilias, 78, 81; as the prime moral imperative, 78, 86, 106, 354, 356; as the root of consummate conduct (*ren*), 79, 357

Xiaojing 孝經. See *Chinese Classic of Family Reverence*

xiaoren 小人 (small, petty persons), 64, 76, 244–245

xin 心 (heartmind, bodyheartminding), 21, 171–172, 232, 270, 272,

307, 310, 312, 338; and the four inclinations in Mencius (*siduan* 四端), 172, 183–187; and holography as *xing* in Mencius

xin 信 (making good on one's word, trust and credibility), 64, 66, 91, 149, 245, 254, 298

xing 性 (native human propensities), 21, 34, 52, 54, 80, 183–187, 256, 390, 400; compared with "human nature," 154–159; and holography with *xin* in Mencius, 194–200; Mencius on, 147–204; a narrative conception of, 147–204, 390; ontological and developmental models, 159–163, 169–170, 164, 167–168; Tang Junyi on, 134, 296

xiushen 修身 (cultivating one's person), 55, 149

Xu Fuguan 徐復觀, 229

xue 學 (teaching and learning), 295–298

Xunzi 荀子, 83, 147, 159, 160, 181, 184, 202

Yan Fu 嚴復, 94
Yan Hui 顏回, 69, 70, 297–298
Yao 堯 (sage-king), 91, 104, 313, 387
Yates, Robin, 361
Yearley, Lee, 162
yi 義 (optimal appropriateness), 21, 66, 76, 83, 103, 143, 160, 201, 202, 255, 256, 292–295, 309, 333, 335, 353, 356, 384; and L. *proprius* 111
yiduobufenguan 一多不分觀 (one is many, many one postulate), 218–231, 321, 324, 349, 391–392. *See also* contextualism

Yijing 易經. See *Book of Changes*
yong 勇 (courage), 149
Yu 禹 (sage-king), 91

Zeng, Master 曾子, 82–83, 88–89, 123–124, 250, 338
Zhang Dainian 張岱年, 176–177, 222
Zhang Dongsun 張東蓀, 304
Zhang Junmai (Carson Chang) 張君勱, 229
Zhang Longxi, 32
Zhang Pengchun (Chang Peng Chun) 張彭春, 229
Zhang Yanhua, 108
Zhao Tingyang 趙汀陽, 1
zhi 智 (wisely, wisdom), 66, 142–143, 149, 174, 200, 202, 246, 256, 309
zhi 志 (intentionality), defined, 188; in Mencius, 187–194, 201
zhixingheyi 知行合一 (inseparability of thinking and doing), 195
zheng 正 (proper); and L. *proprius*, 112, 235
zheng 政 (governing properly); and L. *proprius*, 112, 235
zhengming 正名 (using names/language properly), 239–242
zhong 中 (focusing, coalescing), 137–138, 140
zhong 忠 (doing one's best, conscientiousness), 149, 254, 291; and *shu* 恕 (scenerio rehearsal), 338–339
Zhonggong 仲弓, 67, 69
zhongji 終極 (ultimacies, optimizing harmony), 221–228
Zhongyong 中庸. See *Focusing the Familiar*
Zhou dynasty, 100, 109–110, 304

Zhou Yiqun, 90–94
Zhu Xi 朱熹, 79, 131, 135, 206, 315–316
Zhuangzi 莊子, 49, 50, 236, 306
zhuke 主客 (subjective and objective), 195–196, 232
zhong 忠 (doing one's best, conscientiously), 66, 91

Zigong 子貢, 27, 69, 246, 250, 256, 314, 315, 339
Zilu 子路, 70, 86, 117, 239
ziran 自然 (self-so-ing), 195, 404; causality, 377–378
Zisizi 子思子, 137
Zou Yan 邹衍, 373
Zuo Commentary 左傳, 50, 191